THE AWFUL DISCLOSURES

OF

MARIA MONK:

BEING,

A Narrative of her Sufferings,

DURING A RESIDENCE OF

FIVE YEARS AS A NOVICE, AND TWO YEARS AS A BLACK NUN,

In the Hotel Dieu Nunnery, at Montreal.

TO WHICH IS ADDED,

NOTES, AFFIDAVITS, CONFIRMATIONS,

AND

FACTS OF THE PRESENT DAY;

WHEREIN

MARIA MONK'S DISCLOSURES ARE MOST FULLY PROVED;

AND

THE HIDEOUS NATURE OF THE CONVENTUAL SYSTEM EXPOSED.

LONDON:
PUBLISHED BY HOULSTON & STONEMAN, PATERNOSTER ROW;
G., J. & R. BANKS, 14, BERMONDSEY NEW ROAD;
J. WOOD, PARK HILL, CLAPHAM; J. SCOTT, KING'S ROW, WALWORTH ROAD;
MANCHESTER: W. BREMNER, PICCADILLY; EDINBURGH: J. MENZIES, PRINCES ST.;
DUBLIN: G. HERBERT, LOWER SACKVILLE STREET.

MDCCCLI.

CONTENTS.

AWFUL DISCLOSURES OF MARIA MONK.

CHAPTER I.

Early Recollections—Early Life—Religious Education neglected—First School—Entrance into the School of the Congregational Nunnery—Brief Account of the Nunneries in Montreal—the Congregational Nunnery—The Grey Nunnery—The Black Nunnery—Public Respect for these Institutions—Instructions Received—The Catechism—The Bible 3

CHAPTER II.

Congregational Nunnery—Story told by a Fellow Pupil against a Priest—Other Stories—Pretty Mary—Confess to Father Richards—My subsequent Confession—Instruction in the Catechism . . . 7

CHAPTER III.

Black Nunnery—Preparations to become a Novice in the Black Nunnery Entrance—Occupations of the Novices—The Apartments to which they had access—First Interview with Jane Ray—Reverence for the Superior—A wonderful Nun—Her Reliques—The Holy Good Shepherd, or Nameless Nun—Confession of Novices . . . 9

CHAPTER IV.

Displeased with the Convent Life—Left it—Residence at St. Denis—Relics—Marriage—Return to the Black Nunnery—Objections made by some Novices 14

CHAPTER V.

Received Confirmation—Painful Feelings—Specimen of Instructions received on the subject 20

CHAPTER VI.

Taking the Veil—Interview afterwards with the Superior—Surprise and Horror at the Disclosures—Resolution to submit . . . 22

CHAPTER VII.

Daily Ceremonies—Jane Ray among the Nuns . . . 29

CHAPTER VIII.

Description of Apartments in the Black Nunnery in order—First Floor—Second Floor—Garret—The Founder—Superior's Management with the Friends of Novices—Religious Lies—Criminality of concealing sins at Confessions 33

CHAPTER IX.

Nuns with similar names—Squaw Nuns—First Visit to the Cellar—Description of it—Shocking Discovery there—Superior's Instructions—Private Signal of the Priests—Books used in the Nunnery—Opinions expressed of the Bible—Specimens of what I know of the Scriptures. 42

CHAPTER X.

Manufacture of Bread and Wax Candles, carried on in the Convent—Superstitions—Scapularies—Virgin Mary's Pincussion—Her House—The Bishop's Power over Fire—My Instruction to Novices—Jane Ray—Vascillation of Feeling 50

CHAPTER XI.

Alarming Order from the Superior—Proceed to execute it—Scene in an Upper Room—Sentence of Death and Murder—My own Distress—Reports made to Friends of St. Frances . . . 58

CHAPTER XII.

Description of the Room of the Three States, and the Pictures in it—Jane Ray Ridiculing Priests—Their Criminal Treatment of us at Confession—Jane Rays's Tricks with the Nun's Aprons, Handkerchiefs, and Night-gowns—Apples 64

CHAPTER XIII.

Jane Ray's Tricks continued—The Broomstick Ghost—Sleep Walking—Salted Cider—Changing Beds—Objects of some of her Tricks—Feigned Humility—Alarm 74

CONTENTS.

CHAPTER XIV.

Influencing Novices—Difficulty of convincing persons from the United States—Tale of the Bishop in the City—The Bishop in the Convent—The Prisoners in the cells—Practice in Singing—Narratives—Jane Ray's Hymns—The Superior's best Trick . . . 92

CHAPTER XV.

Frequency of the Priest's Visits to the Nunnery—Their Freedom and Crimes—Difficulty of learning their Names—Their Holy Retreat—Objections in our Minds—Means used to Counteract Conscience—Ingenious Arguments 102

CHAPTER XVI.

Treatment of Young Infants in the Convent—Talking in Sleep—Amusements—Ceremonies at the Public Interment of Deceased Nuns—Sudden Disappearance of the Old Superior—Introduction of the New One—Superstition—Alarm of a Nun—Difficulty of Communication with other Nuns 109

CHAPTER XVII.

Disappearance of Nuns—St. Pierre—Gags—My Temporary Confinement in a Cell—The Cholera Season—How to avoid it—Occupations in the Convent during the Pestilence—Manufacture of Wax Candles—The Election Riots—Alarm among the Nuns—Preparations for Defence—Penances 122

CHAPTER XVIII.

The Punishment of the Cap—The Priests of the District of Montreal have free access to the Black Nunnery—Crimes committed and required by them—The Pope's Command to commit Indecent Crimes—Characters of the Old and New Superiors—The Timidity of the latter—I began to be employed in the Hospitals—Some account of them—Warning given me by a Sick Nun—Penance by Hanging . . 134

CHAPTER XIX.

More Visits to the Imprisoned Nuns—Their Fears—Others temporarily put into the Cells—Relics—The Agnus Dei—The Priest's Private Hospital, or Holy Retreat—Secret Rooms in the Eastern Wing—Reports of Murders in the Convent—The Superior's Private Records—Number of Nuns in the Convent—Desire of Escape—Urgent reasons for it—Plan—Deliberation—Attempt—Success . . 142

CONCLUSION 150

viii   CONTENTS.

	PAGE
APPENDIX	154
FURTHER CONFIRMATIONS AND GENERAL REMARKS	161
ATTEMPTS TO ABDUCT MARIA MONK, FURTHER DISCLOSURES	170

NOTES, CONFIRMATIONS, &c.

Abduction of a young lady in Ireland	17
A priest turning the devil out of Bermondsey	18
Adulterous character of the Romish Priests, and abominable use of the Confessional	87
Buried alive Nuns	87
Britons called upon to purge England of conventual dens	88
Confirmations and authenticated Affidavits in proof of Miss Maria Monk's Awful Disclosures	70, 73, 99, 131, 148
Destruction of the Inquisition at Madrid—Description of its dens, instruments of torture, &c.	46
Dangers arising from sending children to Catholic seminaries	23
Extraordinary proceedings at the Catholic Nunnery in Edinburgh	72
Father Doyle's character displayed	85
Horrors and consequences of the conventual system	21
Luther on the lasciviousness and incontinency of Papists	69
Murder of a wife by her husband	58
Popery in Hartford	71
Progress of beguilement to Romanism	134
Right of Private Judgment	44
Suppression of monasteries in Spain and Portugal	25
Spanish "Bravos"	59
Six Months in a Convent: a narrative of facts relative to the introduction to the Catholic Church, sufferings therein, and escape therefrom, of Rebecca Theresa Reed	114
The Power that upholds Popery	19
The arts and craft used to entrap females	33
The Holy Coat at Trevés	42
The inquisition in the nineteenth century	52
The Female Jesuit, or Spy in the Family	70, 90, 99
The Convent Lodge at Taunton	85
The Monks of Naples	89
The Portrait of Mary in heaven	106

PREFACE.

It is hoped that the reader of the ensuing narrative will not suppose that it is a fiction, or that the scenes and persons that I have delineated had not a real existence. It is also desired that the author of this volume may be regarded, not as a voluntary participator in the very guilty transactions which are described, but receive sympathy for the trials which she has endured, and the peculiar situation in which her past experience and escape from the power of the Superior of the Hotel Dieu Nunnery at Montreal, and the snares of the Roman priests in Canada have left her.

My feelings are frequently distressed and agitated by the recollection of what I have passed through; and by night and by day I have little peace of mind, and few periods of calm and pleasing reflection; futurity also appears uncertain. I know not what reception this little work may meet with, and what will be the effect of its publication here, or in Canada among strangers, friends, or enemies. I have given the world the truth, so far as I have gone, on subjects of which I am told they are generally ignorant; and I feel perfect confidence that any facts which may yet be discovered will confirm my words, whenever they can be obtained. Whoever shall explore the Hotel Dieu Nunnery, at Montreal, will find unquestionable evidence that the descriptions of the interior of that edifice, given in this book were furnished by one familiar with them; for whatever alterations may be attempted, there are changes which no mason or carpenter can make and effectually conceal; and therefore there must be plentiful evidence in that institution of the truth of my description.

There are living witnesses, also, who ought to be made to speak without fear of penance, tortures, and death; and possibly their testimony, at some future time, may be added to confirm my statements. There are witnesses I should greatly rejoice to see at liberty, or rather there were. Are they living now? Or will they be permitted to live after the priests and Superiors have seen this book? Perhaps the wretched nuns in the cells have already suffered for my sake. Perhaps Jane Ray has been silenced for ever, or will be murdered before she has time to add her most important testimony to mine.

But speedy death, in relation only to this world, can be no great calamity to those who lead the life of a nun. The mere recollection of it always makes me miserable. It would distress the reader should I repeat the dreams with which I am often terrified at night; for I sometimes fancy myself pursued by my worst enemies; frequently I seem as if again shut up in the Convent; often I imagine myself present at the repetition of the worst scenes that I have hinted at, or described; sometimes I stand by the secret place of interment in the cellar; sometimes I think I can hear the shrieks of helpless females in the hands of atrocious men; and sometimes almost seem actually to look again upon the calm aad placid features of St. Frances, as she appeared when surrounded by her murderers.

I cannot banish the scenes and characters of this book from my memory. To me it can never appear like an amusing fable, or lose its interest and importance. The story is one which is continually before me, and must return fresh to my mind with painful emotions as long as I live. With time, and christian instruction, and the sympathy and examples of the wise and good, I hope to learn submissively to bear whatever trials are appointed for me, and to improve under them all.

Impressed as I continually am with the frightful reality of the painful communications that I have made in this volume, I can only offer to all persons who may doubt or disbelieve my statement, these two things:—

Permit me to go through the Hotel Dieu Nunnery, at Montreal, with some impartial ladies and gentlemen, that they compare my account with the interior parts of that building, into which no person but the Roman bishops and priests are ever admitted; and if they do not find my description true, then discard me as an impostor—bring me before a court of justice, there I am willing to meet Latargue, Dufresne, Phelan, Bonin, and Richards, and their wicked companions, with the superior, and any of the nuns, before a thousand men.

MARIA MONK.

New York, Jan. 11, 1836.

AWFUL DISCLOSURES

BY

MARIA MONK.

CHAPTER I.

EARLY RECOLLECTIONS.

Early Life—Religious Education neglected—First School—Entrance into the School of the Congregational Nunnery—Brief Account of the Nunneries in Montreal—The Congregational Nunnery—The Black Nunnery—The Grey Nunnery—Public Respect for these Institutions—Instructions received—The Cathechism—The Bible.

My parents were both from Scotland, but had been resident in Lower Canada some time before their marriage, which took place in Montreal; and in that city I have spent most of my life. I was born at St. John's, where they lived for a short time. My father was an officer under the British Government; and, my mother has enjoyed a pension on that account ever since his death. According to my earliest recollections, he was attentive to his family, and had a particular passage in the Bible which often occurred to my mind in after life. I may very probably have been taught by him, as after his death I do not recollect to have received any religious instruction at home, and was not even brought up to read the Scriptures; my mother, although nominally a Protestant, not being accustomed to pay attention to her children, she was rather inclined to think well of the Catholics, and often attended their churches. To my want of religious instructions at home, and the ignorance of my creator, and my duty, which was its natural effect, I think I can trace my introduction to Convents, and the scenes which I am to describe in the narrative. When about six or seven years of age, I went to school to a Mr. Work-

It was supposed that the priest was fearful that his conduct might be betrayed by this young female; and he undertook to clear himself by killing her.

These stories struck me with surprise at first, but I gradually began to feel differently, even supposing them true, and to look upon the priests as men incapable of sin; besides, when I first went to confession, which I did to father Richards, in the old French church, (since taken down,) I heard nothing improper; and it was not until I had been several times, that the priests became more and more bold, and at length indecent in their questions, and even in their conduct, when I confessed to them in the Sacristie. This subject, I believe, is not understood nor suspected among Protestants; and it is not my intention to speak of it very particularly, because it is impossible to do so without saying things both shameful and demoralizing. I will only say here, that when quite a child, I heard from the mouths of the priests at confession what I cannot repeat, with treatment corresponding; and several females in Canada have assured me that they have repeatedly, and indeed regularly, been required to answer the same and other like questions, many of which present to the mind deeds which the most iniquitous and corrupt heart could hardly invent.

There was a frequent change of teachers in the school of the Nunnery, and no regular system was pursued in our instruction. There were many nuns who came and went while I was there, being frequently called in and out without any perceptible reason. They supply school teachers to many of the country towns, usually two for each of the towns with which I was acquainted, besides sending sisters of charity to different parts of the United States. Among those whom I saw most was St. Patrick, an old woman for a nun, (that is, about forty,) very ignorant and gross in her manners, with quite a beard on her face, and very cross and disagreeable. She was sometimes our teacher in sewing, and was appointed to keep order among us. We were allowed to enter only a few of the rooms in the congregational Nunnery, although it was not considered one of the secluded convents.

In the black Nunnery, which is very near the congregational, is an hospital for sick people from the city; and sometimes some of our boarders, such as were indisposed, were sent there to be cured. I was once taken ill myself, and sent there, where I remained a few days.

There were beds enough for a considerable number more. A physician attended it daily, and there are a number of the veiled nuns of that convent who spend most of their time there. They would also sometimes read lectures and repeat prayers to us.

After I had been in the Congregational Nunnery about two years, I left, and attended several different schools for a short time. But I soon became disatisfied, having many and severe trials to endure at home, which my feelings will not allow me to describe; and as my Catholic acquaintances had often spoken to me in favour of their faith, I was inclined to believe it true, although, as I before said, I knew little of any religion. While out of the Nunnery, I saw nothing of religion. If I had, I believe I should never have thought of becoming a nun.

CHAPTER III.

BLACK NUNNERY.

Preparations to become a Novice in the Black Nunnery—Entrance—Occupations of the Novices—The Apartments to which they had access—First interview with Jane Ray—Reverence for the Superior—A wonderful Nun—Her reliques—The Holy Good Shepherd, or Nameless Nun—Confession of Novices.

At length, I determined to become a black nun, and called upon one of the oldest priests in the seminary, to whom I made known my intention.

The old priest to whom I applied was Father Rocque; he is still alive. He was at that time the oldest priest in the seminary and carried the Bon Dieu, (Good God,) as the sacramental wafer is called. When going to administer it in any country place, he used to ride with a man before him, who rang a bell as a signal. When the Canadians heard it, whose habitations he passed, they would come and prostrate themselves to the earth, worshipping it as God. He was a man of great age, and wore large curls, so that he somewhat resembled his predecessor, Father Roue. He was at that time at the head of the seminary. This institution is a large edifice, situated near the congregational and Black Nunneries, being on the east side of Notre-Dame-Street. It is the general rendezvous of all the priests in the District of Montreal; and, I have been told, supplies all the country, as far down as the Three Rivers; which place, I believe, is under the charge of the seminary of Quebec. About one hundred and fifty priests are connected with that of Montreal, as every small place has one priest, and a number of larger ones have two.

Father Roue promised to converse with the superior of the Convent, and proposed my calling again at the end of two weeks:

at which time I visited the seminary again, and was introduced, by him, to the superior of the black Nunnery. She told me she must make some inquiries, before she could give me a decided answer, and proposed to me to take up my abode a few days at the house of a French family, in St. Lawrence suburbs, a distant part of the city. Here I remained about a fortnight; during which time, I formed some acquaintance with the family, particularly with the mistress of the house, who was a devoted Papist, and had a high respect for the superior, with whom she stood on good terms.

At length, on Saturday morning, about ten o' clock, I called, and was admitted into the black Nunnery, as a novice, much to my satisfaction; for I had a high idea of a life in a Convent, secluded, as I supposed the inmates to be, from the world and all its evil influences, and assured of everlasting happiness in heaven. The Superior received me, and conducted me into a large room, where the novices, (who are called in French, *Postulantes*,) were assembled, and engaged in their customary occupation of sewing.

Here were about forty of them, and they were collected in groups in different parts of the room, chiefly near the windows; but in each group was found one of the veiled nuns of the Convent, whose abode was in the interior apartments, to which no novice was to be admitted. As we entered, the Superior informed the assembly that a new novice was come, and she desired any present who might have known me in the world to signify it. Two, Miss Feugnees and a Miss Howard, from Vermont, who had been my fellow pupil in the Congregational Nunnery, immediately recognized me. I was then placed in one of the groups at a distance from them, and furnished by a nun, called Sainte Clotilde, with materials to make a kind of a purse, such as priests use to carry the consecrated wafer in when they go to visit the sick. I well remember my feelings at that time; sitting among a number of strangers, and expecting, with painful anxiety, the arrival of the dinner hour; then, as I knew ceremonies were to be performed, though for which I was but ill prepared, as I had not yet heard the rules by which I was to be governed, and knew nothing of the forms to be repeated in the daily exercises, except the creed in Latin, and that imperfectly. This was during the time of recreation, as it is called: the only recreation there allowed, however, is that of the mind; and of this there is little; we were kept at work, and permitted to speak with each other only in hearing of the old nuns who sat by us. We proceeded to dinner in couples, and ate in silence while a lecture was read. The novices had access to only eight of the apartments of the Convent, and whatever else we wished to know we could only conjecture. The sleeping-room was in the second story, at the end of the western wing; the beds were placed in rows, without curtains or any thing else to obstruct the view, and in one corner was a small room partitioned off, in which was the bed of the night-watch—that is, the old nun who was appointed to oversee us for the night; in each side of the partition were two holes, through which she could look out upon us whenever she pleased. Her bed was a little raised above the level of the others. There was a lamp hung in the middle of our chamber, which showed every thing to her distinctly; and as she had no light in her little room, we never could perceive whether she was awake or asleep. As we knew that the slightest deviation from the rules would expose us to her observation, as well as to that of our companions, in whom it was a virtue to betray one anothers faults, as well as our own, I felt myself under a continual exposure to suffer what I disliked; and had my mind occupied in thinking of what I was to do next, and what I must avoid; though I soon learned the rules and ceremonies we had to pass, which were many, and we had to be very particular in their observance. We were employed in different kinds of work while I was a novice. The most beautiful specimen of the nuns' manufacture which I saw, was a rich carpet made of fine worsted, which had been begun before my acquaintance with the Convent, and was finished while I was there. This was sent as a present to the King of England, as an expression of gratitude for the money annually received from the Government. It was about forty yards in length, and very handsome. We were ignorant of the amount of money thus received. The Convent of Grey Nuns has also received funds from the Government, though, on some account or other, had not for several years.

I was sitting at the window one time with a girl named Jane M'Coy, when one of the old nuns came up and spoke to us in a tone of liveliness and kindness, which seemed strange in a place where everything seemed so cold and reserve. Some remark which she made was evidently intended to cheer and encourage me; and made me think that she felt some interest in me; I do not recollect what she said; but I remember it gave me pleasure. I also remember that her manners struck me singularly. She was rather old for a nun—that is, probably thirty; her figure large, her face wrinkled, and her dress careless. She seemed also to be under less restraint than the others; and this I afterwards found was the case. She sometimes even set the rules at defiance; she would speak aloud when silence was required, and sometimes walk about when she ought to have kept her place; she would even say and do things on purpose to make us laugh, and, although often blamed for her conduct, had her offences frequently passed over, when others would have been punished with penances.

I learnt that this woman had always been singular. She never would consent to take a saint's name on receiving the veil; and had always been known by her own, which was Jane Ray. Her irregularities were found to be numerous; and penances were of so little use in governing her, that she was pitied by some, who thought her insane; she was therefore commonly spoken of as mad Jane Ray; and when she committed a fault, it was often apologised for by the Superior or other nuns, on the ground that she did not know what she did.

The occupations of a novice in the Black Nunnery, are not such as some of our readers may suppose. They are not employed in studying the higher branches of education; they are not offering any advantages for storing their minds, or polishing their manners; they are not taught even reading, writing, or arithmetic; much less any of the more advanced branches of knowledge. My time was chiefly employed, at first, in work and prayers: it is true, during the last year I studied a great deal, and was required to work but very little; but it was the study of prayers in French and Latin, which I had merely to commit to memory, to prepare for the easy repetition of them on my reception, and after I should be admitted as a nun.

Among the wonderful events which had happened in the Convent, that of the sudden conversion of a gay young lady of the city into a nun, appeared to me one of the most remarkable. The story which I first heard, while a novice, made a deep impression upon my mind; it was nearly as follows :—

The daughter of a wealthy citizen in Montreal was passing the Church of Bon Secours one evening on her way to a ball, when she was suddenly thrown upon the steps, or near the door, and received a severe shock. She was taken up, and removed first, I think, into the church, but soon into the Black Nunnery, which she soon determined to join as a nun; instead, however, of being required to pass through a long novitiate, (which usually occupies about two years and a half, and is abridged only where the character is peculiarly exemplary and devout,) she was permitted to take the veil without delay; being declared by God to a priest to be in a state of sanctity. The meaning of this expression is, that she was a real saint, and already, in a great measure, raised above the world and its influences; and incapable of sinning; possessing the power of intercession; and a proper object to be addressed in prayer. This remarkable individual, I was further informed, was still in the Convent, though I never was allowed to see her; she did not mingle with the other nuns, either at work, worship, or meals; for she had no need of food, and not only her soul, but her body, was in heaven a great part of the time. What added, if possible, to the reverence and mysterious awe with which I thought of her, was the fact, I learned she had no name. The titles used in speaking of her were, " the holy saint," " reverend mother," or " *saint bon pasteur*," (the holy good shepherd.)

It is wonderful that we could have carried our reverence for the Superior so far as we did; although it was the direct tendency of many instructions and regulations, indeed the whole system, to permit, even to foster a superstitious regard for her. One of us was occasionally called into her room to cut her nails, or dress her hair; we would often collect the clippings, and distribute them with the utmost care. I once picked up all the stray hairs I could find after combing her head, bound them together, and kept them for some time, until she told me I was not worthy to possess things so sacred. Jane M'Coy and I were once sent to alter a dress for the Superior. I gathered up all the bits of thread, made a little bag, and put them into it for safe preservation. This I wore a long time round my neck, so long indeed, that I wore out a number of strings, which I remember I had replaced with new ones. I believed it to possess the power of removing pain, and have often prayed to it to cure the toothache, &c. Jane Ray sometimes professed to out-go us all in devotion to the Superior, and would pick up the feathers after making her bed. These she would distribute among us, saying, " When the Superior dies, relics will begin to grow scarce, and you had better supply yourselves in season." Then she would treat the whole matter in some way to turn it into ridicule. Equally contradictory would she appear, when occasionally she would obtain leave from the Superior to tell her dreams. With a serious face, which sometimes imposed upon us all, and made us half believe she was in perfect state of sanctity, she would narrate in French some unaccountable vision which she said she had enjoyed; then turning round, would say, " There are some who do not understand me; you all ought to be informed." And then she would say something totally different in English, which put us to the greatest agony for fear of laughing. Sometimes she would say that she expected to be Superior herself one of those days, and other things which I have not room to repeat.

While I was in the Congregational Nunnery, I had gone to the Parish Church whenever I was to confess; for although the nuns had a private confession room in the building, the boarders were taken in parties through the streets, on different days, by some of the nuns, to confess in the church; but in the black Nunnery, as we had a chapel, and priests attending in the confessionals, we never left the building.

Our confessions there, as novicies, were always performed in one way, so that it may be sufficient to describe a single case. Those of us who were to confess at a particular time, took our places on our knees near the confession box, and, after having repeated a number of prayers, &c., prescribed in our book, came up one at a time and kneeled beside a fine wooden lattice-work, which entirely separated the confessor from us, yet permitted us to place our faces almost to his ear, and nearly concealed his countenance from our view, even when so near. I recollect how the priests used to recline their heads on one side, and often covered their faces with their hankerchiefs, while they heard me confess my sins, and put questions to me, which were often of the most improper, and even revolting nature, naming crimes, both unthought of and inhuman. Still, strange as it may seem, I was persuaded to believe that all this was their duty, or at least, that it was done without sin.

Veiled nuns would often appear in the chapel at confession; though, as I understood, they generally confessed in private. Of the plan of their confession-rooms I had no information; but I supposed the ceremony to be conducted much on the same plan as in the chapel, and in the church, viz., with a lattice interposed between the confessor and the confessing.

Punishments were sometimes resorted to while I was a novice, though but seldom. The first time I ever saw a gag, was one day when a young novice had done something to offend the Superior. This girl I always had compassion for, because she was very young, and an orphan. The Superior sent for a gag, and expressed her regret at being compelled, by the bad conduct of the child, to proceed to such a punishment; after which she put it in her mouth, so far as to keep it open, and then let it remain some time before she took it out. There was a leathern strap fastened to each end, and buckled to the back part of the head.

CHAPTER IV.

Displeased with the Convent—Left it—Residence at St. Denis—Relics—Marriage—Return to the Black Nunnery—Objections made by some Novices.

After I had been a novice four or five years, that is, from the time I commenced school in the Convent, one day I was treated by one of the nuns in a manner which displeased me, and because I expressed some resentment, was required to beg her pardon. Not being satisfied with this, although I complied with the command, nor with the coolness with which the Superior treated me, I determined to quit the Convent at once, which I did without asking leave. There would have been no obstacle to my departure, I presume, novice as I then was, if I had asked permission; but I was too much displeased to wait for that, and went home without speaking to any one on the subject.

I soon after, visited the town of St. Denis, where I saw two young ladies with whom I had formerly been acquainted in Montreal; and one of them a former schoolmate at Mr. Workman's school. After some conversation with me, and learning that I had known a lady who kept school in the place, they advised me to apply to her to be employed as her assistant teacher; for she was then instructing the Government school in that place. I visited her, and found her willing, and I engaged at once as her assistant.

The government society paid her £20 a year; she was obliged to teach ten children gratuitously; might have fifteen pence a month, (about a quarter of a dollar) for each of ten scholars more; and then she was at liberty, according to the regulations, to demand as much as she pleased for the other pupils. The course of instruction, as required by the Society, embraced only reading, writing, and what is called cyphering, though, I think, improperly. The only books used, were a spelling book, *l'Instruction de la Jeunesse*, the Catholic New Testament, and *l'Historie de Canade*. When these had been read through, in regular succession, the children were dismissed as having completed their education. No difficulty is found in making the common French Canadians content with such an amount of instruction as this; on the contrary, it is often found very hard indeed to prevail upon them to send their children at all, for they say it takes too much of the love of God from them to send them to school. The teacher strictly complied with the requisitions of the Society in whose employment she was; and the Roman Catholic catechism was regularly taught in the school, as much from choice as from submission to authority, as she was a strict Catholic. I had brought with me the little bag I have before mentioned, in which I had so long kept the clippings of the thread left after making a dress for the Superior. Such was my regard for it, that I continued to wear it constantly round my neck, and to feel the same reverence for its supposed virtues as before. I occasionally had the tooth ache during my stay at St. Denis, and then always relied on the influence of my little bag. On such occasions, I would say,—" By the virtue of this bag, may I be delivered from the toothache!" And I supposed that when it ceased, it was owing to that cause.

While engaged in this manner, I became acquainted with a

man, who soon proposed marriage; and young and ignorant of the world as I was, I heard his offers with favour. On consulting with my friend, she expressed a friendly interest for me, advised me against taking such a step, and especially as I knew little about the man, except that a report was circulated unfavourable to his character. Unfortunately, I was not wise enough to listen to her advice, and hastily married. In a few weeks I had occasion to repent of the steps I had taken, as the report proved true; a report which I thought justified, and indeed required our separation. After I had been in St. Denis about three months, finding myself thus situated, and not knowing what else to do, I determined to return to the Convent, and pursue my former intention of becoming a black Nun, could I gain admittance. Knowing the many inquiries the Superior would make relative to me during my absence, before leaving St. Denis, I agreed with the lady with whom I had been associated as a teacher, (when she went to Montreal, which she did very frequently,) to say to the Lady Superior I had been under her protection during my absence, which would satisfy and stop further inquiry, as I was sensible, should they know I had been married, I should not gain admittance. I soon left and returned to Montreal; and, on reaching the city, I visited the Seminary; and in another interview with the Superior of it, communicated my wish, and desired him to procure my re-admission as a novice. Little delay occurred.

After leaving for a short time, he returned, and told me that the Superior of the Convent had consented, and I was soon introduced into her presence. She blamed me for my conduct in leaving the Nunnery, but told me that I ought to be ever grateful to my guardian angel for taking care of me, and bringing me in safety to that retreat. I requested that I might be secured against the reproaches and ridicule of all the novices and nuns, which I thought some might be disposed to cast upon me, unless prohibited by the Superior; and this she promised me. The money usually required for the admission of novices had not been expected from me. I had been admitted the first time without any such requisition; but now I chose to pay for my re-admission. I knew that she was able to dispense with such a demand, as well in this, as in the former case, and she knew that I was not in possession of any thing like the sum required. But I was bent on paying to the Nunnery; and accustomed to receive the doctrine often repeated to me before that time, that when the advantage of the church was consulted, the steps taken were justifiable, let them be what they would: I therefore, resolved to obtain money on false pretences, confident that if all were known, I should be far from displeasing the Superior. I went to the brigade major, and asked him to give me the money payable to my mother from her pension, which amounted to about thirty dollars; and, without questioning my authority to receive it in her name, he gave it me.(a)

From several of her friends, I obtained small sums under the name of loans; so that altogether I had soon raised a number of pounds, with which I hastened to the Nunnery, and deposited a part in the hands of the Superior. She received the money with evident satisfaction, though she must have known that I could not have obtained it honestly, and I was at once re-admitted as a novice. Much to my gratification, not a word issued from the lips of my old associates, in relation to my unceremonious departure, nor my voluntary return. The Superior's orders, I had not a doubt, had been explicitly laid down; and they certainly were carefully obeyed, for I never heard an illusion made to that subject, during my subsequent stay in the Convent, except, that when alone, the Superior would herself sometimes say a little about it.

There were several young ladies who entered while as novices,

---

(a) Every possible means having been employed to prove that the statements herein made by Maria Monk, are fictitious and false, we purpose to furnish various notes, extracts from current publications, and the testimonies of other parties, corroborative of the real character, and cruel nature of the Convent and Nunnery system: thereby, proving to the unprejudiced reader, that Maria Monk is not singular in her evidence. Multitudes of witnesses to the same end can and will be produced; if Divine Providence permit us to proceed with the work. Under the head of "MYSTERIES OF THE NUNNERY," the following appeared in the *Church and State Gazette*, in February, 1851.—"A letter from the west of Ireland makes some curious revelations in connection with the entrance into a Convent of a young lady, the daughter of a highly-respectable gentleman who, although himself a Roman Catholic, most strongly objects to the undue influence which has been exercised to induce his child to take a step contrary, not only to his wishes, but in a great measure, opposed to the inclination of the 'devotee' herself. Although the names are mentioned without reservation, it would perhaps be premature to give them publicity at this early stage, as the whole affair cannot much longer be concealed from public scrutiny. The facts are briefly these: The lady, who is in her nineteenth year, was prevailed upon to forsake the parental roof, under the belief, duly impressed upon her by certain of the sisterhood, that, like Joan of Arc, she had received a call from heaven; and, without as much as bidding her family farewell or apprising them previously of her intentions, she took shelter in the Convent. Here she was persuaded to write to her father, imploring forgiveness for the step she had taken 'in answering the call of God;' upon the receipt of which, the distracted parents demanded an interview with their child. This was refused. Whereupon, her father intimated to the Superioress of the Convent that he would never give a penny of his money towards the support of the establishment. The answer to this threat, was a hint that they would receive her as a 'lay nun' (that is, a servant), in which capacity they would send her to America or some foreign station. The bewildered parent next appealed to the diocesan, who refused to interpose his authority; but told him he might obtain an interview with his daughter, provided it should be in the presence of a priest; but this gracious concession being declined, all hope of justice in that high quarter was abandoned, and the matter rests for the present—but only for the present. The young lady was to have had the sum of £5,000 as her portion. The sisterhood have decided upon sending their *protegé* to New Zealand in the capacity of a 'lay nun;' but notwithstanding this determination, Mr. —— (the father) continues obdurate, and is resolved, come what will, that the fruits of his industry shall never be spent among the 'pious ladies' who have taken so deep an interest in the fortune of his child."

and became weary, or disgusted with some things they observed, and remained but a short time. One of my cousins who lived at Lachine, named Read, spent about a fortnight in the Convent with me; she, however, conceived such an antipathy to the priests, that she used expressions which offended the Superior. The first day she attended mass, while at dinner with us in full community, she said before us all, " what a rascal that priest was, to preach against his best friend." All stared at such an unusual exclamation; and some one enquired what she meant. "I say," she continued, "he has been preaching against his best friend. Do you suppose that if there were no devil, there would be any priests?" This bold young novice was immediately dismissed; and in the afternoon we had a long sermon from the Superior on the subject.[a]

[a] Facts! Facts! Undeniable facts are the things we like to meet the opponents of the Protestant faith with. The following description of madness, delusion, hypocrisy, and blasphemy, occurred in the very neighbourhood of our office. We quote it entire from the February number of *The British Protestant*. It is from "A SCRIPTURE READER'S JOURNAL." He says, "On Monday, December the 30th, 1850, I visited several Roman Catholics in the neighbourhood of Bermondsey New Road, who received me very kindly, and paid good attention to the word I read and explained. I called on Cornelius Caghlan, a man I mentioned in my journal, whom the priest of Webb Street Chapel sent his visitor to, with a lie in her mouth, and offering to collect money in all parts for him if he would return to his old system again, and have no more to do with Methodists and Protestants, but send for the priest and become a Roman Catholic as before. I read to him and his family several portions of Scripture, that I believe will be profitable to him. When I had done reading and expounding the Word, he said, 'My friend, I must tell you that the priest from Webb Street Roman Catholic Chapel was with me last Friday night, just as we were about to go to bed.' I asked him what time was that: he said, 'between ten and eleven o'clock at night.' I asked what did a priest want here, at that hour, or what did he say? He (Caghlan) said, 'My mother and two sisters came in and sat down; and very soon after the priest came in, accompanied by a very decent man, each having a small bottle in his hand, one containing, I believe, wine or some sort of red liquor, and in the other was holy water. When the priest came in, he said, 'Does Mr. Caghlan live here?' I said, 'I do, sir.' He, (the priest) then said, 'Have you any holy water in the house? for the devil is in this room, and I am come to turn him out of it before I leave here, so that there will be peace and happiness in this house and in the neighbourhood, when I get the devil out.' I then said to the priest, 'We want no holy water here, but the blood of Jesus Christ is the holy water I want, for it will cleanse me from all my sins, and make me holy and happy for ever, and that is what your holy water cannot do.' He (the priest) then said, 'I believe in the blood of Christ too; but it will not do, for it must have other things to help it, good works.' I told him that faith will produce those good works, as a tree produces good fruit. He (the priest) then took the bottle that had the holy water in it, and pouring it on his hand, he sprinkled it all over the whole room, and on my mother and sisters; he then came to put some of it on my head, but I said, 'No, for if I want my head washed, I have plenty of good fresh water in the butt, and it is better than the water you spoilt by putting salt in it.' He then lifted up his hand to throw the water on my head, but I covered my head with the quilt, which he wet very much with the holy water. I then told my wife to call in a policeman, that I might give the priest in charge, but my sister turned the key in the door, and my wife could not get out. The priest then said, 'Come now, confess your sins to me, and I promise you that they will be all forgiven you before I leave this room.' I told him I would confess my sins to God and not to man; for it is God only that can forgive me my sins, and not a priest nor any other man, and that I will prove it in an instant.' I then told my wife to hand me the Bible from the cupboard; the priest put the bottle on the form, and clapped both his hands together, and said, 'This is the lad I

It happened that I one day got a leaf of an English Bible, which had been brought into the Convent wrapped round some sewing silk; purchased at a store in the city. For some reason or other, I determined to commit to memory a chapter it contained; which I soon did. It is the only chapter I ever learnt in the Bible; and I can now repeat it. It is the second of St. Matthew's gospel, "Now when Jesus was born at Bethlehem of Judea," &c. It happened that I was observed reading the paper; and when the nature of it was discovered, I was condemned to do penance for my offence.

Great dislike to the Bible was shown by those who conversed with me about it, and several have remarked to me at different times, that if it were not for that book, Catholics would never be led to renounce their own faith.

I have heard passages read from the Envangile, relating to the death of Christ; the conversion of Paul; a few chapters from St. Matthew; and perhaps a few others. The priest would also sometimes take a verse or two, and preach from it. I have read St. Peter's life, but only in the book called the "Lives of the Saints." He, I understand, has the keys of heaven and hell; and has founded our church. As for St. Paul, I remember, as I was taught to understand it, that he was once a great persecutor of the Roman Catholics, until he became convicted, and confessed to one of the father confessors, I don't know which: for who can expect to be forgiven, who does not become a Catholic and confess ?(a)

came to turn out, that is the lad, the devil I want out of here; I must have him out, and then there will be happiness and peace of mind in this house, and among the neighbours.' My sister also stood up in a great rage, and said, 'As soon as I see it I will tear it in pieces.' I then said to my wife, leave the Bible where it is, for as it frightens them it is better not to shew it to them. The priest bent all his fingers on both hands like grappling irons, and said, 'Come, we must leave him with him, that has his crooks so fast in him, and I am sorry that there is not a scraper at the door.' He then raised up his foot, knee high, and scraped his shoe against the door, when he was doing that wicked deed, the other man pulled the priest's leg away, to prevent him doing such a thing. This was on Friday night, by the Roman Catholic priest of Webb Street Chapel, Bermondsey, December the 27th, 1850.' When I heard all this I took from my pocket, 'The Glories of Mary,' and I read a few pages, particularly the two ladders, one red and one white, to shew him how Roman Catholics trust more in the Virgin Mary and holy water than they do in Christ and his blood. While I was reading to Caghlan his landlord came in, and ordered him to quit the room, for he would have no more visitors, nor prayers, nor preaching in his houses, and that Caghlan should leave this week, for the neighbours would not have him among them. This appears to be another scheme of the priests to break up the prayer meeting he has opened in his room, as Father Kyne has done to my meeting in Angel Court, Long Acre, and he opened a school in my room, that continued only three weeks, when a fever raged in the place, and cut off all my enemies and persecutors, as it says in the 37th Psalm; and so it came to pass, and I saw it, for they were all cut off, and I am left to plead the cause of God my Saviour. This week I visited sixty-two Roman Catholic families, in the various courts and streets in Bermondsey, and out of the sixty-two I was only allowed to read in eight rooms."

(a) Of the power that holds Popery up—and of the power alone that can put it

CHAPTER V.

Received Confirmation—Painful feelings—Specimen of instructions received on the subject.

The day on which I received confirmation, was a distressing one to me. I believed the doctrine of the Roman Catholics; and, according to them, I was guilty of three mortal sins: concealing something at confession, sacrilege, in putting the body of Christ in the sacrament under my feet, and by receiving it while not in a state of grace. And now I had been led into all those sins, in consequence of my marriage, which I never had acknowledged, as it would have cut me off from being admitted as a nun.

On the day, therefore, when I went to the church to be confirmed, with a number of others, I suffered extremely from the reproaches of conscience. I knew, at least I believed, as I had been told, that a person who had been anointed with the holy oil of confirmation on the forehead, and dying in the state in which I was, would go down to hell; and, in the place where the oil had been rubbed, the names of my sins would blaze out on my forehead; these would be a sign by which the devils would know me; and would torment me the worse for them. I was thinking

---

down, the Rev. J. A. James thus speaks:—"A modern eloquent historian in one of his writings said to this effect: 'When I see what Popery is now, and what attacks it has withstood and survived, I do not see by what power it is to be brought down.' Nor do I, till I look up to the Omnipotent One who sits upon the throne. There is something about Popery which makes it treat argument and eloquence as Leviathan does straws and rotten wood. It is sustained, in my opinion, not only by the temporal power that it commands on earth—though that is great, as all the despots of Europe prove—but by *the powers of the infernal world* —and it is heaven only that can conquer hell: God only that can subdue Satan; and he will do it, for he has declared he will. But then he says—'For all these things I will be inquired of.' Prayer is that which moves the hand that moves all things. Prayer is that which, so to speak, awakens the arm of the Lord. I know that Papists pray, and a matter of sport it is for Infidels to see them and the Protestants praying against each other. Yet is there anything in this to be matter of sport? What should the litigants on this question do but carry their disputes to Him who is the God of truth? Yes, Roman Catholics *do* pray. They are besieging heaven with prayers for England's conversion. One thing, however, is enough to give us assurance of the kind of reception *their* prayers must meet with in heaven; and that is, they are addressed to the Virgin Mary, shall I say *more* than to God or Christ? If not, at any rate, to God and Christ through her. Let us, then, betake ourselves to prayer, which is always our best, sometimes our only resource. Never was there a louder call to prayer, than this papal aggression, with all that it implies and indicates, has sent forth. A praying nation is safe. God will be round about such a people as a wall of fire, and a glory in the midst of them. I have confidence in prayer. I have confidence in truth. I have confidence in God. Let us fight against Popery upon our knees, in the sanctuary—in the social meeting—in the family—in the closet. That beautiful, but profligate Popish queen, Mary of Scotland, used to say, 'She was more afraid of the prayers of John Knox, than of the English army.'

"And Satan trembles when he sees,
The weakest saint upon his knees."

of all this, while I sat in the pew, waiting to receive the oil. I felt, however, some consolation, as I often did afterwards when my sins came to my mind; and this consolation I derived from another doctrine of the same church; viz., that a bishop could absolve me from all these sins any minute before my death; and I intended to confess them all to a bishop, before leaving the world. At length, the moment for administering of the "sacrament" arrived; and a bell was rung. Those who had to be confirmed, had brought tickets from their confessors; and these were thrown into a hat, carried around by a priest, who, in turn, handed each to the bishop, by which he learned the name of each of us, and applied a little of the oil to our foreheads; this was immediately rubbed off by a priest, with a bit of cloth, quite roughly.[a]

(a) No. 1 of *Hints to Romanizers*, published by Seeley's, contains an excellent article on "THE CONVENTUAL SYSTEM." We extract as follows—" Fifteen years ago I occupied, in a very solitary part of the town, a house, the garden of which was adjacent to that of a Convent of women. Though my windows overlooked the greatest part of their garden, I had never seen my sad neighbours. In the month of May, on Rogation-day, I heard numerous weak, very weak voices, chanting prayers, as the procession passed through the Convent-garden. The singing was sad, dry, unpleasant, their voices faint, as if spoiled by sufferings. I thought for a moment they were chanting prayers for the dead; but listening more attentively, I distinguished, on the contrary. " *Te rogamus, audi nos,*" the song of hope which invokes the benediction of the God of life upon fruitful nature. This May-song chanted by these lifeless nuns, offered to me a bitter contrast. To see crawling along on the flowery verdant turf these poor girls, who will never bloom again!—The thought of the middle ages, that had at first flashed across my mind, soon died away; for then, monastic life was connected with a thousand other things; but in our modern harmony it is a barbarous contradiction, a false, grating tone? What I then beheld before me was then to be defended neither by nature, nor by history.   *   *   *   It is often from an instinctive tyranny, that the Superiors delight in breaking the ties of kindred. 'The curate of my parish exhorted me to write to my father, who had just lost my mother. I let advent go by (during which time nuns are not permitted to write letters,) and the latter days of the month which are passed in retirement, in the institution, to prepare us for the renewing of our vows, which takes place on new-year's day. But, after the holy term, I hastened to fulfil my duty towards the best of fathers, by addressing to him, both my prayers and good wishes, and endeavouring to offer him some consolation in the afflictions and trials with which it had pleased God to visit him. I went to the cell of the Superior nun, to beg her to read over my letter, fix the convent-seal to it, and send it off; but she was not there. I therefore put it in my cell upon the table, and went to prayers: during this time our Reverend Mother, the Superior, who knew that I had written, because she had sent one of the nuns to see what I was about, beckoned to one of the sisters and bid her to take from me my letter. She did so every time I wrote, seven times running, so that my father died five months afterwards, without ever obtaining a letter from me, which he had so much desired, and had even asked me for on his death-bed, by the curate of his parish.'—*Note of Sister Lemonnier*, in Mr. Tillard's Memoire.   *   *   *   In these dreadful prisons, which are punishments, you may perceive instruments of torture, wheels, iron collars, whips. In what, I should like to know, do convents of our time differ from houses of correction and mad-houses? Many convents seem to unite the three characters. I know but one difference between them; whilst the houses of correction are inspected by the law, and the mad-houses by the police, both stop at the convent doors, the law is afraid, and dares not pass the threshold. Sister Marie Lemonnier was shut up with mad girls; here she found a Carmelite nun, who had been there nine years. The third volume of the *Wandering Jew* contains the real history of Mademoiselle B. She has passed latterly not into a mad-house, but into a convent." Which convent is even worse, in many respects, than a mad-house.

I went home with some qualms of conscience, and often thought with dread of the following tale; which I have heard told to illustrate the sinfulness of conduct like mine. A priest was once travelling; when, just as he was passing by a house, his horse fell on his knees, and would not rise. His rider dismounted, and went in, to learn the cause of so extraordinary an occurrence. He found there a woman near death; to whom a priest was trying to administer the sacrament, but without success; for every time she attempted to swallow it, it was thrown back out of her mouth, into the chalice. He perceived it was owing to unconfessed sin, and took away the holy wafer from her, on which the horse rose from his knees, and he continued his journey.

I often remembered also, that I had been told, that we shall have as many devils biting us, if we go to hell, as we have unconfessed sins on our consciences. I was required to devote myself for about a year, to the study of the prayers, and practice of the ceremonies necessary on the reception of a nun. This I found a very tedious duty; but, as I was released in a great degree, from the daily labours usually demanded of novices, I felt little disposition to complain.

CHAPTER VI.

Taking the Veil—Interview afterwards with the Superior—Surprise and Horror at the Disclosures—Resolution to submit.

I was introduced into the Superior's room on the evening preceding the day on which I was to take the veil, to have an interview with the bishop. The Superior was present; and the interview lasted about half an hour. The bishop, on this, as on other occasions, appeared to me habitually rough in his manner. His address was by no means prepossessing. Before I took the veil, I was ornamented for the ceremony; and was clothed in a rich dress belonging to the Convent, which was used on such occasions; and placed not far from the altar, in the chapel, in the view of a number of spectators who had assembled; in number, perhaps about forty. Taking the veil is an affair which happens so frequently in Montreal, that it has long ceased to be regarded as a novelty: and, although notice had been given in the French parish church as usual, only a small audience assembled, as I have mentioned.

Being well prepared with long training, and frequent rehearsals, for what I was to perform, I stood waiting in my large flowing dress, for the appearance of the bishop. He soon presented himself; entering by the door behind the altar: I then threw myself at his feet, and asked him to confer upon me the veil. He expressed his consent; and then, turning to the Superior, I threw myself prostrate at her feet, according to my instructions; repeating what I had before done at rehearsals; and made a movement as if to kiss her feet. This she prevented; or appeared to prevent; catching me by a sudden motion of her hand, and granted my request. I then kneeled before the holy sacrament; that is—a large round wafer, held by the bishop between his fore finger and thumb, and made my vows. This wafer, I had been taught to regard with the utmost veneration, as the real body of Jesus Christ; the presence of which, made the vows uttered before it, binding in the most solemn manner. After taking the vows, I proceeded to a small apartment behind the altar, accompanied by four nuns; where there was a coffin prepared with my nun name engraven upon it: "Saint Eustace."

My companions lifted it by four handles attached to it, while I threw off my dress, and put on that of a nun of *Sœur Bourgeoise;* and then we all returned to the chapel. I proceeded first, and was followed by four nuns; the bishop, naming a number of worldly pleasures in rapid succession; in reply to which, I as rapidly repeated, "*Je renonce, je renonce, je renonce,*"—I renounce I renounce, I renounce.(a). The coffin was then placed in

(a) We solemnly believe, and are assured, that so corrupt are the doctrines and doings of the convent system, that had we the power, no such pretended religious community should have any sanction whatever. Read the words of the Rev. W. Carus Wilson, in his introductory address to *Narrative of Escape from a Portuguese Convent.* These are his own words:—" Protestant parents! I doubt not you shudder at the very recital of the horrors and abominations of the Portuguese convent; and nothing would more effectually seal your wretchedness for life, than the thought that a beloved daughter could thus be unnaturally lost to you. I doubt not, but your feelings of execration are roused to the very highest pitch against a system which admits of such cruelties: but stop for a moment. Remember, the school is only the ante-room of the nunnery. Popish principles admit of the breaking of faith with heretics; the 'Secreta Monita,' a treatise drawn up for the express purpose of directing the Jesuits in their line of conduct, and which singularly came to light in the pillaging of a monastery some years ago in Germany, and has been translated into English, and published in London, lays it down as a meritorious duty to go any lengths of lying, cruelty or theft, to reclaim a heretic. The promise indeed may be given, not to interfere: and I recollect the case of a clergyman, (with shame be it spoken,) who sent his daughter to be perfected in the French language, in a school at Paris, depending, no doubt, on such a promise. She had previously been educated in the Clergy Daughters' School, now removed to Casterton, and then at Cowen Bridge; where, through grace, she had gathered strength for a time of trial. It pleased God to visit her with a fatal illness in the school, when every measure was resorted to, which priests and 'sisters' could devise for her salvation. But every offer of holy water, of the Virgin's service, and of extreme unction were strenuously rejected, with the noble profession of her faith, amidst this wretched mummery and superstition.—'None but Christ, nothing but Jesus for me.' Here was a striking instance of the snare being escaped; but I ask, can you, with your eyes open, run front of the altar, and I advanced to place myself in it. The coffin was to be deposited, after the ceremony, in an outhouse; to be preserved until my death, when it was to receive my corpse. There were reflections which I naturally made at that time; but I stepped in, extended myself, and lay still. A pillow had been placed at the head of the coffin, to support my head in a comfortable position. A large thick black cloth was then spread over me, and the chanting of Latin immediately commenced. My thoughts were not the most pleasing during the time I lay in that situation. The pall, or "*Drap Mortel,*" as the cloth is called, had a strong smell of incense, which was always disagreeable to me, and then proved almost suffocating. I recollected a story of a novice, who in taking the veil, lay down in her coffin like me; and was covered in the same manner; but, on the removal of the covering, was found dead. When I was uncovered, I rose, stepped out of my coffin, and kneeled: other ceremonies then followed, of no particular interest; after which, the music commenced; and here the whole was finished. I then proceeded from the chapel, and returned to the Superior's room, followed by the other nuns, who walked two by two in their customary manner, with their hands folded on their breasts, and their eyes cast down upon the floor. The nun who was to be my companion in future,

the risk of involving a tenderly-loved daughter in such a horrible and irremediable ruin as this? I feel that I shall not have sent this little work into the world in, vain, if but *one* parent is induced by the reading of it, to abandon his purpose and take the *safer* side, and to prefer for his child a thoroughly Protestant education. What heart does not weep over such an instance, as occurred lately in the country in which I live? Two daughters of a respectable Roman Catholic family, were sent to a distant seminary for education; the period of their return was anxiously anticipated by their fond and affectionate parents; when tidings came, that they had resolved to abandon for ever all their family endearments, and to take the veil. What agony must have thrilled through the soul of the tender mother! Oh! no fancied waters of separation can quench the feelings of pity and campassion which I feel towards her. Well may she be like Rachael, weeping for her children, and refusing to be comforted, because they are not. And yet, there would be the succour of the church readily, and freely administered! Strange, strange infatuation! But how false and unscriptural is the convent system altogether! False, because the history of their proceedings, as well as a correct knowledge of human nature, is at once conclusive, as to their inadequacy to effect the desired object. If that object be the more successful victory over the temptations of the world, how completely is it forgotten that the world is in the *heart*; and that wherever we go, the world, as it respects its real dangers and temptations, goes along with us. The question therefore is, whether the seclusion of a convent is more favourable for a heavenly and devoted course, than the station of life in which God has providentially placed us. I decidedly think not. Take the most favourable instance: that of a young person who is powerfully under a religious influence. Let it be concluded, that she takes the veil from a pure desire to be dead to the world, and alive to God. Is the change of position clearly advantageous for her purpose? I believe that it is with the soul as it is with the body; that as the latter can only be kept in health by exercise—so the former, in all that really regards its highest interests, thrives the best in the active and full discharge of the relative and social duties of life. I believe that while the first effect of real grace is to enlarge and liberalize the heart, the principle of grace is best established and upheld by extension; just as the waters are kept the purest, which, unlike the muddy and stagnant pools, flow in a lengthened stream."

then walked at the end of the procession. On reaching the Superior's door, they all left me; and I entered alone; and found her with a bishop and two priests.

The Superior now informed me, that having taken the black veil, it only remained that I should swear the three oaths customary on becoming a nun; and, that some explanations would be necessary from her. I was now she told me, to have access to every part of the edifice, even to the cellar; where two of the sisters were imprisoned for causes which she did not mention. I must be informed that one of my great duties was to obey the priest in all things; and this I soon learned, to my utter astonishment and horror, was to live in the practice of criminal intercourse with them. I expressed some of the feelings which this announcement excited in me, which came upon me like a flash of lightning; but the only effect was to set her arguing with me in favour of the crime, representing it as a crime acceptable to God, and honourable to me. The priests, she said, were not situated like other men, being forbidden to marry, while they lived secluded, laborious, and self-denying lives, for our salvation. They might indeed, be considered our saviours; as, without their services, we could not obtain pardon of sin, and must go to hell. Now, it was our solemn duty on withdrawing from the world, to consecrate our lives to religion, and to practice every species of self-denial. We could not become too humble, nor mortify our feelings too far; this was to be done by opposing them, and acting contrary to them; and what she proposed was, therefore, pleasing in the sight of God. I now felt how foolish I had been to place myself in the power of such persons as were around me. From what she said, I could draw no other conclusion, but that I was required to act like the most abandoned of beings, and that all my future associates were habitually guilty of the most henious and detestable crimes. When I repeated my expressions of suprise and horror, she told me that such feelings were very common at first, and that many other nuns had expressed themselves as I did, who had long since changed their minds; she even said, that on her entrance into the nunnery, she had felt like me.[a]

(a) Surely such disclosures as are here given, must convince every Protestant reader, of the imperative duty of making Convents and Nunneries throughout the British dominions, the subject of legislative interference. Is it to be endured for a moment, that these abominations can be going forward in our own country with all our boasted light and liberty, while even in the benighted and superstitious countries of Spain and Portugal, they have been seen in their true colors, and summarily annihilated? The *Protestant Magazine* says, "The monastic orders in Spain appear to be in a rapid course of suppression. On the 18th of September the whole of the Convents and Monasteries were shut up at Cadiz, and the inmates obliged to leave, after only five hours' notice. Such a change was, however, effected without any riot or bloodshed, though the women rendered themselves conspicuous by plundering two convents. A letter says, 'There is not now a monk remaining in the city.' Among the items of intelligence received

Doubts, she declared, was among our greatest enemies; they would lead us to question every point of duty, and induce us to waver at every step. They arose only from remaining imperfection; and were always evidences of sin. Our only way was to dismiss them immediately, repent, and confess them: they were deadly sins; and would condemn us to hell, if we should die without confessing them. Priests, she insisted, could not sin. It was a thing impossible. Every thing that they did, and wished, was, of course right. She hoped I would see the reasonableness and duty of the oaths I was to take, and be faithful to them.

She gave another piece of information, which excited other feelings in me, scarcely less dreadful. Infants were sometimes born in the Convent; but they were always baptized, and immediately strangled: this secured their everlasting happiness; for the baptism purified them from all sinfulness, and, being sent out of the world before they had time to do any thing wrong, they were at once admitted into heaven. How happy, she exclaimed, are those who secure immortal happiness to such little beings! Their little souls would thank those who kill their bodies, if they had it in their power.[a]

Into what a place, and among what society, had I been admitted? How differently did a Convent now appear from what I had supposed it to be! The holy women I had always fancied the nuns to be, the venerable Lady Superiors, what were they? And the priests of the seminary adjoining, some of whom indeed I had reason to think, were base and profligate men; what were they all? I now learnt that they were often admitted into the nunnery, and allowed to indulge in the greatest crimes; which they and others called virtues. After having listened for some time to the Superior alone, a number of the nuns were admitted, and took a free part in the conversation. They concurred in everything which she had told me, and repeated, without any signs of shame or compunction, things which criminated themselves. I must acknowledge the truth, and declare that all this had an effect upon my mind. I questioned whether I might not

---

from Lisbon by the last arrivals, the suppression of the monasteries in Portugal holds a high place of importance. On the 28th of May, a decree was published, abolishing for ever the privileges of the monastic orders throughout that kingdom and its dependencies—confiscating their properties, dispersing their societies, and appropriating their service of plate and utensils to the use of the parish churches." We hope England will quickly arouse herself to the clearing out of these dreadful haunts.

(a) Read that well-authenticated Narrative, entitled, "Horrors of the Nunnery," in Nos. 2 and 3 of *The Anti-Popish Reviewer; or, Protestant Lamp for the Christian Churchman;* published by Houlston & Stoneman, Paternoster-row; only One-penny each number; a work that is spreading through the three kingdoms with great rapidity; and will, we hope, be useful in these days, when Rome is craftily plotting our overthrow.

be in the wrong; and felt as if their reasoning might have some foundation. I had been several years under the tuition of Catholics; and was ignorant of the Scriptures, and unaccustomed to the society, example, and conversation of Protestants; had not heard any appeal to the Bible as authority; but had been taught, both by precept and example, to receive, as truth, everything said by the priests. I had not heard their authority questioned; nor anything said of any other standard of faith but their own declarations. I had long been familiar with the corrupt and licentious expressions which some of them use at confessions, and believed that other women were also; I had no standard of duty to refer to; and no judgment of my own which I knew how to use, or thought of using.

All around me insisted that my doubts proved only my own ignorance and sinfulness; that they knew by experience they would soon give place to true knowledge, and an advance in religion; and I felt something like indecision. Still, there was so much that disgusted me in the discovery I had now made of the debased characters around me, that I would most gladly have escaped from the nunnery and never returned. But that was a thing not to be thought of; I was in their power, and this I deeply felt; while I thought there was not one among the whole number of nuns to whom I could look for kindness.

There was one, however, who began to speak to me at length in a tone that gained something of my confidence; the nun whom I have mentioned before as distinguished for her oddity—Jane Ray, who made us so much amusement when I was a novice. Although, as I have remarked, there was nothing in her face, form, or manners, to give me any pleasure, she addressed me with apparent friendliness, and while she seemed to concur with some things spoken by them, took an opportunity to whisper a few words in my ear unheard by them, intimating, that I had better comply with everything the Superior desired, if I would save my life. I was somewhat alarmed before, but I now became much more so; and determined to make no further resistance. The Superior then made me repeat the three oaths, and when I had sworn them, I was shown into one of the community rooms, and remained some time with the nuns, who were released from their usual employments, and enjoying a recreation day on account of the admission of a new sister. My feelings during the remainder of the day, I shall not attempt to describe; but pass on to mention the ceremonies that took place at dinner. This description may give an idea of the manner in which we always took our meals, although there were some parts in which the breakfast and dinner were different.

At eleven o'clock, the bell rang for dinner; and the nuns all took their places in a double row, in the same order as that in which they had left the chapel in the morning; except, that my companions and myself were stationed at the head of the line. Standing thus for a moment, with our hands placed one on the other over the breast, and hidden in our large cuffs, with our heads bent forward, and eyes fixed on the floor. An old nun, who stood at the door, clapped her hands as a signal for us to proceed, and the procession moved on; while we all commenced the repetition of litanies. We walked on in this order, repeating all the way until we reached the door of the dining-room, where we were divided into two lines; those on the right passing down on one side of the long table, and those on the left the other, till all were in; and each stopped in her place. The plates were all ranged, each with a knife and fork, and spoon, rolled up in a napkin, and tied round with a linen band marked with the owner's name. My own plate, knife, and fork, &c. were prepared like the rest; and on the band around them I found my new name written;—"Saint Eustace."

There we stood till all had concluded the litany; when the old nun, who had taken her place at the head of the table next the door, said the prayer before meat, beginning, "*Benedicte*," and we sat down. I do not remember of what our dinner consisted, but we usually had soup and some plain dish of meat; the remains of which were occasionally served up at supper as a fricasee. One of the nuns, who had been appointed to read that day, rose, and began a lecture from a book put into her hand by the Superior; while the rest of us ate in silence. The nun who reads during dinner, stays afterwards to dine. As fast as we finished our meals, each rolled up her knife, fork, and spoon, in her napkin, and bound them together with the band, and sat with hands folded. The old nun then said a short prayer, rose, stepped a little aside, clapped her hands, and we marched towards the door, bowing, as we passed, before a little chapel, or glass box, containing a wax image of the infant Jesus.

Nothing important occurred until late in the afternoon; when, as I was sitting in the community-room, Father Dufresne called me out, saying he wished to speak with me. I feared what was his intention; but I dared not disobey. In a private apartment, he treated me in a brutal manner; and from two other priests I afterwards received similar usage that evening. Father Dufresne afterward appeared again; and I was compelled to remain in company with him till morning. I am assured that the conduct of priests in our Convent, has never been exposed; and is not imagined by the people of the United States. This induces me to say what I do, notwithstanding the strong reasons I have to let it remain unknown. Still I cannot force myself to speak on such subjects except in the most brief manner.

CHAPTER VII.

Daily ceremonies—Jane Ray among the nuns.

On Thursday morning, the bell rung at half-past six to waken us. The old nun who was acting as night-watch, immediately spoke aloud, "*Voici le Seigneur qui vient.*" (Behold the Lord cometh.) The nuns all responded "*Allons—y devant lui.*" (Let us go and meet him.) We then rose immediately, and dressed as expeditiously as possible, stepping into the passage-way at the foot of our beds as soon as we were ready, and taking places each beside her opposite companion. Thus we were soon drawn up in a double row the whole length of the room, with our hands folded across our breasts, and concealed in the broad cuffs of our sleeves. Not a word was uttered. When the signal was given, we all proceeeded to the community-room, which is spacious, and took our places in rows facing the entrance; near which the Superior was seated in a vergiere.

We first repeated, "*Au nom du Pere, du Filis, et du Saint Esprit—Ainsi sait il.*" (In the name of the Father, the Son, and the Holy Ghost,—Amen.) We then kneeled and kissed the floor; then, still on our knees, we said a very long prayer, beginning; "*Divin Jesus, Saveur de mon ame.*" (Divine Jesus, Saviour of my soul.) Then came the Lord's prayer, three hail Mary's, four creeds, and five confessions. (*Confesse a Dieu.*)

Next we repeated the ten commandments. Then we repeated the Acts of the Faith, and a prayer to the Virgin in Latin; (which, like every thing else in Latin, I never understood a word of.) Next we said the litanies of the holy name of Jesus in Latin, which was afterwards to be repeated several times in the course of the day. Then came the prayer for the beginning of the day; then bending down, we commenced the Orison Mental, (or Mental Orison,) which lasted about an hour and a half. This exercise was considered peculiarly solemn. We were told in the nunnery, that a certain saint was saved by the use of it; as she never omitted it. It consisted of several parts. First, the Superior read to us a chapter from a book; which occupied five minutes. Then profound silence prevailed for fifteen minutes; during which we were meditating upon it. Then she read another chapter of equal length on a different subject; and we meditated upon that another quarter of an hour; and after a third reading and meditation, we finished the exercise with a prayer, called an act of contrition; in which we asked forgiveness for the sins committed during the Orison.

During this hour and a half I became very weary; having before been kneeling for some time, and having then to sit in another position more uncomfortable, with my feet under me, and my hands clasped, and my body bent humbly forward, with my head bowed down. When the Orison was over, we all rose to the upright kneeling posture, and repeated several prayers, and the litanies of the Providence; *"Providence de Dieu," &c.* Then followed a number of Latin prayers, which we repeated on the way to mass; for, in the nunnery we had mass daily. When mass was over we proceeded in our usual order to the eating-room to breakfast, practising the same forms which I have described at dinner. Having made our meal in silence we repeated the litanies of the " Holy name of Jesus," as we proceeded to the community-room; and such as had not finished them on their arrival threw themselves upon their knees, and remained there until they had gone through with them, and then kissing the floor, rose again.

At nine o'clock commenced the lecture, which was read by a nun appointed to perform that duty that day; all the rest of us in the room being engaged in work.

The nuns were at this time distributed in different community-rooms, at different kinds of work, and each was listening to a lecture. This exercise continued until ten o'clock, when the recreation bell rang. We still continued our work; but the nuns began to converse with each other on subjects permitted by the rules, in the hearing of the old nuns, one of whom was seated in each of the groups.

At half-past ten the silence bell rang, and this conversation instantly ceased, and the recitation of some latin prayers, commenced, which continued half-an-hour.

At eleven o'clock the dinner bell rang, and then we proceeded to the dining-room, and went through the forms and ceremonies of the preceeding day. We proceeded two by two. The old nun who had the command of us clapped her hands as the first couple reached the door, when we stopped. The first two dipped their fingers into the font, touched the holy water to the breast, forehead, and each side, thus forming a cross, said, " In the name of the Father, Son, and Holy Ghost. Amen," and then walked on to the dining-room, repeating the litanies. The rest followed their example. On reaching the door the couples divided, and the two rows of nuns marching up, stopped and faced the table against their plates. There we stood repeating the close of the litany aloud. The old nun then pronounced "*Benedicite*," and we sat down. One of our number began to read a lecture, which continued during the whole meal. She stays to eat after the rest have retired. When we had dined each of us folded up her napkin, and again folded her hands. The old nun then repeated a short prayer in French, and stepping aside from the head of the table, let us pass out as we came in. Each of us bowed in passing the little chapel near the door, which is a glasscase containing a waxen figure of the infant Jesus. When we reached the community room we took our places in rows, and kneeled upon the floor, while a nun read aloud, "*Douleurs de Notre sainte Marie*," (the sorrows of our holy Mary,) at the end of each verse we responded "*Ave Maria.*" We then repeated again the litanies of the Providences, and the "*Benissante.*" Then we kissed the floor; and rising, took our work, with leave to converse on permitted subjects (this is what is called recreation,) till one o'clock. We then began to repeat litanies, one at a time in succession; still engaged at sewing for an hour.

At two o'clock commenced the afternoon lectures; which lasted till near three. At that hour one of the nuns stood up in the middle of the room, and asked each of us a question out of the catechism; and such as were unable to answer correctly were obliged to kneel down until that exercise was concluded upon as many dry peas as there were verses in the chapter out of which they were questioned. This seems like a penance of no great importance; but I have sometimed kneeled on peas until I suffered great inconvenience, and even pain. It soon makes one feel as if needles were running through the skin. Whoever thinks it a trifle had better try it.

At four o'clock recreation commenced, when we were allowed, as usual, to speak to each other while at work. At half past four we began to repeat prayers in Latin, while we worked; and concluded about five o'clock, when we commenced repeating the "prayers for the examination of conscience;" the "prayer after confession;" the "prayer before sacrament;" and the "prayer after sacrament." Thus we continued our work until dark; when we laid it aside, and began to go over the same prayers which we had repeated in the morning, with the exception of the Orison Mentale; instead of that long exercise, we examined our consciences, to determine whether we had performed the resolution we had made in the morning; and such as had kept it repeated an "*acte de joie*," or expression of gratitude; while such as had not said an "*acte de contrition.*" When the prayers were concluded, any nun who had been disobedient in the day, knelt and asked pardon of the Superior, and her companions, "for the scandal she had caused them;" and then requested the Superior to give her a penance to perform. When all the penances had been imposed, we all proceeded to the eating room to supper, repeating litanies on the way. At supper the ceremonies were the same as at dinner, except that there was no lecture read. We ate in silence, and went out bowing to the *chapelle*, and repeating litanies. Returning to the community-room, which we had left, we had more prayers to repeat, which are called " *La corounne*, (crown) which consist of the following parts.—

First,—Four "*Paters.*" Second,—Four "*Ave Marias.*" Third,—Four "*Gloria Patrias.*" Fourth,—"*Benisser, Santeys.*"

At the close of these we kissed the floor; after which we had recreation till half-past eight o'clock; being allowed to converse on permitted subjects, but closely watched, and not allowed to sit in the corner.

At half past eight a bell was rung, and a chapter was read to us in a book of meditations, to employ our minds upon, during our waking hours at night. Standing near the door we dipped our fingers in the holy water; crossed, and blessed ourselves, and proceeded up to the sleeping-room in the usual order, two by two. When we had got into bed, we repeated a prayer beginning with; "*Mon Dieu, je vous donne mon coeur.*" " My God, I give you my heart." And then an old nun, bringing some holy water, sprinkled it on our beds to frighten away the devil; while we took some and crossed ourselves again. At nine o'clock the bell rang, and all who were awake repeated a prayer, called the offrande; those who were asleep were considered as excused.

After my admission among the nuns, I had more opportunity than before to observe the conduct of mad Jane Ray. She behaved quite differently from the rest, and with a degree of levity irreconcilable with the rules. She was, as I have described her, a large woman, with nothing beautiful or attractive in her face, form, or manners; careless in her dress, and of a restless disposition, which prevented her from steadily applying herself to anything for any length of time, and kept her perpetually roving about, and almost perpetually talking to somebody or other. It would be very difficult to give an accurate description of this singular woman, dressed in the plain garments of the nuns, bound by the same vows, and accustomed to the same life, resembling them in nothing else, and frequently interrupting all their employments. She was apparently almost always studying, or pursuing some odd fancy; now rising from sewing to walk up and down, or straying in from another apartment, looking about, addressing some of us, and passing out again, or saying something to make us laugh. But what shewed she was no novelty was the little attention paid to her, and the levity with which she was treated by the old nuns, even the Superior every day passed over irregularities in this singular person, which she would have punished with penance, or at least have met with reprimands in any other. From what I saw of her I soon perceived that she betrayed two distinct traits of character,—a kind disposition towards such as she chose to prefer, and a pleasure in teasing those she disliked, or such as had offended her..

CHAPTER VIII.

Description of Apartments in the Black Nunnery in order—First Floor—Second Floor—Garret—The Founder—Superior's Management with the Friends of Novices—Religious Lies—Criminality of concealing sins at Confessions.

I WILL now give from memory, a general description of the interior of the Convent of Black Nuns; except the few apartments which I never saw. I may be inaccurate in some things, as the apartments and passages of that spacious building are numerous and various; but I am willing to risk my credit for truth and sincerity on the general correspondence between my description, and things as they are. And this would, perhaps, be as good a case as any, by which to test the truth of my statements, were it possible to obtain access to the interior. It is well known that none but veiled nuns, the bishops, and priests, are ever admitted; and, of course, that I cannot have seen what I profess to describe, if I have not been a black nun. The priests who read this book, will acknowledge to themselves the truth of my description; but will, of course, deny it to the world, and probably exert themselves to destroy my credit. I offer to every reader the following description; knowing that time may possibly throw open those secret recesses, and allow the entrance of those who can satisfy themselves with their own eyes, of its truth. Some of my declarations may be thought deficient in evidence; and this, they must of necessity be, in the present state of things. But here is a kind of evidence on which I rely, as I see how unquestionable and satisfactory it must prove, whenever it shall be obtained.

If the interior of the Black Nunnery, whenever it shall be examined, is materially different from the following description, then I can claim no confidence of my readers. If it resembles it, they will, I presume, place confidence in some of those declarations, on which I may never be corroborated by true, and living witnesses. I am sensible that great changes may be made in the furniture of apartments; that new walls may be constructed, or old ones removed; and I have been credibly informed, that masons have been employed in the Nunnery since I left it. I well know, however, that entire changes cannot be made; and that enough must remain, as it was to substantiate my description, whenever the truth shall be known.(a)

(a) By divine permission, we purpose to give at great length, many published and incontestible descriptions of Nunnery Disclosures. For the present take the following from the Rev. Carus Wilson's *Escape from a Convent*, published by Seeley. "Doblado's letters from Spain describe the arts which are used by the

THE FIRST STORY.

Beginning at the extremity of the western wing of the Convent, towards Notre-Dame Street, on the first story, there is—

First, the nun's private chapel; adjoining which, is a passage to a small projection of the building, extending from the upper story to the ground, with very small windows. Into the passage we were sometimes required to bring wood from the yard, and pile it up for use.

partizans of monasticism to entrap their unsuspecting victims. The first nascent wish of taking the veil is eagerly watched and seized by a confessor. * * * Pious parents tremble at the thought of standing between God and their daughter, and often with a bleeding heart lead her to the foot of the altar. There is an extreme eagerness in the Catholic professors of celibacy, both male and female, to decoy young persons into the toils from which they themselves cannot escape. * * * The whole process which condemns a female to live a secluded sister all her life, is studiously made to represent a wedding. The unconscious victim, generally in her fifteenth year, finds herself for some time previous to her taking the veil, the queen—nay, the idol of the whole community which has obtained her preference. She is constantly addressed by the name of bride, and sees nothing but gay preparations for the expected day of her spiritual nuptials. Attired in a splendid dress, and decked with all the jewels of her family and friends, she takes public leave of her acquaintance; visits, on her way to the convent, several other nunneries, to be seen and admired by the recluse inhabitants, and even the crowd which collects in her progress follows her with tears and blessings. As she approaches the church of her monastery, the dignified ecclesiastic who is to perform the ceremony, meets the intended novice at the door, and leads her to the altar, amid the sound of bells and musical instruments. The monastic weeds are blessed by the priest in her prescence; and having embraced her parents and nearest relations, she is led by the lady who acts as bride's maid, to the small door next to the double grating, which seperates the nuns' choir from the body of the church. A curtain is drawn while the abbess cuts off the hair of the novice, and strips her of her worldly ornaments. On the removal of the curtain, she appears in the monastic garb, surrounded by the nuns, bearing lighted tapers, her face covered with the white veil of probationship, fixed on the head by a wreath of flowers. After the *Te Deum*, or some other hymn of thanksgiving, the friends of the family adjourn to the locutory, or visiting-room, where a collection of ices and sweetmeats is served in presence of the mock bride, who, with the principal nuns, attends behind the grating which separates the visitors from the inmates of the convent. In the more austere convents the parting visit is omitted, and the sight of the novice in the white veil, immediately after having her hair cut off, is the last which, for a whole year, is granted to the parents. They again see her on the day when she binds herself with irrevocable vows, never to behold her more, unless they should live to see her again crowned with flowers, when she is laid in the grave. * * Letters from Spain vividly exhibit the evil tendency of monasteries. One letter says,—Many convents have been founded under the title of reformed, where, without regard to the sex of the votaries, young and delicate females are subjected to a life of privation and hardship, as the only infallible method of obtaining the favour of heaven. Their dress is a tunic of sackcloth, tied round the waist with a knotted rope. The rule allows them no linen either for clothing or bedding; woollen of the coarsest kind frets their bodies, day and night, even during the burning summers of the south of Spain. A mantle of the same sackcloth is the only addition which the nuns make to their dress in winter, while their feet shod with open sandals, and without either socks or stockings, are exposed to the sharp winter blasts, and the deadening chill of the brick floors. A band of coarse linen two inches in breadth, is worn by the Capuchin nuns, bound tight six or eight times round the head, in remembrance, it is said, of the crown of thorns; and such is the barbarous spirit of the rule, that it does not allow the band to be taken off even under an excess of fever. A young woman who takes the veil in any of the reformed convents, renounces the sight of her nearest relations. The utmost indulgence as to communication with parents and brothers extends to a short conversation once a month, in the presence of one of the elder nuns, behind a thick curtain spread on the inner side of the iron grating, which completely interrupts the view. The religious vows, however, among the Capuchin nuns put a final end to all communication between parents and children."

Second, a large community-room, with plain benches fixed against the wall to sit, and lower ones in front, to place our feet upon. There is a fountain in the passage near the chimney, at the further end, for washing the hands and face, with a green curtain sliding on a rod before it. This passage leads to the old nun's sleeping-room on the right, and the Superior's sleeping-room just beyond it, as well as to a staircase which conducts to the nun's sleeping-room, or dormitoire above. At the end of the passage, is a door opening into—

Third, the dining-room; this is larger than the community-room, and has three long tables for eating, and a *chapelle*, or collection of little pictures, a crucifix, and a small image of the infant Saviour in a glass case. This apartment has four doors, by the first of which we are supposed to have entered, while one opens to a pantry, and the third and fourth to the two next apartments.

Fourth, a large community room, with tables for sewing; and a staircase on the opposite left-hand corner.

Fifth, a community-room for prayer; used by both nuns and novices. In the further right-hand corner, is a small room, partitioned off, called the room for the examination of conscience, which I had visited while a novice, by permission of the Superior, and where nuns and novices occasionally resorted to reflect on their character, usually in preparation for the sacrament, or when they had transgressed some of the rules. This little room was hardly large enough to contain a half-dozen persons at a time.

Sixth, next, beyond, is a large community-room for Sundays. A door leads to the yard, and thence to a gate in the wall on the cross street.

Seventh, adjoining this is a sitting-room, fronting on the cross street; with two windows, and a store-room on the side opposite them. There is but little furniture, and that is very plain.

Eighth, from this room, a door leads into what I may call the wax-room, as it contains many figures in wax, not intended for sale. There we sometimes used to pray, or meditate on the Saviour's passion. This room projects from the main building; leaving it, you enter a long passage, with cupboards on the right, in which are stored crockery-ware, knifes and forks, and other articles of table furniture, to replace them worn out or broken, all of the plainest description; also shovels, tongs, &c. This passage leads to—

Ninth, a corner room, with a few benches, &c. and a door leading to a gate on the Street. Here some of the medicines were kept; and persons were often admitted on business, or to obtain medicines with tickets from the priests; and waited till the Superior, or an old nun, could be sent for. Beyond this room we never were allowed to go; and I cannot speak from personal knowledge of what came next.

THE SECOND STORY.

Beginning as before, at the western extremity of the north wing, but on the second story, the farthest apartment in that direction which I ever entered, was—

First, the nun's sleeping-room, or dormitoire, which I have already described. Here is an access to the projection mentioned in speaking of the first story. The stairs by which we came up to bed are at the farther end of the room; and near them a crucifix and fount of holy water. A door at the end of the room opens into a passage, with two small rooms, and closets between them containing bed-clothes. Next you enter—

Second, a small community-room, beyond which is a passage with a narrow staircase, seldom used, which leads into the fourth community-room in the first story. Following the passage just mentioned, you enter by a door—

Third, a little sitting-room furnished in the following manner: with chairs, a sofa, on the north side, covered with a red figured cover and fringe; a table in the middle, commonly bearing one or two books, an inkstand, pens, &c. At one corner is a little projection into the room, caused by a staricase leading from above to the floor below, without any communication with the second story. This room has a door opening upon a staircase leading down to the yard, on the opposite side of which is a gate opening into the cross street. By this way the physician is admitted, except when he comes later than usual. When he comes in, he sits a little while, until a nun goes into the adjoining nun's sick room, to see if all is ready, and returns to admit him. After prescribing for the patients, he goes no farther, but returns by the way he enters; and these two are the only rooms into which he is ever admitted.

Fourth, the nun's sick room adjoins the little sitting-room on the east, and has, I think, four windows towards the north, with beds ranged in two rows from end to end, and a few more between them, near the opposite extremity. The door from the sitting-room swings to the left, and behind it is a table; while a glass-case, on the right, contains a wax figure of the infant Saviour, with several sheep. Near the north-eastern corner of this room are two doors, one of which opens into a long and narrow passage, leading to the head of the great staircase that conducts to the cross street. By this passage the physician sometimes finds his way to the sick-room, when he comes later than usual. He rings the bell at the gate, which I was told had a concealed pull, known only to him and the priests, proceeds up stairs, and through the passage, rapping three times at the door of the sick-room, which is opened by a nun in attendance, after she has given one rap in reply. When he has visited his patients, and prescribed for them, he returns by the same way.

Fifth, next beyond this sick-room is a large unoccupied apartment, half divided by two partial partitions, which leave an open space in the middle. Here some of the old nuns commonly meet in the daytime.

Sixth, a door from this apartment opens into another, not appropriated to any particular use, but containing a table, where medicines are sometimes prepared by an old nun, who is usually found there. Passing through this room, you enter a passage, with doors on its four sides: that on the left, which is kept fastened in the inside, leads to the staircase and gate; that in front to private sick-rooms, soon to be described.

Seventh, that on the right leads to another, appropriated to nuns suffering with the most loathsome disease. There were usually a number of straw mattrasses in that room, as I well knew, having helped to carry them in after the yard-man had filled them. A door beyond enters into a store-room, which extends also beyond this apartment. On the right, another door opens into another passage; crossing which, you enter by a door—

Eighth, a room with a bed and screen in one corner, on which nuns were laid to be examined before their introduction into the sick room last mentioned. Another door, opposite the former, opens into a passage, in which is a staircase leading down.

Ninth, beyond this is a spare room, sometimes used to store apples, boxes of different things, &c.

Tenth, returning now to the passage which opens on one side upon the stairs to the gate, we enter the only remaining door, which leads into an apartment usually occupied by some of the old nuns, and frequently by the Superior.

Eleventh and Twelfth, beyond this are two more sick rooms, in one of which those nuns stay who are waiting their accouchment; and in the other, those who have passed it.

Thirteenth, the next is a small sitting-room, where a priest waits to baptise the infants previous to their murder. A passage leads from this room on the left, by the doors of two succeeding apartments, neither of which have I ever entered.

Fourteenth, the first of them is the " holy retreat," or room occupied by the priests, while suffering the penalty of their licentiousness.

Fifteenth, the other is a sitting-room, to which they have access. Beyond these the passage leads to two rooms, containing closets for the storage of various articles, and two others where persons are received who come on business.

The public hospitals succeed, and extend a considerable distance, I believe to the extremity of the building. By a public entrance in that part priests often come into the Nunnery; and I have often seen some of them thereabouts, who must have entered by that way. Indeed, priests often get into the "holy retreat" without exposing themselves to the view of persons in other parts of the Convent, and have been first known to be there, by the yard-nuns being sent to the Seminary for their clothes.

The Congregational Nunnery was founded by a nun called Sister Bourgeoise. She taught a school in Montreal, and left property for the foundation of a Convent. Her body is buried, and her heart is kept under the Nunnery, in an iron chest, which has been shown to me, with the assurance that it continues in perfect preservation, although she has been dead more than one hundred and fifty years. In the chapel is the following inscription: "Sœur Bourgeoise, Fondatrice du Convent." (Sister Bourgeoise, Founder of the Convent.) Nothing was more common than for the Superior to step hastily into our community-rooms, while numbers of us were assembled there, and hastily communicate her wishes in words like these:—

"Here are the parents of such a novice: come with me, and bear me out in this story." She would then mention the outlines of a tissue of falsehoods she had just invented, that we might be prepared to fabricate circumstances, and throw in whatever else might favour the deception. This was justified, and, indeed, highly commended by the system of faith in which we were instructed.

It was a common remark always at the initiation of a new nun into the Black Nun department, that is, to receive the black veil, that the introduction of another novice into the Convent as a veiled nun, always caused the introduction of a veiled nun into heaven as a saint, which was on account of the singular disappearance of some of the older nuns always at the entrance of new ones!

To witness the scenes which often occurred between us and strangers, would have struck a person most powerfully, if he had known how truth was set at nought. The Superior, with a serious and dignified air, and a pleasant voice and aspect, would commence a recital of things most favourable to the character of the absent novice, and representing her as equally fond of her situation, and beloved by the other inmates. The tale told by the Superior, whatever it was, however unheard before might have been any of her statements, was then attested by us, who in every way we could think of, endeavoured to confirm her declarations beyond the reach of doubt.

Sometimes the Superior would entrust the management of such a case to some of the nuns, whether to habituate us to the practise in which she was so highly accomplished, or to relieve herself of what would have been a serious burden to most other persons, or to ascertain whether she could depend upon us, or all together, I cannot tell. Often, however, have I seen her throw open a door, and say, in a hurried manner, "Who can tell the best story?"

One point, on which we received frequent and particular instructions was, the nature of falsehoods. On this subject I have heard many a speech, I had almost said, many a sermon ; and I was led to believe that it was one of great importance, one on which it was a duty to be well informed, as well as to act. " What!" exclaimed a priest one day—" what, a nun of your age, and not know the difference between a wicked and a religious lie ?" He then went on, as had been done many times previously in my hearing, to show the essential difference between the two different kinds of falsehoods. A lie told merely for the injury of another, for own interest alone, or for no purpose at all, he painted as a sin worthy of penance ; but a lie told for the good of the church or Convent was meritorious, and of course the telling of it a duty. And of this class of lies there were many varieties and shades. This doctrine had been inculcated upon me and my companions in the nunnery, more times than I can enumerate ; and to say that it was generally received, would be to tell a part of the truth. We often saw the practice of it, and were frequently made to take part in it. Whenever any thing which the Superior thought important, could be most conveniently accomplished by falsehood, she resorted to it without scruple.

There was a class of cases, in which she more frequently relied on deception than any other. The friends of novices frequently applied at the Convent to see them, or at least to enquire after their welfare. It was common for them to be politely refused an interview, on some account or other, generally a mere pretext; and then the Superior generally sought to make as favourable an impression as possible on the visitors. Sometimes she would make up a story on the spot, and tell the strangers; requiring some of us to confirm it, in the most convincing way we could. At other times she would prefer to make over to us the task of deceiving, and we were commended in proportion to our ingenuity and success.

Some nun usually showed her submission by immediately stepping forward. She would then add, perhaps, that the parents of such a novice whom she named, were in waiting, and it was necessary that they should be told such and such things. To perform so difficult a task well, was considered a difficult duty, and it was one of the most certain ways to gain the favour of the Superior.

Whoever volunteered to make a story on the spot was sent immediately to tell it, and the other nuns present were hurried off with her, under strict injunctions to uphold her in everything she might state. The Superior, as there was every reason to believe, on all such occasions when she did not herself appear, hastened to the apartment adjoining that in which the nuns were going, there to listen through the thin partition, to hear whether all performed their parts aright. It was not uncommon for her to go rather further, when she wanted to give such explanations as she could have desired. She would then enter abruptly, and ask, " Who can tell a good story this morning ?" and hurry us off without a moment's delay, to do our best at a venture, without waiting for instructions. It would be curious, could a stranger from the " wicked world" outside the Convent, witness such a scene. One of the nuns, who felt in a favourable humour to undertake the task would step promptly forward, and signify her readiness in the usual way : by a knowing wink of one eye, and a slight toss of the head. " Well, go and do the best you can," the Superior would say : " and all the rest of you mind and swear to it." The latter part of the order, at least, was always performed; for in every case all the nuns present appeared as unanimous witnesses of every thing that was uttered by the spokeswoman of the day.

We were constantly hearing it repeated, that we must never again look upon ourselves as our own ; but must remember, tha we were solemnly and irrevocably devoted to God. Whatever was required of us, we were called upon to yield under the most solemn considerations. I cannot speak on every particular with equal freedom ; but I wish my readers clearly to understand the condition in which we were placed, and the means used to reduce us to what we had to submit to. Not only were we required to perform the several tasks imposed upon us at work, prayers, and penances, under the idea that we were performing solemn duties to our Maker, but every thing else which was required of us, we were constantly told, was something indispensable in his sight. The priests, we admitted, were the servants of God, especially appointed by his authority, to teach us our duty, to absolve us from sin, and to lead us to heaven. Without their assistance, we had allowed, we could never enjoy the favour of God ; unless they administered the sacrament to us, we could not enjoy everlasting happiness. Having consented to acknowledge all this, we had no objection to urge against admitting any other demand that might be made for or by them. If we thought an act ever so criminal, the Superior could tell us that the priests acted under the direct sanction of God, and *could not sin.* Of course, then, it could not be wrong to comply with any of their requests, because they could not demand any thing but what was right. On the contrary, to refuse to do any thing they asked, would necessarily be sinful. Such doctrines admitted, and such practices performed, it will not be thought wonderful when I mention that we often felt something of their preposterous character.

Sometimes we took pleasure in ridiculing some of the favourite themes of our teachers; and I recollect one subject particularly, which at one period afforded us repeated merriment. It may seem irreverent in me to give the account, but I do it to show how things of a solemn nature were sometimes treated in the Convent, by women bearing the title of saints. A Canadian novice, who spoke very broken English, one day remarked that she was performing some duty " for the God." This peculiar expression had something ridiculous to the ears of some of us; and it was soon repeated again and again, in application to various ceremonies which we had to perform. Mad Jane Ray seized upon it with avidity, and with her aid it soon took the place of a bye-word in conversation; so that we were constantly reminding each other that we were doing this thing and that thing, how trifling and unmeaning soever, " for the God." Nor did we stop here; when the Superior called upon us to bear witness to one of her religious lies, or to fabricate the most spurious one the time would admit, to save her the trouble, we were sure to be reminded, on our way to the stranger's room, that we were doing it " for the God." And so it was when other things were mentioned, every thing which belonged to our condition was spoken of in similar terms. I have hardly detained the reader long enough on this subject to give him a just impression of the stress laid on confession. It is one of the great points to which our attention was constantly directed to keep a strict and constant watch over our thoughts; to have continually before our minds the rules of the Convent, to compare the one with the other, remember every devotion, and tell all, even the smallest, at confession, either to the Superior, or to the priest. My mind was thus kept in a continual state of activity, which proved very wearisome: and it required the constant exertion of our teachers, to keep us to the practice they inculcate.

Another tale recurs to me, of those which were frequently told us, to make us feel the importance of unreserved confession. A nun of our Convent, who had hidden some sin from her confessor, died suddenly, and without any one to confess her. Her sisters assembled to pray for the peace of her soul, when she appeared, and informed them, that it would be of no use, but rather troublesome to her, as her pardon was impossible. The doctrine is, that prayers made for souls guilty of unconfessed sin, do but sink them deeper in hell; and this is the reason I have heard given for not praying for Protestants. The authority of the priests in every thing, and the enormity of every act which opposes it, were also impressed upon our minds in various ways, by our teachers. A " Father" told us the following story, one day, at catechism. A man once died who had failed to pay some money which the priest had asked of him; he was condemned to be burnt in purgatory until he should pay it, but had permission to come back to this world, and take a human body to work in. He made his appearance therefore again on earth, and hired himself to a rich man as a labourer. He worked all day with the fire working in him, unseen by other people; but while he was in bed that night, a girl in an adjoining room perceiving the smell of brimstone, looked through a crack in the wall, and saw him covered with flames. She informed his master, who questioned him the next morning, and found that his hired man was secretly suffering the pains of purgatory, for neglecting to pay a certain sum of money to the priest. He, therefore, furnished him with the amount due; it was paid, and the servant went off immediately to heaven. The priest cannot forgive any debt due unto him, because it was the Lord's estate.

While at confession I was urged to hide nothing from the priest; and have been told by them, that they already knew what was in my heart, but would not tell, because it was necessary for me to confess it. I really believed that the priests were acquainted with my thoughts; and often stood in great awe of them. They often told me they had power to strike me dead at any moment.[a]

CHAPTER IX.

Nuns with similar names—Squaw Nuns—First Visit to the Cellar—Description of it—Shocking Discovery there—Superior's Instructions—Private Signal of the Priests—Books used in the Nunnery—Opinions expressed of the Bible—Specimens of what I know of the Scriptures.

I FOUND that I had several namesakes among the nuns, for there were two others who had already bore away my new name, *Saint Eustace*. This was not a solitary case, for there were five Saint Marys, and three Saint Munros, beside two novices of that name. Of my namesakes I have little to say, for they re-

[a] In appending notes to this work, our object is to shew a very fearful fact; and that fact is this—that the Church of Rome in her principles—in her delusions—in her dreadful beguilements and falseness—in her blasphemies and idolatries—is the same to this day, where she can carry on her trade of superstition founded in ignorance. Read the following extract from a Lecture delivered at the Beaumont Institution, Mile End Road, Jan. 10th, 1851, by the Rev. George Smith, of Poplar: published by Gorbell, Commercial Road, East; and on p. 19 of it, you find the following: "Now, the theory of the church of Rome is that there ought to be judgment about religion, but that the church ought to judge; that you ought not to judge at all about it; that you are just to take what the church shall tell you, and believe it thoroughly, simply because the church has said it. That is the theory. 'Aye,' but people are apt to say, 'that is hardly the fact now, in the middle of the nineteenth century.' Well, go and talk to any Roman Catholic that you like. Go and converse with any man who will be frank

sembled most of nuns; being so much cut off from intercourse with me and the other sisters, that I never saw anything in them, nor learnt anything about them, worth mentioning.

Several of my new companions were squaws, who had taken the veil at different times. They were from some of the Indian settlements in the country, but were not distinguishable by any striking habits of character from other nuns, and were generally not very different in their appearance when in their usual dress, and engaged in their customary occupations. It was evident they were treated with much kindness and lenity by the Superior and the old nuns: and this I discovered was done in order to render them as well contented and happy in their situation as possible; and should have attributed the motives for this partiality to their wishing, that they might not influence others to keep away, had I not known they were like ourselves, unable to exert such an influence. And, therefore, I could not satisfy my own mind why this difference was made. Many of the Indians were remarkably devoted to the priests, believing everything they were taught. And as it is represented to be not only a high honor,

---

enough to tell you the truth, and he will admit that it is the real practice as well as the theory. I will give you an instance of it. I was a few years ago in the north of Germany, in that old city of Treve, of which many, perhaps all, of you have heard. It was said that a series of miracles had just been performed in the cathedral of that city. Pilgrims flocked in thousands and tens of thousands from every part of Germany, and from every part of continental Europe, to that shrine, and it was said that they were healed. There was an old lady, a princess, who hobbled into the church upon a pair of crutches, and they made her believe (for she was a very nervous woman,) that she was perfectly healed, and contrived to help her to hobble out, but as soon as she got outside the church she was unable to walk. They took the crutches from her, however, and hung them up in the church. I saw them in the cathedral. I stood upon the high altar of that cathedral at Treves, and there I saw a frame about four feet in length and three feet in height. It was made of mahogany. The front of it was glazed; and inside there was a dirty, uncomfortable-looking kind of thing, that they called a 'holy coat.' They had inscribed on the case in German, two passages of scripture (for the church can quote scripture when she likes). One was: 'Now the coat was whole, without seam, wove from the top throughout.' The other text was: 'If I may but touch the hem of his garment I shall be made whole.' And what think you? To this wretched relic there were myriads of people coming. 'The lame, the halt, and the blind,' were all variously hobbling to this place. If a man had a bad foot, they put it through a hole to touch the coat; if he had a weak arm, his hand was put in. A great number of things of that kind were done, very ridiculous, and very painful; aye, very absurd indeed, if they did not involve a blasphemous enormity. I stood upon that altar a short time after these so-said miracles had been performed; and I said to a Roman Catholic gentleman with whom I was travelling at the time, 'What is your opinion of these said miracles?' 'Oh,' said he, 'I have no opinion whatever about them.' I said, 'I marvel at that. Do you hold your judgment in abeyance about them?' 'Thoroughly so,' said he. 'Why?'. 'Because the church has not yet pronounced upon them.' I give you my honour for the truthful repetition of the words that fell from his lips. 'Then,' I said, 'if the church were to say they were genuine miracles?' 'I should then believe them.' 'And if the church were to say that they are not genuine miracles?' 'Then I should believe that they were untrue.' Now, my friends, can you conceive anything more pitiable than an intelligent, rational being, giving up his intellect, his soul, his understanding, thus to be tied and bound, and put under the authority of the church?"

but a real advantage to a family, to have one of its members become a nun, Indian parents will often pay large sums of money for the admission of their daughters into a Convent. The father of one of the squaws, I was told, paid to the Superior nearly her weight in silver on her reception, although he was obliged to sell nearly all his property to raise the money. This he did voluntarily, because he thought himself overpaid by having the advantage of her prayers, self-sacrifice, &c., for himself and remainder of his family. The squaws sometimes served to amuse us; for when we were partially dispirited or gloomy, the Superior would occasionally send them to dress themselves in their Indian garments, which usually excited us to meriment. Among the squaw nuns whom I particularly remember, was one of the *Saint Hypolites*, not the one who figured in a dreadful scene, described in another part of this narrative, but a woman of far more mild and human character.[a]

Three or four days after my reception; the Superior sent me into the cellar for coal; and after she had given me directions, I proceeded down a staircase with a lamp in my hand. I soon found myself upon the bare earth in a spacious place, so dark that I could not at once distinguish its form or size; but I observed that it had very solid stone walls, and was arched overhead, at no great elevation. Following my directions, I proceeded on-

---

(a) The demoralising influence of the Roman Catholic system is very nicely set forth in the following extract from Mr. Geo. Smith's Lecture (of Poplar,) which we have noticed before. Speaking of the advantages of "THE RIGHT OF PRIVATE JUDGMENT," he says—"There is a healthful intelligence in the piety of our age; there is a healthful intelligence in the Protestant mind. I think I could almost determine, when I was in Switzerland, whether I was in a Popish or a Protestant canton by the very look of the people. There was something so squalid, so downcast, so priest-ridden, about the very attitude of the Roman Catholics, that one saw from it the economy to which they belonged; and there was such a healthful, noble, intelligent demeanour on the part of the Protestant people, that even the peasantry stood up in the dignity of their common manhood, and ventured to think and to speak for themselves. What constitutes the difference between the Scotch and the Irish mind? What constitutes the difference between a Highlander of the north, or a poor Paddy from the south or the west of Ireland? It is not want of intellect on the part of the Irish; it is not want of wit; it is not want of nobleness of feeling; it is not want of warm-heartedness. Never, never, did I find more genuine hospitality than I have found in the west and south of Ireland. Never did I see nobler qualities on the part of the peasantry than there. Talk to them of everything else, and they are sharp, and shrewd, and ready; but talk to them about religion, and you find the weight of priestly authority pressing them down to the ground. All that intelligent piety that you have, all that large knowledge of divine truth that many of you possess, that distinctive view that you have of justification by faith, (not confounding it, as every Romanist, according to the Council of Trent, must confound it with sanctification,) that broad line of distinction presented to you between one truth and another, and that intelligent comprehension of it, you all owe to the right and the duty of private judgment. Hold it fast; let no man rob you of it; don't be cajoled out of it; don't be brought into bondage by any one; don't let any sanctimonious priest come into your dwelling to inveigle himself into your affections and confidence; don't be robbed of this privilege; it is above all price, ' He who steals my purse steals trash—'twas mine, 'tis his,' and it may be another's; but he who robs me, or attempts to do so, of the right of private judgment, perpetrates a felony upon my mind, and should be stamped as a robber, by the verdict of the universe."

wards from the foot of the stairs, where appeared to be one end of the cellar. After walking about fifteen paces, I passed three small doors, on the right, fastened with large iron bolts on the outside, pushed into posts of stonework, and each having a small opening above, covered with a fine grating, secured by a smaller bolt. On my left were three similar doors, resembling these, and placed opposite them. Beyond these the space became broader; the doors evidently closed small compartments, projecting from the outer wall of the cellar. I soon stepped upon a wooded floor, on which were heaps of wool, coarse linen, and other articles, apparently deposited there for occasional use. I soon crossed the floor, and found the bare earth again under my feet. A little further on, I found the cellar again contracted in size, by a row of closets, or smaller compartments, projecting on each side. These were closed by doors of a different description from the first, having a simple fastening, and no opening through them. Just beyond, on the left side, I passed a staircase leading up, and then three doors, much resembling those first described, standing opposite three more, on the other side of the cellar. Having passed there, I found the cellar again enlarged as before, and here the earth appeared as if mixed with some whitish substance, which attracted my attention. As I proceeded, I found the whiteness increased, until the surface looked like snow; and, in a short time, I observed before me a hole dug so deep into the earth that I could perceive no bottom. I stopped to observe it—it was circular, twelve, perhaps, or fifteen feet across; in the middle of the cellar, and unprotected by any kind of curb, so that one might have easily have walked into it in the dark. The white substance which I had observed, was spread all over the surface around it, and lay in such quantity on all sides, that it seemed as if a great deal of it must have been throw into the hole. It immediately occurred to me that the white substance was lime, and that this was the place where the infants were buried after being murdered, as the Superior informed me. I knew that lime is often used by Roman Catholics in burying places; and in this way, I accounted for its being scattered about the spot in such quantities. This was a shocking thought to me, but I can hardly tell how it affected me, as I had already been prepared to expect dreadful things in the Convent; and had undergone trials which prevented me from feeling as I should formerly have done in similar circumstances. I passed the spot, therefore, with dreadful thoughts, it is true, about the little corpses which might be in that secret burying place: but with recollections also of the declarations which I had heard about the favour done their souls in sending them straight to heaven, and the necessary virtues accompanying all the actions of the priests.

Whether I noticed them or not, at the time, there is a window or two on each, nearly against the hole, in at which are sometimes thrown articles brought to them from without, for the use of the Convent. Through the window on my right, which opens into the yard, towards the cross Street, lime is received from carts; I then saw a large heap of it near the place.

Passing the hole, I came to a spot where was another projection on each side, with three cells like those I first described. Beyond them, in another broad part of the cellar were heaps of vegetables, and other things; on the right and on the left I found the charcoal I was in search of. This was placed in a heap against the wall, as I might then have observed, near a small high window, like the rest, at which it is thrown in. Beyond this spot, at a short distance, the cellar terminated.(a)

The top, quite to that point, is arched overhead, though at different heights; for the earth on the bottom is uneven, and in

---

(a) THE TAKING OF THE INQUISITION AT MADRID; WITH A FULL DISCOVERY OF ITS DENS, INSTRUMENTS OF TORTURE, AND THE STATE OF ITS UNHAPPY VICTIMS WHEN FOUND, is given by Edward Smith, in his new work just published by Aylott and Jones, entitled *The Desolations of the Abominations*, &c., of which the following is a correct copy,—" As proof of the unchangeable character of the votaries of Rome, the taking of the Inquisition at Madrid in 1809 may be quoted. Col. Lehmanowsky, the officer who was employed to demolish it, had spoken rather freely of the priests and Jesuits and of the Inquisition, which endangered his life; he being one night nearly taken by some guards of the Inquisition. He then went to Marshal Soult, the Governor of Madrid, and reminded him of the Emperor Napoleon's decree to suppress the institution. Marshal Soult replied that he might go and destroy it, and granted him the troops he required for that purpose. The Inquisition was about five miles from the city, surrounded with a wall of great strength, and defended by a company of soldiers. On being summoned to surrender, the answer was given by firing at the French troops, which was the signal of attack; and after a powerful resistance a breach was made in the walls, and the imperial troops rushed in. 'Here' says Col. Lehmanowsky, 'we met with an incident which nothing but Jesuitical effrontery is equal to. The Inqisitor-general and the father confessors, all came out of their rooms, and with long faces and their arms crossed over their breasts, as though they had been deaf to all the noise of attack and defence, and had just learned what was going on, they addressed themselves in the language of rebuke to their own soldiers, saying, ' Why do you attack our friends the French ?' Their intention, no doubt, was to make us think that this defence was unauthorized by them, but their artifice did not succeed. I caused them to be placed under guard, and all their soldiers to be secured as prisoners. We then proceeded to examine all the rooms of the stately edifice. We passed through room after room, but could discover no evidences of iniquity being practised there—nothing of those peculiar features which we expected to find in an Inquisition. Here was beauty and splendour, and the most perfect order on which my eyes had ever rested. The architecture, the proportions, were perfect. There was everything to please the eye, and gratify a cultivated taste; but where were those horrid instruments of torture of which we had been told, and where those dungeons in which human beings were said to be buried alive? we searched in vain. The holy fathers assured us they had been belied; that we had seen all; and I was prepared to give up the search convinced that this Inquisition was different from others of which I had heard. But Col. De Lile (who commanded one of the other regiments,) was not so ready to give up the search, and advised to pour water upon one of the marble floors, and watch if there was any place through which it escaped. This was done, much to the dissatisfaction of the inquisitors; and after careful examination, it was found that the water passed through fast by the side of one of the marble slabs, as though there was an opening beneath. All hands were now at work for farther some places several feet higher than in others. Not liking to be alone in so spacious and gloomy a part of the Convent, especially after the discovery I had made, I hastened to fill my basket with coal, and to return.

Here then I was in a place which I had considered as the nearest imitation of heaven to be found on earth, among a society where deeds were perpetrated which I had believed to be most criminal, and had now found the place in which harmless infants were unfeelingly thrown out of sight, after being murdered. And yet, such is the power of instruction and example, although not satisfied, as many around me seemed to be, that this was all righteous and proper, I sometimes was half inclined to believe it, for the priests could do no sin, and this was done by the priests.

discovery, while the priests remonstrated against our desecrating their holy and beautiful house. While thus engaged, a soldier struck a spring with the butt of his musket, and the slab flew up. Then the faces of the inquisitors grew pale as Belshazzar when the handwriting appeared on the wall: they trembled all over. Beneath the marble slab there was a staircase. I took a candle from the altar, four feet in length, that I might explore the room below. As I was doing this, I was arrested by one of the inquisitors, who laid his hand gently on my arm, and with a very demure and holy look, said, 'My son, you must not take these lights with your bloody hands: they are holy.' 'Well,' I said, 'I will take a holy thing to shed light on iniquity;' and proceeded down the staircase. As we reached the foot of the stairs, we entered a large square room, which was called the Hall of Judgment. In the centre of it was a large block, and a chain fastened to it. On this they had been accustomed to place the accused, chained to his seat. On one side of the room was an elevated seat, called the Throne of Judgment, for the inquisitor-general; and on either side were seats, less elevated, for the holy fathers when engaged in the solemn business of the Holy Inquisition. From this room we proceeded to the right, and obtained access to small cells, extending the entire length of the edifice; and here such sights were presented as we hoped never to see again. These cells were places of solitary confinement, where the wretched objects of inquisitorial hate were confined year after year, till death released them from their sufferings; and there their bodies were suffered to remain until they were entirely decayed, and the rooms had become fit for others to occupy. To prevent this being offensive to those who occupied the Inquisition, there were flues or tubes extending to the open air, sufficiently capacious to carry off the odour. In these cells we found the remains of some who had paid the debt of nature; some had been dead but a short time, while of others, nothing remained but their bones, still chained to the floor of their dungeon. In other cells, we found living sufferers of both sexes, and of every age, from three-score years and ten down to fourteen or fifteen years—all naked as when born into the world, and all in chains! The soldiers immediately went to work to release these captives from their chains, and took from their knapsacks clothing to cover them. They were exceedingly anxious to bring them out to the light of day; but the Colonel, aware of the danger, had food given them, and then brought them gradually to the light, as they were able to bear it. We then proceeded to explore another room, on the left. Here we found the instruments of torture, of every kind which the ingenuity of men or devils could invent. Col. L. here described four of these horrid instruments. The first was a machine by which the victim was confined, and then, beginning with the fingers, every joint in the hands, arms, and body was broken or drawn out, one after another, until the victim died. The second was a box, in which the head and neck of the victim were so closely confined by a screw, that he could not move in any way. Over the box was a vessel, from which one drop of water a second fell upon the head of the victim—every successive drop falling upon precisely the same place on the head, suspended the circulation in a few moments, and put the sufferer in the most excruciating agony. The third was an infernal machine, laid horizontally, to which the victim was bound; the machine then being placed between two beams, in which were scores of knives so fixed that, by turning the machine with a crank, the flesh of the

Among the first instructions I received from the Superior, were such as prepared me to admit priests into the nunnery, from the street, at irregular hours. It is no secret that priests enter and go out; but if they were to be watched by any person in St. Paul's-street all day long, no irregularity might be suspected; and they might be supposed to visit the Convent for the performance of religious ceremonies merely. But if a person were near the gate about midnight, he might sometimes form a different opinion: for when a stray priest is shut out of the Seminary, or is otherwise put in the need of seeking a lodging, he is always sure of being admitted into the Black Nunnery. Nobody but a priest can even ring the bell at the sick-room door; much less can any but a priest gain admittance. The pull of the bell is entirely concealed, somewhere on the outside of the gate I have been told. He makes himself known as a priest by a peculiar kind of hissing sound, made by the tongue against the teeth while they are kept closed and the lips open. The nun within, who delays to open the door until informed what kind of an applicant is there, immediately recognizes the signal, and replies with two inarticulate sounds, such as are often used instead of yes, with the mouth closed.

The Superior seemed to consider this part of my instructions

sufferer was torn from his limbs all in small pieces. The fourth surpassed the others for fiendish ingenuity. Its exterior was a beautiful woman, richly dressed, with arms extended, ready to embrace its victim. Around her feet a semi-circle was drawn. The victim who passed over this fatal mark, touched a spring, which caused the diabolical engine to open; its arms clasped him, and a thousand knives cut him into as many pieces in the deadly embrace. Colonel L. said, that the sight of these engines of infernal cruelty kindled the rage of the soldiers to fury. They declared that every inquisitor and soldier of the Inquisition should be put to the torture. Their rage was ungovernable. Colonel L. did not oppose them, they might have turned their arms against him, if he had attempted to arrest their work. They began with the holy fathers. The first they put to death in the machine for breaking joints. The torture of the inquisitor, put to death by the dropping of water on his head, was most excruciating. The inquisitor-general was brought before the infernal engine, called the 'Virgin.' He begs to be excused. 'No,' said they, 'you have caused others to kiss her, and now you must do it.' They interlocked their bayonets so as to form large forks, and with these pushed him over the deadly circle. The beautiful image instantly prepared for the embrace, clasped him in its arms, and he was cut into innumerable pieces. Colonel L. said that he witnessed the torture of four of them—his heart sickened at the awful scene—and he left the soldiers to wreak their vengeance on the last guilty inmate of that prison-house of hell. In the meantime, it was reported through Madrid, that the prisons of the Inquisition were broken open, and multitudes hastened to the spot. It was like a resurrection! About a hundred, who had been buried for many years, were now restored to life. There were fathers, who found their long-lost daughters; wives were restored to their husbands, sisters to their brothers, and parents to their children; and there were some who could recognize no friend among the multitude. The scene was such as no tongue can describe. When the multitude had retired, Colonel L. caused the library, paintings, furniture, &c. to be removed; and having sent to the city for a waggon load of powder, deposited a large quantity in the vaults beneath the building, and placed a slow match in connexion with it. All had withdrawn to a distance; and in a few moments there was a joyful sight to thousands. The walls and turrets of the massive structure rose majestically towards the heavens, impelled by the tremendous explosion, and fell back to the earth an immense heap of ruins."

quite important, and taught me the signals. I had often occasion to use them; I have been repeatedly called to the door, in the night, while watching in the sick-room; and on reaching it, heard the short hissing sound I have mentioned; then, according to standing orders, unfastening a door, admitted a priest, who was at liberty to go when he pleased. I will name Mr. Bierze, from St. Denis.

The books used in the nunnery, at least such as I recollect of them, were the following. Most of these are lecture books, or such as are used by the daily readers, while we are at work and meals. These were all furnished by the Superior, out of her library, to which we never had access. She was informed when we had done with one book, and then exchanged it for such another as she pleased to select. *Le Miroir du Chretien* (Christian Mirror,) History of Rome, History of the Church, Life of Sœur Bourgeoise, (founder of the Convent,) in two volumes, *L' Ange Conducteur* (the Guardian Angel,) *L' Ange Chretien*, (the Christian Angel,) *Les Vies des Saints*, (Lives of the Saints) in several volumes. Dialogues, a volume consisting of conversations between a Protestant Doctor, called Dr. D. and a Roman Catholic clergyman, on the articles of faith, in which, after much ingenious reasoning, the former was confuted. One large book, the name of which I have forgotten, occupied us nine or ten months at our lectures, night and morning *l' Instruction de la Jeunesse*, (the instruction of Youth,) containing much about Convents, and the education of persons in the world, with a great deal on confession, &c. *Examen de la Conscience*, (Examination of Conscience,) is a book frequently used.

I may here remark, that I never saw a bible in the Convent, from the day I entered as a novice, until that on which I effected my escape. The Catholic New Testament, commonly called the Evangile, was read to us two or three times a year. The Superior directed the reader what passage to select; but we never had it in our hands to read when we pleased. I often heard the Protestant Bible spoken of in bitter terms, as a most dangerous book, and one which never ought to be in the hands of common people.

CHAPTER X.

Manufacture of Bread and Wax Candles, carried on in the Convent—Superstitions—Scapularies—Virgin Mary's Pincussion—Her House—The Bishop's Power over Fire—My instruction to Novices—Jane Ray—Vacillation of feeling.

LARGE quantities of bread are made in the Black Nunnery every week; for, besides what is necessary to feed the nuns, many of the poor are supplied. When a priest wishes to give a loaf of bread to a poor person, he gives him an order, which is presented at the Convent. The making of bread is, therefore, one of the most laborious employments in the institution.

The manufacture of wax candles was another important branch of business in the nunnery. It was carried on in a small room, on the first floor, thence called the *ciergerie*, or wax room, *cierge* being the French word for *wax*. I was sometimes sent to read the daily lecture and catechism to the nuns employed there, but found it a very unpleasant task; as the smell rising from the melted wax gave me a sickness at the stomach. The employment was considered as rather unhealthy, and those were assigned to it who had the strongest constitutions. The nuns who were commonly employed in that room, were Saint Marie, Saint Catherine, Saint Charlotte, Saint Frances, Saint Hyacinthe, Saint Hypolite, and others. But with these, as with other persons in the Convent, I was never allowed to speak, except under circumstances before mentioned. I was sent to read, and was not allowed to answer the most trivial question, if one were asked me. Should a nun say, "What o'clock is it?" I never should have dared to reply, but was required to report her to the Superior.

Much stress was laid on the *sainte scapulaire*, or holy scapulary. This is a small band of cloth or silk, formed and wrought in a particular manner, to be tied around the neck, by two strings fastened to the ends. I have made many of them; having been sometimes sent to make them in the Convent. On one side is worked a kind of double cross (thus, ++) and on the other I. H. S., the meaning of which I do not exactly know. Such a band is called a scapulary, and many miracles are attributed to its power. Children, on first receiving the communion, are often presented with scapularies, which they are taught to regard with great reverence. We are told of the wonders effected by their means, in the addresses made to us, by priests, at catechism or lectures. I will repeat one or two of the stories which occur to me.

A Roman Catholic servant woman, who had concealed some of her sins at confession, acted so hypocritical a part as to make her mistress believe her a *devotee*, or strict observer of her duty. She even imposed upon her confessor to such a degree, that he gave her a scapulary. After he had given it, however, one of the saints in heaven informed him in a vision, that the holy scapulary must not remain on the neck of so great a sinner, and that it must be restored to the church. The belief was, that the devil could not endure to have so holy a thing on one of his servants, and had pulled so hard to get it off, as to draw the silken thread, with which it was tied, through her neck; after which, by some divine power, it was restored to the church.

Another story was as follows. A poor Roman Catholic was once taken prisoner by the heretics. He had a *saint's scapulaire* on his neck, when God, seeing him in the midst of his foes, took it from the neck by a miracle, and held it up in the air above the throng of heretics; more than one hundred of whom were converted, by seeing it thus supernaturally suspended.

I had been informed by the Superior, on my first admission as a nun that there was a subterranean passage leading from the cellar of our Convent into that of the Congregational Nunnery; but, though I have so often visited the cellar, I had never seen it. One day, after I had been received three or four months, I was sent to walk through it on my knees, with another nun, as a penance. This, and other penances, were sometimes put upon us by the priests, without any reason assigned. The common way, indeed, was to tell us of the sin for which a penance was imposed, but were left many times to conjecture. Now and then the priest would inform us at a subsequent confession, when he happened to recollect something about it, as I thought, and not because he reflected or cared much upon the subject.

The nun who was with me led through the cellar, passing to the right of the secret burial-place, and showed me the door of the subterranean passage, which was at the extremity towards the Congregational Nunnery. The reasons why I had not noticed it before, I presume were, that it was made to shut close and even with the wall; and all that part of the cellar was whitewashed. This door, which is of wood, and square, opens with a latch into a passage about four feet and a half high. We immediately got upon our knees, commenced saying the prayers required, and began to move slowly along the dark and narrow passage. It may be fifty or sixty feet in length. When we reached the end, we opened a door, and found ourselves in the cellar of the Congregational Nunnery, at some distance from the outer wall; for the covered way is carried in towards the middle of the cellar, by two low partitions covered at the top. By the side of the door, was placed a list of names of the Black Nuns, with a slide that might be drawn over any of them. We covered our names in this manner, as evidence of having performed the duty assigned us; and then returned downwards, on our knees, by the way we had come. This penance I repeatedly performed afterwards; and by this way, as I have occasion elsewhere to mention, nuns from the Congregational Nunnery sometimes entered our Convent for worse purposes.(a)

We were frequently assured, that miracles are still performed; and pains were taken to impress us deeply on this subject. The

(a) In Dr. Achilli's excellent work entitled "Dealings with the Inquisition," published by Arthur Hall and Co; under the head of "THE INQUISITION IN THE NINETEENTH CENTURY," we find the following striking facts recorded to prove that cruelty, barbarity, idolatry, and wickedness, are still practised by the Church of Rome. This note may seem out of place here; but we wish to back up not merely Maria Monk's statements, but the whole Protestant force against the Papal agression. The fact is, we are resolved, in the strength of the Lord, to do all we can to *expose* the crafty foe, the Lord alone can conquer him; and this he has promised to do. Dr. A. (on page 97) says,—"I do not know what to think of the impudence of a certain writer, unquestionably not an ordinary personage, who, a short time ago, published an article in the 'Dublin Review,' July 1850, entitled 'The Inquisition,' the object of which was to persuade the world that, after all, this Inquisition, respecting which so much unjust clamour (!) had been raised, contained nothing but what might honestly be considered necessary for the present state of society and the interests of religion. Every religion, it was stated, had been intolerant. What by us, in the present day, is denominated intolerance, 'entered into the very spirit of the Jewish religion.' (P. 423.) The learned writer, who, by the way, we verily believe to be at this present time a cardinal, and, to his shame, an Englishman, leads the reader to the conclusion that the Almighty himself, the true founder of the Jewish religion, has countenanced intolerance. He then proceeds to observe: 'Of the five great religions which divided the Gentile world—the Greek, the Roman, the Egyptian, the Persian, and the Indian—there is not one which can claim exemption from the charge.' (Ib.) His inference, therefore, is, that it is no wonder that Christianity also is in a similar state; and this involves the farther conclusion that Christianity itself, in this respect, is a system of religion similar to these five great religious systems which divided the pagan world. This is the doctrine held out to us by a Cardinal Archbishop! Like the preceding religions, Christianity, according to him, has always been more or less intolerant. With respect to papacy, it is most true that in practice it has always been more or less so, but in theory it has been always the same. In fact, Thomas Aquinas, the leading theologian and doctor of the Church of Rome, lays down the following doctrine, which his Eminence and others of his school seem very ready to act upon. 'It is,' says he, 'much more grievous to corrupt faith, which is the source and life of the soul, than to corrupt money, which but tends to the relief of the body. Hence, if coiners and other malefactors are justly put to death by the secular authority, much more may heretics not only be excommunicated, but even justly put to death.' For example, if you, reader, a Christian of intelligent mind, should deny that the bread and the wine, in consequence of a few words uttered over them, should cease to be actually bread and wine—you, in that case, have corrupted the faith of the Thomasine school, which is that of the Church of Rome; and the reverend Inquisitor speedily lays hold of you, with sufficient argument before him to condemn you to death, for the glory of God. These barbarities were formerly common in Spain and Italy; but now!!—Is the theory of the Church of Rome, I ask, still in favour of these practices? I ask, whether it be possible for Cardinal W——, who is an Englishman, to renounce this doctrine, and at the same time remain consistent to his principles? Is it not manifestly a con-

Superior often spoke to us of the Virgin Mary's pincushion, the remains of which are pretended to be preserved in the Convent, though it has crumbled quite to the dust. We regarded this

tradiction? It is his duty, (the Bishops swear to observe the laws of the Inquisition,) then at a Roman Catholic, and an Archbishop, to condemn you to death, whenever he may have the power so to do, if you refuse to believe that the bread and the wine, over which the priest has breathed the words, '*Hoc est corpus meum*,' have not form with ceased to be bread and wine. Yes, his Eminence, faithful to his oath, and functioned by the theological and legal decision of the Thomasine doctors, music necessity consign you to the flames. Are flames no longer resorted to, as attracting too vividly the attention of the public? It matters not; poison will get rid of a heretic equally well, and more secretly. The reverend Jesuits, Busemban, Sa, Escobar, and others, readily give their vote to that effect. When, in the year 1842, I was for the first time delivered over to the Inquisition, the General of the Dominicans, the oldest of the Inquisitors, (Father Ancarani, an Inquisitor of forty-five years standing,) exclaimed before the council : 'This heretic,' speaking of myself, 'we had better burn him alive.' Such was the humanity of one who had grown grey among the corruptions and evil practices of his profession! His proposition, however, was not seconded, it being the first time I had been accused; but what might not have been my fate if this old man had been living, and appointed to judge me in the year 1850? In fact, I heard last year, whilst I was in Rome, that another of these precious theologians, less fierce and furious than the Dominican, suggested a more moderate proceeding, in the following terms:—' I should advise that Achilli be so dealt with as to prevent the possibility of his ever troubling us any more.' (This, most reverend personage is a man of mild temper, apparently incapable of cruelty. He was at that time one of the Counsellors of the Inquisition.) This, unquestionably, evinced no intention of setting me at liberty. And at a later period, after I had written my letters to the Pope, and published many other things in opposition to the Romish doctrines, the same *monsignore*, speaking of me to one of his adherents, who was more my friend than his, observed : ' I was right in the advice I gave in 1842, that Achilli should be so dealt with as to prevent the possibility of his ever troubling us any more. Had it been followed, we should not have had the present annoyance. And who knows what worse he may not have in store for us?' What, then, is the Inquisition of the nineteenth century? The same system of intolerance which prevailed in the barbarous ages. That which raised the Crusade, and roused all Europe to arms at the voice of a monk. (Bernard of Chiaravalle,) and of a hermit, (Peter the Hermit). That which—in the name of a God of peace, manifested on earth by Christ, who, through love for sinners, gave himself to be crucified—brought slaughter on the Albigenses and the Waldenses; filled France with desolation, under Domencico, di Guzman; raised in Spain the funeral pile and the scaffold, devastating the fair kingdoms of Granada and Castile, through the assistance of those detestable monks, Raimond de Pennefort, Peter Arbues, and Cardinal Torquemada. That which, to its eternal infamy, registers in the annals of France the fatal 24th of August, and the 5th of November in those of England. That same system which at this moment flourishes in Rome, which has never yet been either worn out or modified, and which, at this present time, in the jargon of the priests, is called 'the Holy, Roman, Universal, Apostolic Inquisition.' Holy, as the place where Christ was crucified is holy; Apostolic, because Judas Iscariot was the first Inquisitor; Roman and Universal, because from Rome it extends over all the world. Here, then, we see the Roman Inquisition extending into the most remote countries, In India, for example —who would ever believe that the Inquisition was at work there? So far from Rome? in the dominions of the English! The bare assertion would meet with ridicule. 'Oh! the Inquisition in India! No, no, we cannot believe that. In name, indeed, it may be there, but never in actual reality.' Fortunately, however, I have a letter by me, which I received in this country in March last. The original has been seen by many persons; among others, by Sir Culling E. Eardley, through whom, indeed, I received it. It came to hand very opportunely. It is written in English, and, if not elegant in its phraseology, it is at least sincere, and to be depended upon. It is as follows:—'DEAR AND REVEREND SIR,—I hope you will excuse me, if I, who am a stranger to you, take the liberty to relic with such veneration, that we were afraid even to look at it; and we often heard the following story related when the subject was introduced.—

"A priest in Jerusalem once had a vision, in which he was

address you the present letter. But the same God who delivered you from the brutal hands of your persecutors, (for which I congratulate you,) has given me courage to rise from my lethargy in which I was; and, kneeling before his presence, I heard a voice, saying, Write to Mr. A. [Achilli] for advice, and fly again from this Babylon. Therefore, full of confidence, I take the pen, in order to relate to you all my story. 'I am a Roman Catholic priest, and, as soon as I was ordained, being very anxious to preach the gospel to poor Hindoos, I left Rome, on the 2nd of March, 1840, being then twenty-three years of age, and was sent by *Propaganda Fide* to India; and there, being able to speak the English language, I was appointed, by the Roman Catholic bishop of Bombay, as military chaplain, and was sent to a military camp at Belgaum, where I was a very zealous and bigoted Roman Catholic priest, till God was pleased to open my eyes in the following manner: A Protestant clergymen of the Church of Scotland, named Taylor, celebrated the marriage ceremony to two Catholics; and this hurt my feeling very much; therefore I thought it my duty to write him a letter in very *impolite* (as the style does not interfere with the sense, it has not been deemed necessary to correct the foreign idioms in this letter,) manner, as is the custom of all Roman Catholic priests to do, to which he answered very kindly, and sent me also some Protestant books to read;—of course I refused to read them, and I returned them to him. But God put it into his heart to call as he did on me. He spoke to me a new language which I had never before heard;—it was the language of a true Christian—(how a sinner is justified before God). This language, by the grace of God touched my heart in such a manner that I took a Protestant book and began to read. It was 'The Spirit of the Papacy,' which opened my eyes, and I began to perceive the errors of the Church of Rome. Then, quite another man, I opened the Holy Bible, and confirmed myself that the Catholic religion is in perfect contradiction to the word of God, and that the Protestant Church was the Church in which God called me; therefore I opened my mind to the Rev. Mr. Jackson, who was the military Protestant chaplain at Belgaum, and a great friend of mine. He advised me to write to Dr. Carr, bishop of Bombay, which I did; and his Lordship was pleased to answer me in a very polite manner, begging me to write my sentiments about the real presence of our Lord Jesus Christ in the Sacrament, and a treatise on the spiritual power of the Pope, which I also did; and then he wrote to me to go to Bombay, where I embraced the Protestant religion, that is to say the pure religion of the Gospel. A Spanish Jesuit priest, named Francis Xavier Serra, whom I never saw before, called on me, in a secular dress; and, speaking the Italian language well, he told me that he was an Italian layman, and having heard that I was an Italian too, he called on me: but he did not mention any thing about religion, saying he did not care about it;—and he was very kind to me. He called on me four or five times; till one day, being a very agreeable evening, he begged me to take a round with him, which I did. And we went near the Catholic church, and, to my great surprise, I was taken by four men, and forced to go to the vicar-general, where they forced me to write a letter to the Protestant minister, Mr. Valentine, in whose house I lived, stating my intention to return to the Catholic religion; which, I am very sorry to say, I did. They then closed me in a room, till Sunday, when the vicar took me by force to the pulpit, and dictated to me what I was to say to the congregation; and he obliged me to declare that I left the Catholic religion for worldly motives; which was quite contrary to my sentiments. When night came, they took me from the room in which I was closed, and delivered me to a captain of a French ship, as a prisoner, with the order to take care of me to Marseilles, where he delivered me to the bishop, who, with a French priest, sent me to Rome. From Rome I was sent, as a punishment, to a convent at Perugia, where I remained for five years, till I got again my liberty, and returned to Rome; this was in November 1848. I am sure, Sir, you are not surprised to hear the treachery made to me at Bombay by that Jesuit, and by the vicar. Besides you must know that the vicar, whose name is Father Michele informed that the house in which the virgin had lived should be removed from its foundations, and transported to a distance. He did not think the communication was from God, and therefore disregarded it; but the house was soon after missed, which convinced him that the vision was true, and he told where the house might be found. A picture of the house is preserved in the nunnery, and was sometimes shown us. There are also wax figures of Joseph sawing wood, and Jesus as a child, picking up the chips. We were taught to sing a little song relating to this, the chorus of which I remember;

> " Saint Joseph charpentier,
> Petit Jesus ramassait les copeaux
> Pour fair bouillir la marmite!"

(St. Joseph was a carpenter, little Jesus collected chips to make the pot boil.)

I began to speak of miracles, and I recollect a story of one, about a family in Italy saved from shipwreck by a a priest, who were in consequence converted, and had two sons honoured with the priest's office.

I had heard before I entered the convent about a great fire which had destroyed a number of houses in the Quebec suburbs, and which some said the Bishop extinguished with holy water. I once heard a Catholic and a Protestant disputing on this subject; and when I went to the Congregational Nunnery, I sometimes heard the children, alluding to the same story, say, at an alarm of fire, "Is it a Catholic fire? Then why does not the Bishop run?"

Among the topics on which the Bishop addressed the nuns in the Convent, this was one. He told us the story one day, that he could have sooner interfered and stopped the flames, but that

---

Antonio, for his bad character, had been put in gaol for six months, by the British Government at Bombay. Now, Sir, I live in a most miserable estate of mind, being from my heart a Protestant, yet I am obliged to observe the Roman Catholic forms: which is quite contrary to my feelings. I am very sorry that I had not in India the Christian courage which you have demonstrated just now in Rome : but you must know that they threatened me with brutal menaces, and that I was too young. I am at present firmly resolved to fly from this Babylon, and embrace again the pure doctrine of the Gospel; to remain in the faith, by the grace of God, till my death, and to preach it throughout the world. I have the honour, &c., Your Brother in Jesus Christ, N. N. Rome, the 26th Feb. 1850.' This adventure at Bombay proves that the Inquisition is not only in existence, but sufficiently daring to carry on its operations even within the British dominions : and we see the manner in which it acts. In Bombay, the recantation of this poor priest is all that is known (as an English missionary, who was there at the time, told me) : it was said, indeed, that he had since left the country; but no one knew of the treachery of the Jesuit, or of the tricks of the apostolic vicar. Similar events occur more or less frequently in various parts of the world."

at last, finding they were about to destroy too many Catholic houses, he threw holy water on the fire, and extinguished it. I believed this, and also thought he was able to put out any fire, but that he never did it, except when inspired.

The holy water which the Bishop had consecrated was considered much more efficacious than any blessed by a common priest; and this it was which was used in the convent in sprinkling in our beds. It had virtue in it, to keep off any evil spirits.

Now that I was a nun, I was occasionally sent to read lectures to the novices, as other nuns had been while I was a novice. There were but few of us who were thought capable of reading English well enough, and, therefore, I was more frequently sent than I might otherwise have been. The superior often said to me, as I was going among the novices:

"Try to convert them—save their souls—you know you will have a higher place in heaven for every one you convert."

For whatever reason, mad Jane Ray seemed to take great delight in crossing and provoking the Superior and old nuns; and often she would cause an interruption when it was most inconvenient and displeasing to them. The preservation of silence was insisted upon rigidly, and penances of such a nature were imposed for breaking it, that it was a constant source of uneasiness with me, to know that I might infringe the rules in so many ways, and that inattention might at any moment subject me to something very unpleasant. During the periods of meditation, therefore, and those of lecture, work, and repose, I kept a strict guard upon myself to escape penances, as well as to avoid sin; and the silence of the others, convinced me that they were equally watchful, and from the same motives.

My feelings, however, varied at different times, and so did those of many, if not all my companions, excepting the older ones, who took their turns in watching us. We sometimes felt disposed for gaiety, and threw off all idea that talking was sinful, even when required by the rules of the Convent. And even when I felt that I might perhaps be doing wrong, I reflected that confession, and certainly penance, would soon wipe off the guilt.

I may remark here, that I ere long found out several things important to be known to a person living under such rules. One of these was, that it was much better to confess to a priest a sin committed against the rules, because he would not require one of the penances I most disliked, viz., those which exposed me to the observation of the nuns, or which demanded self-debasement before them, like begging their pardon, kissing the floor or the

Superior's feet, &c., and besides, he, as a confessor, was bound to secrecy, and could not inform the Superior against me. My conscience being as effectually unburthened by confession to the priest, as I had been taught to believe, therefore I preferred not to tell my sins to any one else; and this course I found was pre-preferred by others for the same good reasons.

To Jane Ray, however, it sometimes appeared to be a matter of perfect indifference, who knew her violation of rule, or to what penance she exposed herself.

Often and often, while perfect silence prevailed among the nuns, at meditation, or while nothing was to be heard except the voice of the reader appointed for the day, no matter whose life or writings were presented for our contemplations, Jane would break forth with some remark or question, that would attract general attention, and often cause a long and total interruption. Sometimes she would make some harmless remark or enquiry aloud, as if through mere inadvertency; and then her loud and well known voice, so strongly associated with every thing singular and ridiculous, would arrest the attention of us all, and generally incline us to smile, and even force us to laugh. The Superior would then usually utter some hasty remonstrance, and many a time I have heard her pronounce some penance upon her; but Jane had ever some apology ready, or some reply calculated to irritate us still farther, or to prove to every one that no punishment would be effectual on her. Sometimes this singular woman would appear to be actuated by different feelings and motives; for although she usually delighted in drawing others into difficulty, and has thrown many a severe penance even upon her greatest favourites, on other occasions she appeared totally regardless of consequences herself, and preferred to take all the blame, anxious only to shield others.

I have repeatedly known her to break silence in the community, as if she had no object, or none beyond that of causing disturbance, or exciting a smile, and as soon as it was noticed, exclaim, " Say it's me, say it's me."

Sometimes she would even expose herself to punishments in place of another who was guilty; and thus I found it difficult fully to understand her. In some cases she seemed decidedly out of her wits, as the Superior and priests commonly preferred to represent her; but generally I saw in her what prevented me from counting her insane. Amongst her most common tricks were such as these:—she gave me the name of the " Devout English Reader," because I was often appointed to make the lecture to the English girls; and sometimes, after taking a seat near me, under pretence of deafness, would whisper in my hearing, because she knew my want of self-command when excited to laughter. Thus she often exposed me to penances for a breach of decorum, and set me to biting my lips, to avoid laughing outright in the midst of a solemn lecture. "Oh! you devout English Reader!" would sometimes come upon me suddenly from her lips, with something in it so ludicrous, that I had to exert myself to the utmost to avoid observation. This came so often at one time, that I grew uneasy, and told her I must confess it, to unburden my conscience. I had not done so before, because she would complain of me for giving way to temptation.

Sometimes she would pass behind us as we stood at dinner ready to sit down, and softly moving back our chairs, leave us to fall down upon the floor. This she repeatedly has done; and while we were laughing together, she would spring forward, kneel to the Superior, and beg her pardon and a penance.

CHAPTER XI.

Alarming Order from the Superior—Proceed to execute it—Scene in an upper Room—Sentence of Death and Murder—My own Distress—Reports made to Friends of St. Frances.

But I must now come to one deed in which I had some part, and which I look back upon with greater horror and pain than any occurrence in the Convent, in which I was not the principal sufferer. It is not necessary for me to attempt to excuse myself in this or any other case. Those who have any disposition to judge fairly, will exercise their own judgment in making allowances for me, under the fear and force, the command and examples before me.(b) I, therefore shall confine myself, as usual, to

---

(b) The awfully debased and degraded state of society, where the word of God is rejected, and Popish delusions countenanced, may be seen, in some measure, from the following facts. The Rev. Carius Wilson, in his work before referred to, and which is one of deep interest, says,—"I heard an anecdote of a married couple, who had lived for some time very unhappily. The husband at last attempted to murder the wife; and she escaped to her own friends, who took up the cause, and the man was put in prison. It is customary for justice to yield to mercy, whenever the injured party intercedes for the aggressor. The husband's relatives therefore came and implored the wife to exert her prerogative, and beg the life of her husband. She seemed resolved that he should die, and it was long before she would listen to any proposal for releasing him. Her relations at last joined her husband's, and made the same request; when, overpowered by their united entreaties, she consented to implore his release. The next attempt made by their united families was to persuade the wife to return to her husband's house; and she at length yielded to their solicitations and his promises of future kindness, and a day was fixed for her return. The husband, attended by his relations, and the wife by her's, met at an appointed place. The sight of

the simple narration of facts. The time was about five months after I took the veil; the weather was cool, perhaps in September or October; one day the Superior sent for me and several other nuns, to receive her commands at a particular room. We found

her husband revived affection in her bosom, and she rushed forward to his arms, 'Take that,' said he, in a tone of savage revenge, and she sank on the ground, whilst the dagger he had plunged into her breast gave the death blow. No attempt was made by any of the attendants to secure the murderer. 'Poor fellow, let him go!' was the only observation; whilst a way was opened to facilitate his flight. This want of moral feeling is not to be wondered at where the Word of God is so hid, that the true light never shineth, and where 'men love darkness rather than light, because their deeds are evil.' The above anecdote I believe to be true, as it was related by the Rev. J. H—, a gentleman of great integrity, who was at that time chaplain to the British Factory in Lisbon. He also gave an account of the way in which persons were despatched in a more private manner, by means of a 'bravo.' And I am willing to narrate this circumstance, as it throws more light upon the degraded tone of moral feeling, as well as upon the deluded state of many, not, I fear, only in Portugal, but also in other countries, where there is that greatest of all famines, 'not a famine of bread, nor a thirst of water, but of hearing the word of the Lord.' A young Englishman of family and fortune, had a quarrel one night with a Portuguese nobleman, at the Opera House. He sent him a challenge the following morning, which the nobleman refused to accept. The young Englishman received this refusal when at a dinner party, where he drank too freely; and on his return to his lodgings, was observed by his French valet to be much out of humour. The servant taking advantage of his master's state of excitement from intoxication, ventured to ask what had disturbed him? When he named the affront he had received from the Portuguese, and his refusal to fight, the French servant added fuel to the flame, and urged revenge. His master did not at first understand his drift; till the man named a 'bravo,' and offered to get the work done for him at once. The gentleman, unable to reason and to see the sin and unmanliness of the step, urged by his anger, told his valet 'he might do what he pleased,' and went to bed. He slept till late the next morning; but as soon as his servant appeared, he inquired the first thing as to the subject of their conversation the night before, having an indistinct recollection of the man's proposal of a bravo, but unable to remember all that had passed. The servant soon refreshed his memory; and the young Englishman was horror-struck at the consent he had given to the murder of a fellow-creature. He begged him to think no more of the subject; and added his regret that his excited state the night before should have led him so astray. 'Sir,' said the servant, 'I fear it is too late; I have seen the bravo this morning, and he has promised to do the job.' The gentleman entreated his man to see the bravo immediately; and to offer him any sum to spare the nobleman's life. His valet replied, 'I cannot see him again till to-morrow morning where I met him to-day.' 'How came you to hear of him?' said his master; 'and where did you meet him?' 'An acquaintance of mine, whom I saw after I left you last night, directed me to a church, where I should see a person of middle stature, dressed in black, and kneeling before a particular altar. He told me I should observe a peculiar fixedness in his devotions; and on speaking to him after they were over, I should find him answer to the name he gave me. I therefore went very early this morning, and I saw the bravo; but so intent did he seem at his prayers, that I felt, over and over again, I must be mistaken in the man: however I waited till I saw him leaving the church; and I spoke to him by name, he answered me, and appeared to understand immediately the subject of my errand. He knew the Portugese nobleman well, and said that the long passages leading to his house would afford every facility for the execution of our purpose. I asked him the sum. He replied a moidore; (twenty-seven shillings of British money,) and he told me that if I would meet him at that same church tomorrow, at the same hour, he would tell me if he had succeeded with his victim.'—The young Englishman finding it useless to send his valet to seek the bravo before the time appointed, passed a day and night of such wretchedness as few, perhaps, have experienced. With the dawn of day he sent off his servant to the Bishops and some priests with her; and speaking in an unusual tone of fierceness and authority, she said, "Go to the room for the examination of conscience, and drag St. Frances up stairs." Nothing more was necessary than this unusual command, with the tone and manner which accompanied it, to excite in me most gloomy anticipations. It did not strike me as strange that St. Frances should be in the room to which the Superior directed us. It was an apartment to which we were often sent to prepare for the communion, and to which we voluntarily went, whenever we felt the compunctions which our ignorance of duty, and the misinstructions we received, inclined us to seek relief from self-reproach. Indeed, I had seen her there a little before. What terrified me was, first, the Superior's angry manner; second, the expressions she used, being a French term, whose peculiar use I had learnt in the convent, and whose meaning is rather softened when translated into drag; third, the place to which we were directed to take the interesting young nun, and the persons assembled there, as I supposed, to condemn her. My fears were such, concerning the fate that awaited her, and my horror at the idea that she was in some way to be sacrificed, that I would have given any thing to be allowed to stay where I was. But I feared the consequences of disobeying the Superior, and proceeded with the rest towards the room for the examination of conscience. The room to which we were to proceed from that, was in the second story, and the place of many a scene of a shameful nature. It is sufficient for me to say, after what I have said in other parts of this book, things had here occurred which made me regard the place with the greatest disgust. St. Frances had appeared melancholy for some time. I well knew that she had cause, for she had been repeatedly subject to trials which I need not name, our

---

the church, with full directions to offer any sum to save the nobleman's life. The man soon returned,—his countenance told the tale—his application was too late. The butcher only waited his reward. There was the same serenity of countenance at the altar— the same uplifted eye. His conscience alone seemed in a deep slumber. When the valet named his master's relentings, 'It is too late now,' said the bravo; 'he died by my hand last night, at eleven o'clock, on his way to the opera.' My informant told me the poor young Englishman left Lisbon immediately: and one would expect that he never more was guilty of the sin of drunkenness, which had been with him the moving spring to murder. It is true, that had the nobleman accepted his challenge, and fallen in a duel, it would still have been murder in the sight of God: though in the eye of man midnight assassination is considered dastardly, whilst the openly fought duel is thought to be a courageous and honourable action. Colonel Gardiner had more courage, when with his Bible in his hand, he refused to accept a challenge, saying, 'I am not afraid to fight but I am afraid to sin.' May these 'tales of other times' (though indeed not far distant) lead us to pray more earnestly 'for all sorts and conditions of men; that God's way may be known upon earth; his saving health among all nations.' And may all those who know and love the way of salvation study to throw their talents into the spiritual treasury; that the word of God may have free course, and be glorified."

common lot. When we reached the room where we had been bidden to seek her, I entered the door, my companions standing behind me, as the place was so small as hardly to hold five persons at a time. The young nun was standing alone, near the middle of the room; she was probably about twenty, with light hair, blue eyes, and a very fair complexion. I spoke to her in a compassionate voice, but at the same time with such a decided manner, that she comprehended my full meaning.

"Saint Frances, we are sent for you." Several others spoke kindly to her, but two addressed her very harshly. The poor creature turned round with a look of meekness, and without even speaking a word, resigned herself to our hands. The tears came into my eyes. I had not a moment's doubt that she considered her fate as sealed, and was already beyond the fear of death. She was conducted or rather hurried to the staircase, which was near by, and then seized by her limbs and clothes, and in fact almost dragged up stairs, in the sense the Superior had intended. I laid my own hands upon her, I took hold of her too, more gentle indeed than some of the rest; yet I encouraged and assisted them in carrying her. I could not avoid it. My refusal would not have saved her, nor prevented her being carried up; it would only have exposed me to some severe punishment, as I believe some of my companions would have seized the first opportunity to complain of me.

All the way up the staircase, Saint Frances spoke not a word, nor made the slightest resistance. When we entered with her the room to which she was ordered, my heart sunk within me. The Bishop, the Lady Superior, and five priests, viz., Bonin, Richards, Savage, and two others, I now ascertained, were assembled for trial, on some charge of great importance.

When we had brought our prisoner before them, Father Richards began to question her, and she made ready but calm replies. I cannot pretend to give a connected account of what ensued; my feelings were wrought up to such a pitch, that I knew not what I did, or what to do; I was under a terrible apprehension that, if I betrayed the feelings which overcame me, I should fall under the displeasure of the cold-blooded persecutors of my poor innocent sister; and this fear on the one hand, with the distress I felt for her on the other, rendered me almost frantic. As soon as I entered the room, I had stepped into a corner, on the left of the entrance, where I might partially support myself, by leaning against the wall, between the door and the window. This support was all that prevented me from falling to the floor, for the confusion of thoughts were so great, that only a few words I heard spoken on either side made any lasting impression upon me. I felt as if struck with some insupportable blow, and death would not have been more frightful to me. I am inclined to the belief, that Father Richards wished to shield the poor prisoner from the severity of her fate, by drawing from her expressions that might bear a favourable construction. He asked her, among other things, if she was now sorry for what she had been overheard to say, (for she had been betrayed by one of the nuns,) and if she would not prefer confinement in the cells, to the punishment which was threatened. But the bishop soon interrupted him, and it was easy to perceive, that he considered her fate as sealed, and was determined that she should not escape. In reply to some of the questions put to her, she was silent; to others I heard her voice reply, that she did not repent of words she had uttered, though they had been reported by some of the nuns, who had heard them; that she had firmly resolved to resist every attempt to compel her to the commission of crimes which she detested. She added, that she would rather die than cause the murder of harmless babes.

"That is enough, finish her!" said the Bishop.

Two nuns instantly fell upon the woman, and in obedience to directions given by the Superior, prepared to execute her sentence. She still maintained all the calmness and submission of a lamb. Some of those who took part in this transaction, I believe, were as unwilling as myself: but of others, I can safely say, that they delighted in it. Their conduct certainly exhibited a most blood thirsty spirit. But, above all others present, and above all human fiends I ever saw, I think Saint Hypolite was the most diabolical; she engaged in the horrid task with all alacrity, and assumed from choice the most revolting parts to be performed. She seized a gag, forced it into the mouth of the poor nun, and when it was fixed between her extended jaws, so as to keep them open at their greatest possible distance, took hold of the straps fastened at end of the stick, crossed them behind the helpless head of the victim, and drew them tight through the loop prepared as fastening. The bed, which had always stood in one part of the room, still remained there; though the screen which had usually been placed before it, and was made of thick muslin, with only a crevice through which a person behind might look out, had been folded upon its hinges in the form of a W., and placed in a corner. On the bed the prisoner was laid with her face upward, and then bound with cords so that she could not move. In an instant another bed was thrown upon her. One of the priests, named Bonin, sprung like a fury first upon it, with all his force. He was speedily followed by the nuns, until there was as many upon the bed as could find room; and all did what they could, not only to smother but bruise her. Some stood up and jumped upon the poor girl with their feet, some with their knees; and others, in different ways, seemed to seek how they might best beat the breath out of her body, and mangle it, without coming in direct contact with it, or seeing the effects of their violence. During this time my feelings were almost too strong to be endured. I felt stupified, and scarcely was conscious of what I did. Still, fear for myself remained in a sufficient degree to induce me to some exertion; and I attempted to talk to those who stood next, partly that I might have an excuse for turning away from the dreadful scene.

After the lapse of fifteen or twenty minutes, and when it was presumed that the sufferer had been smothered and crushed to death, Father Bonin and the nuns ceased to trample upon her, and stepped from the bed. All was motionless and silent beneath it.

They then began to laugh at such inhuman thoughts as occurred to some of them; rallying each other in the most unfeeling manner, ridiculing me for my feelings which I in vain endeavoured to conceal. They alluded to the resignation of our murdered companion; and one of them tauntingly said, " she would have made a good Catholic Martyr." After spending some moments in such conversation, one of them asked if the corpse should be removed. The Superior said it had better remain a little while. After waiting a short time longer, the feather-bed was taken off, the cords unloosed, and the body taken by the nuns and dragged down stairs. I was informed that it was taken into the cellar, and thrown unceremoniously into the hole which I have already described, covered with a great quantity of lime; and afterwards sprinkled with a liquid, of the properties and name of which I am ignorant. This liquid I have seen poured into the hole from large bottles, after the necks were broken off; and have heard that it is used in France, to prevent the effluvia rising from cemeteries.

I did not soon recover from the shock caused by this scene; indeed, it still recurs to me with most gloomy impressions. The next day, there was a melancholy aspect over everything, and recreation time passed in the dullest manner; scarcely anything was said above a whisper. I never heard much said afterwards about Saint Frances.

I spoke with one of the nuns a few words one day, but we were all cautioned not to expose ourselves very far, and could not place much confidence in each other. The murdered nun had been brought to her shocking end through the treachery of one of our number, in whom she confided. I never knew with certainty who had reported her remarks to the Superior; but suspicion fastened on one, and I never could regard her but with detestation. I was more inclined to blame her, than some of those employed in the execution; for there could have been no necessity for the betrayal of her feelings. We all knew how to avoid exposing each other.

I was often sent by the Superior to overhear what was said by novices and nuns: when they seemed to shun her, she would say, "go and listen, they are speaking English;" and though I obeyed her, I never informed her against them. If I wished to clear my conscience, I would go to a priest and confess, knowing that he dared not communicate what I said to any person, and that he would not choose as heavy penances as the Superior.

We were always at liberty to choose another confessor when we had any sin to confess, which we were unwilling to tell one to whom we should otherwise have gone.

Not long after the murder just related, a young woman came to the nunnery, and asked for permission to see St. Frances. It was my former friend, with whom I had been an assistant teacher, Miss Louise Bousquet, of St. Denis. From this, I supposed the murdered nun might have come from that town, or its vicinity. The only answer was, that St. Frances was dead.

Some time afterward, some of St. Frances's friends called to enquire after her; and they were told she died a glorious death: and further told, that she made some heavenly expressions; which were repeated in order to satisfy her friends.

CHAPTER XII.

Description of the Room of the Three States, and the Pictures in it—Jane Ray ridiculing Priests—Their Criminal Treatment of us at Confession—Jane Ray's Tricks with the Nun's Aprons, Handkerchiefs, and Nightgowns—Apples.

The pictures in the room of the Three States were large, and painted by some artist who understood how to make horrible ones. They appeared to be stuck to the walls. The light is admitted from small and high windows, which are curtained, and is rather faint, so as to make every thing look gloomy. The story told us was, that they were painted by an artist, to whom

God had given power to represent things exactly as they are in heaven, hell, and purgatory.

In heaven, the picture of which hangs on one side of the apartment, multitudes of nuns and priests are put in the highest places, with the Virgin Mary at the head; St. Peter and other saints far above the great number of good Catholics of other classes, who were crowded in below.

In purgatory are multitudes of people; and one part, called "*The place of lambs*," are infants who died unbaptized; "*The place of darkness*," is that part of purgatory in which adults are collected; and there they are surrounded with flames, waiting to be delivered by the prayers of the living.

In hell, the picture of which, and that of purgatory, were on the wall opposite that of heaven, the human faces were the most horrible that can be imagined. Persons of different descriptions were represented, with the most distorted features, ghastly complexions, and every variety of dreadful expression; some with wild beasts gnawing at their heads, others furiously biting the iron bars which kept them in, with looks which could not fail to make a spectator shudder.

I could hardly persuade myself, that the figures were not living; and the impression they made on my feelings was powerful. I was often shewn the place where nuns go who break their vows, as a warning. It is the hottest place in hell, and worse, in every point of view, even than that to which all Protestants are assigned; because they are not so much to be blamed, as we were sometimes assured, as their ministers and the Bible, by which they are perverted.

Whenever I was shut up in that room, as I was several times, I prayed for "les ames des fideles trepasses:" the souls of those faithful ones who have long been in purgatory, and have no relations living to pray for them.

My feelings were often of the most painful description, while I remained alone with those frightful pictures.

Jane Ray was once put in, and uttered the most dreadful shrieks. Some of the old nuns proposed to the Superior to have her gagged. "No," she replied, "go and let out that devil, she makes me sin more than all the rest."

Jane could not endure the place; and she afterwards gave names to many of the worst figures in the pictures. On catechism-days she would take a seat behind a cupboard door, where the priest could not see her, while she faced the nuns, and would make us laugh. "You are not so attentive to your lesson as you used to be," he would begin to say, while we were endeavouring to suppress our laughter.

Jane would then hold up the first letter of some priest's name, whom she had before compared with one of the faces in "hell," and look so that we could hardly preserve our gravity.

I remember she named the wretch, who was biting at the bars of hell, with a serpent gnawing his head, with chains and padlock on, Father Dufresne; and she would say—" Does he not look like him, when he comes into catechism with his long solemn face, and begins his speeches with, 'My children, my hope is, that you have lived very devout lives.'"

The first time I went to confession after taking the veil, I found abundant evidence that the priests did not treat even that ceremony, which is called a solemn sacrament, with respect enough to lay aside the detestable and shameless character they so often shewed on other occasions. The confessor sometimes sat in the room for the examination of conscience, and sometimes in the Superior's room, and always alone, except the nun who was confessing. He had a common chair placed in the middle of the floor; and instead of being placed behind a grate, or lattice, as in the chapel, had nothing before or around him. There were no spectators to observe him, and of course any such thing would have been unnecessary.

A number of nuns usually confessed on the same day, but only one could be admitted into the room at a time. They took their places just without the door, on their knees, and went through the preparation prescribed by the rules of confession; repeating certain prayers, which always occupy a considerable time. When one was ready, she rose from her knees, entered, and closed the door behind her; and no one even dare touch the latch until she came out.

I shall not tell what was transacted at such times, under the pretence of confessing, and receiving absolution from sin: far more sin was often incurred than pardoned; and crimes of a deep dye were committed, while trifling irregularities, in childish ceremonies, were treated as serious offences. I cannot persuade myself to speak plainly on such a subject, as I must offend the virtuous ear. I can only say, that suspicion cannot do any injustice to the priests, because their sins cannot be exaggerated.

Some idea may be formed of the manner in which even such women as many of my sister nuns regarded the father confessors, when I state, that there was often a contest among us to avoid entering the apartment as long as we could, endeavouring to make each other go first, as that was what most of us dreaded.

During the long and tedious days, which filled up the time between the occurrences I have mentioned, nothing, or little took place to keep up our spirits. We were fatigued in body with labour, or with sitting, debilitated by the long continuance of our religious exercises, and depressed in feelings by our miserable and hopeless condition. Nothing but the humours of mad Jane Ray could rouse us for a moment from our langour and melancholy.

To mention all her devices would require more room than is here allowed, and a memory of almost all her words and actions for years. I had early become a favourite with her, and had opportunity to learn more of her character than most of the other nuns. As this may be learned from hearing what she did I will here recount a few of her tricks, just as they happen to present themselves to my memory, without regard to the order of time.

She one day, in an unaccountable humour, sprinkled the floor plentifully with holy water, which brought upon her a severe lecture from the Superior, as might have been expected. The Superior said it was a heinous offence; she had wasted holy water enough to save many souls from purgatory; and what would they not give for it! She then ordered Jane to sit in the middle of the floor, and when the priest came he was informed of her offence. Instead, however, of imposing one of those penances to which she had often been subjected, but with so little effect, he said to her, "Go to your place, Jane; we forgive you for this time."

I was once set to iron aprons with Jane; aprons and pocket-handkerchiefs are the only articles of dress which are ever ironed in the Convent. As soon as we were alone, she remarked, "Well, we are free from the rules while we are at this work;" and, although she knew she had no reason for saying so, she began to sing, and I soon joined her, and thus we spent the time while we were at work, to the neglect of the prayers we ought to have said.

We had no idea that we were in danger of being overheard; but it happened that the Superior was overhead all the time, with several nuns, who were preparing for confession: she came down and said, "How is this?" Jane Ray cooly replied that we had employed our time in singing hymns, and referred to me. I was afraid to confirm so direct a falsehood in order to deceive the Superior, though I had often told more injurious ones of her fabrication, or at her orders, and said very little in reply to Jane's request.

The Superior plainly saw the trick that was attempted, and ordered us both to the room for the examination of conscience, where we remained till night without a mouthful to eat. The time was not, however, unoccupied: I received such a lecture from Jane as I have very seldom heard; and she **was** so angry with me, that we did not speak to each other for **two** weeks.

At length she found something to complain of against me, had me subjected to a penance, which led to our begging each other's pardon; and we became perfectly satisfied, reconciled, and as good friends as ever.

One of the most disgusting penances we ever had to submit to, was that of drinking the water in which the Superior had washed her feet. Nobody could ever laugh at this penance except Jane Ray. She would pretend to comfort us by saying she was sure it was better than mere plain clear water.

Some of the tricks which I remember, were played by Jane with nuns' clothes. It was a rule that the oldest aprons in use should go to the youngest received, and that the old nuns were to wear all the new ones. On four different occasions Jane stole into the sleeping room at night and, unobserved by the watch, changed a great part of the aprons, placing them by the beds of nuns to whom they did not belong. The consequence was, that in the morning they dressed themselves in such haste, as never to discover the mistake they made until they were all ranged at prayers; and then the ridiculous appearance which many of them cut disturbed the long devotions. I laugh so easy that on such occasions I usually incurred a full share of penances. I generally, however, got a new apron when Jane played this trick; for it was part of her object to give the best aprons to her favourites, and put off the ragged ones on some of the old nuns whom she most hated.

Jane once lost her pocket handkerchief. The penance for such an offence is, to go without any for five weeks. For this she had no relish, and requested me to pick one from some of the nuns on the way upstairs. I succeeded in getting two: this, Jane said, was one too many; and she thought it dangerous for either of us to keep it, lest a search should be made. Very soon the two nuns were complaining that they had lost their handkerchiefs, and wondering what could have become of them, as they were sure they had been careful. Jane seized an opportunity, and slipped one into a straw bed, where it remained until the bed was emptied to be filled with new straw.

As the winter was coming on, one year, she complained that we were not as well supplied with warm night-clothes as two of the nuns she named, whom she said she "abominated." She soon after found means to get possession of their fine warm flannel night-gowns, one of which she gave to me, while the other was put on at bed-time. She presumed the owners would have a secret search for them; and in the morning hid them in the stove, after the fire had gone out, which was kindled a little before the hour of rising, and then suffered to burn down.

This she did every morning, taking them out at night, through the winter. The poor nuns who owned the garments were afraid to complain of their loss, lest they should have some penance laid on them; and nothing was ever said about them. When the weather began to grow warm in the spring, Jane returned the night-gowns to the beds of the nuns from whom she had borrowed them; and they were probably as much surprised to find them again, as they had been before at losing them.

Jane once found an opportunity to fill her apron with a quantity of fine apples, called *fameuses*, which came in her way, and, hastening up the sleeping-room, hid them under my bed. Then coming down she informed me, and we agreed to apply for leave to make our elevens, as it is called. The meaning of this is, to repeat a certain round of prayers, for nine days in succession, to some saint we choose to address for assistance, in becoming more charitable, affectionate, or something else. We easily obtained permission, and hastening up stairs to begin our nine day's feast on the apples, when, much to our suprise, they had all been taken away; and there was no way to avoid the disagreeable fate we had brought upon ourselves. Jane, therefore, began to search the beds of the other nuns; but not finding any trace of the apples, she became doubly vexed, and stuck pins in those which belonged to her enemies. When bed-time came, they were much scratched in getting into bed, which made them break silence, and that subjected them to penances.

NOTES, FACTS, CONFIRMATIONS, &c.

The public generally are but little aware of the opposition that has been raised against the Disclosures of Maria Monk; nor of the host of evidence produced to prove the correctness of her assertions. Abundance of paragraphs like the following, and many more powerful, will be given as we pass on. This is from the volume of Confirmations. "The following extract of a letter from a worthy gentleman in Montreal, who has taken some pains to investigate this matter, will enable the reader to understand something of the state of feeling, respecting this subject in and about that city. After detailing the efforts of himself and another gentleman in making inquiries of those who ought to know something of Miss Monk's past history, he writes as follows:—'Now the fact is just here, everybody is afraid to know any thing about this matter: and all her relatives seem backward to say what they might on the subject. Romanism is so far predominant here, that there are only a very few who have correct principle and moral courage enough to think, speak, or act aright in the concern. Political, pecuniary, and relative interests and connexions have occasioned such a commingling of Romanism and Protestantism, that it is difficult to reach the black heart of the Roman beast, nominal Protestants are so much in the way. A bookseller said to me yesterday, that he and all the other booksellers in the town were afraid to keep Maria Monk's book in their stores, lest a mob should attack them.'"

Martin Luther, in his book entitled "Table Talk," **speaks thus** "Of the Lasciviousness and Incontinency of the Papists." "**Paul the third** (before he was Pope) had a sister; the same he gave to his predecessor, the Pope, for a concubine, and thereby deserved to be made a Cardinal. **Such** confounded pranks have the Popes played, as surpass all human thought. **The** Priests were forced to give (as their pander) a florin for every child they begat; the same was called a milk-penny. In the council at Lateran, in the year 1515, (which began in the life of Pope Julius, and ended under Pope Leo) it was first concluded that the resurrection of the dead should thenceforth be believed, and that a Cardinal lawfully might keep five whores, but not more, to be his chamberlains for accomplishing of his wicked lust, but the same was afterwards altered by Pope Leo. Surely some fearful fall and destruction attendeth them, and those that undertake to maintain and defend them; therefore let us pray. The suspicions and idolatries in Popedom were such horrible abominations, that if I had not seen them with mine eyes, but only had read thereof, I should never have believed them. The Pope placeth his Cardinals in all kingdoms, the same are peevish milksops, effeminate, and unlearned ass-heads; they lie lolling in kings' courts among the ladies and women. The Pope hath possessed all countries with Cardinals, and with his papistical Bishops. Germany is taken captive with popish Bishops, for I can make an account of above forty bishoprics, besides abbies and cathedrals (which are richer than the bishoprics.) Again, there are in Germany but eight-and-twenty principalities, so that the popish Bishops are far more rich and powerful than the Princes of the empire. On a time the Bishop of Magdeburg (reading by chance in the Bible of the Prophets) said 'Can I find nothing in this Book but how we priests are railed at?' and indeed the writings of the Prophets are fierce thunder-bolts against false Prophets and popish Bishops. The Princes of the empire regard not much, neither do they look thereunto, how and after what deceitful manner the Pope devoureth and swalloweth up the whole world, according to Daniel's prophecy."

A very splendid work entitled. "The Female Jesuit," is just issued. We shall, next number, notice its contents more fully. We here give one short extract as follows,—" I cannot now describe to you the feelings of horror I endured when I became a *postulant*. In the first instance I was cruelly deceived, for though I had been with the Society fifteen years I had not the most remote idea of the humiliating and trying ordeal they were called to pass through. I knew nothing of their customs, &c. till I entered the community. You may imagine my feelings of grief, and also suprise, when I was told to give up (with other things) the only earthly treasure I valued—my beloved mamma's portrait. Oh! uncle, you say I shall no longer value it. Did you know the tears and wishes that were spent in parting with that dear relic of a fond mother, you would not say so; or if you have still left any consideration for my feelings and affections, you will soon make me the happy possessor of that which, if it were in the power of any earthly good to create happiness, this would to me; parting with which was so great a trial to me, that it appeared as if it were to tear away every fibre of what I loved. I was never told I should be required to do this. The daily routine of a nun's life soon became most irksome and wearisome to me."

In an early number of the "AMERICAN PROTESTANT VINDICATOR" we find the following remarks in reference to Maria Monk's Awful Disclosures:—"We are deafened with clamour for proof to substantiate Maria Monk's history; but that demand is tantamount to the declaration—'I will not believe.' In anticipation of speedy death, and an immediate appearance at the dread tribunal of Jehovah, Maria Monk communicated to Mr. Tappan, the Chaplain at Bellevue—one of the benevolent institutions belonging to the city of New York, the principal facts in her Awful 'Disclosures.' After her unexpected recovery she personally appeared at Montreal, expressly and openly, to promulge her allegations of atrocious crimes against the chief Roman ecclesiastics in that city, who were armed with power, and having nearly the whole population her infuriated enemies. There she remained almost four weeks, constantly daring the Roman priests and nuns in vain. It is true Dr. Robertson, in his affidavit, says that he was willing 'To take the necessary steps for a full investigation if a direct charge were made against any particular individual of a criminal nature.' Now if Maria Monk's charges are not direct—of a criminal nature—and against particular individuals—what charges can be so characterised? The fact is this:—Dr. Robertson would no more dare to issue a warrant for the apprehension of Lartigue, or any of the inferior

Roman priests in Montreal than he would dare publicly to strike the Commander of the Garrison, or the Governor of Canada upon military parade. If any papist had stated to him the same facts concerning a protestant, or protestant minister, and offered to confirm them by his worthless oath, he would have issued his process at once; but Dr. Robertson knows that, in the present state of Canadian society, Roman priests can do what they please; and no man dares to reprove, much less to "Take any necessary steps for a full investigation" of their crimes. If the jesuits and nuns at Montreal are anxious for a full and impartial scrutiny of the Hotel Dieu Convent, Maria Monk is ready to oblige them with some facilities for that object; provided she may carry them out to all their extent and application. Mr. Ogden has one affidavit, and knows the whole matter; as can incontestibly be proved by Mr. A P. Hart, an Attorney of Montreal; and we recommend Dr. Robertson to issue his warrant for the apprehension of Lartigue, Bonin, Dufresne, and Richards, they are enough to begin with; and if Mr. Ogden will carry the facts with which he is acquainted to the Grand Jury, one witness in New York is ready to appear; and Dr. Robertson will find his hands full of employment if he will only "Take the necessary steps" to procure two or three other persons who shall be pointed out to him in the Hotel Dieu Nunnery. Therefore, until Dr. Robertson commences some incipient measures as a magistrate towards "The necessary steps for a full investigation," as he says, we shall be forced to believe that the printer made a mistake in his affidavit, and put willing for unwilling. The cavilling call, however, for additional evidence to be adduced by Maria Monk is manifestly futile. That testimony is within the jurisdiction of the priests alone who are criminated. Maria Monk reiterates her charges against the Roman ecclesiastics of Canada, and their nuns; and has solemnly sworn that they are true. What more can she do? What more can be required of her? Nothing but to search the premises, to see whether the statements which she has made are correct. A Committee of the New York Protestant Association are willing to accompany her to Montreal; to walk through the Hotel Dieu Nunnery in company with any gentlemen of Montreal, and investigate the truth without favour or partiality. Maria Monk is willing to submit the whole affair to that short, and easy, and sensible test, in which there is no possibility of deception. It does not depend upon credibility of witnesses, conflicting evidence, personal friendship, or religious prejudices; it is reduced to that unerring criterion—the sight and the touch. But, it is retorted, that will not be granted; then we repeat another proposal.—Let the Priest Conroy come forth girded in all the panoply of the Roman court, and appear as the champion of the Canadian Jesuits; let him institute an action, civil, or criminal, or both, against the publishers of such atrocious crimes which, as they pretend, are falsely alleged against the priests. If Lartigue, and his Montreal inferior priests, are implicated in the most nefarious felonies, Maria Monk has published him as a virtual accomplice. Why does he not put her truth to the test by subjecting her to a criminal process? Why does he not commence a suit against the booksellers who published her 'Awful Disclosures?'"

(a) Files of the "American Protestant Vindicator," have now come to hand. They are full of the controversy and confirmations arising out of Maria Monk's publications. We shall give the whole of the interesting matter in succeeding numbers, if we are encouraged. In proof of the spirit of the American Journal, read the following:—Popery in Hartford. I have often read your paper with deep interest, and believe that it is one of the most efficient means now in operation for diffusing a knowledge of, and exposing the abominations of the Romish Church in the United States. For it is a fact, however humiliating it may appear, that they exist here, even in the land of the pilgrims, and among their free institutions, to an alarming extent. And what is still greater cause for alarm is, that few seem to realize it. We frequently hear men and even professed Christians say, that Popery is not so bad and so much to be feared as many over zealous sectarians suppose. In illustration of this, the following fact will be deemed sufficient. Several years since, a Popish Priest came to Hartford for the purpose of establishing a church. He collected a considerable number of Irishmen and formed them into a Society; they then purchased a house on condition that they should move it from the ground on which it then stood. But this church, consisting chiefly of the labouring class of foreigners who necessarily laboured under embarrassing pecuniary circumstances, they applied to the citizens for aid, and raised a considerable sum from the contributions of the Protestant churches, sufficient I believe to complete the work. They have held their meetings in this house from time to time until now; the basement story has, I believe, been occupied by an Irish family, and the priest who has appropriated several rooms to himself for confessional and school rooms, and what else I would not undertake to show. But I will relate a circumstance which took place some months since. There were two young men, both residents in Hartford, one whose veracity is not to be doubted, passing the house at a late hour of the night, their attention was called to the house by the voice of a female within. They stopped; the cries became louder; they at length came to the determination to investigate the matter and find out the real cause. They then went to the door from which the sound proceeded, and stood in breathless silence, when they distinctly heard a female utter these words, "Don't, Father——, Don't." The cry was repeated; and the voice of —— was heard, but in so low and grum a tone as to render it unintelligible. They tried to gain admittance; but the door was fastened, and the key hole stopped. They stood and heard it for some time, then left the place, believing that she was still resisting the solicitations of her spiritual guide, and that he was still urging her to compliance. What his designs were I shall not undertake to shew. But I would inquire, what earthly motives can be assigned for her being there at so late an hour of so dark a night, or what motive is sufficient to justify so indelicate an act on the part of a female? The priests have no wives. They are not allowed to marry. She was at confession, some papist might say. Will they admit that their church has become so exceedingly corrupt as to render it necessary for their priests to hear confessions and absolve sins until so late an hour in the night? Surely this church is not so numerous as to require it; therefore this reason if assigned would be but a poor one and poorly understood. But I will leave the reader to judge for himself; and if he judges from analogy, I have little doubt as regards the decision. For Popery is the same in the United States as in Austria, Ireland or France, or wherever it exists. Their institutions and designs are the same, and their priests alike vicious. But what astonishing incredulity on the part of Protestants; notwithstanding all the recent disclosures which have been made, many still persist in saying that the Romish Church is not so corrupt as she once was. Alas! how few are the signs of reformation. It will answer better for old men to comfort themselves with this belief, perchance they may slumber under the sod before we shall be compelled to witness the sad demonstration of the fallacy of this unwarrantable belief. But never should any man who has the least regard for his country, or for the honour of his God, slumber when he knows that a storm is gathering which threatens to prostrate the object of his regard in the dust. Protestantism and Roman Catholicism are utterly opposed to each other as it regards their object and effect. And when we consider the fact stated above, that the Protestants in Hartford helped the Catholics to a church, does it not bespeak the awful lethargy and indifference which exists towards them? Let Christians and philanthropists instead of furnishing them with means by which their very heart's blood is to be drawn from them, awake and unite their energies and efforts in the suppression of an evil, which threatens the fairest prospects of our beloved country. SIGMA.

The *Glasgow Examiner* gives the following account of Extraordinary Proceedings of the Roman Catholic Nunnery at Edinburgh. "We have omitted from our report at the Free Commission on Wednesday, a statement of a very startling nature made by Mr. George Lyon in the course of the discussion on Popery, which may be worth quoting here, as if true, it would perhaps form of itself one of the most effective arguments against the further toleration of these monastic institutions which it is possible to procure. 'Not many days ago,' said Mr. Lyon, a little excited in manner, 'a cab stopped at the nunnery out the way there, with three gentlemen in it and a wretched young woman. Two ladies were passing by at the time. She was forcibly taken out of the cab, with shrieks that pierced the ears of these two ladies who were passing. She clung to the spokes of the wheels of the cab, but was dragged from them, and immured in the nunnery; the gate was locked upon her, and the gentlemen, if gentlemen they could be called, were seen returning in the cab.' This extraordinary statement failed not to produce, as in the circumstances it was well calculated to do, a very profound impression on the rev. court."

We have noted before, that we have received from America, several numbers of the "AMERICAN PROTESTANT VINDICATOR;" in these papers, all the arguments adduced as evidence of the falsity of Maria Monk's Disclosures are "*weighed in the balances*;" and their untruthfulness proved. The authorities of the Hotel Dieu Nunnery, did first state that no such person as Maria Monk ever inhabited that convent. The following extract from a number of the "*Protestant Vindicator*" will shew what reliance is to be placed on this statement.—"Dr. Chapin of Westhampton, and lately a missionary in Canada, has furnished the Hampshire Gazette with an article on Maria Monk's disclosures. He has been in Montreal, has visited the Hotel Dieu Nunnery. 'Saw a number of both sexes confessing to the priests'—heard it said that Maria Monk's 'character was very bad from her youth up,' 'that she had been partially deranged.' *Proof.* The informant 'had seen her tied to a bed post like a dog!' No small confirmation of the Awful Disclosures! 'The French Cathedral,' exclaims the enraptured Mr. Chapin, 'within or without, is the proudest structure which I ever beheld!—the largest in America—the exterior how lofty! Within, how vast and magnificent! The transparencies are truly splendid, glorious!' The conclusion of the whole matter, in the mind of Mr. Chapin, is: 'The disclosures are a base fabrication.' Verily! the Cathedral of St. Peter's at Rome, must have been 'gorgeous' in the eyes of our Protestant clergyman, had he been honored with an admittance into it three centuries ago. Query. Whether he would not have thought the 'Awful Disclosures' of Martin Luther, 'a base fabrication?'—Whatever else has or has not been disclosed by the book of Maria Monk, three things have been made abundantly apparent. 1. Not a few of our patrician Protestants, 'gentlemen of property and standing,' gowned and ungowned, have become perfectly fascinated and enraptured with the external pomp and magnificence of the 'Man of Sin.' 2. They feel any attack upon the Popish priesthood, as sensitively as if it was made upon themselves, and much more so than they do any insult to the Lord's despised poor. 3. There is nothing too contradictory to be swallowed by these men—no barbarities that can move their compassion for the victims of Romanism, or lessen the strength of their sympathy for the instigators of them. 'A base fabrication,' a book, like that of Maria Monk, attributed to a poor maniac girl! A female, of 'very bad character from her youth up,' selected for the society of the faithful, and for their own especial intimacy and spiritual communion by a chaste, an innocent and slandered priesthood! Very doubtful whether Maria Monk had ever been in the Nunnery, but its official inmates have '*seen her tied to a bed post like a dog!*' The man that could coolly pen the account of such treatment of an unfortunate girl; and retain his sympathy and credence for the barbarian that could throw this in her teeth to degrade and insult her, and render her testimony contemptible, would need little transformation in order to sit down with complacency at an *auto de fe*, and console himself for the horrors of the torture by the 'proud,' 'splendid,' 'glorious' palace of the Grand Inquisitor!" Here is testimony from one of their own fraternity to prove that Maria Monk *was* an inmate of the Hotel Dieu Nunnery. A Colonel Stone, once a *professing* Protestant, paid a visit to the Nunnery, with a view to compare Maria Monk's description of the building, with the building itself. We shall publish some parts of his contradictory statements, wherein he attempts to prove Maria Monk an impostor; and shall also add the testimony of other persons against Colonel Stone, proving beyond doubt, (which the said Colonel Stone's evidence goes more to prove than falsify,) that all that Miss Monk has here stated, is but too true.— The faithfulness of this Narrative is proved first, by the affidavit of William Miller, City and County of New York, "William Miller being duly sworn, doth say,—I knew Maria Monk when she was quite a child, and was acquainted with all her father's family. My father, Mr. Adam Miller, kept the Government school at St. John's, Lower Canada, for some years. Captain William Monk, Maria's father, lived in the garrison, a short distance from the village, and she attended the school with me for some months, probably as much as a year. Her four brothers also attended with us. Our family were on terms of intimacy, as my father had a high regard for Captain Monk; but the temper of his wife was such even at that time, as to cause much trouble. Captain Monk died very suddenly, as was reported, in consequence of being poisoned. Mrs. Monk was then keeper of the Government House in Montreal, and received a pension, which privilege she hath since enjoyed. In the Summer of 1832, I left Canada, and came to this city. In about a year afterward, I visited Montreal, and on the day when the Governor reviewed the troops, I believe about the end of August, I called at the

Government House, where I saw Mrs. Monk and several of the family. I enquired where Maria was, and she told me that she was in the nunnery. This fact I well remember, because the information gave me great pain, as I had unfavourable opinions of the nunneries. On reading the 'Awful Disclosures,' I at once knew she was the eloped nun, but was unable to find her until a few days since, when we recognized each other immediately. I give with pleasure my testimony in her favour, as she is among strangers, and exertions have been made against her. I declare my personal knowledge of many facts stated in her book, and my full belief in the truth of her story, which shocking as it is, cannot appear incredible to those persons acquainted with Canada. William Miller. Sworn before me, this 3rd day of March, 1836, Benjamin D. K. Craig, Commissioner of Deeds, &c."

CHAPTER XIII.

Jane Ray's Tricks continued—the Broomstick Ghost—Sleep-walking—Salted Cider—Changing Beds—Objects of some of her tricks—Feigned Humility—Alarm.

ONE night Jane, who had been sweeping the sleeping room for a penance, dressed up the broomstick, when she had completed her work, with a white cloth on the end so tied as to resemble an old woman with long arms sticking out. This she stuck through a broken pane of glass, and placed it so that it appeared to be looking in at the window, by the font of holy water. There it remained till the nuns came up to bed. The first who stopped at the font to dip her finger in caught a glimpse of the singular object, and started with terror. The next was equally terrified as she approached, and the next, and the next.

We all believed in ghosts; and it was not wonderful that such an object should cause alarm, especially as it was but a short time after the death of one of the nuns. Thus they went on, each getting a fright in turn, yet all afraid to speak. At length, one more alarmed, or with less presence of mind than the rest, exclaimed—" Oh, mon Dieu! je ne me coucherais pas!" When the night watch called out " Who's that?" she confessed she had broken silence, but pointed at the cause; and then all the nuns assembled at a distance from the window: Jane offered to advance boldly, and ascertain the nature of the apparition, which they thought a most resolute intention. We all stood looking on when she stepped to the window, drew in the broomstick, and showed us the ridiculous puppet which had caused so many superstitious fears.

Some of her greatest feats she performed as a sleep walker. Whether she ever walked in her sleep or not, I am unable with certainty, to say. She, however, often imposed upon the Superior and old nuns, by making them think so, when I knew she did not; and yet I cannot positively say that she always did. I have remarked that one of the old nuns was always placed in our sleeping-room at night to watch us. Sometimes she would be inattentive, and sometimes fall into a doze. Jane Ray often seized such times to rise from her bed, and walk about, occasionally seizing one of the nuns in bed, in order to frighten her. This she generally effected; and many times we have all been awakened by screams of terror. In our alarm, some of us frequently broke silence, and gave occasion to the Superior to lay us under penances. Many times, however, we escaped with a mere reprimand, while Jane usually received expressions of compassion: "Poor creature! she would not do so if she were in perfect possession of her reason." And Jane displayed her customary artfulness, in keeping up the false impression. As soon as she perceived that the old nun was likely to observe her, she would throw her arms about, or appear unconscious of what she was doing; falling upon a bed, or standing stock still, until exertions had been made to rouse her from her supposed lethargy.

We were once allowed to drink cider at dinner, which was quite an extraordinary favour. Jane, however, on account of her negligence of all work, was denied the privilege, which she much resented. The next day, when dinner arrived, we began to taste our new drink, but it was so salt we could not swallow it. Those of us who first discovered it, were as usual afraid to speak; but we set down our cups, and looked around, till the others made the same discovery; which they all soon did, and most of them in the same manner. Some, however, at length, taken by surprise, uttered some ludicrous exclamation, on tasting the salted cider, and then an old nun looking across, would cry out—

"Ah! tu casses la silence." (Ah! you have broken silence.) And thus we soon got a laughing beyond our power of supporting it. At recreation that day, the first question asked by many of us was, "How did you like your cider?"

Jane Ray never had a fixed place to sleep in. When the weather began to grow warm in the spring, she usually pushed some bed out of its place, near a window, and put her own beside it; and when the winter approached, she would choose a spot near the stove, and occupy it with her bed in spite of all remonstrance. We were all convinced that it was generally best to yield to her.

She was often set to work in different ways: but whenever she was dissatisfied with doing any thing, would devise some trick that would make the Superior, or old nuns, drive her off; and whenever any suspicion was expressed of her being in her right mind, she would say that she did not know what she was doing; and all the difficulty arose from her repeating prayers too much, which wearied and distracted her mind.

I was once directed to assist Jane Ray in shifting the beds of the nuns. When we came to those of some of the sisters whom she most disliked, she said, now we will pay them for some of the penances we have suffered on their account; and taking some thistles, she mixed them with the straw. At night, the first of them that got into bed felt the thistles and cried out. The nightwatch exclaimed as usual, "You are breaking silence there." And then another screamed, as she was scratched by the thistles, and another. The old nun then called upon all that had broken silence to rise, and ordered them to sleep under their beds as a penance, which they silently complied with. Jane and I afterwards confessed, when it was all over, and took some trifling penance which the priest imposed.

Those nuns who fell most under the displeasure of mad Jane Ray, as I have intimated before, were those who had the reputation of being most ready to inform of the trifling faults of others, and especially those who acted without any regard to honour, by disclosing what they had pretended to listen to in confidence. Several of the worst-tempered "saints" she held in abhorrence; and I have heard her say, that such and such she abominated. Many a trick did she play upon these, some of which were painful to them in their consequences, and a good number of them have never been traced to this day. Of all the nuns, however, none other was regarded by her with so much detestation as Saint Hypolite; for she was always believed to have betrayed Saint Frances, and to have caused her murder. She was looked upon by us as the voluntary cause of her death, and of the crime which those of us committed who unwillingly took part in her execution. We, on the contrary, being under the worst of fears for ourselves, in case of refusing to obey our masters or mistress, thought ourselves chargeable with less guilt, as unwilling assistants in a scene which it was impossible for us to prevent or delay. Jane has often spoken with me of the suspected informer, and always in terms of the greatest bitterness.

The Superior sometimes expressed commiseration for mad Jane Ray, but I never could tell whether she believed her insane or not. I was inclined to think that she was willing to put up with some of her tricks, because they served to divert our minds from the painful and distressing circumstances in which we were placed. I knew the Superior's powers and habits of deception also, and that she would deceive us as willingly as any one else.

Sometimes she proposed to send Jane to St. Anne's, a place

near Quebec, celebrated for the pilgrimages made to it by persons differently afflicted. It is supposed that some peculiar virtue exists there, which will restore health to the sick; and I have heard stories told in the corroboration of the common belief. Many lame and blind persons, with others, visit St. Anne's every year, some of whom may be seen travelling on foot, and begging their food. The Superior would sometimes say, that it was a pity that a woman like Jane Ray, capable of being so useful, should be unable to do her duties in consequence of a malady which she thought might be cured by a visit to St. Anne's. Yet to St. Anne's, Jane was never sent, and her wild and various tricks continued as before. The rules of silence which the others were so scrupulous in observing, she set at nought every hour; and as for other rules, she regarded them with as little respect when they stood in her way. She would now and then step out and stop the clock by which our exercises were regulated, and sometimes in this manner lengthened out our recreations till near twelve. At last the old nuns began to watch against such a trick, and would occasionally go out to see if the clock was going.

She once made a request that she might not eat with the other nuns; which was granted, as it seemed to proceed from a spirit of genuine humility which made her regard herself as unworthy of our society.

It being most convenient, she was sent to the Superior's table to make her meals after her; and it did not at first occur to the Superior that Jane, in this manner, profited by the change, by getting much better food than the rest of us. Thus there seemed to be always something deeper than any body at first suspected, at the bottom of every thing she did. She was once directed to sweep a community-room, under the sleeping-chamber. This office had before been assigned to the other nuns, as a penance; but the Superior, considering that Jane Ray did little or nothing, determined thus to furnish her with some employment. She declared to us that she would not sweep it long, as we might soon be assured. It happened that the stove by which the community-room was warmed in the winter, had its pipe carried through the floor of our sleeping chamber, and thence across it, in a direction opposite that in which the pipe of our stove was carried. It being then warm weather, the first mentioned pipe had been taken down, and the hole left unstopped. After we had all retired to our beds, and while engaged in silent prayers, we were suddenly alarmed by a bright blaze of fire, which burst from the hole in the floor, and threw sparks all around us. We thought the building was burning, and uttered cries of terror, regardless of the penances, the fear of which generally kept us silent.

The utmost confusion prevailed; for although we had solemnly vowed never to flee from the Convent, even if it was on fire, we were extremely alarmed, and could not repress our feelings. We soon learned the cause, for the flames ceased in a moment or two; and it was found that mad Jane Ray, after sweeping a little in the room beneath, had stuck a quantity of wet powder on the end of her broom, thrust it up through the hole in the ceiling into our apartment, and with a lighted paper set it on fire.

The date of this alarm I must refer to a time soon after the election riots; for I recollect that she found means to get possession of some of the powder which was prepared at that time for an emergency to which some thought the Convent was exposed.

She once asked for pen and paper; and then the Superior told her if she wrote to her friends she must see it: she replied that it was for no such purpose: she wanted to write her confession, and thus make it once for all. She wrote it, handed it to the priest, and he gave it to the Superior who read it to us. It was full of offences which she had never committed, evidently written to throw ridicule on confessions, and one of the most ludicrous productions I ever saw.

Our bedsteads were made with narrow boards laid across them, on which the beds were laid. One day, while we were in the bedchamber together, she proposed that we should misplace these boards. This was done, so that at night nearly a dozen nuns fell down upon the floor on getting into bed. A good deal of confusion naturally ensued, but the authors were not discovered. I was so conscience-stricken, however, that a week afterwards, while we were examining our consciences together, I told her I must confess the sin the next day. She replied, "Do as you like, but you will be sorry for it."

The next day when we came before the Superior, I was just going to kneel and confess, when Jane, almost without giving me time to shut the door, threw herself at the Superior's feet and confessed the trick, and a penance was immediately laid upon me for the sin I had concealed.

There was an old nun who was a famous talker, whom we used to call La Mere, (Mother). One night, Jane Ray got up, and secretly changed the caps of several of the nuns; and hers among the rest. In the morning there was great confusion, and such a scene as seldom occurred. She was severely blamed by La Mere, having been informed against by some of the nuns; and at last became so much enraged, that she attacked the old woman, and even took her by the throat. La Mere called on all present to come to her assistance, and several nuns interfered.

Jane seized the opportunity afforded in the confusion, to beat some of her worst enemies quite severely; and afterward said, that she had intended to kill some of the rascally informers.

For a time, Jane made us laugh so much at prayers, that the Superior forbade her going down with us to morning prayers; and she took the opportunity to sleep in the morning. When this was found out, she was forbidden to get into her bed again after leaving it; and then she would creep under it and take a nap on the floor. This she told us of one day, but threatened us if we ever betrayed her. At length she was missed at breakfast, as she would sometimes oversleep herself, and the Superior began to be more strict, and always inquired, in the morning, whether Jane Ray was in her place.

When the question was general, none of us answered; but when it was addressed to some nun near her, by name, as "Saint Eustace, is Jane Ray in her place?" then we had to reply.

Of all the scenes that occurred during my stay in the Convent, there was none which excited the delight of Jane more than one which took place in the chapel one day at mass, though I never had any particular reason to suppose that she had brought it about.

Some person, unknown to me this day, had put some substance or other, of a most nauseous smell into the hat of a little boy, who attended at the altar, and he, without observing the trick, put it upon his head. In the midst of the ceremonies he approached some of the nuns, who were almost suffocated with the odour; and as he occasionally moved from place to place, some of them began to beckon him to stand farther off, and to hold their noses with looks of disgust. The boy was quite unconscious of the cause of the difficulty, and paid them no attention; but the confusion became so great, through the distress of some, and the laughing of others, that the Superior ordered the boy to withdraw.

All attempts, however, to engage us in any work, prayer, or meditation, were found ineffectual. Whenever the circumstances in the chapel came to mind, we would laugh out. We had got into such a state, that we could not easily restrain ourselves. The Superior used sometimes to send Jane to instruct the novices in their English prayers. She would proceed to her task with all seriousness; but sometimes chose the most ridiculous, as well as irreverent passages from songs, and other things, which she had somewhere learned, which would set us, who understood her, laughing. One of her rhymes, I recollect, began with—

"The lord of love—look from above,
Upon this turkey hen!"

Jane for a time slept opposite me; and often in the night would rise, unobserved, and slip into my bed, to talk with me, which she did in a low whisper, and return again with equal caution.

She would tell me of the tricks she had played, and such as she meditated; and sometimes make me laugh so loud, that I had much to do in the morning with begging pardons and doing penances.

One winter's day, she was sent to light a fire; but after she had done so, remarked privately to some of us, " My fingers were too cold—you'll see if I do it again."

The next day, there was a great stir in the house, because it was said that mad Jane Ray had been seized with a fit while making a fire, and she was taken up apparently insensible, and conveyed to her bed. She complained to me, who visited her in the course of the day, that she was likely to starve, as food was denied her; and I was persuaded to pin a stocking under my dress and secretly put food into it from the table. This I afterwards carried to her, and relieved her wants.

One of the things which I blamed Jane most for was a disposition to quarrel with any nun who seemed to be winning the favour of the Superior. She would never rest until she brought such an one into some difficulty.

We were allowed but little soap; and Jane, when she found her supply nearly gone, would take any piece she could find. One day there was a general search made for a large piece that was missed; when, soon after I had been searched, Jane Ray passed me, and slipped it into my pocket; she was soon after searched herself, and then secretly came for it again.

While I recal these particulars of our nunnery, and refer so often to the conduct and language of one of the nuns, I cannot speak of some things, which I believed or suspected, on account of my want of sufficient knowledge. But it is a pity you have not Jane Ray for a witness; she knows many things of which I am ignorant. She must be in possession of facts that should be known. Her long residence in the Convent, her habits of roaming about, and of observing every thing, must have made her acquainted with things which would be heard with interest. I always felt as if she knew everything. She would often go and listen, or look through the cracks into the Superior's room, while any of the priests were closeted with her, and sometimes would come and tell me what she witnessed. I found myself bound to confess in such cases, and always did so.

She knew, however, that I only told it to the priest or to the Superior, and without mentioning the name of my informant, which I was at liberty to withhold, so that she was not found out. I often said to her, "Dont tell me, Jane, for I must confess it." She would reply, " It is better for you to confess it than for me." I thus became, against my will, informed of scenes supposed by the actors of them to be secret.

Jane Ray once persuaded me to accompany her into the Superior's room, to hide with her under the sofa, and await the appearance of a visitor whom she expected, that we might overhear what passed between them. We had not been long concealed, when the Superior came in alone, and sat for some time; when, fearing she might detect us in the stillness which prevailed, we began to repent of our temerity. At length, however, she suddenly withdrew, and thus afforded us a welcome opportunity to escape.

I was passing one day through a part of the cellar, where I had not often occasion to go, when the toe of my shoe hit something. I tripped and fell down. I rose again, and holding my lamp to see what had caused my fall, I found an iron ring, fastened to a small square trap-door. This I had the curiosity to raise, and saw four or five steps leading down; but there was not light enough to see more, and I feared to be noticed by somebody and reported to the Superior; so closing the door again I left the spot. At first I could not imagine the use for such a passage, but it afterwards occurred to me that it might open to the subterranean passage to the Seminary, for I never before could account for the appearance of many of the priests, who often appeared and disappeared among us, particularly at night, when I knew the gates were closed. They could, as I now saw, come up to the door of the Superior's room at any hour; then up stairs into our sleeping room, or where they chose. And often they were in our beds before us.

I afterwards ascertained that my conjectures were correct and that a secret communication was kept up in this manner between the two institutions, at the end towards Notre Dame-street, at a considerable depth under ground. I often afterwards met priests in the cellar, when sent there for coal and other articles, as they had to pass up and down the common cellar stairs on their way.

My wearisome daily prayers and labours, my pain of body, and depression of mind, which were so much increased by penances I had suffered, and those which I constantly feared, and the feelings of shame, remorse, and horror, which sometimes arose, brought me to a state which I cannot describe.

In the first place, my frame was enfeebled by the uneasy postures I was required to keep for so long a time during prayers. This alone, I thought was sufficient to undermine my health and destroy my life. An hour and a half every morning I had to sit on the floor of the community-room, with my feet under me, my body bent forward, and my head hanging on one side; in a posture expressive of great humility, it is true, but very fatiguing to keep for such an unreasonable length of time. Often I found it impossible to avoid falling asleep in this posture, which I could do without detection, by bending a little lower than usual. The signal to rise, or the noise made by the rising of the other nuns, then awoke me, and I got up with the rest unobserved.

Before we took the posture just described, we had to kneel for a long time without bending the body, keeping quite erect, with the exception of the knees only, with the hands together before the breast. This I found the most distressing attitude for me, and never assumed it without feeling a sharp pain in my chest, which I often thought would soon lead me to my grave—that is, to the great common receptacle for the dead, under the chapel. And this upright kneeling posture we were obliged to resume as soon as we rose from the half sitting posture first mentioned; so that I usually felt myself exhausted and near to fainting, before the conclusion of the morning services.

I found the meditations extremely tedious, and often did I sink into sleep, while we were all seated in silence on the floor. When required to tell my meditations, as it was thought to be of no great importance what we said, I sometimes found I had nothing to tell but a dream, and told that, which passed off very well.

Jane Ray appeared to be troubled still more than myself with wandering thoughts; and when blamed for them would reply, " I begin very well; but directly I begin to think of some old friend of mine, and my thoughts go a-wandering from one country to another."

Sometimes I confessed my falling asleep; and often the priests have talked to me about the sin of sleeping in time of meditation. At last, one of them proposed to me to prick myself with a pin, which is often done, and so roused myself for a time.

My close confinement in the Convent, and the want of opportunities to breathe the open air, might have proved more injurious to me than they did, had I not been employed a part of my time in more active labours than those of sewing, &c. to which I was chiefly confined. I took part occasionally in some of the heavy work, as washing, &c.

The events which I am now to relate occurred about five months after my admission into the Convent as a nun; but I cannot fix the time with precision, as I know not of anything which took place in the world about the same period. The circumstances I clearly remember; but as I have elsewhere remarked, we were not accustomed to keep any account of time.

Information was given to us one day, that another novice was to be admitted among us; and we were required to remember and mention her often in our prayers, that she might have faithfulness in the service of her holy spouse. No information was given us concerning her beyond this fact: not a word about her age, name, or nation. On all similar occasions the same course was pursued; and all that the nuns ever learnt concerning one another was what they might discover by being together, and which usually amounted to little or nothing.

When the day of her admission arrived, though I did not witness the ceremony in the chapel, it was a gratification to us all on one account, because we were always released from labour, and enjoyed a great recreation day.

Our new sister, when she was introduced to the "holy" society of us "saints," proved to be young, of about the middle size, and very good looking for a Canadian; for I soon ascertained that she was one of my own countrywomen. The Canadian females are generally not handsome—I never learnt her name nor any thing of her history. She had chosen St. Martin for her nun name. She was admitted in the morning, and appeared melancholy all day. This, I observed, was always the case; and the remarks made by others, led me to believe that they, and all they had seen, had felt sad and miserable for a longer or shorter time. Even the Superior, as it may be recollected, confessed to me that she experienced the same feelings when she was received. When bed time arrived she proceeded to the chamber with the rest of us, and was assigned a bed on the side of the room opposite my own, and a little beyond. The nuns were all soon in bed, the usual silence ensued, and I was making my customary mental prayer, and composing myself to sleep, when I heard the most piercing and heart-rending shrieks proceed from our new comrade. Every nun seemed to rise as if by one impulse, for no one could hear such sounds, especially in such total silence, without being greatly excited. A general noise succeeded, for many voices spoke together, uttering cries of surprise, compassion, or fear. It was in vain for the night-watch to expect silence; for once we forgot rules and penances, and gave vent to our feelings, and she could do nothing but call for the Superior.

I heard a man's voice mingled with the cries and shrieks of the nun. Father Quiblier of the Seminary, I had felt confident, was in the Superior's room at the time when we retired; and several of the nuns afterward assured me that it was he. The Superior soon made her appearance, and in a harsh manner commanded silence. I heard her threaten gagging her, and then say, "You are no better than anybody else, and if you do not obey, you shall be sent to the cells."

One young girl was taken into the Convent during my abode there, under peculiar circumstances. I was acquainted with the whole affair, as I was employed to act a part in it.

Among the novices, was a young lady, of about seventeen, the daughter of an old rich Canadian. She had been remarkable for nothing that I know of, except the cheerfulness of her disposition. The Superior once expressed to us a wish to have her take the veil, though the girl herself never had any such intention that I know of. Why the Superior wished to receive her I could not conjecture. One reason might have been, that she expected to receive a considerable sum from her father. She was, however, strongly desirous of having the girl in our community, and one day said—" Let us take her in by a trick, and tell the old man she felt too humble to take the veil in public."

Our plans then being laid, the unsuspecting girl was induced by us, in sport, as we told her, and made her believe, to put on such a splendid robe as I had worn on my admission, and to pass through some of the ceremonies of taking the veil. After this, she was seriously informed, that she was considered as having entered the Convent in earnest, and must henceforth bury herself to the world, as she would never be allowed to leave it. We put on her a nun's dress, though she wept, and refused, and expressed the greatest repugnance. The Superior threatened, and promised, and flattered by turns, until the poor girl had to submit; but her appearance long showed that she was a nun only by compulsion.

In obedience to the directions of the Superior, we exerted ourselves to make her contented, especially when she was first received; when we got round her, and told her we had felt so for a time, but having since become acquainted with the happiness of a nun's life, were perfectly content, and would be willing never to leave the Convent. An exception seemed to be made in her favour, in one respect; for I believe no criminal attempt was made upon her, until she had been for tome time an inmate of the nunnery.

Soon after her reception, or rather her forcible entry into the Convent, her father called to make enquiry about his daughter. The Superior first spoke with him herself, and then called us to repeat her plausible story, which I did with accuracy. If I had wished to have said any thing else, I never should have dared.

We told the foolish old man, that his daughter, whom we all affectionately loved, had long desired to become a nun, but had been too humble to wish to appear before spectators, and had, at her own desire, been favoured with a private admission into the community.

The benefit conferred upon himself and his family, by this act of self-consecration I reminded him, must be truly great and valuable; as every family who furnishes a priest or a nun, is justly looked upon as receiving the peculiar favour of heaven on that account. The old Canadian firmly believing every word I was forced to tell him, took the event as a great blessing, and expressed the greatest readiness to pay more than the customary fee to the Convent. After the interview, he withdrew, promising soon to return, and pay a handsome sum to the Convent, which he peformed with all dispatch and the greatest cheerfulness. The poor girl never heard that her father had taken the trouble to call and see her, much less did she know any thing of the imposition passed upon him. She remained in the Convent when I left it.

The youngest girl who ever took the veil of our sister-hood, was only fourteen years of age, and considered very pious. She lived but a short time. I was told that she was ill treated by the priests, and believed her death was in consequence.

NOTES, FACTS, CONFIRMATIONS, &c.

THE CONVENT LODGE AT TAUNTON.—We wish our readers distinctly to understand that we do not intend (in the issue of this work) to confine ourselves to the mere narrative of Maria Monk, but to attach thereto the essence of all ancient and modern works, as well as notices of, and extracts from, all current publications that may add to the interest and value of this production, as also tend to illustrate the real "CHARACTER OF THE CONVENT." The following prospectus of the Convent Lodge at Taunton, has come forth in Miss Talbot's case:—"The Lodge, Taunton. The age of admission to thirteen years old inclusive. Twenty-eight young ladies only are admitted. They must be children of Roman Catholic parents. For board, washing, sheets, towels, stationery, and school books, forty guineas per annum, half of which is always paid in advance, and two guineas entrance. Education comprises the principles and practices of the Catholic religion, the English and French languages, history, geography, writing, arithmetic, plain and fine needlework, &c. The uniform dress on Sundays—white muslin and blue sash; every day in summer, a gingham, procured at Taunton Lodge; in winter, a dark blue merino, straw bonnet, trimmed with blue ribbon: other articles of dress as each young lady may have been accustomed to. No vacation; and no deduction is made for absence, if by way of indulgence; if absence is occasioned by illness, a deduction is then made. If parents take their children home, it can only be for a month once in a year."

FATHER DOYLE'S CHARACTER IN MISS TALBOT'S CASE.—Priestly perfection has not had many average examples fuller of instruction than that of Dr. Doyle. He now appears in the High Court of Chancery as guardian of an orphan, and to appreciate the fidelity with which he has discharged his office as an angel ministrant, we must go back to the first point visible of his tutelar ministration. A nobleman, wedded in an evil hour to a Protestant lady, had been by some influence or other separated from the pollution of her society. In good time, the honourable is on his death-bed, where it behoves him to make amends for the sins of his life, and there stands Dr. Doyle instructing him how to go through the solemn transaction. Notwithstanding his high rank, unlike poor M. Carre, who was but a lone foreigner in Somers-town, the dying man forgets all worldly connexions, and, under the tutelage of this ministering spirit, consigns his estate to the executorship of his will, by which will he gives the self-same doctor all his personal property, and intrusts him with the guardianship of his two children, one of them, the boy, to be in the priest's power at once, and the other, the little girl, to be nursed by her own mother, until ten years of age, and then torn from her bosom, to be led into some by-way of existence by the hand of this same priest Doyle, *sole guardian* of both infants. But when children are thrown into the *creche* of stern old mother Church, they are almost sure to perish. These infants are to have a fortune, if they can get it. The late Charles, Earl of Shrewsbury, left them each 30,000*l.*, " contingently upon their attaining twenty-one years of age; or, in the case of the female, upon her marriage, with a gift over to the present Earl of Shrewsbury, in the event of their dying under age, and, as to Augusta Talbot, unmarried." This brings the Earl and Countess of Shrewsbury upon the stage, to figure in the drama, and to become subservient to the plot. Guardian Doyle has them also under his vigilant supervision, when an order of the Court of Chancery empowers them to take part in the " care and management" of these infants, with the provision that he should travel with them as tutor to the boy. The mother of Augusta dies, and she, poor orphan, is forthwith consigned to a cheap conventual school at Taunton, to be kept there for 40*l.* per annum; to be instructed, first and chiefly, " in the principles and *practices* of the Catholic religion," with a common, very common, secular education, and to wear the " uniform dress on Sundays," on week days in summer and winter, with no holidays. Guardian Doyle wisely husbands the legacy of the old Earl, and thereby assures larger accumulations. Following his elder ward, John Talbot, to that most happy country, Naples—where the paths into eternity are notoriously numerous—he is soon found waiting at his death-bed, as he was at that of the father, and at the early age of sixteen, this infant passes from the scene, leaving the actor one the fewer, under the skilful care and management of guardian Doyle. Fully instructed in the doctrine and practices of the Catholic religion—as far, at least, as it concerns an orphan lady to know its practices—she is taken out suddenly into the world of fashion and confusion, whirled for a few weeks in the vortex of wildest frivolity at the West end, showed up to a crowd of strangers, exhibited as heiress of 80,000*l.* at least, hurried across the Channel, and proposed by the Earl and Countess to be wife of a strange French Count de Rochefoucauld. And in this snare she is nearly caught, for she was not made for a nunnery. She has no objection to a marriage; but her training at Taunton Lodge, the want of maternal guidance, the habitual negligence of her obeul relatives, have left her in a condition of incapacity to choose a husband. The Lord Chancellor of England being her legal protector, happily interposes, and, although disappointed, she wisely submits to his judgment, refuses the suitor, and offends her relatives, the Earl and Countess of Shrewsbury. Consequently, the Earl himself, having made arrangements by his chaplain, takes her back to Taunton Lodge, where she is immured as a postulant—nominally, not really, say the Lady Superior and Bishop Hendren, of Clifton, the ecclesiastical superior—but she really is treated as a postulant for nunship. The Earl has enjoined that she be kept in strict monastic seclusion, only to be seen alone by the guardian angel of the Shrewsburys and Talbots, Dr. Doyle. The next point would soon be gained. In a few months Miss Talbot will be of age, and therefore at her own disposal *legally*. In the character of a free agent she would dispose of her property, now accumulated to 85,000*l*. But, not being a free agent *morally*, she would resign it all, and take *the vow of poverty*. As one about to die to the world, she might bequeath it all to the Earl, according to the letter of his father's will, which gave him the money on the contingency of her death. But as the death will not be bodily, but civil, she might give it all to the Church within whose arms she is to expire; or, Doyle and Shrewsbury might share the spoil. At any rate, *she was to be the victim*, under the vow of power canonically prescribed and taken—for Popish priests may administer oaths, although Protestant ministers neither can nor ought. It was under the care and management of Dr. Doyle that the father died: the son died in his minority under the same: the daughter was imprisoned, and on her way to be a nun, as fast as girl could be, under the same. The Lord Chancellor and Solicitor General—and his lordship well knows the circumstances and history of both branches of the family—clearly see that Miss Augusta Talbot was entrapped.—*Christian Times.*

We will here give an extract from Da Costa, a Portuguese Roman Catholic writer, who had suffered in the inquisition, in consequence of being accused of Freemasonry. It illustrates the adulterous character of Roman priests, and also the abominable character of the Confessional. Pope Paul IV., from some cause or other, was induced to issue a bull, ordering an investigation into the crime of *solicitant,* as it is called—that is, when the confessional is used by the priests for licentious purposes. This had reference to the kingdom of Spain. The following is an extract from the bull:—" Whereas certain ecclesiastics in the kingdom of Spain, and in the cities and dioceses thereof, having the cure of souls, or exercising such cure for others, or otherwise deputed to hear the confessions of such penitents, have broken out into such heinous acts of iniquity, as to abuse the sacrament of penance in the very act of hearing the confessions, not fearing to injure the same sacrament, and him who instituted it, our Lord God and Saviour Jesus Christ, by enticing and provoking, or trying to entice and provoke females to lewd actions at the very time when they were making their confessions." " When this bull," says Da Costa, " was first introduced into Spain, the inquisitors published a solemn edict in all the churches belonging to the archbishopric of Seville, that any person knowing, or having heard of any friar or clergyman's having committed the crime of abusing the sacrament of Confession, or in any manner having improperly conducted himself during the confession of a female penitent, should make a discovery of what he knew, within thirty days, to the holy tribunal; and very heavy censures are attached to those who should neglect or despise this injunction. When this edict was first published, such a considerable number of females went to the palace of the inquisition, only in the city of Seville, to reveal the conduct of their infamous confessors, that twenty notaries, and as many inquisitors, were appointed to minute down their several informations against them; but these being found insufficient to receive the depositions of so many witnesses; and the inquisitors being thus overwhelmed, as it were, with the pressure of such affairs, thirty days more were allowed for taking the accusations, and this lapse of time also proving inadequate to the intended purpose, a similar period was granted, not only for a third but a fourth time. The ladies of rank, character, and noble families, had a difficult part to act on this occasion, as their discoveries could not be made of any particular time and place. On one side, a religious fear of incurring the threatened censures, goaded their consciences so much as to compel them to make the required accusations; on the other side, a regard to their husbands, to whom they justly feared to give offence, by affording them any motives for suspecting their private conduct, induced them to keep at home. To obviate these difficulties, they had recourse to the measure of covering their faces with a veil, according to the fashion of Spain, and thus went to the inquisitors in the most secret manner they could adopt. Very few, however, escaped the vigilance of their husbands, who, on being informed of the discoveries and accusations made by their wives, were filled with suspicions; and yet, notwithstanding this accumulation of proofs against the confessors, produced to the inquisitors, this holy tribunal, contrary to the expectations of every one, put an end to the business, by ordering that all crimes of this nature, proved by lawful evidence, should from thenceforth be consigned to perpetual silence and oblivion."—*Nar. &c., by Hippolyto Joseph Da Costa Pereira Furtudo de Mendonea, vol. i, pp.* 117—119. Here then are the " holy confessors and the holy confessional" depicted to the life, so far as decency will allow the picture to be drawn. It were an easy task, would decency permit, to prove, and that too from Roman Catholic historians, that the priesthood of Rome is composed of the most licentious body of men that ever infested human society. And yet the writers of the " Awful Exposure " have the brazen impudence to make the following declaration on page 56 of their book. "Now the priests of Montreal and of Canada, do enjoy, at least, public esteem for morality, and if necessary, the testimony of every adult in the province would be gladly yielded to their excellent character." The father of lies could not fabricate a purer untruth than this.

BURIED ALIVE.—Hobart Seymour is a good authority. In his "*Pilgrimage to Rome,*" he thus describes one part of the ceremony of taking the veil, which exactly corroborates the statements made by Maria Monk. Mr. Seymour says:— " The young creature, as a part of the ceremonial of admission into a nunnery, is laid alive in her coffin, and when once admitted she is in fact as dead and buried to her friends, for she is never again allowed to see any of them. Once a-year, on an appointed day, the parents of the " buried alive" may attend at the nunnery, and the young creature within may hear their loved and familiar voices, but she must never see them; and, as no kind of intercourse is ever permitted, she can never know whether they are living or dead, except as she hears or does not hear their voices on that day. If a parent has died during the year, the abbess assembles the nuns. She tells them that the parent of one of them is dead, and desires all to pray for the soul of the departed; but she never reveals the name of the dead, so that all the nuns are left in a state of intense and agonising suspense till the one day comes round, and all listen to catch the tones of their parent's voices, and the absence of the longed-for voice tells the tale of the bereaved recluse!"

BRITONS CALLED UPON TO PURGE ENGLAND OF CONVENTUAL DENS.—Mr. John Bensley, of North Shields, has written a noble letter to the editor of the *Christian Times*, with reference to convents. We transcribe the substance of it. Mr. Bensley says:—I rejoice that nunneries are engaging public attention. I confess that the facts lately revealed, have stirred my soul to its depths. That English nuns are left to the tender mercies of the Council of Trent, which decrees that " No nun after taking the veil is to be allowed to go out of the monastery, even for a moment, under any pretext," ought to excite the burning indignation of every Briton. That woman, tender woman, innocent of the infraction of law, may be immured in a dark Papal prison, on the free soil of England, is enough to startle "the ends of the earth," which have heard of the fame of our freedom. This is a legal anomaly, over which the angel of liberty may well weep! We might meet the Popish law by saying, We cannot allow it any longer to neutralise our national statutes. Touching this matter, we now practically acknowledge the supremacy of the Pope. But we can confront the Papacy with its hypocritical plea of "religious liberty." Popery urges the voluntary act of the nun in taking the veil. We reply, that the true idea of religious liberty is the power of constantly following the decision of the judgment and the dictates of the conscience. Suppose, then, the views and feelings of the unhappy nun undergo a complete revolution—that she wishes for an exit from, as ardently as she desired an entrance into, a nunnery; to retain her by force is the foulest tyranny, a flagrant violation of both civil and religious freedom, and of the dearest rights of our common humanity! I am here pleading for the true liberty of the members of the Romish communion. The transparent sophism, that as the vow of perpetual seclusion was voluntarily taken by the recluse, she should be retained, will weigh as small dust in the balance in the estimation of honest Englishmen. How deeply affecting was the occurrence at Nottingham a few weeks since. "A female confined in a nunnery adjoining the Roman Catholic Church of St. Barnabas, Derby-road, Nottingham, endeavoured to effect her escape, but was observed by a person who retails milk in that part of the town, and she was again immured within the convent." Let us listen for a moment to Father Gavazzi, on Mosaic Institutions: "The average mortality prevalent in Italian cloisters, showed its pernicious working on body and soul. The poor victims, forced to take that step for family reasons, lead, of course, a career of hopeless gloom; but when the voluntary vestal repents—as we know occurs in a majority of instances—what bitter regret wastes and corrodes the blighted years of self-imposed incarceration. The car of Juggernaut rolled over willing suicides, and crushed out their life-blood in an ecstacy of fanaticism; but here the sustaining enthusiasm has perished; and the crushing process is continued through days and nights of dismal despondency till death claims the bride of despair. Is there no law in this land of enlightened humanity to arrest the recruiting sergeants of this infamous enrolment of credulous girls to swell that melancholy mass of misery, delusion, and remorse?" No! eloquent Father; but we trust there will be very soon. On the supposition that nunneries are still allowed to stand on British soil, the law should interpose so as effectually to secure the liberty of their inmates. The proposed act appears to me to provide for far too infrequent visitations. The utmost caution and greatest vigilance are required in dealing with so crafty and unprincipled a foe to human freedom as the Papacy. I think also that the act should decree that the visitors have an introduction too, so as to enable them to identify, every nun who takes the veil. I fear not the charge of uncharitableness, when I contend that the whole system of monasticism should be treated with "suspicion." But if emancipation from the wretched slavery which runs riot in these dark dens be rejected by Romish dignitaries and priests, then in the name of liberty, of religion, of all that is dear to humanity, let these institutions be annihilated by the power of the law! This would doubtless bring upon us the bitterest execrations of Rome. Perhaps the whole nation would be "cursed" in the infernal "form" prescribed against all who open the prison doors to the captive nun. We might even be condemned by those who would tolerate the most hideous despotism, under the pretence of supporting the loveliest freedom! But the truest Christians and the most genuine liberals would cordially sustain a government in such an act of righteousness, while we should feel assured of the smile of that God of justice and benevolence, who so signally crowned with victory our illustrious forefathers, in their heroic resistance of Papal domination.

Under the title of "THE MONKS OF NAPLES," Dr. Achilli, in his beautiful volume, published by Arthur Hall & Co., thus describes that singular class of men. Separated from human ties, apart from the laws of nature, there is no race of beings, in my estimation, so useless to society, so immoral, and so absurd, in a religious point of view, as they who call themselves monks. The Jesuits are monks, as well as those instituted by St. Francis of Assisi; both have the same degree of worth, and the same defects. I used to believe that the monks reckoned among their virtues kindness, gentleness, humility, and moderation; I imagined that they were full of charity towards their neighbour; and believing nothing of them but what was good, I thought when I entered into their society I should be living among saints. Who would have supposed that all their imaginary virtues should fade before my eyes, from the time I became bound to them by vows which prevented my return? Every day the pleasant delusion became less and less, and bitter experience continually operated to undeceive me, at various periods of my sojourn among them. I had paid strict attention to the proceedings of the Dominicans, both in Rome and Tuscany; and from what I had observed I was led to form a resolution to escape from them, and to renounce their society for ever. * * * Cardinal Feretti was kind in endeavouring to persuade me to seek an asylum among the monks of Naples, after leaving those of Rome. "Are you not of opinion, Monsignore," said I to him, " that these monks of Naples are *birbanti*, (vagabonds,) as well as those of Rome?" "Nay, I think they are worse," replied he. "But it is precisely on that account that you ought to stay among them. If we did not do all we could to keep a few good persons among this class of gentry, we should have a community of a character qualified to inspire us with fear, and to compromise us utterly. I believe the monks of Naples are more ignorant and more turbulent than any others; and I repeat, it is for that very reason I request you to place yourself among them, where you would be most useful, both through your example and your teaching." "But they will drive me to despair." "In that case, then, you must leave them." "But why, in the mean time, should I be made to endure such a tribulation?" "To do good; to be useful to your brethren, for the glory of God——" "Well, be it so. I will consent to make the experiment, commending myself to him." In the meanwhile, the Dominican monks had had recourse to all their powers of persuasion to induce me to take up my abode among them Solicited on one side to enter the monastery of St. Dominic, and on the other that of St. Peter the Martyr, I chose the latter. * * * There were in other monasteries, belonging to the same Order, many despicable monks, who united in their own persons every vice that can be found in human nature. These appeared to hate the faintest trace of honesty or virtue, and were always ready to plot, to calumniate, and to stick at nothing to promote their own interest. I frequently took occasion to reprove them, and threatened, more than once, to make public their infamous proceedings, unless they thought proper to desist from their practices. But all my remonstrances were in vain. And at length I lost all patience: I fought manfully against them for a long time, but the general of the Order, Ancarini, was on their side, and lent them his powerful protection. I therefore felt that I had nothing more to do but to hold out, to the end of my year of Priorate, and then to give in my *rescritto* to the proper officer; which I accordingly did, in the month of August, 1839, and finally separated myself from the Order. I remember Father Talia, who was exceedingly esteemed among the clergy of Naples, expressed himself in the following terms before the Cardinal Archbishop:—" I do not believe that your Eminence will suppose that I am actuated by an overweening desire for liberty, in emancipating myself from the Order of these monks; I would rather persuade you that my doing so has been occasioned by the pure love of truth and virtue, which the monks altogether refuse either to acknowledge or to practise. Your Eminence may say that I am an old man, and as such might have been contented to have finished the remainder of my days in the cloister; but 1 would observe that my spirit is not affected by age, and that before I terminate my earthly career, I, a man, though old in body not in mind, would leave behind me to the youth of the present generation, an example of Christian courage; shewing that when an institution becomes corrupt, it is one's duty to abandon it, early or late, as it may be; for as the homely proverb expresses it, 'Better late than never.'" To this the Cardinal replied, that he was willing to admit that the good Father had his own reasons for quitting the Dominican habit; that he could not suspect a man like him to be actuated by light mindedness; and that his friendship towards him would always remain the same. And the good old man felt himself not a little comforted with these kind assurances. The monks, however, and more particularly those to whom our desertion from the order was a bitter reproof, were by no means humbled; on the contrary, they were exceedingly irritated at our proceedings, and set themselves to consider how they could most persecute and injure us; in which intent they were greatly encouraged by the assistance they derived from Rome; I mean from the head of the order, which unfortunately was at that time represented by the Monk Angelo Ancarini, a man of the most dark and gloomy character that ever disgraced humanity. His history might all be told in these few words: he was, during forty-five years, an inquisitor of the Holy Office,

We close these extracts by one which shews the murderous spirit which these monks still manifest towards the faithful followers of truth. Dr. A. says:— On hearing that the inquisition had laid hold of me, these wretched monks of Naples began to chant their hymn of victory: "He who made war against us," said they, "is fallen; he who branded us with dishonour is fallen to rise no more. The inquisition will root out from the earth the very memory of his name." Another circumstance is worth relating. The two principal agents in my accusation were Ancarini and Cardinal Lambruschini. "We ought to burn this heretic alive," said Ancarini, at one of the sittings of the inquisition; at another he was a little more moderate, and only suggested my being sent to the galleys for life. The Cardinal asserted that I was not only a heretic, but a conspirator as well. In a meeting of cardinals at the Holy Office, this dreamer assured their eminences and the pope, that he could bring proof that I was a heretic in religion, a Freemason, a Carbonari, a member of a secret society, and I know not what besides.

"THE FEMALE JESUIT."—We mentioned in our last, a beautiful Volume just issued, entitled—"*The Female Jesuit;*" and promised a further notice. We commence by quoting the following from the Preface of the work, which, by the bye, is a quotation from Hogan; there Hogan says,—

"Soon after my arrival in Philadelphia," he writes, "I became acquainted with a Protestant family. I had the pleasure of dining occasionally with them, and could not help noticing a seemingly delicate young man, who waited at the table. There was something in the countenance and whole appearance of this individual which struck me as singular. I could see no indication of positive wickedness or signal depravity in the external configuration of the young man's head. The expression of the eye indicated meekness, humility, and habitual obedience, rather than anything else; but I could see, nevertheless, in the closely compressed lips and furtive glance, which I could only occasionally catch—and even then by a sort of stealth—something that puzzled me. I know not why, but I could not like him. There was no cause, as far as I could see, why I should dislike the young man. Constitutionally, I was myself rather fearless than otherwise. I cannot recollect that, with equal means of defence, I ever feared any one. * * * I could never find the eye of this man fixed upon me without an involuntary feeling of dread. I met him often in the streets; he always seemed neat and tidy in his person; he was civil and respectful in his deportment; never seemed to forget that society had its grades, and that circumstances had clearly designated his own. With that he seemed well contented, never, as far as I could see, seeming to feel the least desire of intruding upon that of others. This being rather a rare case in the United States, twenty years ago—at any rate, when it was difficult to get servants who knew their places, struck me as another singular feature in his manner and character, and did not at all tend to remove the unpleasant impressions which his appearance made upon my mind. Not long after this, a messenger called at my rooms to say that 'Theodore ——' was taken ill, and wished to see me. I was then officiating as a Romish priest, and calling to see him, was shown up stairs to the door of a garret room, into which, after a loud rap, and announcing my name, I was admitted to the *sick* young *man*. He had returned to his bed before I entered, and was wrapped in a large overcloak. I asked him whether he wanted to see me, and for what purpose. He deliberately turned out of his bed, locked the door again, very respectfully handed me a chair, and asked me to sit down, as he had something very important to tell me. He wrapped himself again in his cloak, lay on the outside of the bed, and spoke to me in a firm, decided tone to the following effect :—' Sir, you have taken me for a young man, but you are mistaken. I am a girl, but not so young as I appear to you in my boy's dress. I sent for you because I want to get a *character*, and confess to you before I leave the city.' I answered, 'You must explain yourself more fully before you do either.' I moved my chair further from the bed, and tightened my grasp upon a sword-cane which I carried in my hand. 'Feel no alarm,' said this young woman; I am as well armed as you are'—taking from under her jacket an elegant poignard: 'I will not hurt you. I am *a lay sister belonging to the order of Jesuits in Stonyhurst, England*, and I wear this dagger to protect myself.' There was no longer any mystery in the matter. I knew now where I was, and the character of the being that stood before me. I discovered from her that she arrived in New Orleans to the priests and nuns of that city. She had the necessary 'Shibboleth' from the Jesuits of Stonyhurst, to their brothers and sisters, who were then, and are now, numerous in that city. They received her with all due caution, as far as could be seen by the public, but privately in the warmest manner. Jesuits are active and diligent in the discharge of their duties to their superiors, and of course this *sister*, who was chosen from among many for her zeal and craft, lost no time in entering on her mission. The *Sisters of Charity* in New Orleans took immediate charge of her, recommended her as chambermaid to one of the most respectable Protestant families in the city; and having clothed her in an appropriate dress, she entered upon her employment. She was active, diligent, and competent. The young ladies of the family were delighted with her; she appeared extremely pious, but not ostentatiously so. She seemed desirous to please in all things; talked but seldom of religion, but took care that her devotional exercises should be noticed, though she seemed to avoid such a thing. Her conduct was in every way unexceptionable. So great a favourite did she become in the family, that in a short time she became acquainted with all the circumstances and secrets, from those of the father down to those of the youngest child. According to a custom universally in vogue among the Jesuit spies, she kept notes of every occurrence which might tend to elucidate the character of the family, never carrying them about her, but depositing them, for safe-keeping, with the Mother Abbess, especially deputed to take charge of them. She soon left this family under some pretext or other, obtained from them an unqualified recommendation for honesty and competency, which, with the previous and secret arrangements of the *Sisters of Charity*, obtained for her without delay a place in another Protestant family. Here, too, she was without fault, active, honest, and industrious to all appearance. Little did these families know that, while they and their children were quietly reposing in the arms of sleep, this apparently innocent waiting-maid or chambermaid was, perhaps, in the dead hour of the night, reducing to paper their conversation of the day previous, and preparing it, at least as much of it as could answer any Jesuitical purpose, to be recorded among the secret archives of the Jesuit college of Stonyhurst, from which they were to be transcopied to those of the parent college in Rome. Thus did this *lay sister* continue to go from place to place, from family to family, until she became better acquainted with the politics, the pecuniary means, religious opinions, (whether favourable or not to the propagation of Popery in this country,) than even the very individuals with whom she resided. No one suspected her, all believed her innocent and industrious; the only fault they could find with her was, that she seemed too fond of going from one place to another. For this, however, the *Sisters of Charity* had some salvo or other. On arriving in Baltimore, she, of course, called upon the nuns of that city, who were prepared for her reception, and had already a situation engaged for a 'chambermaid whom they expected from New Orleans, and who was coming highly recommended by some of the first families in that city.' She took possession of a place as soon as convenient, spent several months in that city, discharging all her duties faithfully, no one finding any fault with her, except her restlessness in not staying long with any family. Having now become acquainted with the secret and circumstances of almost every Protestant family of note in Baltimore, and made her report to the Mother Abbess of the nunnery of her order in that city, she retired to the district of Columbia;

and, after advising with the Mother Abbess of the convent, she determined to change her apparent character and appearance. By advice of *that venerable lady, the Holy Prioress* on whom many of the wives of our national representatives, and even grave senators, look as an example of *piety and chastity*, she cut short her hair, dressed herself in a smart-looking waiter's jacket and trousers, and with the best recommendations for intelligence and capacity, she, in her new dress, applied for a situation as waiter at Gadsby's Hotel, in Washington city. This smart and tidy-looking young man got instant employment: and now we have the *lay* sister in quite a different character. His intelligent countenance—we must not say *her* in future—soon attracted the notice of some of our most eloquent statesmen. He appeared so humble, so obedient, and so inattentive to anything but his own business, that those senators on whom he waited, not suspecting that he had the ordinary curiosity of servants in general, were entirely thrown off their guard, and in their conversations with one another seemed to forget their usual caution. Such in a short time was their confidence in him, that their most important papers and letters were left loose upon their tables, satisfied with saying, as they were going out, 'Theodore, take care of my room and papers.' Now the Jesuit was in her glory; now the lay sister had an opportunity of knowing many of our national secrets, as well as the private characters of some of our eminent statesmen; now it was known whether Henry Clay was a gambler; whether Daniel Webster was a libertine; whether John C. Calhoun was an honourable, but credulous man. Now it was known what value was put upon Popish influence in this country, and what were the hopes of Papist foreigners in the United States. In fact, this lay sister in male uniform, and but a waiter in Gadsby's Hotel, was thus enabled to give more correct information of the actual state of things in this country, through the General of the Jesuit Order in Rome, than the whole corps diplomatic from foreign countries then resident at our seat of government. After relating to me in her sick room—as the family in which she lived fancied it was—all these circumstances, she deliberately said to me, 'I want a written character from you. You must state in it that I have *complied with my duty;* and as it is necessary that I should wear a cap for a while, having cut off my hair, you must say that you visited me in my sick room, that I confessed to you, received the *viaticum*, and had just recovered from a violent fever, in which I lost my hair. My business is not yet done,' said she. 'I must go to New York, where the *Sisters of Charity* will find a place for me as waiting-maid.' It is needless to say with what reluctance any man could comply with such a request as this; and my having done so, is a stronger evidence than I have heretofore given of the indomitable strength of early education."

CHAPTER XIV.

Influencing novices—Difficulty of convincing persons from the United States—Tale of the Bishop in the City—The Bishop in the Convent—The Prisoners in the Cells—Practice in Singing—Narratives—Jane Ray's Hymns—The Superior's best Trick.

It was considered a great duty to exert ourselves to influence novices in favour of the Roman Catholic religion; and different nuns, were at different times, charged to do, what they could, by conversation, to make favourable impressions on the minds of some, who were particularly indicated to us by the Superior. I often heard it remarked, that those who were influenced with the greatest difficulty, were young ladies from the United States; and on some of those, great exertions were made.

Cases in which citizens of the States were said to have been converted to the Roman Catholic faith, were sometimes spoken of, and always as if they were considered highly important.

The Bishop, as we were told, was on the public square, on the day of an execution, when, as he said, a stranger looked at him in some peculiar manner, which made him confidently believe God intended to have him converted by his means. When he went home, he wrote a letter for him, and the next day found him again in the same place, and gave him the letter, which led to his becoming a Roman Catholic. This man, it was added, proved to be a citizen of the States.

The Bishop, as I have remarked, was not very dignified on all occasions, and sometimes acted in such a manner as would not have appeared well in public.

One day I saw him preparing for mass; and because he had some difficulty in getting on his robe, shewed evident signs of anger. One of the nuns remarked:—" The Bishop is going to perform a passionate mass."—Some of the others exclaimed: " Are you not ashamed to speak so of my lord ?" And was rewarded with a penance.

But it might be hoped that the Bishop would be free from the crimes of which I have declared so many priests to have been guilty. I am far from entertaining such charitable opinions of him; and I had good reasons, after a time.

I was often required to sleep on a sofa, in the room of the present Superior, as I have already mentioned.

One night, not long after I was first introduced there for that purpose, and within the first twelve months of my wearing the veil, having retired as usual, at about half-past nine, not long after we had got into bed, the alarm bell from without, which hangs over the Superior's bed, was rung. She told me to see who was there; and going down, I heard the signal given, which I have before mentioned, a peculiar kind of hissing sound made through the teeth. I answered with a low " Hum—hum ;" and then opened the door. It was Bishop Lartique, the present Bishop of Montreal. He said to me, " Are you a Novice or a Received?" meaning a Received Nun. I answered " a Received." He then requested me to conduct him to the Superior's room, which I did. He went to the bed drew the curtains behind him, and I lay down again upon the sofa, until morning, when the Superior called me, at an early hour, about day-light, and directed me to show him to the door, to which I conducted him, and he took his departure.

I continued to visit the cellar frequently, to carry up coals for the fires, without anything more than a general impression that there were two nuns imprisoned in it. One day, while there on my usual errand, I saw a nun standing on the right of the cellar, in front of one of the cell doors I had before observed; she was apparently engaged with something within. This attracted my attention. The door appeared to close in a small recess, and was fastened with a stout iron bolt on the outside, the end of which was secured by being let into a hole in the stonework which formed the posts. The door, which was of wood, was sunk a few inches beyond the stonework, which rose and formed an arch overhead. Above the bolt was a small window supplied with a fine grating, which swung open, a small bolt having been removed from it on the outside. The nun I had observed seemed to be whispering with some person within, through the little window; but I hastened to get my coal, and left the cellar, presuming that was the prison. When I visited the place again, being alone, I ventured to the spot, determined to learn the truth, presuming that the imprisoned nuns, of whom the Superior had told me on my admission, were confined there. I spoke at the window where I had seen the nun standing, and heard a voice reply in a whisper. The aperture was so small, and the place so dark, that I could see nobody; but I learnt that a poor wretch was confined there a prisoner I feared that I might be discovered; and after a few words which I thought could do no harm, I withdrew.

My curiosity was now alive, to learn everything I could about so mysterious a subject. I made a few enquiries of Saint Xavier, who only informed me that they were punished for refusing to obey the Superior, Bishop, and Priests. I afterwards found that other nuns were acquainted with the fact I had just discovered. All I could learn, however, was, that the prisoner in the cell whom I had just spoken with, and another in the cell just beyond. had been confined there several years without having been taken out; but their names, connexions, offences, and everything else relating to them, I could never learn, and am still as ignorant of as ever. Some conjectured that they had refused to comply with some of the rules of the Convent, and who would not consent to sign deeds of it. Some of the nuns informed me, that the severest of their sufferings arose from fear of supernatural beings.

I often spoke with one of them in passing near their cells, when on errands in the cellar, but never ventured to stop long, or to press my enquiries very far. Besides, I found her reserved, and little disposed to converse freely; a thing I could not wonder at, when I considered her situation, and the characters of persons around her. She spoke like a woman in feeble health, and of broken spirits. I occasionally saw other nuns speaking to them, particularly at meal times, when they were regularly furnished with food, which was such as we ourselves ate.

Their cells were occasionally cleaned, and then the doors were opened. I never looked into them, but was informed that the ground was their only floor. I presumed that they were furnished with straw to lie upon, as I always saw a quantity of old straw scattered about that part of the cellar, after the cells had been cleaned. I once enquired of one of them, whether they could converse together, and she replied that they could, through a small opening between their cells, which I could not see.

I once enquired of the one I spoke with in passing, whether she wanted any thing, and she replied, "Tell Jane Ray I want to see her a moment, if she can slip away." When I went up I took an opportunity to deliver my message to Jane, who concerted with me a signal to be used in future, in case a similar request should be made through me. This was a sly wink at her with one eye, accompanied with a slight toss of my head. She then sought an opportunity to visit the cellar, and was soon able to hold an interview with the poor prisoners, without being noticed by any one but myself. I afterwards learned that Jane Ray was not so mad but she could feel for those miserable beings, and carry through measures for their comfort. She would often visit them with sympathizing words, and, when necessary, conceal part of her food while at table, and secretly convey it into their dungeons. Sometimes we would combine for such an object; and I have repeatedly aided her in thus obtaining a larger supply of food than they had been able to obtain from others.

I frequently thought of the two nuns confined in the cells, and occasionally heard something said about them, but very little. Whenever I visited the cellar, and thought it safe, I went up to the first of them and spoke a word or two, and usually got some brief reply, without ascertaining that any particular change took place with either of them. The one with whom I alone conversed, spoke English perfectly well, and French, I thought, as well. I supposed she must have been well educated, for I could not tell which was her native language. I remember that she frequently used these words when I wished to say more to her, and which alone showed that she was constantly afraid of punishment: " O, there's somebody coming—do go away !" I have been told that the other prisoner also spoke English.

It was impossible for me to form any certain opinion about the size or appearance of those two miserable creatures, for their cells were perfectly dark, and I never caught the slightest glimpse even of their faces. It is probable they were women not above the middle size, and my reason for this presumption is the following: I was sometimes appointed to lay out the clean clothes for all the nuns in the Convent on Saturday evening, and was always directed to lay by two suits for the prisoners. Particular orders were given to select the largest-sized garments for several tall nuns; but nothing of the kind was ever said in relation to the clothes for those in the cells.

I had not been long a veiled nun, before I requested of the Superior permission to confess to the "Saint Bon Pasteur," (Holy Good Shepherd,) that is, the mysterious and nameless nun whom I had heard of while a novice. I knew of several others who had confessed to her at different times, and of some who had sent their clothes to be touched by her when they were sick; and I felt a desire to unburden my heart of certain things which I was loath to acknowledge to the Superior, or any of the priests.

The Superior made me wait a little while, until she could ascertain whether the "Saint Bon Pasteur" was ready to admit me; and, after a time, returned and told me to enter the old nun's room. That apartment has twelve beds, arranged like the berths of a ship, by threes; and as each is broad enough to receive two persons, twenty-four may be lodged there, which was about the number of old nuns in the Convent during most of my stay in it. Near an opposite corner of the apartment was a large glass case, with no appearance of a door, or other opening, in any part of it; and in that case stood the venerable nun, in the dress of the community, with her thick veil spread over her face, so as to conceal it entirely. She was standing, for the place did not allow room of sitting, and moved a little, which was the only sign of life, as she did not speak. I fell on my knees before her, and began to confess some of my imperfections, which lay heavy on my mind, imploring her aid and intercession, that I might be delivered from them. She appeared to listen to me with patience, but still never returned a word in reply. I became much affected as I went on; at length I began to weep bitterly; and when I withdrew, was in tears. It seemed to me that my heart was remarkably relieved after this exercise; and all the requests I had made I found, as I believed, strictly fulfilled. I often, afterward, visited the old nun's room for the same purpose, and with similar results; so that my belief in the sanctity of the nameless nun, and my regard for her intercession, were unbounded.

What is remarkable, though I was repeatedly sent into the room to dust it out, or to put it in order, I remarked that the glass-case was vacant, and no signs were to be found either of the nun or of the way by which she had left it; so that the solemn conclusion rested upon my mind, that she had gone on one of her frequent visits to heaven.

A priest would sometimes come in the daytime to teach us to sing; and this was done with some parade or stir, as if it were considered, or meant to be considered, as a thing of importance.

The instructions, however, were entirely repetitions of the words and tunes, nothing being taught even of the principles of the science. It appeared to me, that although hymns alone were sung, the exercise was chiefly designed for our amusement, to raise our spirits a little, which were apt to become depressed. Mad Jane Ray certainly usually treated the whole thing as a matter of sport, and often excited those of us who understood English to a great degree of mirth. She had a very fine voice which was so powerful as generally to be heard above the rest. Sometimes she would be silent when the other nuns began; and the Superior would often call out "Jane Ray, you don't sing." She always had some trifling excuse ready, and commonly appeared unwilling to join the rest.

After being urged or commanded by the Superior, she would then strike up some English song, or profane parody, which was rendered ten times more ridiculous by the ignorance of the lady Superior, and the majority of the nuns. I cannot help laughing now when I remember how she used to stand with perfect composure and sing,

"I wish I was married and nothing to rue,
With plenty of money and nothing to do."

"Jane Ray, you don't sing right," the Superior would exclaim. "Oh," she would reply, with perfect coolness, "that is the English for,

"Seigneur Dieu de clemence,
Recoise ce grand pecheur."

and as sung by her, a person ignorant of the language would naturally be imposed upon. It was extremely difficult for me to conceal my laughter. I have always had greater exertion to make in repressing it than most other persons; and mad Jane Ray often took advantage of this.

Saturday evening usually brought with it much unpleasant work for some of us. We received the Sacrament every Sunday; and in preparation for it, on Saturday evening we asked pardon of the Superior, and of each other, "for the scandal we had caused them since we last received the sacrament," and then asked the Superior's permission to receive it on the following day. She enquired of each nun, who necessarily asked her permission, whether she, naming her as Saint somebody, had concealed any sin that should hinder her receiving it? and if the answer was in the negative, she was granted her permission.

On Saturdays we were catechised by a priest, being assembled in a community-room. He sat on the right of the door in a chair. He often told us stories, and frequently enlarged on the duty of enticing novices into the nunnery. "Do you not feel happy," he would say, "now that you are safely out of the world, and sure of heaven? But remember how many poor people are yet in the world.—Every novice you influence to take the black veil, will add to your honour in heaven. Tell them how happy you are."

The Superior played one trick while I was in the Convent, which always passed for one of the most admirable she ever carried into execution. We were pretty good judges in a case of the kind; for, as may be presumed, we were rendered familiar with the arts of deception, under so accomplished a teacher.

There was an ornament on hand in the Nunnery, of an extraordinary kind, which was prized at ten pounds; but it had been made and exposed to view so long, that it became damaged, and quite unsaleable. We were one day visited by an old priest from the country, who was evidently intoxicated; and as he withdrew to go to his lodgings in the Seminary, where the country priests often stay, the Superior conceived a plan of disposing of the old ornament. "Come," said she, "we will send it to the old priest, and swear he has bought it!"

We all approved of the ingenious device, for it evidently might be classed among the pious frauds we had so often recommended to us, both by precept and example; and the ornament was sent to him the next morning as his property when paid for. He soon came into the Convent, and expressed the greatest suprize that he had been charged with purchasing such a thing, for which he had no need and no desire.

The Superior heard his declaration with patience, but politely insisted that it was a fair bargain: and we then surrounded the old priest with the strongest assertions that such was the fact, and that nobody would have ever thought of his purchasing it, unless he had expressly engaged to do so. The poor old man was entirely put down. He was certain of the truth; but what could he do to resist or disprove a direct falsehood pronounced by the Superior of a Convent, and sworn to by all her holy nuns? He finally expressed his conviction that we were right: he was compelled to pay his money.

NOTES, FACTS, CONFIRMATIONS, &c.

The following is extracted from the volume entitled, "Confirmations of Maria Monk's Disclosures." These confirmations we hope to continue throughout the whole course of this work; beside which original documentary evidence is coming to hand. On page 170, the writer says—"For the truth of the following statement of facts, I hold myself responsible. A Catholic young woman, ardently devoted to her religion, by the name of Miss N——, lived in the family of Mr. M——, in New York. In her appearance she was quite prepossessing, and probably of virtuous character, up to the time to which this narrative refers. A short time before Good Friday, which was the first day of last April, she was observed to be uncommonly devoted to the ceremonies of the church. About this time, she said to a young lady of the family, 'My father Confessor is a going to bestow upon me a wonderful gift, about next Good Friday, if I am faithful to go frequently to confession, and confess all my sins, and answer all the questions which he asks me.' What is it, a new gown?' replied the lady. 'Oh, no, not a carnal gift, but a spiritual one; I am to be exalted, and to be made a spiritual sister.' Miss N. increased her visits to the confessional, going more frequently as the time of her 'exaltation' drew near. At length the time arrived. Miss N. was to go to confess at that time in the evening. She went, but did not return until early the next morning. Sad disappointment and shame were depicted on her countenance. To the question, asking her where she had passed the night, she declined giving a direct answer. On one occasion she said, that she staid in the church all night; but then it should be known that the house of her father Confessor was in the immediate neighbourhood of the church. Miss N. remained in the family of Mr. M. but a few days after this. I leave my readers to make their own inferences. But I would ask, if it be not the duty of the friends of virtue and good order, to discountenance a practice so corrupting and so ruinous to all that is virtuous in the female character, as is that of confession to a corrupt priest. Destroy the confessional, and you at once destroy that fatal power, which the priests now have over their deluded followers; and until this is done, all your efforts to enlighten and elevate Catholics, will be thwarted by these enemies of the human race. Let, then, every lawful means be used to accomplish this end, remembering that it is at the confessional those chains are forged, applied, and riveted, which hold in bondage so large a portion of the human family; a bondage more dreadful than that of the African slave, because it is the bondage of the soul, which God made in his own glorious image."

From "Partridge and Oakey's Female Jesuit" we come to make another extract. We have had a convent lady—a mysterious personage—call at our office:—We expect something will come out of this. For the present, we briefly extract her departure from the Convent:—"It was about nine o'clock on the following morning, when the I—— omnibus rolled on, and gradually set down the greater part of its passengers, till four only remained. Among these was the young lady of the convent. It was Marie, whom we introduced in the last chapter. She was reading her Catholic prayer-book, as is the custom of the nuns all leisure moments, when out of it accidentally dropped a little cross. It was picked up by a gentleman who sat opposite to her, and courteously returned without a remark. Shortly after, the two other passengers got out, and they were left alone. He then entered into conversation with her, and, presuming that she was a member of the Roman Catholic Church, he gradually led the way to what he conceived to be its errors. The gentleman in question was neither young nor handsome, but the expression of his countenance was strikingly benevolent, and his manner most kind and fatherly. The first thought that he might be one of her own Church, seeking to test her fidelity, was soon discarded, and his evident earnestness and sincerity won her entire confidence. She frankly acknowledged her doubts, and stated her circumstances. He expressed his surprise how she or any one could read the Bible and continue to be a Roman Catholic. She burst into tears, and told him that she had never seen a Bible, and would not be allowed to possess one. He seemed much shocked, and earnestly entreated her to seek advice of some Protestant minister. She told him she had long wished to meet with one, but knew not where or how. He said she could go to some Protestant place of worship, and remain to speak to the minister. She told him that it would not be permitted, and that she could not do it unobserved. He then recommended her to seek one that very day. She expressed her willingness to do so. 'To whom should she go?' and he began to think. There was a Dr. ——, a very good man, but he did not know where he lived, and feared it was a long way off. There was a Mr.——, but he too lived at some distance. There was another minister a Mr. L——, who had not long been in London; the chapel at which he officiated was near: she had better go to him. She asked whether she might indeed place confidence in this Mr. L——. He assured her that she might. She thanked him, and resolved to follow the advice of her kind friend and adviser, feeling an impression that he had been sent to her by heaven, in answer to her prayer. The omnibus stopped. He expressed his regret that he could not show her the way, having business in another direction, and bade her farewell. It was a feast and gala night in the convent of S——, whither Marie was going. Her young attendant's services would be required, so, availing herself of this pretext, on getting out of the omnibus she sent the girl on, promising to follow as soon as she had completed the business about which she had been sent. She, herself, went to execute a commission, and then commenced her search for Mr. L. Unacquainted with the neighbourood, and timid from her convent life, she wandered about for three hours, getting into courts and places which terrified her, and receiving one answer from all whom she asked, 'that there was no such chapel in the square.' It was getting dusk, and fatigue and fasting added to her dejection. At length she met with a girl who knew the place, and kindly undertook to be her guide. It was not in the square, but in one of the many streets leading out of it. She rang at the side door, and asked for Mr. L——, and was told that he was not there, and that he lived between three and four miles off. If Marie had not been inspired with energy and perseverance from above, she would surely have given up in despair. But she was not to be dismayed, even by this discouraging reply. She inquired farther, and found that there was to be a service at seven o'clock, and that Mr. L—— would be there a few minutes before that time. Resolving to return, she hastened to where she had some other business to transact, and was informed that the lawyer to whom she was sent, would not be home till after seven. This suited very well, as it allowed time to renew her inquiries for Mr. L.——, in the interval, and furnished an excuse for a late return to the convent. She walked about for another hour, to while away the time, and returned to —— street a little after six. It was Mr. L——'s custom to spend the Thursday in visiting his people, and to take tea with one of them before going to service. That evening, as he went his rounds, he felt so unwell that he gave up his usual plan, went straight to the vestry, and asked the pew-opener to send him tea there. He arrived about six. But for this unusual circumstance, he would not have been there till just before the service began, and too late to speak to Marie. She arrived a little after six, and was shown into the vestry. Her agitation was extreme, and she glanced round as though the walls had eyes and ears, but his calm and gentle manner soon inspired her with confidence. There was not time for any lengthened conversation; such as there was, soothed and comforted her. He gave her a little New Testament, the first she had ever held in her hand, and directed her to come to his house the next day, if she could obtain her liberty for a few hours. From the vestry Maria posted on to the house of the Catholic lawyer, and thence hastened back to the convent. She had paced about for hours, and had not tasted food since early in the morning. All at the convent were too busy to make more than general enquiries, and after taking a little refreshment, she retired to her room. She took her Testament from her pocket, and placed it under her pillow, that it might not be discovered during her sleep. But sleep was not for Marie. Thoughts of the past, and dreams of the future, crowded through her excited brain. All the circumstances of her previous life passed in rapid review before her, and a lifetime yet to come floated on her imagination. What was to become of her, if after all she did not make her escape, or how she was to be provided for if she did; fears of discovery regarding the past evening, and cogitations as to how she could get away for a few hours on the morrow, kept her in such a whirl of emotion, that she would have been overpowered had it not been for the firm persuasion which possessed her, that the extraordinary meeting with the stranger in the omnibus was the hand of God pointing out her way, and that he would not leave her till he had accomplished her deliverance. Marie was no longer friendless though she knew it not; there were those in whose minds an interest had that night been awakened which was soon to ripen into warm attachment, and who talked of her and prayed for her as she lay on her restless couch. And where was he who had opened to her the door of hope, who had seemed to her as an angel from heaven directing her way? Did he think of her and pray for her that night? Did he tell the tale of his interview with her to some dear home circle who could mingle their prayers with his on her behalf? Does he ever think of her now? Does he ever wish to know what became of her? It is her hope that he may chance to see this book, and learn how, while instant in season and true to his Master's work, his Christian fidelity and love were blessed to her deliverance. And if any of the public journals or reviews should notice her little history, she makes it her request to them that they will repeat the circumstance of his meeting with her, and tell him the gratitude she shall ever feel towards him, and how she longs once again to see him and thank him for herself; or how if she may not thank him on earth, she hopes to do so in eternity."

In a former number, in giving some extracts from the AMERICAN PROTESTANT VINDICATOR, we mentioned the name of a Col. Stone, as having taken an active part in condemning Maria Monk as an impostor. We here annex another quotation from the same paper. Col. Stone states that the interior of the Nunnery, which he pretended to examine, does not correspond with Maria Monk's description of the same; and then adds, " No alterations whatever have been made within the Hotel Dieu Nunnery since the time Maria Monk says she left that place." The Editor of the aforesaid paper says:—"This is one of the reckless assertions which this new advocate of the Jesuits and nuns of Montreal, has permitted himself to make in his narrative of his late investigations. Now, although I have been put in possession of the most satisfactory testimony, that every reflecting man at all acquainted with this controversy, and the evidence of the case, is fully persuaded that Col. Stone has been completely 'hoaxed' by the Montreal nuns and Jesuits; yet I deem it my duty to detail every *new* portion of evidence on this point. A few days ago, a gentleman called on me, with whose brother, a resident of this city, I am acquainted. The gentleman is an architect at present residing in Montreal; an intelligent gentleman, of the highest reputation, and of an unimpeachable veracity. The points on which my friend gave me fresh evidence were these: 1. His daughter, an amiable young lady, was a schoolmate of Maria Monk; he and his wife also knew Maria Monk: the intimacy was kept up between his daughter and M. Monk, after the latter was in '*the Nunnery*,' and after she had taken the veil of the *Novice*. Miss —— frequently, along with others, saw Maria Monk in the streets in the novice's habit; and she, and he himself, and his wife, all knew personally the fact that Maria Monk entered the Hotel Dieu Nunnery, *and took the nun's veil.* This fact I heard this gentleman state, in an explicit manner. Yet Col. Stone pronounces from the overwhelming evidence of his seeing a certain dozen of rooms, out of some dozen score, more or less, that most truly, and of verity it doth appear that the said *Maria Monk* never was even *in* the nunnery! What a philosopher! The evidence of this young lady fully corresponds with that of Mrs. H. already published in the second edition of the Awful Disclosures of Maria Monk. 2. I drew his particular attention to 'the alterations' that are said to have been made lately in the nunnery. He gave me the following answer:—'It must be evident that Col. Stone has not lived in Montreal; it is perfectly evident that he was a transient visitant; and not only so, but that he had when there, put himself under the Bishop's party's guidance. Why, every discreet man who professes to be a Protestant, and who thinks according to the evidence of his own eyes, must smile at the absolute silliness of that editor of your city. The very priests laugh at his weakness and the facility of his being made a tool, and a *hoax-monger!*' I tell you what I saw with my own eye, and what all my hands to the number of some twenty persons saw, when we did our part of a lofty building, adjacent to the Hotel Dieu Nunnery. From our scaffoldings we had a complete view of the rear of the nunnery, from Notre Dame St. There we saw, during last May, June, and July, between fifteen and twenty men busily employed within the nunnery's outer walls, carrying in timber, stones, and mortar. The work went on briskly for *three* months; how much longer I do not profess to say. I do not say they began in May, and stopped in July. But while at our work, we saw them briskly employed for that time.—'Now' continued he,—'they reared and erected *no building on the outside,* so far as any one of us could see. They carried their materials *within the great building.* And if fifteen or twenty men could be so busy, during such a length of time, *in the inside*, and yet make no alterations, it is fairly beyond sober credence. I only state what we saw with our own eyes, and do testify on our honour.' 3. I also put the usual question to him respecting the *extent* of the nunnery 'Sir,' I said to him, 'you are an architect: I ask you as one who can, by your eye, take a survey of a building and form a tolerable accurate idea of its extent ; or perhaps you have stepped the front, what is the extent of that nunnery ?' He replied—'Mons. Bouchette's dimensions quoted by you and Col. Stone, are unquestionably accurate. I am well acquainted with the size of that nunnery. I have lived near it twenty-one years, And I tell you, and you may tell the public that the man who can take it on him to say, that he has fully explored all that immense building, from garret to cellar, *in about three hours*, must be either *a fool or a knave !* I leave you to judge which, for I never saw Col. Stone, and know nothing of him. I had much conversation with my friend, also, on the subterranean passage, and on the extent of credit given to Maria Monk, in Montreal. As to the first, he was surprised that any man should ever question the under ground passage ; and he hesitated not to say, that had Col. Stone been a little with him, during his twenty-one years residence in Montreal, that gentleman never could, without a gross outraged offered to his conscience, have denied that secret way. In addition to those statements, I may simply add, what I heard lately, a distinguished lady, one of a party recently from a visit to the nunnery, detail in the presence of the family where she was then on a visit. ' In visiting the apartments of the Hotel Dieu Nunnery, we reached' said she, ' what seemed to be *the end* and termination of that building, or wing. But my son, not satisfied with this, began to examine. He at last discovered *a key hole in the pannel work.* Determined to explore, he placed his eye close to the key hole, and discovered what seemed to him, alighted apartments behind this wall; and *the yellow fresh paint stuck on his brow and nose.* This created much laughter ; as it was with much difficulty he could get it off.' Yet the far-famed McDonald's *man with the steel pointed cane*, carefully examined every wall, every chamber, every closet, from the garret to the cellar, and solemnly declares that *no paint yielded to his cane; that there was no fresh paint to be seen or found ; no alterations whatever !"*

CHAPTER XV.

Frequency of the Priest's Visits to the Nunnery—Their Freedom and Crimes—Difficulty of learning their Names—Their Holy Retreat—Objections in our minds—Means used to Counteract Conscience—Ingenious Arguments.

SOME of the priests from the Seminary were in the Nunnery every day and night, and often several at a time. I have seen nearly all of them at different times, though there are about a hundred and fifty in the district of Montreal. There was a difference in their conduct; though I believe every one of them was guilty of licentiousness; while not one did I ever see who maintained a character any way becoming the profession of a priest. Some were gross and degraded in a degree which few of my readers can ever have imagined; and I should be unwilling to offend the eye, and corrupt the heart of any one, by an account of their words and actions. Few imaginations can conceive deeds so abominable as they practised, and often required of some of the poor women, under the fear of severe punishments, and even death. I do not hesitate to say, with the strongest confidence, that although some of the nuns became lost to every sentiment of virtue and honour, especially one of the Congregational Nunnery whom I have before mentioned, St. Patrick, the greater part of them loathed the practices to which they were compelled to submit, by their Superior and priest, who kept them under so dreadful a bondage.

Some of the priests I saw I never knew by name; and the names of others I did not learn for a time, and at last learnt only by accident.

They were always called " *mon pere*," (my father ;) but sometimes when they had purchased something in the ornament room, they would give their real names, with directions where it should be sent. Many names, thus learnt, and other ways, were whispered about from nun to nun, and became pretty generally known. Several of the priests some of us had seen before we entered the Convent.

Many things of which I speak, from the nature of the case, must necessarily rest chiefly upon my own word, until further evidence can be obtained; but there are some facts for which I can appeal to the knowledge of others. It is commonly known in Montreal that some of the priests occasionally withdraw from their customary employments, and are not to be seen for some time, it being understood that they have retired for religious study, meditation, and devotion, for the improvement of their hearts. Sometimes they are thus withdrawn from the world for weeks; but there is no fixed period.

This was a fact I knew before I took the veil; for it is a frequent subject of remark, that such or such Father is on a " holy retreat." This is a term which conveys the idea of a religious seclusion from the world for sacred purposes. On the re-appearance of a priest, after such a period, in the church or in the streets, it is natural to feel a peculiar impression of his devout character—an impression very different from that conveyed to the mind of one who knows matters as they really are. Suspicions have been indulged by some in Canada on this subject, and facts are known by at least a few. I am able to speak from personal knowledge; for I have been a nun of Sœur Bourgeoise.

The priests are liable, by their dissolute habits, to occasional attacks of disease, which render it necessary, or at least prudent, to submit to medical treatment.

In the Black Nunnery they find private accomodations, for they are free to enter one of the private hospitals whenever they please; which is a room set apart on purpose for the accomodation of the priests, and is called a retreat-room.—But an excuse is necessary to blind the public, and this they find in the pretence they make of being in a " Holy Retreat." Many such cases have I known; and I can mention the names of priests who have been confined in this "Holy Retreat." They are very carefully attended by the Superior and old nuns, and their diet consists mostly of vegetable soups, &c., with but little meat, and that fresh. I have seen an instrument of surgery lying upon the table in that holy room, which is used only for particular purposes.

Father Tombau, a Roman priest, was on one of his holy retreats about the time when I left the nunnery. There are sometimes a number confined there at the same time. The victims of these priests frequently share the same fate.

I have often reflected how greviously I had been deceived in my opinion of a nun's condition!—All the holiness of their lives, I now saw, was merely pretended. The appearance of sanctity and heavenly-mindedness, which they had shown among us novices, I found was only a disguise to conceal such practices as would not be tolerated in any decent society in the world; and as for peace and joy like that of heaven, which I had expected to find among them, I learned too well that they did not exist there.

The only way in which such thoughts were counteracted, was by the constant instructions given us by the Superior and the priests, to regard every doubt as a mortal sin. Other faults we might have, as we were told, over and over again, which, though worthy of penances, were far less sinful than these. For a nun to doubt that she was doing her duty in fulfilling her vows and oaths, was a henious offence; and we were exhorted always to suppress our doubts, to confess them without reserve, and cheerfully to submit to severe penances on account of them, as the only means of mortifying our evil dispositions, and resisting the temptations of the devil. Thus we learnt, in a good degree, to resist our minds and consciences, when we felt the rising of a question about the duty of doing anything required of us.

To enforce this upon us, they employed various means. Some of the most striking stories told us at catechism by the priests, were designed for this end. One of these I will repeat. "One day," as a priest assured us, who was hearing us say the catechism on Saturday afternoon, "As one Monsieur * * *, a well-known citizen of Montreal, was walking near the cathedral, he saw satan giving orders to certain evil spirits who had assembled around him. Being afraid of being seen, and yet wishing to observe what was done, he hid himself where he could observe all that passed. Satan dispatched his devils to different parts of the city, with directions to do their best for him; and they returned in a short time, bringing in reports of their success in leading persons of different classes to the commision of various sins which they thought would be agreeable to their master.

Satan, however, expressed his dissatisfaction, and ordered them out again; but just then a spirit from the Black Nunnery came, who had not been seen before, and stated that he had been trying for seven years to persuade one of the nuns to doubt, and had just succeeded. Satan received the intelligence with the highest pleasure; and turning to the spirits around him, said, " you have not half done your work—he has done much more than all of you."

In spite, however, of our instructions and warnings, our fears and penances, such doubts would obtrude; and I have often indulged them for a time, and at length, yielding to the belief that I was wrong in giving place to them, would confess them, and undergo with cheerfulness, such new penances as I was loaded with. Others, too, would occasionally entertain and privately express such doubts; though we all had been most solemnly warned by the cruel murder of St. Frances. Occasionally some of the nuns would go further, and resist the restraints and punishments imposed upon them; and it was not uncommon to hear screams, sometimes of a most piercing and terrific kind, from nuns suffering under discipline.

Some of my readers may feel disposed to exclaim against me, for believing things which will strike them as so monstrous and abominable. To such, I would say, without pretending to justify myself :—You know little of the position in which I was placed: in the first place, ignorant of any other religious doctrines; and, in the second, met at every moment by some ingenious argument, and the example of a large community, who received all the instructions of the priests as of undoubted truth, and practiced upon them. Of the variety and speciousness of the arguments used, you cannot have any correct idea. They were often so ready with replies, examples, anecdotes, and authorities, to enforce their doctrines, that it seemed to me, they could never have learnt it all from books, but must have been taught by wicked spirits. Indeed, when I reflect upon their conversations, I am astonished at their art and address, and find it difficult to account for their subtlety and success in influencing my mind, and persuading me to anything they pleased. It seems to me that hardly anything would be safe in their hands. If you were to go to confession twice, I believe you would feel very different from what you do now. They have such a way of avoiding one thing and speaking of another; of affirming this, and doubting and disputing that; of quoting authorities, and speaking of wonders and miracles recently performed, in confirmation of what they teach, as familiarly known to persons whom they call by name, and whom they pretend to call as witnesses, though they never give you an opportunity to speak with them;—these and many other means, they use in such a way, that they always blinded my mind, and, I should think would blind the minds of others.

NOTES, FACTS, CONFIRMATIONS, &c.

THE PORTRAIT OF MARY IN HEAVEN.—From the French of Napoleon Roussel, Ward and Co. have published a series of neat little tracts. One is under the above title. It is a correspondence between Maria-Saint-Romain and Joseph-de-Saint-Pierre. The Abbess writes to the Painter requesting a portrait of the Virgin to hang in her cell to help her devotions. The Painter is led to the best of books to see what help he can get as regards form and features. The Painter's reply to the Abbess is worth its weight in gold, and we must, therefore, give some portion of it to our readers. The following are faithful extracts.—"*The Painter to the Abbess*: Cloister of the Assumption, Jan. 4, 1566. My Sister,—Here is, at length, the work completed!—and a conscientiously faithful work, if ever there was one. But it is not enough to assert fidelity—I must also prove it: for the portrait which I send you is such, that you might question its likeness if I did not set before you at length the authorities on which rest my pretensions to have achieved the most accurate portrait of the blessed Mary, as now in heaven, which has ever existed. I will, therefore, enter into detail on the subject. One of the most important points to know, in order to picture a face to yourself is the person's age. On the arrival of your Bible I therefore directed my first enquiries to Mary's age. I opened the Gospel according to St. Luke, and from the first page I observed that Elizabeth, who conceived only six months before Mary, was then 'Well stricken in years;' which made me at first suspect that Mary, her cousin, could not be very young at the period when the daughter of her uncle or aunt was very old. The second circumstance which came to my aid in fixing the age of Mary, is that when the miraculous conception took place she was already betrothed. We do not risk too much in supposing that Mary was then twenty years old. Setting out thence, let us continue the reckoning. Mary was betrothed at twenty. After the betrothal Joseph perceived her condition, therefore when she brought her Son into the world, she must have been twenty and a half. From the first chapter of St. Luke I pass to the second. And I see that Mary is still living, because she forgets the child Jesus in the temple of Jerusalem. Moreover, I see from verse 42, that Jesus was then twelve years old. Therefore I conclude that Mary was at that time thirty-two and a half. From the second I proceed to the third chapter; and therein I learn that Jesus was baptised by John, and began his holy ministry at thirty years. Now Mary was still living, since, as you know, and as we shall see later, she outlived Jesus on the earth. I draw farther this very clear and simple conclusion, that if the mother was twenty years and a half old at the birth of her child, when Jesus had attained the age of thirty, Mary must have arrived at that of fifty and six months. Now how long did the ministry of Jesus Christ last? It was easy to calculate this by searching out from the beginning to the end of the same gospel, the number of different times during that ministry that Jesus went to celebrate the feast of the Passover at Jerusalem. Thus in St. John ii. 12, 13, I see that Jesus descends to Capernaum, because the Passover was near. If Mary was fifty years and a half old when Jesus began to preach, and if his ministry lasted three years and a half, Mary, when standing at the foot of the Saviour's cross, was exactly fifty-four. Here the Gospel finishes; but the Acts of the Apostles commence, and there I find Mary again, at prayer with the disciples. Elsewhere I observed that, according to the order of Jesus, the apostle John must have received Mary into his dwelling. How long did she remain there? This the Holy Scriptures no where say, for there is no farther mention of her whatever. Whether Mary lived one, two, three, ten, or twenty years, I know not. In the silence of the holy Scriptures I suppose she dwelt in this inferior world only five or six years more, which makes her just sixty. It is at that age that Mary would ascend to heaven.'
* * * * * * After a lengthened enquiry into the fact that Jesus had natural brothers and sisters the Painter says, 'Finally, if Jesus were the only child of Mary, why does not the holy Scripture say so? It says, indeed, and

that several times, that Jesus is the *only Son of God;* why does it not say also, at least once, that he is the only Son of Mary? If the words are different it is because the facts are different also. We must suppose that authors, inspired by the Holy Spirit, knew how to choose their expressions, and that they speak with equal truth when they call Jesus only Son of God, and first-born Son of Mary. From these considerations we must come to this conclusion :—Mary, after having conceived by the Holy Spirit, carried in her virgin womb a body free from pollution, and brought into the world the only Son of God, had accomplished her supernatural task, and from that time re-entered into the ordinary course of nature; i. e. became in all things the chaste wife of her husband Joseph. Now then, according to this thirteenth chapter of St. Matthew, Jesus had at this period four brothers and some sisters. The plural of the word sisters represents at least the number two; I therefore draw this final inference : Mary had as children :—Jesus, her first-born; his four brothers; and his two sisters. In other words, Mary was mother of seven children. Now, understand, my sister that I felt it right to take account in my picture of this important circumstance, and slightly emaciate the features already aged. But if Mary's advanced age of sixty years, and her seven times renewed maternity, came to my aid to give her the respectable features of a holy and good mother, grown old in the experience of life, and alas! in grief also, since the sufferings and death of her first-born Son must have transpierced her soul like a sword; still none of this could yet teach me anything of the expression of her face. Were her features beautiful and regular? or had they nothing very remarkable in them? The answer to this question appeared to me difficult to find. I even searched the whole New Testament without discovering anything in it to put me on the track of a direct solution. On the whole, I observed in every page a marked disdain for what has to do with mere outward form. Thus God willed that his divine Son should be born in a manger; should live with artisans; should die on a cross; all through the Gospel the flesh is abased, and the spirit exalted, therefore appearance is despised, and reality required; throughout, the body of the christian is counted for little, and his soul for much. Consequently, I inclined towards the opinion that such was also the case with the body of Jesus Christ, when a passage of the Old Testament came to confirm me in it. Notice how Isaiah describes the exterior of the Messiah :—' He hath no form nor comeliness; and when we shall see him there is no beauty that we should desire him.' Isa. liii, 2. That is what Isaiah the prophet says. Ah! doubtless, my sister, to me as to you, Jesus is the Son of God, and himself God; he is a model of sanctity, of moral beauty, of magnanimity, of high-souled devotion. Doubtless Jesus is worthy of all our worship. I placed myself before my canvas and seized my pencil, when a new idea struck me. It is for Mary as she is now, and not as she was in her childhood or youth, that you have asked me, and you are right; for it is not Mary at her marriage, but Mary after her entrance into heaven who now intercedes for us. Here I had no longer anything in the holy Scripture to guide me. The Church, indeed, speaks of the Assumption of the Virgin, but the Word of God is silent upon it. What could I do?—as a good Catholic submit to the church. I admitted without further hesitation what that good mother teaches; i. e. that Mary at the close of her earthly life (according to our calculation at sixty years of age) was raised to heaven in body and soul, and placed beside her Son. This once accepted as a fact how should I represent Mary arriving in Paradise? Of course, with the features which she had on quitting the earth, since she did not die, but departed with the same body; but was not the body in any way modified? Such is the question which I thought I could put to my guide—hitherto so sure—the Word of God. I again went entirely through the New Testament, and here is what I found respecting my subject :—' In the life to come,' said Jesus to the Sadducees, ' those who are worthy of the resurrection shall neither marry nor be given in marriage because they are like the angels.' Thus Mary, as now in heaven, can neither marry, nor be given in marriage; she is in a manner neither man nor woman. Jesus says, ' She is like the angels.' Now how are the angels to be represented? or, at least, what is the essential difference which distinguishes these celestial creatures from human creatures? On the one hand, we must believe that their forms are analagous to ours, because it is thus that they are often presented to the personages of the Old and New Testament; but, on the other hand, we are told in the 6th chapter of Isaiah, that in the presence of God 'the angels veil their faces with their wings.' Whence I draw this conclusion, if not certain, at least probable, that our celestial body must differ in some respects from the present one; and that to us, as well as to the angels, this admirable method of traversing space, and of ranging from sun to sun,

and from world to world, will be given, that we may accomplish the commands of our God. As to the drapery with which I have covered Mary, I was guided, not by our imaginary portraits, in which she is painted gracefully attired in light blue robes; nor have I introduced into her garments those folds, here tightened to define the form, there let loose to hang tastefully: but I have the rather conformed myself to the indications furnished by the Book of Revelation, where great multitudes of saints are seen enveloped in long white robes. And now, my sister, I have completed the vindication of my portrait. I hope that you will be pleased with it; for I have accomplished what I promised—a portrait of Mary, the most faithful of all that have ever been painted.'
A year passed away, and the Abbess replied,—Dear brother in our Lord and Saviour, Jesus Christ—With feelings of the purest and most vivid joy I address you. Without question you have rendered me the greatest of services; it is only just that I should endeavour to render as great a one to you in my turn. You believed you were sending me an inanimate portrait, you gave me a living being; you thought to make me acquainted with a woman, our mediatrix with Christ, you have revealed to me God the Saviour. But this needs explanation. I will unfold the matter from the beginning. You will understand how, on the receipt of your packet, my first glance was at the picture. The sight confounded me! I read your letter; and, although with difficulty, I yielded to your arguments. Afterwards I hung up the blessed portrait in my cell; yes, *blessed*, as you will see. The more I contemplated those emaciated features, that figure enfeebled by age, the more was I disenchanted, and the more was my veneration for Mary weakened. I felt displeased with myself. 'For, after all,' I reflected, ' she is still the very same being, and Mary is not the less powerful with God, for being neither young nor beautiful.' Vainly did I again and again school myself with these fine reasonings; I was conscious of a continual diminution and failure of affection for my patroness; and at length I came to perceive that what I had hitherto loved in the Virgin was her young, beautiful, girlish face, and her graceful and pure form; but not her moral character and intercession with Jesus Christ. Having once made this confession, I wished to know for myself this Mary whom I still respected, but whom I could no longer adore without difficulty. I opened the Bible which you had sent me. There, too, as before the picture, I felt my old ideas vanish one after the other; and the young, sweet, beautiful Virgin, the mediatrix between Jesus and men, and, moreover, the Queen of heaven, was changed into a humble servant of the Lord; happy because she had been received into favour, and who, far from being able to contribute to the salvation of others, herself required to be saved. The following is the passage which struck me most vividly—' My soul doth magnify the Lord, and my spirit hath rejoiced in God my Saviour.' See Luke i. 46, 47. If God be her Saviour, I said to myself, then Mary was previously lost; then she was not sinless; but I continue to quote this portion of the Gospel—' For he hath regarded the low estate of his handmaiden.' You perceive Mary speaks of her low estate. She adds: ' Henceforth all generations shall call me blessed. For he that is mighty hath done unto me great things.' Thus, then, if Mary was exalted, it was by God, and not by herself. But listen again to what the angel Gabriel says to her at verse 30 of the same chapter—' Mary, thou hast found grace before God.' Now, you understand that to find grace it is necessary to have sinned : you feel that it would, for instance, be ridiculous to say that God has bestowed grace or pardon on Jesus Christ; ridiculous, because he did not sin. Notwithstanding, do not think my great joy comes from the discovery that Mary was only a favoured and blessed woman, like every woman who is pardoned and saved. No; but directly I had dethroned this idol from the sovereignty of my heart, the place was prepared for him who should always have filled it. Yes; in seeking to know Mary from the Bible, I learned better to appreciate Jesus Christ, my only and well-beloved Saviour. And that which I find in him is not what I formerly sought in Mary, a carnal body, chiselled in this or that form : but a soul, a heart, a love, which nothing here below can worthily express. Ah! dear brother, when I saw the Son of God quit the heavens to come and live on the earth; when I followed him at every step instructing the people, curing the sick, visiting the poor, from whom he expected nothing; blaming the great, at the risk of their displeasure; and, above all, when I heard this Saviour say to me : 'Come unto me, you who are heavy laden, and I will give you rest; he who believes in me shall not die; I give my life for the sheep.' And, lastly, when having thus listened to him, I beheld him ascend a cross to expiate my sins, and exclaim in death, ' Father, forgive them, for they know not what they do!' Oh, then I felt my heart burn within me, emotion overcame me, my eyes overflowed with tears, and I cried:

'My Lord and my God; I am at length saved.' Since then, every thing has seemed new to me; those Christian truths which I already called mine, seem, like beautiful images which have suddenly received life and motion. The Gospel, Christ, heaven, God, became realities to me. I felt in my heart a divine guest explaining the word of God, rendering the good which had hitherto been so difficult to me easy, and disgusting me with the evil formerly so sweet. I am as though I had been transported into a new world, where the ideas, the feelings, all things are different from the world of yesterday; and this new world began to surround me on the day when I truly felt that I was fully and freely saved by Jesus Christ. And you, dear brother, will you not also finish the way which you have already half travelled? You have restored the Virgin to her place, will you not also restore our Lord and Saviour Jesus Christ to His? Ah, believe me, true peace, true joy, is there alone. Take this Bible [not the same, for I keep that myself]; read it every day, praying for the Holy Spirit; and, be assured, you will soon find a better than Mary, the Mediatrix; *you will meet Jesus himself*, our God and Saviour!" [Reader—in this way may every idol be dethroned from thy heart, and Jesus alone revealed and exalted there.—ED.]

CHAPTER XVI.

Treatment of young Infants in the Convent—Talking in sleep—Amusements—Ceremonies at the public Interment of deceased Nuns—Sudden Disappearance of the Old Superior—Introduction of the new one—Superstition—Alarm of a Nun—Difficulty of Communication with other Nuns.

It will be recollected, that I was informed, immediately after taking the veil, that infants were occasionally murdered in the Convent. I was one day in the nun's private sick room, when I had an opportunity, unsought for, of witnessing deeds of such a nature. It was, perhaps, a month after the death of St. Frances. Two little twin babes, the children of St. Catherine, were brought to a priest, who was in the room, for baptism. I was present while the ceremony was performed, with the Superior and several of the old nuns, whose names I never knew, they being called Ma tanta, (Aunt).

The priests took turns in attending to confession and catechism in the Convent, usually three months at a time, though sometimes longer periods. The priest then on duty was Father Larkin. He is a good looking European, and has a brother who is a Professor in the College. He first put oil upon the heads of the infants, as is the custom before baptism. When he had baptized the children, they were taken, one after another, by one of the old nuns in the presence of us all. She pressed her hands upon the mouth and nose of the first so tight that it could not breathe; and in a few minutes, when the hand removed, it was dead! She then took the other, and treated it in the same way. No sound was heard, and both the children were corpses. The greatest indifference was shown by all present during this operation;

for all, as I well knew, were long accustomed to such scenes. The little bodies were then taken into the cellar, thrown into the pit I have mentioned, and covered with a quantity of lime.

I afterwards saw a new-born infant treated in the same manner in the same place; but the actors in this scene I choose not to name, nor the circumstances, as every thing connected with it is of a peculiarly trying and painful nature to my own feelings. These were the only instances of infanticide I witnessed; and it seemed to be merely owing to accident that I was then present. So far as I know, there were no pains taken to preserve secrecy on this subject; that is, I saw no attempt made to keep any inmate of the Convent in ignorance of the murder of the children. On the contrary, others were told, as well as myself on their first admission as veiled nuns, that all infants born in the place, were baptized and killed without loss of time; and I had been called to witness the murder of the three just mentioned, only because I happened to be in the room at the time.

That others were killed in the same manner, during my stay in the nunnery, I am well assured.

How many were there I cannot tell, and having taken no account of those I heard of, I cannot speak with precision; I believe, however, that I learnt through nuns, that at least eighteen or twenty infants were smothered, and secretly buried in the cellar while I was a nun.

One of the effects of the weariness of our bodies and minds, was our proneness to talk in our sleep. It was both ludicrous and painful to hear the nuns repeat their prayers in the course of the night, as they frequently did in their dreams. Required to keep our minds continually on the stretch, both in watching our conduct, in remembering the rules and our prayers, under the fear of the consequences of any neglect, when we closed our eyes in sleep, we often went over again the scenes of the day; and it was no uncommon thing for me to hear a nun repeat one or two of our long exercises in the dead of night. Sometimes, by the time she had finished, another, in a different part of the room, would happen to take a similar turn, and commence a similar recitation; and I have known cases in which several such unconscious exercises were performed, all within an hour or two.

We had now and then a recreation-day, when we were relieved from our customary labour, and from all prayers except those for morning and evening, and the short ones said at every striking of the clock. The greater part of our time was then occupied with different games, particularly back-gammon and drafts, and in such conversation as did not relate to our past lives, and the outside of the Convent. Sometimes, however, our sports would be interrupted on such days by the entrance of one of the priests, who would come in and propose that his fete, the birthday of his patron saint, should be kept by " the saints." We saints!

Several nuns died at different times while I was in the Convent; how many I cannot say, but there was a considerable number. I might rather say many in proportion to the number in the nunnery. The proportion of deaths I am sure was very large. There were always some in the nun's sick-rooms, and several interments took place in the chapel.

When a Black Nun is dead, the corpse is dressed as if living, and placed in the chapel in a sitting posture, within the railing round the altar, with a book in the hand as if reading. Persons are then freely admitted from the street, and some of them read and pray before it. No particular notoriety is given, I believe, to this exhibition out of the Convent, but such a case usually excites some attention.

The living nuns are required to say prayers for delivery of their deceased sister from purgatory, being informed, as in all other such cases, that if she is not there, and has no need of our intercession, our prayers are in no danger of being thrown away, as they will be set down to the account of some of our deceased friends, or at least to that of the souls which have no acquaintances to pray for them.

It was customary for us occasionally to kneel before a dead nun thus seated in the chapel and I have often performed that task. It was always painful: for the ghastly countenance being seen whenever I raised my eyes, and the feeling that the position and dress were entirely opposed to every idea of propriety in such a case, always made me melancholy.

The Superior sometimes left the Convent, and was absent for an hour, or several hours at a time, but we never knew of it till she had returned, and were not informed where she had been. I one day had reason to presume that she had recently paid a visit to the priest's farm, though I had not direct evidence that such was the fact. The priest's farm is a fine tract of land belonging to the Seminary, a little distance from the city, near the Lachine road, with a large old-fashioned edifice upon it. I happened to be in the Superior's room on the day alluded to, when she made some remark on the plainness and poverty of her furniture. I replied that she was not proud, and could not be dissatisfied on that account.

" No; but if I was, how much superior is the furniture at the priest's farm; the poorest room there is furnished better than the best of mine."

I was one day mending the fire in the Superior's room, when a priest was conversing with her on the scarcity of money; and I heard him say that very little money was received by the priests for prayers, but that the principal part came with penances and absolutions.

One of the most remarkable and unaccountable things that happened in the Convent, was the disappearance of the old Superior. She had performed her customary part during the day, and had acted and appeared just as usual. She had shown no symptoms of ill health, met with no particular difficulty in conducting business, and no agitation, anxiety, or gloom had been noticed in her conduct. We had no reason to suppose that during that day she had expected any thing particular to occur, any more than the rest of us. After the close of our customary labours and evening lecture, she dismissed us to retire to bed, hurried on our clothes as usual, and proceeded to the community-room in double line, to commence the morning exercises. There, to our suprise, we found Bishop Lartique; but the Superior was no where to be seen. The Bishop soon addressed us instead of her, and informed us, that a lady near him, whom he presented to us, was now the Superior of the Convent, and enjoined upon us the same respect and obedience which we paid to her predecessor.

The lady he introduced to us was one of our oldest nuns, Saint Du***, a very large, fleshly, woman, with swelled limbs which rendered her very slow in walking, and often gave her great distress. Not a word was dropped from which we could conjecture the cause of this change, nor of the fate of the old Superior. I took the first opportunity to enquire of one of the old nuns, whom I dared to talk to, what had become of her; but I found them as ignorant as myself, though suspicious that she had been murdered by the orders of the Bishop. Never did I obtain any light on her mysterious disappearance. I am confident, however, that if the Bishop wished to get rid of her privately, and by foul means, he had ample opportunities and power at his command. Jane Ray, as usual, could not allow such an occurrence to pass by without intimating her own suspicions more plainly than other of the nuns would have dared to do. She spoke out one day in the commumity-room and said, "I'm going to have a hunt in the cellar for my old Snperior."

"Hush, Jane Ray!" exclaimed some of the nuns, "you'll be punished."

"My mother used to tell me (replied Jane) never to be afraid of the face of a man."

It cannot be thought strange that we were superstitious. Some were more easily terrified than others by unaccountable sights and sounds; but all of us believed in the power and occasional appearance of spirits, and were ready to look for them at almost any time. I have seen several instances of alarm caused by such superstition, and have experienced it myself more than once. I was one day sitting mending aprons, beside one of the old nuns, in the community-room, while the litanies were repeating; as I was very easy to laugh, Saint Ignace, or Agnes, came in, walked up to her with much agitation, and began to whisper in her ear. She usually talked but little, and that made me more curious to know what was the matter with her. I overheard her say to the old nun, in much alarm, that in the cellar from which she had just returned, she had heard the most dreadful groans that ever came from any being. This was enough to give me uneasiness. I could not account for the appearance of an evil spirit in any part of the Convent, for I had been assured that the only one ever known there, was that of the nun who had died with an unconfessed sin; and that others were kept at a distance by the holy water that was rather profusely used in different parts of the nunnery. Still, I presumed that the sounds heard by Saint Ignace must have proceeded from some devil: and I felt great dread at the thought of visiting the cellar again. I determined to seek further information of the terrified nun; but when I addressed her on the subject, at recreation-time, the first opportunity I could find, she replied that I was always trying to make her break silence, and walked off to another group in the room, so that I could obtain no satisfaction.

It is remarkable that in our nunnery, we were almost entirely cut off from the means of knowing any thing even of each other. There were many nuns whom I know nothing of to this day, after having been in the same rooms with them every day and night for four years. There was a nun, whom I supposed to be in the Convent, and whom I was anxious to learn something about from the time of my entrance as a novice; but I was never able to learn anything concerning her, not even whether she were in the nunnery or not, whether alive or dead. She was the daughter of a rich family residing at Point aux Trembles, of whom I had heard my mother speak before I entered the convent. The name of her family, I think, was Lafayette, and she was thought to be from Europe. She was known to have taken the black veil; but as I was not acquainted with the name of the Saint she had assumed, and I could not describe her in " the world," all my enquiries and observations proved entirely in vain.

I had heard before my entrance into the Convent, that one of the nuns had made her escape from it during the last war, and once enquired about her of the Superior. She admitted that such was the fact; but I was never able to learn any particulars concerning her name, origin, or manner of escape.

NOTES, FACTS, CONFIRMATIONS, &c.

We have been requested to make notes in this edition of Maria Monk, from a work entitled "Six Months in a Convent: a Narrative of Facts; by Rebecca Theresa Reed." A new edition has recently been published, with an introductory Preface from the pen of the Rev. H. H. Beamish, A.M. Partridge and Oakey, Paternoster-row.—We shall proceed to make some extract from this work, according to request. The narrative commences in the following interesting style:—

"In the summer of 1826, while passing the Nunnery on Mount Benedict, Charlestown, Massachusetts, in company with my school-mates, the question was asked by a young lady, who I think was a Roman Catholic, how we should like to become nuns. I replied, after hearing her explanation of their motives for retirement, &c., ' I should like it very well;'' and gave as my principal reasons, their apparent holy life, my love of seclusion, &c. The conversation which passed at that time made but little impression upon my mind. But soon after, the '*Religieuse*' (by the term *Religieuse* I mean those who constituted the Ursuline community,) came from Boston, to take possession of Mount Benedict as their new situation. We were in school, but had permission to look at them as they passed. One of the scholars remarked, that they were Roman Catholics, and that our parents disapproved of their tenets. The young lady who before asked the question how we should like to become nuns, and whose name I have forgotten, was affected even to tears in consequence of what passed, and begged them to desist, saying, ' they were saints; God's people; and the chosen few ;' that, ' they secluded themselves that they might follow the Scriptures more perfectly, pray for the conversion of sinners, and instruct the ignorant (by the term *ignorant* is meant what they term heretics,) in the principles of religion. This conversation with the solemn appearance of the nuns, affected me very sensibly, owing probably to the peculiar state of my feelings. The impressions thus made remained on my mind several months; and at the age of thirteen years and four months, I asked my parents if they were willing I should become an inmate of the convent. This proposition my parents were inclined to treat as visionary; but they soon discovered themselves to be in an error. Nothing of consequence was said upon the subject; but soon after, owing to the delicacy of my health, and other reasons, it was deemed expedient for me to visit my friends in New Hampshire; and being fond of retirement, this arrangement accorded very well with my feelings. While in New Hampshire I spent many many pleasant hours, which I think of with delight. Memory oft brings to view and faithfully delineates those hours of retirement and happiness which I imagined I should spend were I an inhabitant of a cloister. While writing this narrative, I often lament my little knowledge of history; for, had I been more acquainted with it, I do not think I ever should have united myself to an institution of this nature. But to proceed: I never could prevail on my parents to say much on this subject. I kept silence, resolving in my own mind to become acquainted with some one who would introduce me to the superior of the Ursuline community, but did not ask any one till after the death of my mother. Previous to that event, I had become acquainted with Miss M. H., a domestic in Mr. H. J. K's family, near my father's house, in Charlestown. After my mother's decease, while residing with my father, my sisters being absent, Miss H. came to our house and begged me to keep her as a domestic a little while, as she had no place. She had walked a great way for the purpose of seeing Mr. K., who had moved away. This was in the fall of 1830. After consulting with my father, I concluded to let her stay. She found me in great trouble and grief, in consequence of the absence of my two younger sisters, whom I very dearly loved, and who had gone to reside with my sisters at Boston. After family prayers were over, and I was about retiring, I stepped from my room to see if Miss H. had extinguished her lamp; when, to my surprise, I found her kneeling and holding a string of beads. I asked her what she was doing. She did not speak for some time. When she did, she said she was saying her 'Hail Marys.' (*Catholic Prayer, translated from the Latin.*—' Hail Mary! full of grace; our Lord is with thee! Blessed art thou among women, and blessed is the fruit of thy womb, Jesus! Holy Mary, mother of God, pray for us, sinners, now at the hour of our death. Amen.') I asked her what the ' Hail Marys' were, at the same time taking hold of the beads. She then said, ' I say my prayers on these to the Blessed Virgin.' My friends will of course excuse my curiosity at this time, for I had never before learned their manner of praying to saints and angels. Before I left her she showed me an *Agnus Dei*, (Lamb of God; a small piece of wax sewed up in silk, in the form of a heart,) which she wore to preserve herself from the temptations of Satan. I cannot remember all the conversation which passed the next day on the subject; but I learned that she had been acquainted with the nuns at Boston, and was also acquainted with the superior. The first pleasant day, I asked her to accompany me to the superior, which she did, and appeared by her questions to know my motive. She introduced me to the superior in the following manner:—We were invited by a lay sister (those nuns who are occupied in domestic affairs) to sit; who, after retiring, in a few moments made her appearance, requesting Miss H. to see her in another room. Soon after the superior came in, and embraced me with much seeming affection, and put the following questions to me :—how long since the death of my mother ; whether I ever attended the Catholic Church, or knew any thing of the principles of their religion ; what I had heard respecting them ; of their order ; my views of it ; what progress I had made in my studies ; whether I had attended much to history ; knew anything of embroidery, drawing, or painting, or any other ornamental work ; whether I had ever assisted in domestic affairs. After which questions, taking my hand, she said, ' O, it feels more like a pancake than any thing else.' (This may appear laughable ; but as I intend to publish all which will be for the benefit of the reader, I cannot refrain from mentioning this ; in order to show the course of flattery, &c., made use of by the superior and those connected with the establishment, to draw the inexperienced into their power, and make them converts to the religion of the Pope.) She inquired in what capacity I desired to enter the institution, whether as a recluse or a scholar ; whether I had done attending school, &c. I replied, that I did not consider my education complete ; that I wished to go into the school attached to the nunnery, on the same terms as other pupils, until I had made sufficient progress to take the veil, and become a recluse ; that my father was averse to my becoming a *nun*, but I was of opinion that he would concur with my Episcopal friends in not objecting to my becoming a *pupil*. In the course of the interview, the superior conversed much upon the Scriptures, and intimated that I ought to make any sacrifice, if necessary, to adopt the religion of the cross ; repeating the words of our Saviour, ' He that loveth father or mother more than me, is not worthy of me,' &c. At a subsequent interview, the superior desired me to see the bishop or clergy, remarking, she believed I had a vocation for a religious life, and the bishop would tell me whether I had or not. She also asked if I was acquainted with a Catholic friend who would introduce me to the bishop, and mentioned a Mr. R., who would introduce me to him. I was unacquainted with Mr. R., but had seen him at my sister's house in Boston. She said that the bishop or Mr. R. would also discuss the matter with my father, and reconcile him to Catholicity. After consulting some friends who were in favour of the Catholic religion, I consented to see Mr. R., who, being requested, called at my father's, gave me some Scripture proofs of the infallibility of the Romish Church ; as, 'Thou art Peter, and upon this rock I build my church, and the gates of hell shall not prevail against it ;' and ' whose sins ye retain, they are retained, and whose sins ye remit, they are remitted.' 'He that will not hear the church, let him be to thee as an heathen man and a publican.' He (Mr. R.) desired I would secret the paper upon which the texts were quoted. He then took his leave, saying he would call to see me in town soon, at the Misses S., when he would introduce me to the bishop. I will here remark, that previous to my joining the community, I heard of many miracles wrought by Catholic priests. Mrs. G. brought a lady one day in a chaise to show me her eyes, which were restored by means of a priest, Dr. O'F. She, as Mrs. G. stated, was totally blind ; but having faith in miracles, she knelt to her confessor, requesting him to heal her. After touching her eyes with spittle and holy oil, she 'immediately received her sight.'"

We pass over a lengthened detail of preliminary circumstances, and frequent interviews with the bishop and the superior, and notice only in our way, the following description of her introduction to the Catholic Church :—

"The ordinance of baptism was administered to me by Mr. B., himself, and a Mrs. P. standing sponsors for me ; my former baptism being considered by the Catholics *invalid*. At the time of my baptism I was anointed with oil ; a piece of salt was put in my mouth, the priest breathing three times upon me, and touching my eyes, ears, and nose with spittle, speaking Latin all the while. They profess to take these ceremonies from the Scriptures. While in Charlestown, I stood sponsor for Mrs. G.'s daughter, of whom I shall speak in the course of this narrative."

Omitting again several particulars, we find Miss Reed now in the convent. Some sketches of her drawing will further confirm the nature of these secret bastiles.

"After preparing myself for a public reception, I visited the superior ; when she said, if I would place myself under her care from this time, she would protect me for ever ; and particularly from the persecution of the ' heterodox ;' and she looked to heaven above for her reward. She then stated that the bishop had concluded to receive me, not as a member of the public department, but as a ' novitiate,' which would screen me from the questions of the Protestant scholars. She also added, that I should be received as the other sisters were, and that we were to support ourselves by our talents and industry. She then desired me to kneel down and take the following obligation :—' I do, with the grace and assistance of Almighty God, renounce the world for ever, and place myself under your protection, from this day to consecrate myself to his honour and glory, in the house of God, and to do whatever obedience prescribes, and to tell no one of this obligation but Mr. B., in confession.' After this, the superior summoned two of the 'Choir Religieuse,' who conducted me to the garden, where they left me to amuse myself. Presently the superior joined me, wishing to know how I liked the garden, the flowers, &c. Observing a pocket album in my hand, she asked me what I had hoarded up there; some worldly goods? She took it, and examining it, desired to know if I wished to keep some money I had in it (fifteen dollars). I replied no; as I was going to join them, I would intrust it to her care. She also requested me to sing one tune. I complied; and sung, 'There's nothing true but Heaven.' Her observation was, she would wish me to commence immediately with music. I then left the convent, and attended the sacraments of Confession and Communion : and on Sabbath morning, August 7th, 1831, I was attended to the gate of the convent by my friend, Mrs. G. I was shown into the public parlour by the lay sister, and was requested to kneel and continue my devotion until the superior made her appearance. She soon came, and made a sign for me to follow her. She led the way into a long room, darkened, at one end of which stood a large crucifix, made of bone, which I was afterwards informed was made of the bones of saints. The superior told me, in a whisper, it was the time of silence; but, after arranging my dress, she took from her toilet a religious garb, which she placed upon my head, and bade me kiss it, saying it had been blessed by the bishop. She then pronounced a short Latin prayer, while I was kneeling, at the same time giving me her blessing."

We have now a long account of the foolish mummeries called Catholic Devotion, to which Miss Reed had to attend. After which she says—

"I shall now continue my narrative of the remainder of the first day. The evening bell for the Latin office now rang, and we now assembled at the choir, where we performed such ceremonies as I before named, until time of retiring. Next morning being holy day morning, the bell rang at three, instead of four, as it usually does, for meditation in the choir. After Litany, the bell rang for diet in the refectory, every morning, except Friday; on which day we assembled for confession to the superior. The manner of confession to the superior is as follows: the room is first darkened, and one lighted wax taper placed upon the superior's throne; and she is considered as filling the place or station of the Blessed Virgin. After taking their places in the greatest order and silence, the Religieuse responds. Then the lecturess reads from a book called Rules for the Ursuline Order, by Saint Ursula, about complaining of the cold, our clothing, food, &c. &c. They sit on their feet during the reading, a posture *extremely painful*. The reading finished, the superior whispers to the Sisters to approach her separately, which they do; each one in her turn approaches, and repeats the following: 'Our Mother, we acknowledge that we have been guilty of breaking the rules of our *Holy Order*, by lifting our eyes while walking in the passage-ways; in neglecting to take holy water on entering the community and choir; failing in respect to our superior, and veneration to our Father; failing in religious decorum, and in respect to our vows—poverty and obedience; for which we most humbly ask pardon of God, penance and forgiveness of you, our Holy Mother.' As each one finishes, the 'Holy Mother' gives her advice and penances, and her blessing; they then kiss her feet, and sometimes make the cross with their tongues on the floor; then making their inclination, they retire to the choir to perform the penances. This ceremony is very solemn. It is performed until eight o'clock A.M., when we receive our portions, sitting on the floor. Our diet consisted of the plainest kind of food, principally vegetables and vegetable soups, Indian puddings, and, very seldom, meat. Our tea was made of herbs, sometimes of the bitterest kind. We partook of this diet in imitation of the Holy Fathers of the Desert, to mortify our appetites. Pumpkins, stewed with molasses and water, served us sometimes as a dessert. Occasionally we had mouldy bread to eat. A very insignificant piece of butter was sometimes placed on our plates. The superior's diet was far better than ours; sometimes it was sumptuous, wine not excepted. I ascertained this, as I, occasionally, in turn, went round to gather the fragments. She sent me, on two occasions, some apple parings to eat, as a part of my portion. Sometimes the Religieuse deny themselves any diet; prostrate, kiss the feet of those who remain at table, performing various kinds of penance, while the others are eating and listening to the reading. Those who have permission to deny themselves in the morning, take their work-baskets as they pass to the refectory; where they sew by candle-light, as the lecturess is reading. This has a solemn and impressive appearance. * * * * Soon after I became an inmate of the convent, the bishop came into the community and said, 'How does that little nun? and what have you done with sister Stimson?' The superior answered that she was not fit for the order, and she had sent her on to the Sisters of Charity. He then, addressing me, asked how I liked Mount Benedict. I said, 'Very well, my lord.' He then said, 'O, but you will have to strive with the temptations between the good and evil spirits;' and he then explained all the horrors of Satan, and asked me where Saint Teresa, my namesake, was, and if I had read her life; and told me to say, as she did, these words :—' Now come, all of you; I, being a true servant of God, will see what you can do against me;' by way of challenge to the evil ones, and beg her intercession. He told me my sister had been to see if I had taken the veil, or had any thought of taking it; and he said I might rest contented, as my friends would trouble me no more. He then told me the difference between a holy life and a worldly life;

said the devil would assail me as he did Saint Teresa, and make me think I ought to go back to the world, and make me offers of worldly pleasures, and promise me happiness. In order to prevent this, I must watch and pray all the time, and banish entirely worldly thoughts from my mind, and throw holy water at the evil spirits, and challenge them to come if they dare. Perceiving the unpleasant effect this had on my feelings, he portrayed in lively colours the happiness which would flow from my resisting the evil spirits, and what a crown of glory would be placed on my head by the angels. According to my confessor's orders, I took upon myself many austere penances, &c.; but the superior, noticing my exhaustion from this cause, released me from my austerities for a time, saying, I was a favoured one; and she gave me permission to rest while the others rose to say *midnight matins*, and hear Mass. On the exaltation of the holy cross, the bishop gave us his blessing, we all kneeling in the community. In conversation with the sisters, he remarked one had not a very pleasant countenance; and he asked me how I was pleased with my teacher, saying, he hoped she put a more pleasant countenance on while instructing me. Soon preparations were made for my taking the vows of a Religieuse, a Novena (nine days' devotion) being said for me, and for my perfection in religious life, and prayers for the conversion of my friends. About this time my sponsor, the priest, visited the convent, and talked, as I then thought, like a godlike person. My reception was to take place privately, because we wished to keep my father ignorant of the manner in which I had been received; and because he might hear of it, should it take place publicly; as he before said I was not eighteen, and he could prevent my going there. They said he could not prevent me, as I was now of age. I was perfectly happy at this time, and presented the superior with some lines of poetry, which gave her proof of my sincerity and contentment. She appeared very much pleased with the verses, embraced me very affectionately, and expressed her hearty approbation of my perseverance in performing the duties of the order, and said the request for her entreaties that I might persevere in a religious life should be granted, and she would show the lines to the bishop. She accordingly did so, when he was present one day, and he said he must write my conversion, for it was so much like St. Teresa's, my namesake. After this she gave orders to have all my worldly dresses, being ten in number, and other articles of wearing apparel, altered for those young ladies whom she clothed and educated; and for me she ordered a long habit to be prepared, which was to be blessed by the bishop; also a veil, which they said denoted purity and innocence.   *   *   *

I told Mary Francis if she did not explain to me the cause of her grief I should certainly tell the superior; for I could receive no benefit from her instructions while she was so confused, and the superior had reprimanded me for not learning my lessons; and I promised if she would tell me I would not inform the superior. She replied, that she could not answer me *then*, but would think of it, and give me an answer in the afternoon. Accordingly, in the afternoon, a Religieuse being present, watching us, she communicated what I desired to know by writing on a slate, and desired to know if I was happy. I answered, that I did not like the superior so well as formerly. She then wrote, that while at prayer and meditation she concluded it was her duty, particularly as I was dissatisfied, to give me some advice, and considered her promise before made as not binding; and receiving from me a promise of secrecy, she proceeded to say that she hoped she should be pardoned if any thing wrong was said by her, as my whole happiness depended on the words she should communicate. 'I am,' she said, 'kept here by the superior, through selfish motives, as a teacher, under a slavish fear, and against my will. I have written several letters to my father, and have received no satisfactory answer; and I have for a long time felt dissatisfied with my situation. The superior has failed in fulfilling her promise, not complying with the conditions on which I was received; which were, that as she was in need of a teacher, particularly in French and music, I might take the white veil, and leave whenever I chose; and my taking the veil, 'as it was only a custom,' should not compel me; and that my obligations should not be binding. My father thinks I can leave at any time, for I do not believe he has received my letters, and that letter you have heard read as Miss L.'s is a forged one.' At my lesson in the afternoon I again conversed with Mary Francis concerning the letter, and requested her to inform me how my happiness was concerned. She said still that the letter read to the community was a forged one; that Mrs. I. was her aunt and sincere friend; and did her father know her sufferings, and the treatment she received from the superior, he would prosecute her; that she feared the superior as she did a serpent. She then advised me not to bind myself, after my three months' 'test or trial,' to *that* order, by complying with the rules of 'reception,' any farther than would leave me at liberty to go to another if I chose; and I must not think, because they were wicked, that the inmates of all convents were so. I assured her that although I had thought there were none good but Catholics, I now believed there were good and bad among all sects. I related to her then, and during the next afternoon, all the particulars. She appeared very much surprised to learn that my friends had been opposed to my coming, as the superior had told her that they had put me there for life. She said she had been taken from the public apartment, because she had been seen weeping by the young ladies, that should the superior refuse to let her go, she should, if possible, make her escape; and named a Religieuse (Miss Mary Angela) who had made her escape before. She desired me, if she should be so fortunate as to make her escape, to ask, in private confession, permission to see my friends, and consult them about going to the 'Sisters of Charity;' and if they were willing that I should go, she would procure me a situation, and by letter inform me of it. She was in great distress on account of *that* letter, which plainly unfolded the motives of the superior."

POOR SISTER MARY MAGDALENE.

What think your readers of Convent kindness after the following which Miss Reed gives us.—" I must again speak of the sufferings of Mary Magdalene. One day she came from the refectory, and being so much exhausted as to be hardly able to ascend the stairs, I offered to assist her. The Superior reprimanded me for it ; saying, her weakness was feigned, and my pity was false pity. She said to sister Magdalene in a tone of displeasure, if she did not make herself of use to the 'Community,' she would send her back to Ireland; on which sister Mary Magdalene rose and said ' Mamere, I would like ———.' The Superior cut short what she was going to say by stamping upon the floor; and demanding who gave her permission to speak, imposed on her the penance of kissing the floor. The Superior, after this, imposed hardships which she was hardly able to sustain, frequently reminding her that she had but a short time to work out her salvation, and that she must do better if she did not wish to suffer in purgatory. The Superior questioned me about my feelings—wished to know why I looked so solemn. I told her I was ill from want of exercise, that I was not accustomed to their mode of living, &c. She said I must mention it to my confessor, which I did. The next time the bishop visited us, he was in unusually high spirits, and very sociable ; and he related several stories, which are not worthy of notice in this place. He again asked sister Magdalene when she thought of going to that happy place to receive her crown of glory. She replied, ' Before the celebration of our divine Redeemer's birth, my lord.' He said she ought to be very thankful that she was called so soon. When I was summoned to the Superior, she enquired, as usual, into the state of my feelings; and when I said I desired to see my friends, she replied, 'Why, my dear Agnes, do you wish to see worldly friends? Whom do you call your friends? Am not I your friend? Is not the bishop your friend? If your worldly friends wished to see you, would they not come and see you?' I replied, 'Yes.' A few days after this I was taken very ill, and went to the infirmary. Miss Mary Magdalene and myself were closely watched. I then asked the Superior's permission to write to my friends, and desire them to come and see me, which she granted ; and also told me to write whatever I pleased. I began to be much dissatisfied with this convent. Not long after this, at private confession, I was questioned very particularly in regard to my views of remaining there for life. I told my confessor that I was convinced that order was too austere for me, and immediately burst into tears. He endeavoured to comfort me by saying I was not bound to that order for life; I could go to another order. I asked him if I might see my friends, He answered, 'Yes.' After receiving a promise from him that I should go to any other order I chose, I consented to take the vows. He gave me to understand that I need take no other vows than I should at the convent of the Sisters of Charity. My reception took place the next day. I refused the white veil because the Sisters of Charity did not wear it, and it was omitted. The choir was first darkened, and then lighted with wax tapers. The ceremony commenced with chaunts, prayers, responses, &c. A book was placed in my hands, which contained the vows I was to take. As near as I can recollect the following is the substance of them :—' O Almighty and everlasting God, permit me, a worm of the dust, to consecrate myself more strictly to thee this day, in presence of thy most holy mother and saint Ursula, and all of thy saints and martyrs, by living two years a recluse, and by instructing young ladies after the manner of saint Ursula, and by taking upon myself her most holy vows of poverty, chastity, and obedience, which, with thy grace and assistance I will fulfil.' They all responded 'Amen,' and repeated a long office in Latin. I still continued to wear the black garb, which the bishop blessed ; also a long habit and a string of rosary beads, which were also blessed by the bishop. He wished to know one day how Miss Mary Agnes did, after taking the white vows; to which the Superior replied, 'Very well.' As time passed on the Superior became more severe in her treatment, because I objected to pursue my music. My mind had been in such an unhappy state, that I for a long time found it impossible to study ; and, further, I did not wish to receive instruction, for I had determined not to stay there. I therefore succeeded in obtaining the Superior's permission to occupy my time chiefly with the needle, and assured her that I would again study when I felt better. On one of the holy days the bishop came in, and, after playing upon his flute, addressed the Superior, styling her Mademoiselle, and wished to know if Mary Magdalene wanted to go to her long home. The Superior beckoned her to come to them, and she approached on her knees. The bishop asked her if she felt prepared to die. She replied, 'Yes, my lord; but, with the permission of our mother, I have one request to make.' They told her to say on. She said she wished to be anointed before death, if his lordship thought her worthy of so great a favour. He said, 'Before I grant your request I have one to make; that is, that you will implore the Almighty to send down from heaven a bushel of gold, for the purpose of establishing a college for young men on Bunker Hill.' He said he had bought the land for that use, and that all the sisters who had died had promised to present his request, but had not fulfilled their obligations; and,' says he, 'you must shake hands in heaven with all the sisters who have gone, and be sure and ask them why they have not fulfilled their promise, for I have waited long enough; and continue to chaunt your office with us while here on earth, which is the sweet communion of saints.' After she had given her pledge, and kissed his feet, he told the several members of the community to think of what they should like best. I was first called to make my request. I had never seen anything of this kind before, and my feelings were such as I cannot describe; and continuing silent, the Superior bade me name it. I then said I lacked humility, and should wish for that virtue. The Religieuse then made their requests: one asked for grace to fulfil the vow of poverty; another, for obedience; a third, more fervent love for the mother of God; a fourth, more devotion to her patron saint; a fifth, more devotion in approaching the altar and host; and so on. The Superior ended it by making the same request as the bishop, adding, the purpose intended was, that the gospel of our Lord and Saviour might be more extensively propagated, and that all Dissenters might be made to turn to the true church and believe. The conversation then turned upon the Pope, and the bishop said the Pope would, perhaps, before long, visit this country; and when things were more improved, and his new church finished, he should write to the Pope. Not long after this, Mary Magdalene was anointed for death, and took her vows for life, but she continued to wear the white veil. She lived rather longer than was expected, but her penances were not remitted. She would frequently kneel and prostrate all night long in the cold infirmary, saying her rosary, and other penances. She wore next her heart a metallic plate, in imitation of a crown of thorns, from which I was given to understand she suffered a sort of martyrdom. This I often saw her kiss and lay on the altar of the crucifix as she retired. Another penance was, the reclining upon a mattress more like a table than a bed. The next day, it being my turn to see that all the vessels which contained holy water were filled, &c., I had an opportunity of looking at Mary Magdalene. Her eyes were partly open, and her face very purple; she lay pretty still. I did not dare to speak to her, supposing she would think it a duty to tell of it, as it would be an infraction of the rules. The next night I lay thinking of her, when I was suddenly startled, hearing a rattling noise, as I thought, in her throat. Very soon sister Martha (the sick lay nun) arose, and coming to her said, 'Jesus! Mary! Joseph! receive her soul;' and rang the bell three times. The spirit of the gentle Magdalene had departed. The Superior came, bringing a lighted wax taper, which she placed in the hand of the deceased. She closed the eyes, and placed the crucifix on the breast. Sister Martha had whispered us to rise, and the Superior, observing my agitation, said, 'Be calm, and join with us in prayer: she is a happy soul.' 'I knelt accordingly, repeating the litany, until the clock struck two, when we all assembled in the choir, in which was a fire and wax tapers burning. After meditation, matins, lauds, and prayers, and a Novena (a particular supplication) that our requests might be granted, we assembled for diet, and, for the first time, we had some toasted bread. We also had recreation granted in the time of silence. The Superior sent for us, and instructed us how to appear at the burial of our sister Mary Magdalene, and accompanied us to view her corpse. She was laid out in the habit of a professed nun, in a black veil; her hands were tied together, and her vows placed in them. The Superior remarked that this was done by the bishop's request. At the evening recreation the bishop appeared in high spirits, and rejoiced that so happy a soul had at last arrived in heaven; and commenced the 'Dies illæ,' on the piano forte, accompanied by the voices of the others. He told me I should have Miss Mary Magdalene for my intercessor, for she was to be canonised. The Mother-Superior permitted me to embrace the sisters, and gave me the mother-assistant for my mother. She then presented us with the relics of saints, that by their means we might gain indulgences. She mentioned a 'retreat' as being necessary for our perseverance in a religious life. The second day after this the coffin was placed in the choir, and the funeral services were performed in the following manner: Dr. O'Flaherty sang the office, while the bishop chanted it. Father Taylor officiated at the altar. Four or five of the altar-boys were present, and dressed in their altar robes, &c.; two of them held wax tapers, a third holy water, a fourth a crucifix. One swung incense in the censer over the corpse, and another at the same time sprinkled holy water upon it. We performed our part by saying the 'Dies illæ.' The coffin was then carried to the tomb by two Irishmen. [My feelings were much hurt to witness the manner in which the lid of the coffin was forced down to its place. The corpse had swollen much, and become too large for the coffin.] The bishop, priests, and others followed, singing, and carrying lighted tapers and a large crucifix. The corpse was also followed by some of the young ladies from the public schools, while the Religieuse remained in the convent. After depositing the coffin in the tomb the clergy retired to dinner. I had until this time kept the secret of my friend Mary Francis; but the bishop perceiving that I grew more discontented, endeavoured to comfort me, by saying that I was not bound to that order; but he wished to know more particularly my reasons for disliking it, and began to threaten me with judgments; and observing my agitation, said he must know what lay so heavily on my mind. He asked me if it was anything connected with the sickness and death of Mary Magdalene. I told him "No, not that in particular; I do not like the Superior.' He said I must tell him instantly all the wicked thoughts that had disturbed my mind, and asked me various improper questions, the meaning of which I did not then understand, and which I decline mentioning. I was so confused that I inadvertently spoke Mary Francis' name, and begged his pardon for listening to her; and he immediately exclaimed, 'Ah! I know all; confess to me what she told you, and do not dare to deceive me; you cannot deceive God. I told him nearly all that had passed between Mary Francis and myself."

What horrible hypocrisy, cruelty, and infernal deceit these poor nuns are exposed to! Read the following:—

"One day as I was sitting alone in the refectory, in the time of silence, the superior came in, and after kneeling and extending her arms in the form of a cross, she kissed the floor, and rising, walked towards the door; returning, she seated herself on the bench beside me. I asked her if I should bring a chair; she answered 'No,' and inquired how I felt, and why I changed colour while at the table. I replied that my mouth was very sore, and that it hurt me to read. She wished to know what made my mouth sore. I told her I thought it was something I had eaten. She said, *laughingly*, it was the canker, and asked if it was not sent as a judgment for some sin. I replied I did not know; I had not felt very well for some days, and thought it was partly owing to the want of exercise. She then sent sister Martha to conduct me into a room at the farther part of the convent, for the first time called a "*mangle room.*" There were some sisters there kneeling in devotion, and one turning a machine used for pressing clothes, instead of ironing them, called a *mangle*. She presented me with some altar laces, and told me to have them prepared for the altar the next day at the ringing of the bell. While there I was watched very narrowly; but as I had gathered from the superior's conversation, at different times, that the gates were watched by the porters and dogs, which were of great value to the convent, I did not dare, then, to make my escape, but appeared as cheerful as possible.   *   *   *   *
One day I went to the chapel, and was arranging things for Mass, which was to take place the next day. While busily employed, I heard the adjoining door open, and the Bishop's voice distinctly. I kept as still as possible, lest I should be discovered. While in this room I overheard the following conversation between the Bishop and the Superior:—The Bishop, after taking snuff in his usual manner, began by saying, 'Well, well, what does Agnes say? how does she appear?' I heard distinctly from the Superior in reply, that 'According to all appearances, she is either possessed of insensibility or great command.' The Bishop walked about the room, seeming much displeased with the Superior, and cast many severe and improper reflections upon Mary Francis, who, it was known, had influenced me; all which his lordship will well remember. He then told the Superior that the establishment was in its infancy, and that it would not do to have such reports go abroad as these persons would carry; that Agnes must be taken care of; that they had better send her to Canada, and that a carriage would cross the line in two or three days. He added, by way of repetition, that it would not do for the Protestants to get hold of those things, and make another 'fuss.' He then gave the Superior instructions how to entice me into the carriage, and they soon both left the room, and I heard no more. The reader may well judge of my feelings at this moment; a young and inexperienced female, shut out from the world,

and entirely beyond the reach of friends, threatened with speedy transportation to another country, and involuntary confinement for life, with no power to resist the immediate fulfilment of the startling conspiracy I had overheard. It was with much difficulty that I controlled my feelings; but aware of the importance of not betraying any knowledge of what had taken place, I succeeded in returning to the refectory unsuspected. I now became firmly impressed, that unless I could contrive to break away from the convent soon, it would be for ever too late; and that every day I remained, rendered my escape more difficult. What I have now to relate is of importance. A few days after, while at my needle in the refectory, I heard a carriage drive to the door of the convent, and heard a person step into the Superior's room. Immediately the Superior passed lightly along the passage which led to the back entry, where the men-servants or porters were employed, and reprimanded them in a loud tone for something they were doing. She then opened the door of the refectory, and seemed indifferent about entering, but at length seated herself beside me, and began conversation, by saying, 'Well, my dear girl, what do you think of going to see your friends?' I said, 'What friends, Mamere?' Said she, 'You would like to see your friends Mrs. G., and father B., and talk with them respecting your call to another order.' Before I had time to answer, she commenced taking off my garb, telling me she was in haste, and that a carriage was in waiting to convey me to my friends. I answered, with as cheerful a countenance as I could assume, 'O Mamere, I am sorry to give you so much trouble; I had rather see them here first.' While we were conversing, I heard a little bell ring several times. The Superior said, 'Well, my dear, make up your mind; the bell calls me to the parlour.' She soon returned, and asked, if I had made up my mind to go. I answered, 'No, Mamere.' She then said, I had failed in obedience to her; and as I had so often talked of going to another order, with such a person as Mary Francis, I had better go immediately: and again she said, raising her voice, 'You have failed in respect to your Superior; you must recollect that I am a lady of *quality*, brought up in opulence, and accustomed to all the luxuries of life.' I told her that I was very sorry to have listened to any thing wrong against her dignity. She commanded me to kneel, which I did; and if ever tears were a relief to me they were then. She stamped upon the floor violently, and asked, if I was innocent, why I did not go to communion. I told her I felt unworthy to go to communion at that time. The bell again rang, and she left the room; and in a few moments returning, desired me to tell her immediately what I thought of doing; for as she had promised to protect me for ever, she must know my mind. She then mentioned that the carriage was still in waiting. I still declined going, for I was convinced their object was not to carry me to Mrs. G. and Priest B., to consult about another order, but directly to Canada."

MISS REED'S ESCAPE.

"Some days after the conversation which I heard between the bishop and superior while behind the altar, I was in the refectory, at my work, and heard the noise of the porters, who were employed sawing wood, and I conjectured the gate might be open for them. I thought it a good opportunity to escape, which I contemplated doing in this manner, viz.: to ask permission to leave the room, and as I passed the entry, to secrete about my habit a hood which hung there, that would help to conceal part of my garb from particular observation; then to feign an errand to the infirmarian from the superior, as I imagined I could escape by the door of the infirmary. This plan formed, and just as I was going, I heard a band of music, playing, as it seemed, in front of the convent. I heard the young ladies assembling in the parlour, and the porters left their work, as I supposed, for the noise of the saws ceased. I felt quite revived, and was more confident I should be able to escape without detection, even should it be necessary to get over the fence. I feigned an errand, and asked permission of Miss Mary Austine to leave the room, which she granted. I succeeding in secreting the hood, and the book in which Miss Mary Francis had left her address, and then knocked at the door three times which led to the lay aparments. A person came to the door, who appeared in great distress. I asked her where sister Bennet and sister Bernard were; she left me to find them. I gave the infirmarian to understand that the superior wished to see her, and I desired her to go immediately to her room. These gone, I unlocked and passed out at the back door, and as the gate appeared shut, I climbed upon the *slats* which confined the grape vines to the fence; but they gave way, and falling to the ground, I sprained my wrist. I then thought I would try the gate, which I found was fastened, and as there was no one near it, I ran through, and hurried to the nearest house. In getting over the fences between the convent and this house, I fell and hurt myself badly. On reaching the house, I fell exhausted upon the door step; but rising as soon as possible, I opened the door, and was allowed to enter. I inquired if Catholics lived there: one answered 'No.' For some time I could answer none of their questions, being so much exhausted. As soon as they understood that I requested protection, they afforded me every assistance in their power. I had only been a few moments there, when I heard an alarm-bell ringing at the convent. On looking out of the window, we saw two of the porters searching in the canal with long poles. After searching some time they returned to the convent, and I saw their dogs scenting my course. While at that house I looked in a glass, and was surprised, nay, frightened, at my own figure; it was so *pale* and *emaciated*. Notwithstanding my wrist being sprained, I wrote a few lines to Mrs. G., whom I still supposed my friend, begging her to come to my relief, for I did not wish my father and sisters to see me in my present condition. I thanked God that he had inclined his ear unto me, and delivered me out of the hands of the wicked. But here was not an end of my afflictions. Mrs. G. came in the evening to convey me to her house. She would not allow me to say any thing about my escape at Mr. K's, and wished me to return to the convent that night. I resolved not to go. After whispering a long time to me about the importance of secrecy, she left Mr. K's, as we supposed, for home; but she soon returned, saying she at first intended to leave me at Mr. K's, but had concluded to take me home with her, as she desired some further conversation. Her manners appeared very strange, yet I did not distrust her friendship. Before leaving Mr. K's, she requested me to obtain from them a promise not to say any thing about my escape, which I did. After I arrived at Mrs. G's, I showed her my wounds, and my feet, which had been frozen, and told her I did not find the convent what I had expected. She seemed to sympathize with me, and to do all in her power for my recovery. She did not urge me to say much, as I was quite weak. The next morning, the convent boy on horseback came galloping up to the house, and delivered to Mrs. G. a letter from the superior, and was very particular, as he said he had orders not to give it to any one except to her. She refused to tell me its contents, and sent directly for a chaise, to go to the convent. When Mrs. G. returned from the convent, she said the superior had too exalted an opinion of me to think I would say any thing against the institution, and she had sent me a present, as she still considered me one of her flock; and if I had gone astray, she should do every thing she could for me, in a temporal as well as in a spiritual sense, if I would repent. My words were just these: 'I cannot receive any present from the superior; she is a wicked woman, and I do not believe her friendship pure.'"

After detailing much opposition which befel her, Miss Reed thus concludes her affecting narrative of which we have given but small portions.

"If, in consequence of my having for a time strayed from the *true religion*, I am enabled to become an humble instrument in the hands of God in warning others of the errors of Romanism, and preventing even *one* from falling into its *snares*, and from being *shrouded* in its delusions, I shall feel richly rewarded."

CHAPTER XVII.

Disappearance of Nuns—St. Pierre—Gags—My temporary confinement in a Cell—The Cholera Season—How to avoid it—Occupations in the Convent during the Pestilence—Manufacture of Wax Candles—The Election Riots—Alarm among the Nuns—Preparations for Defence—Penances.

I AM unable to say how many nuns disappeared while I was in the Convent. There were several. One was a young lady called St. Pierre, I think, but am not certain of her name. There were two nuns by this name. I had known her as a novice with me. She had been a novice about two years and a half before I became one. She was rather large without being tall, and had rather dark hair and eyes. She disappeared unaccountably, and nothing was said of her except what I heard in whispers from a few of the nuns, as we found moments when we could speak unobserved.

Some told me they thought she must have left the Convent; and I might have supposed so, had I not some time afterward found some of her things lying about, which she would, in such a case, doubtless have taken with her. I had never konwn any thing more of her than what I could observe or conjecture. I had always, however, the idea that her parents or friends were wealthy, for she sometimes received clothes, and other things, which were very rich.

Another nun named St. Paul, died suddenly; but as in other cases, we knew so little, or rather were so entirely ignorant of the cause and circumstances, that we could only conjecture; and being forbidden to speak freely on that or any other subject, thought little about it. I have mentioned that a number of veiled nuns thus mysteriously disappeared during my residence amongst them. I cannot, perhaps, recall them all, but I am confident there were as many as five, and I think more. All that we knew in such cases was, that one of our number who appeared as usual when last observed, was no where to be seen, and never again.— Mad Jane Ray, on several occasions, would indulge in her bold, and, as we thought, dangerous remarks. She had intimated that some of those, who had been for a time in the Convent, were by some means removed to make room for new ones; and it was generally the fact, that the disappearance of one and the introduction of another into our community, were nearly at the same time. I have repeatedly heard Jane Ray say, with one of her significant looks, " When you appear, somebody else disappears !"

It is unpleasant enough to distress or torture one's self: but there is something worse in being tormented by others, especially where they resort to force, and show a pleasure in compelling you, and leave you no hope to escape, no opportunity to resist. I had seen the gags repeatedly in use, and sometimes applied with a roughness which seemed rather inhuman; but it is one thing to see, and another thing to feel. They were ready to recommend a resort to compulsory measures, and ready to run for the gags. These were kept in one of the community rooms, in a drawer between two closets; and there a stock of about fifty of them was always kept in deposit. Sometimes a number of nuns would prove refractory at a time; and I have seen battles commenced, in which several appeared on both sides. The disobedient were, however, soon overpowered; and to prevent their screams from being heard beyond the walls, gagging commenced immediately. I have seen half a dozen lying gagged and bound at once. I have been subjected to the same state of involuntary silence more than once; for sometimes I became excited to a state of desperation, by the measures used against me, and then conducted in a manner perhaps not less violent than some others. My hands had been tied behind me, and a gag put into my mouth, sometimes with such force and rudeness, as to separate my lips, and cause the blood to flow freely.

Treatment of this kind is apt to teach submission, and many times I have acquiesced under orders received, or wishes expressed, with a fear of recurrence to some severe measures.

One day I had incurred the anger of the Superior in a greater degree than usual, and it was ordered that I should be taken to one of the cells. I was taken by some of the nuns, bound and gagged, carried down the stairs into the cellar, and laid upon the floor. Not long afterward I induced one of the nuns to request the Superior to come down and see me; and on making some acknowledgement, I was released. I will, however, relate this story rather more in detail.

On that day I had been engaged with Jane Ray, in carrying into effect a plan of revenge upon another person, when I fell under the vindictive spirit of some of the old nuns, and suffered severely. The Superior ordered me to the cells, and a scene of violence commenced which I will not attempt to describe, nor the precise circumstances which lead to it. Suffice it to say, that after I had exhausted all my strength, by resisting as long as I could against several nuns, I had my hands drawn behind my back, a leathern band passed first round my thumbs, then round my hands, and then round my waist, and fastened. This was drawn so tight that it cut through the flesh of my thumbs, making wounds, the scars of which still remain. A gag was then forced into my mouth, not indeed so violently as it sometimes was, but roughly enough; after which I was taken by main force, and carried down into the cellar, across it almost to the opposite extremity, and brought to the last of the second range of cells on the left hand. The door was opened, and I was thrown in with violence, and left alone, the door being immediately closed and bolted on the outside. The bare ground was under me, cold and as hard as if it had been beaten down even. I lay still in the position in which I had fallen, as it would have been difficult for me to move, confined as I was, and exhausted by my exertions; and the shock of my fall, and my wretched state of desperation and fear, disinclined me from any further attempt. I was in almost total darkness, there being nothing perceptible except a slight glimmer of light which came in through the little window far above me.

How long I remained in that condition I can only conjecture. It seemed to me a long time, and must have been two or three hours. I did not move, expecting to die there, and in a state of distress which I cannot describe, from the tight bandage about my hands and the gag holding my jaws apart at their greatest extension. I am confident I must have died before morning, if, as I then expected, I had been left there all night. By-and-by, however, the bolt was drawn, the door opened, and Jane Ray spoke to me in a tone of kindness.

She had taken an opportunity to slip into the cellar, unnoticed, on purpose so see me. She unbound the gag, took it out of my mouth, and told me she would do any thing to get me out of that dungeon. If she had had the bringing of me down, she would not have thrust me so brutally, and she would be resented on those who had. She offered to throw herself on her knees before the Superior, and beg her forgiveness. To this I would not consent; but told her to ask the Superior to come to me as I wished to speak to her. This I had no idea that she would condescend to do; but Jane had not been long gone before the Superior came, and asked if I repented in the sight of God for what I had done. I replied in the affirmative; and after a lecture of some length on the pain I had given the Virgin Mary by my conduct, she asked whether I was willing to ask pardon of all the nuns for the scandal I had caused them by my behaviour. To this I made no objection; and I was then released from my prison and my bonds, went up to the community-room, and kneeling before all the sisters in succession, begged the forgiveness and prayers of each.

Among the marks which I still bear of the wounds received from penances and violence, are the scars left by the belt with which I repeatedly tortured myself, for the mortification of my spirit. These are most distinct on my side; for although the band, which was four or five inches in breadth, and extended round the waist, was stuck full of sharp iron points in all parts, it was sometimes crowded most against my side, by resting in my chair, and then the wounds were usually deeper there than anywhere else.

My thumbs were several times cut severely by the tight drawing of the band used to confine my arms; and scars are still visible upon them.

The rough gagging which I several times endured, wounded my lips very much; for it was common, in that operation, to thrust the gag hard against the teeth, and catch one or both the lips, which were sometimes cruelly cut. The object was to stop the screams made by the offender as soon as possible; and some of the old nuns delighted in tormenting us. A gag was once forced into my mouth which had a large splinter upon it; and this cut through my under lip, in front, leaving to this day a scar about half an inch long. The same lip was several times wounded as well as the other; but one day worse than ever, when a narrow piece was cut from off the left side of it, by being pinched between the gag and the under fore-teeth: and this has left an inequality in it which is still very observable.

One of the most shocking stories I heard, of events that had occurred in the nunnery before my acquaintance with it, was the following, which was told me by Jane Ray. What is uncommon, I can fix the date when I heard it. It was on New Year's day, 1834. The ceremonies, customary in the early part of that day, had been performed after mass in the morning, the Superior had shaken hands with all the nuns, and given us her blessing, for she was said to receive power from heaven to do so only once a year, and then on the first day of the year. Besides this, cakes, raisins, &c., are distributed to the nuns on that day.

While in the community-room, I had taken a seat just within the cupboard door, where I often found a partial shelter from observation with Jane, when a conversation incidently began between us. Our practice often was, to take places there besides one of the old nuns, awaiting the time when she should go away for a little while, and leave us partially screened from the observation of others. On that occasion, Jane and I were left for a time alone; when, after some discourse on suicide, she remarked that three nuns once killed themselves in the Convent. This happened, she said, not long after her reception, and I knew, therefore, that it was several years before, for she had been received a considerable time before I became a novice. Three young ladies, she informed me, took the veil together, or very near the same time, I am not certain which. I know they have four robes in the Convent, to be worn during the ceremony of taking the veil; but I have never seen more than one of them used at a time.

Two of the nuns were sisters, and the other their cousin. They had been received but a few days, when information was given one morning that they had been found dead in their beds, amid a profusion of blood. Jane Ray said she saw their corpses, and that they appeared to have killed themselves by opening veins in their arms with a knife they had obtained, and all had bled to death together. What was extraordinary, Jane Ray added, that she had heard no noise, and that she believed nobody had suspected that any thing was wrong during the night. St.

Hypolite, however, had stated, that she found them in the morning, after the other nuns had gone to prayer, lying lifeless in their beds.

For some reason or other, their death was not made public; but their bodies, instead of being exhibited in full dress in the chapel, and afterward interred with solemnity beneath it, were taken unceremoniously into the cellar, and thrown into the hole I have so often mentioned.

There were a few instances, and only a few, in which we knew any thing that was happening in the world; and even then our knowledge did not extend out of the city. I can recall but three occasions of this kind. Two of them were when the cholera prevailed in Montreal; and the other was the election riots. The appearance of the cholera, in both seasons of its ravages, gave us abundance of occupation. Indeed, we were borne down more by hard labour at those times than ever before or afterward during my stay. The Pope had given early notice that the burning of wax candles would afford protection from the disease, because so long as any person continued to burn one, the Virgin Mary would intercede for him. No sooner, therefore, had the alarming disease made its appearance in Montreal, than a long wax candle was lighted in the Convent for each of the inmates, so that all parts of it in use were artificially illuminated day and night. Thus a great many candles were constantly burning, which were to be replaced from those manufactured by the nuns. But this was a trifle. The Pope's message having been promulgated in the Grey Nunnery, the Congregational Nunnery, and to Catholics at large through the pulpits, an extraordinary demand was created for wax candles, to supply which we were principally depended upon. All who could be employed in making them were therefore set at work, and I, among the rest, assisted in different departments, and witnessed all.

Numbers of the nuns had long been familiar with the business; for a very considerable amount of wax had been annually manufactured in the Convent; but now the works were much extended, and other occupations in a great degree laid aside. Large quantities of wax were received in the building, which was said to have been imported from England; kettles were placed in some of the working-rooms, in which it was clarified by heat over coal fires, and, when prepared, the process of dipping commenced. The wicks, which were quite long, were placed hanging upon a reel, taken up and dipped in succession, until, after many slow revolutions of the reel, the candles were of the proper size. They were then taken to a part of the room where tables were prepared for rolling them smooth. This is done by passing a roller over them, until they become even and polished, after which they are laid by for sale. These processes caused a constant bustle in several of the rooms; and the melancholy reports from without, of the ravages of the cholera, with the uncertainty of what might be the result with us, notwithstanding the promised intercession of the Virgin; and the brilliant lights constantly burning in such numbers around us, impressed the scenes I used to witness very deeply on my mind. I had very little doubt, myself, of the strict truth of the story we had heard about the security conferred upon those who burnt candles, and yet I sometimes had serious fears arise in my mind. These thoughts, however, I did my utmost to regard as great sins, and evidence of my own want of faith.

It was during that period that I formed a partial acquaintance with several Grey Nuns, who used to come frequently for supplies of candles for their Convent. I had no opportunity to converse with them, except so far as the purchase and sale of the articles they required. I became familiar with their countenances and appearances, but was unable to judge of their characters or feelings. Concerning the rules and habits prevailing in the Grey Nunnery, I therefore remained as ignorant as if I had been a thousand miles off; and they had no better opportunity to learn any thing of us beyond what they could see around them in the room where the candles were sold.

We supplied the Congregational Nunnery also with wax candles, as I before remarked; and in both those institutions, it was understood a constant illumination was kept up. Citizens were also frequently running in to buy candles, in great and small quantities, so that the business of storekeeping was far more laborious than common.

We were confirmed in our faith in the intercession of the Virgin; when we found that we remained safe from the cholera; and it is a remarkable fact, that not one case of that disease existed in the Nunnery, during either of the seasons in which it proved so fatal in the city.

When the election riots prevailed in Montreal, the city was thrown into general alarm; we heard some reports, from day to day, which made us anxious for ourselves. Nothing, however, gave me any serious thoughts, until I saw uncommon movements in some parts of the nunnery, and ascertained, to my own satisfaction, that there was a large quantity of gunpowder stored in some secret place within the walls, and that some of it was removed, or prepared for use, under the direction of the Superior.

Penances.—I have mentioned several penances in different parts of this narration, which we had sometimes to perform. There is a great variety of them; and, while some, though trifling in appearance, became very painful, by long endurance or frequent repetition, others are severe in their nature, and would never be submitted to, unless through fear of something worse, or or a real belief in their efficacy to remove guilt. I will mention here such as I recollect, which can be named without offending a virtuous ear; for some there were, which, although I have been obliged to submit to, either by a misled conscience, or the fear of severe punishments, now that I am better able to judge of my duties, and at liberty to act, I would not mention or describe.

Kissing the floor is a very common penance; kneeling and kissing the feet of other nuns is another; as are kneeling on hard peas, and walking with them in the shoes. We had repeatedly to walk on our knees through the subterranean passage, leading to the Congregational Nunnery; and sometimes to eat our meals with a rope round our necks. Sometimes we were fed only with such things as we most disliked. Garlic was given to me on this account, because I had a strong antipathy against it.

Eels were repeatedly given some of us, because we felt an unconquerable repugnance to them, on account of reports we heard of their feeding on dead carcases in the river St. Lawrence. It was no uncommon thing for us to be required to drink the water in which the Superior had washed her feet. Sometimes we were required to brand ourselves with a hot iron, so as to leave scars; at other times to whip our naked flesh with several small rods, before a private altar, until we drew blood. I can assert with the perfect knowledge of the fact, that many of the nuns bear the scars of these wounds.

One of our penances was to stand for a length of time with our arms extended, in imitation of the Saviour on the cross. The *Chemin de la croix*, or Road to the Cross, is, in fact, a penance, though it consists of a variety of prostrations, with the repetition of many prayers, occupying two or three hours. This we had to perform frequently, going into chapel, and falling before each chapelle in succession, at each time commemorating some particular act or circumstance reported of the Saviour's progress to the place of crucifixion. Sometimes we were obliged to sleep on the floor in the winter, with nothing over us but a single sheet; and sometimes to chew a piece of window glass to a fine powder, in the presence of the Superior.

We had sometimes to wear leathern belts stuck full of sharp metallic points, round our waists, and the upper part of our arms, bound on so tight, that they had penetrated the flesh, and drew blood.

Some of the penances were so severe, that they seemed too

much to be endured: and when they were imposed, the nuns who were to suffer them, shewed the most violent repugnance. They would often resist, and still oftener express their opposition by exclamations and screams.

Never, however, was any noise heard from them for a long time, for there was a remedy always ready to be applied in cases of the kind. The gag which was put into the mouth of the unfortunate St. Frances, had been brought from a place where there were forty or fifty others, of different shapes and sizes. These I have seen in their depository, which is a drawer between two closets, in one of the community-rooms. Whenever any loud noise was made, one of these instruments was demanded, and gagging commenced at once. I have known many, many intances, and sometimes five or six nuns gagged at once. Sometimes they would become so much excited before they could be bound and gagged, that considerable force was necessary to be exerted; and I have seen the blood flowing from mouths into which the gag had been thrust with violence.

Indeed I ought to know something on this department of nunnery discipline; I have had it tried upon myself, and can bear witness that it is not only most humiliating and oppressive, but often extremely painful. The mouth is kept forced open, and the straining of the jaws at their utmost stretch, for a considerable time is very distressing.

One of the worst punishments which I ever saw inflicted, was that with a cap; and yet some of the old nuns were permitted to inflict it at their pleasure. I have repeatedly known them to go for a cap, when one of our number had transgressed a rule, sometimes though it were a very unimportant one. These caps were kept in a cupboard in the old nuns' room, whence they were brought when wanted.

They were small, made of a reddish looking leather, fitted closely to the head, and fastened under the chin with a kind of buckle. It was the common practice to tie the nun's hands behind, and gag her before the cap was put on, to prevent noise and resistance. I never saw it worn by any one for a moment, without throwing them into severe sufferings. If permitted, they would scream in the most shocking manner, and always writhed as much as their confinement would allow. I can speak from personal knowledge of this punishment, as I have endured it more than once; and yet I have no idea of the cause of the pain. I never examined one of the caps, nor saw the inside, for they are always brought and taken away quickly; but although the first sensation was that of coolness, it was hardly put on my head before a violent and indescribable sensation began, like that of a blister, only much more insupportable; and this continued until it was removed. It would produce such an acute pain as to throw us into convulsions; and I think no human being could endure it for an hour. After this punishment, we felt its effects through the system for many days. Having once known what it was by experience, I held the cap in dread; and whenever I was condemned to suffer the punishment again, felt ready to do anything to avoid it; but when tied and gagged, with the cap on my head again, I could only sink upon the floor, and roll about in anguish until it was taken off.

This was usually done in about ten minutes, sometimes less, but the pain always continued in my head for several days. I thought that it might take away a person's reason if kept on a much longer time. If I had not been gagged I am sure I should have uttered awful screams. I have felt the effects for a week. Sometimes fresh cabbage leaves were applied to my head to remove it. Having had no opportunity to examine my head I cannot say more.

NOTES, FACTS, CONFIRMATIONS, &c.

CONFIRMATIONS OF MARIA MONK'S DISCLOSURES.— In a former number, we promised to give some extracts from the Confirmations of Miss Monk's Statements. These Confirmations and further Disclosures, make a thick volume. The most striking of these, (with notes and critical enquiries,) we shall give, in connection with proofs from other journals.—" The character and conduct of Miss Monk furnish the strongest evidence in support of the general truth of her claims, as a professed ex-nun. 1. *Her incapacity to have acted the part of an impostor, is, in the highest degree, evident to all who are personally acquainted with her.*—The cogency of this argument is acknowledged by her opponents. Hence they deny that she is the authoress of the disclosures attributed to her. They maintain that she is a *mere tool*, in the hands of others, who have fabricated and published them in her name. But this, I trust, has been shown to the satisfaction of the reader, to be untrue. It has been shown, that she, and she alone, is the authoress of the dark tale, which she has published to the astonishment of the people of this country. Miss Monk is young, and possesses a mind altogether undisciplined by study. Her education is inferior to that of ordinary country girls. Habits of study she has none. Her knowledge of books is, or was when she first arrived in New York, next to nothing. And if the 'Awful Exposure' gives us a true history of her life, she has never been either a nun, or a Roman Catholic; but ' has led the life of a stroller and a prostitute.' If this be true, it is asked how a girl of her age, character, and attainments, could possibly fabricate such a book as her 'Awful Disclosures?' The supposition beggars all belief, but that of blindness. If she has fabricated them, Rome, with its numberless saints, may be fearlessly challenged to produce a miracle any thing like as great. Besides, on the supposition that she had fabricated her 'Disclosures,' it is impossible that she should have been able to act the part of an impostor, up to the present time, without being detected. Many minds have been at work, for more than a year past, endeavouring to develope her true character. Both friends and foes have been thus employed. Had she been an impostor, it would have been discovered, long before this day. She constitutionally possesses transparency of character, to an uncommon degree. Hence the predominant workings of her mind are very apparent to a penetrating observer. She has very little of that systematic concealment and forethought, so necessary to a successful impostor. Her openness of character, constitutionally considered, is almost the first thing observed by an intelligent stranger who may chance to see and converse with her. Hence, if such a person has been sceptically disposed in regard to the general truth of her claims, his scepticism, in perhaps nineteen cases out of twenty, has been removed by a free conversation with her. Such an individual readily perceives, that her mental constitution is such, as totally to disqualify her to act the part of protracted imposture. The argument, therefore, under this head, is twofold—being founded, on her incapacity to create her 'Disclosures', and on the supposition that she possessed such ability, her incapacity to have successfully concealed her imposture up to the present time. 2nd. *Her minute and extensive nunnery knowledge, connected with the ease and dexterity with which she can perform the many ceremonies of a convent,* can be accounted for, on no other supposition, than that of her having been a nun, as she states. Her practical knowledge of Popery and Jesuitism, of priests and nuns, of the furniture and diversified apartments of the Hotel Dieu, of the ceremonies and practices of that establishment, is, such as could have been acquired by her, only by a residence of years in that convent. She is as familiar with the mummery of Popish observances, as a school-boy is with his alphabet—such as penances, hymns, Latin prayers, &c. &c., though she is as ignorant of the meaning of Latin words, as she is of the Chinese language. The same is true with reference to the ease with which she performs the various bodily ceremonies, some of which she speaks of in her book, such as falling upon her knees, and standing erect upon them, &c. &c. With the Romish catechisms she is perfectly familiar. In a word, she is, in regard to these matters, all that we might suppose her to be, on the supposition that she has, for years, been a resident in the convent. Speaking in the language of common life, 'she has learned her trade.' And no man in his senses, can understandingly deny it. How, then, can this evidence be resisted? 3. *Her ignorance of life, disconnected from convents,* can be accounted for, only on the supposition of her having lived a conventual life. I speak now with special reference to what she was, when she first arrived in New York, in the spring of 1835. At that time, her acquaintance with matters and things, as they appear in the domestic circle, and in ordinary life, was very limited. She was evidently a comparative stranger to them; whilst all her movements and manners were such, as bespoke her former life to have been that of a cloistered nun. Says Mr. Hilliker, in his affidavit:—' We observed also, that she always folded her hands under her apron when she walked, as she has described the nuns as doing, in her 'Awful Disclosures.' 4. *The marks on her person,* which were produced by suffering by penances, and other violent treatment, afford an argument in support of her claims. She has several of these, as she states in her first volume. She speaks of having worn a broad belt round her waist, 'stuck full of sharp points, for the mortification of her spirit.' The writer of this has been informed by a respectable lady, who examined Miss Monk's waist, that the scars produced by this belt, are very manifest. To use her own language, 'it looks distressing.' The marks of gagging are seen on her lips; and there are scars also on her thumbs, which were 'cut severely by the tight drawing of the band used to confine her arms.' These are the signs of Romish penance and violence. But the 'Awful Exposure' tells us she has never been a Roman Catholic.' *The circumstances,* in connexion with which she was first discovered by Mr. Hilliker, and his associates, after her arrival in the city of New York, afford an argument in proof of Miss Monk's honesty; as is seen in Mr. Hilliker's affidavit.* She was discovered by Mr. Hilliker and his companions in a retired place, above the city of New York, where she had secreted herself for several days, and where she had evidently made up her mind to die. She was not far from death when thus found; and it was with much difficulty that she was prevailed upon to leave the place of her concealment. Nay, she declined leaving it, until she saw that the gentlemen were determined to take her by force, unless she would go voluntarily. She had already become so feeble as to need to be supported by two of the gentlemen, in walking the distance of half a mile, to the almshouse. She was in a strange country, under circumstances peculiarly distressing.* After Mr. Hilliker had conversed with her some time alone, and assured her that he was a married man, and that he wished to befriend her in every way he could, she stated to him, that she was an eloped nun, and that she became *enciente* in the convent. He states that he found her in tears, and that she wept for two hours afterwards. He has mentioned several circumstances in his affidavit, all of which bear the marks of honest sincerity, on the part of Miss Monk. It is impossible to account for them on any other supposition than that she told the truth, as to her elopement from the nunnery. It is impossible, that such circumstances should mislead, for they cannot testify falsely, as guilty man can, and often does, do. 6. *The circumstances* in connexion with which Miss Monk first divulged the principal facts recorded in her book, are such as to afford the strongest evidence in support of her claims to public confidence. These are detailed in the statement of the Rev. Mr. Tappin.*

---

* Mr. Hilliker's affidavit and the Rev. Mr. Tappin's testimony we shall insert in our next number.

She made known these facts to him by way of penitential confession, while sick in the alms-house, and as she supposed, ready to die. Mr. Tappin states that it was perfectly manifest to his mind, that she had no idea of criminating others, or that her statements would ever be made public. She and others thought, that she was on the borders of the grave, and she wished to quiet her troubled conscience by confessing what she supposed to be her grossest sins. She was still a Roman Catholic; it was therefore in perfect accordance with the religion she had been taught, thus to confess. There are two things worthy of special notice in connexion with Miss Monk's confession to the Rev. Mr. Tappin:—1st. *The manifest absence of every sinister motive,* by which she could have been influenced in making these communications to him. What earthly motive could have influenced her? Revenge to the priests? Certainly not; for she had no idea that her confessions would go beyond the mind of him whom she then considered as her confessor. The same reply may be given to the insinuation, that she did it in order to mitigate her unfortunate situation, in being the mother of an illegitimate child; or that she did it for the purpose of securing any earthly good whatever. 2nd. The only motives which appeared to be present, at the time, to her mind, were such as arise from *the apprehension of speedy dissolution, connected with the solemn retributions of eternity.* Was it, then, within the limits of possibility, under such circumstances, for her to have acted the part of a diabolical impostor? Is not the supposition utterly incredible? How then can it be otherwise, than that she is honest in putting forth her claims as an ex-nun? I would only add that the hand of God is extremely manifest in bringing to light Miss Monk's statements respecting the Hotel Dieu Nunnery, in a manner so convincing to every reflecting mind. Let, then, her sad tale be believed; and let it produce the benign effects, in counteracting vice and error, which, under the government of the Supreme disposer of all events, it is adapted to do. 7. *The consistency of Miss Monk's conduct with the demands of truth,* furnishes an argument favourable to her claims. She has acted just as one might suppose she would have done, on the supposition that she was honest in giving her disclosures to the world. Her circumstances have been peculiarly trying, arising in part from her comparative ignorance of the world, connected with the discredit which has been thrown upon her statements, and the consequent violent denunciations which have been heaped upon her by Protestants, especially editors of newspapers, who have taken very little pains to investigate the subject. Often has she felt, as if she had scarcely a real friend on earth—as if all the world was against her, making her the helpless victim of its combined contempt and indignation. Yet amidst all her trials, she has exhibited, to those around her, that she felt an unwavering consciousness of standing upon the truth; and that the God of truth would one day vindicate her honesty. Being possessed naturally of an unusual degree of sensibility, and feeling her forlorn situation, it is true, she has often wept in secret places, for having published her dark story, not because of its untruth, but because of the cruel treatment she has received in consequence of it. She has invariably manifested a very strong desire that the truth of her charges against the Roman priests and nuns of Lower Canada, might be tested by some equitable tribunal. Hence her visit to Montreal for this purpose, in the August of 1835, and before she ever thought of publishing a book. She then and there solemnly appealed to the civil authorities, to investigate their truth. She was accompanied by two American gentlemen, of the legal profession, who assisted her in presenting her charges in due form, attested on oath, to the Attorney General for prosecution. And after spending some three or four weeks, in fruitless attempts to secure the object of her visit, she returned to New York. While at Montreal, it was denied by the Priests that she had ever been an inmate of the Hotel Dieu. She at once offered a fair test of the fact, which, by a very little trouble, would have settled the point beyond the power of contradiction. She proposed a description of the interior of the convent—its furniture, its inmates and different apartments, and their uses—and staked her all upon its correctness. But the application of it was not allowed by her opponents; on what ground, no mortal can conjecture, unless it were that they were afraid to abide the results. On the fourteenth day of last July, I received a letter from the Rev. Mr. Perkins of Montreal, informing me, that on the following day a committee of gentlemen were to apply the test, which she had proposed nearly one year before. The thought immediately occurred to me, if she be an impostor I can now discover it, by communicating to her this unexpected intelligence. I applied the test, in the best manner to accomplish the end in view, that I was capable of; and the result was such, as decidedly deepened my convictions of her honesty. Other particulars might be mentioned, were it necessary, all going to show the consistency of her conduct, with the supposition, that she feels herself standing upon the rock of truth."

CHAPTER XVIII.

The punishment of the Cap—The Priests of the District of Montreal have free access to the Black Nunnery—Crimes committed and required by them—The Pope's Command to commit indecent crimes—Characters of the Old and New Superiors—The timidity of the latter—I began to be employed in the Hospitals—Some account of them—Warning given me by a sick Nun—Penance by Hanging.

This punishment was occasionally resorted to for very trifling offences, such as washing the hands without permission; and it was generally applied on the spot, and before the other nuns in the community-room.

I have mentioned before that the country, so far down as Three Rivers, is furnished with Priests by the Seminary of Montreal; and that these hundred and fifty men are liable to be occasionally transferred from one station to another. Numbers of them are often to be seen in the streets of Montreal as they may find a home in the Seminary.

They are considered as having an equal right to enter the Black Nunnery whenever they please; and then, according to our oaths, they have complete control over the nuns. To name all the works of shame of which they are guilty in that retreat would require much time and space, neither would it be necessary to the accomplishment of my object, which is the publication of but some of their criminality to the world, and the development, in general terms, of scenes thus far carried on in secret within the walls of that Convent, where I was so long an inmate.

Secure against detection by the world they never believed that an eye-witness would ever escape to tell of their crimes, and declare some of their names before the world; but the time has come, and some of their deeds of darkness must come to the day. I have seen in the Nunnery the priests from more, I presume, than a hundred country places, admitted for shameful and criminal purposes; from St. Charles, St. Denis, St. Marks, St. Antoine, Chambly, Bertier, St. Johns, &c., &c.

How unexpected to them will be the disclosures I make! Shut up in a place from which there has been thought to be but one way of egress, and that the passage to the grave, they considered themselves safe in perpetrating crimes in our presence, and in making us share in their criminality as often as they chose, and conducted more shamelessly than even the brutes.

These debauchees would come in without ceremony, concealing their names both by night and day. Being within the walls of that prison-house of death, where the cries and pains of the injured innocence of their victims could never reach the world for relief or redress for their wrongs, without remorse or shame they would glory, not only in satiating their brutal passions, but even in torturing, in the most barbarous manner, the feelings of those under their power; telling us, at the same time, that this mortifying the flesh was religion, and pleasing to God. The more they could torture us, or make us violate our own feelings, the more pleasure they took in their unclean revelling; and all their brutal obscenity they called meritorious before God.

We were sometimes invited to put ourselves to voluntary sufferings in a variety of ways, not for a penance, but to show our devotion to God. A priest would sometimes say to us—" Now which of you have love enough for Jesus Christ to stick a pin through your cheeks?"

Some of us would signify our readiness, and immediately thrust one through up to the head. Sometimes he would propose that we should repeat the operation several times on the spot! and the cheeks of a number of nuns would be bloody.

There were other acts occasionally proposed and consented to, which I cannot name in a book. Such the Superior would sometimes command us to perform; many of them things not only useless and unheard of, but loathsome and indecent in the highest possible degree. How they could ever have been invented I never could conceive. Things were done worse than the entire exposure of the person, though this was occasionally required of several at once in the presence of the priests.

The Superior of the Seminary would sometimes come and inform us that he had received orders from the Pope to request that those nuns who possessed the greatest devotion and faith should be requested to perform some particular deeds, which he named or described in our presence, but of which no decent or moral person could ever endure to speak. I cannot repeat what would injure any ear not debased to the lowest possible degree. I am bound by a regard to truth, however, to confess that deluded women were found among us who would comply with those requests.

There was a great difference between the characters of our old and new Superior, which soon became obvious. The former used to say she liked to walk, because it would prevent her from becoming corpulent. She was, therefore, very active, and constantly going about from one part of the Nunnery to another, overseeing us at our various employments. I never saw in her any appearance of timidity: she seemed, on the contrary, bold and masculine, and sometimes more than that, cruel and cold-blooded in scenes calculated to overcome any common person.

Such a character she had particularly exhibited at the murder of St. Frances.

The new Superior, on the other hand, was so heavy and lame that she walked with much difficulty, and consequently exercised a less vigilant oversight of the nuns. She was also of a timid disposition, or else had been overcome by some fright in her past life; for she was apt to become alarmed in the night, and never liked to be alone in the dark. She had long performed the part of an old nun, which is that of a spy upon the younger ones, and was well known to us in that character, under the name of Ste. Margarite. Soon after her promotion to the station of Superior, she appointed me to sleep in her apartment, and assigned me a sofa to lie upon. One night, while I was asleep, she suddenly threw herself upon me, and exclaimed, in great alarm, "*Oh! mon Dieu! mon Dieu! qui'est que ea?*" (Oh! my God! my God! what is that?) I jumped up and looked about the room, but saw nothing, and endeavoured to convince her that there was nothing extraordinary there. But she insisted that a ghost had come and held her bed curtain, so that she could not draw it. I examined it, and found that the curtain had been caught by a pin in the vallance, which had held it back; but it was impossible to tranquilise her for some time. She insisted on my sleeping with her the rest of the night, and I stretched myself across the foot of her bed, and slept there till morning.

During the last part of my stay in the Convent I was often employed in attending in the hospitals. There are, as I have before mentioned, several apartments devoted to the sick, and there is a physician of Montreal, who attends as physician to the Convent. It must not be supposed, however, that he knows any thing concerning the private hospitals. It is a fact of great importance to be distinctly understood, and constantly borne in mind, that he is never, under any circumstances, admitted into the private hospital-rooms; of those he sees nothing more than any stranger whatever. He is limited to the care of those patients who are admitted from the city into the public hospital, and one of the nuns' hospitals, and these he visits every day. Sick poor are received for charity by the institution, attended by some of the nuns, and often go away with the highest ideas of our charitable characters and holy lives. The physician himself might, perhaps, in some cases share in the delusion.

I frequently followed Dr. Nelson through the public hospital, at the direction of the Superior, with pen, ink, and paper in my hands, and wrote down the prescriptions which he ordered for the different patients. These were afterwards prepared and administered by the attendants. About a year before I left the Convent, I was first appointed to attend the private sick rooms, and was frequently employed in that duty up to the day of my departure. Of course, I had opportunities to observe the number and classes of patients treated there; and in what I am to say on the subject, I appeal, with perfect confidence, to any true and competent witness to confirm my words, whenever such a witness may appear.

It would be vain for any body who has merely visited the Convent from curiosity, or resided in it as a novice, to question my declarations. Such a person must necessarily be ignorant of even the existence of the private rooms, unless informed by some one else. Such rooms, however, there are, and I could relate many things which have passed there during the hours I was employed in them, as I have stated.

One night I was called to sit up with an old nun, named St. Clare, who, in going down stairs, had dislocated a limb, and lay in a sick room adjoining an hospital. She seemed to be a little out of her mind a part of the time, but appeared quite in possession of her reason most of the night. It was easy to pretend that she was delirious; but I considered her speaking the truth, though I felt reluctant to repeat what I heard her say, and excused myself from mentioning it even at confession, on the ground that the Superior thought her deranged.

What led her to some of the most remarkable parts of her conversation was, a motion I made, in the course of the night, to take the light out of her little room into the adjoining apartment, to look once more at the sick persons there. She begged me not to leave her for a moment in the dark, for she could not bear it. "I have witnessed so many horrid scenes," said she, "in this Convent, that I want somebody near me constantly, and must always have a light burning in my room. I cannot tell you," she added, "what things I remember, for they would frighten you too much. What you have seen are nothing to them. Many a murder have I witnessed; many a nice young creature has been killed in this Nunnery. I advise you to be very cautious—keep every thing to yourself—there are many here ready to betray you."

What it was that induced the old nun to express so much kindness to me I could not tell, unless she was frightened at the recollection of her own crimes, and those of others, and felt grateful for the care I took of her. She had been one of the night watches, and never before showed me any particular kindness. She did not indeed go into detail concerning the transactions to which she alluded, but told me that some nuns had been murdered under great aggravations of cruelty, by being gagged, and left to starve in the cells, or having their flesh burned off their bones with red hot irons.

It was uncommon to find compunction expressed by any of the nuns. Habit renders us insensible to the sufferings of others, and careless about our own sins. I had become so hardened myself, that I find it difficult to rid myself of many of my former principles and views of right and wrong.

I was one day set to wash some of the empty bottles from the cellar, which had contained the liquid that was poured into the cemetery there. A number of these had been brought from the corner where so many of them were always to be seen, and placed at the head of the cellar stairs, and there we were required to take them and wash them out. We poured in water and rinsed them; a few drops which got upon our clothes soon made holes in them. I think the liquid was called vitriol, or some such name; and I heard some persons say that it would soon destroy the flesh and even the bones of the dead. At another time, we were furnished with a little of the liquid, which was mixed with a quantity of water, and used in dying some cloth black, which was wanted at funerals in the chapels. Our hands were turned very black by being dipped into it, but a few drops of some other liquid were mixed with fresh water, and given us to wash in, which left our skin of a bright red.

The bottles of which I spoke were made of very thick dark-coloured glass, large at the bottom, and from recollection, I should say held something less than a gallon.

I was once much shocked, on entering the room for the examination of conscience, at seeing a nun hanging by a cord from a ring in the ceiling, with her head downward. Her clothes had been tied round with a leathern strap to keep them in their place, and then she had been fastened in that situation, with her head some distance from the floor. Her face had a very unpleasant appearance, being dark-colored and swollen by the rushing in of the blood; her hands were tied, and her mouth stopped with a large gag. The nun proved to be no other than Jane Ray, who for some fault had been condemned to this punishment.

This was not however, a solitary case; I heard of numbers who were "hung," as it was called, at different times; and I saw St. Hypolite and St. Luke undergoing it. This was considered a most distressing punishment, and it was the only one which Jane Ray could not endure, of all that she had tried.

Some of the nuns would allude to it in her presence, but it usually made her angry. It was probably practised in the same place while I was a novice; but I never heard or thought of such a thing in those days. Whenever we wished to enter the room for the examination of conscience we had to ask leave; and, after some delay, were permitted to go, but always under a strict charge to bend the head forward and keep the eye fixed on the floor.

NOTES, FACTS, CONFIRMATIONS, &c.

For further confirmation of the nature of the Confessional, we now give an extract from Miss Eliza Smith's volume, entitled "THE PROGRESS OF BEGUILEMENT TO ROMANISM." The volume is full of unquestionable facts. It is published by Seeleys, in Fleet-street. The following extract commences on page 66. Miss Smith's own words are these—

"The Romish religion teaches, that if you omit to name anything in confession, however repugnant or revolting to purity, which you even doubt may come under the category of mortal sins, your confession, or confessions, however so many, which have been made subsequently to such omissions, are nothing worth, in fact sacrilegious; and all require to be made over again before the absolution can avail; while it also inculcates that sins of *thought* should be confessed, in order that the confessor may judge of their mortal or venial character. What sort of a spiritual chain this links around the strictly conscientious, I would attempt to pourtray if I *could;* but it must have been *worn* to understand its torturing character. Suffice it to say, however, that I had been for some months in the habit of confessing to this bad priest himself, ere I became aware of his real character—and though I had certainly sometimes suspected him, yet being from circumstances compelled to make use of his ministry, I had never of course named my injurious suspicions to him: and I further candidly acknowledge that from utter incapacity to allude to such subjects, and dreading their baneful effects on my own mind, I had on several previous occasions passed by thoughts and circumstances which I had *doubted* my confessors would call sin, so that now I was involved in a labyrinth of perplexity and disquiet from which I saw no escape, but through the medium of a general confession, dating from the first time I could recall such omission. To this I made up my mind. But this confessor's scrupulosity exceeded everything I had ever encountered hitherto. He told me many things were mortal sins, that I had hardly deemed sin at all before; and thus a host of anxieties for my *first* general confession was awakened within me. I had no resource, therefore, but to remake *that*, and thus I afresh entered on the bitter path I had deemed I should never have occasion to tread again. But if that first confession had lacerated my feelings, what, *what* was it, to *this* one? words have no power, language has no expression, for the emotions which characterized the task from the commencement of it to the close. Had I been really less sincere, and remorseful for what I deemed my faults than I was, it *must* have awakened me, deeply sunk in darkness as I had become. The difficulty I felt in entering on the subjects I was compelled to do, and the distress I manifested,—which I suppose is natural to my sex, though I *have* met with some among them strangely familiar with such topics,—furnished my confessor, of course, with a plea for his assistance in the questioning department; and some of the images supplied, and feelings elicited, I would fain cancel as foul blots in memory. I soon found that he made mortal sins of what my *first* confessor had thought but lightly of, or professed to do so, and he did not scruple to pronounce that I had never *yet* made a good confession at all. My ideas therefore became more complicated and confused as I proceeded, until at length I began to feel hopeless of ever accomplishing my task in any degree satisfactorily; and my mind and memory were positively racked to recal every itoa of every kind, real or imaginary, that may hereafter be occasion of uneasiness should it be omitted. The most simple childish follies were recounted, and magnified into mortal sin; and as day after day I knelt, sometimes for hours at the feet of that man, answering queries, and listening to reproofs, calculated to bow my very soul in the dust, I then felt as though I should never raise my head again. The confession lasted at intervals over the space of a fortnight, that is, I went perhaps to him thrice in the week, for that time, and to chronicle a small part of what passed there would sully the paper. O how can the judgment ever be so perverted as to call such pollution purity;—how can the mind ever be so darkened as to believe that such an awful parody upon the divine perogative of the Immaculate and spotless Lamb of God, can be aught but the most fearful mockery? Even I, benighted as I was, sometimes trembled, I knew not why. Never shall I forget my sensations on two or three occasions at that time. Once, my confessor having been unexpectedly called away, I went to the Church-porch for air, while awaiting his return. How I gasped for some relief to my overwrought mind! the memory even now oppresses me. But that was soon superseded by feelings more insupportable still; as he came with his unchanged smile and broad gaze to summon me back to my terrible task. Even this however sank into significance a day-or-two afterwards, when I went to proceed with my confession. I was desired to *repeat* what had most harrowed my feelings over again. I replied, I had confessed it once already, and ventured some demur; when I was told in the most merciless manner, that *if I had,* he had forgotten it, and the command enforced, with the consolatory assurance, that the repetition would *only serve to humble me.* A feeling almost akin to suffocation for the moment overwhelmed me, and I felt as if the words would choke me. I leaned against the confessional for support, but with promptings and suggestions he at length gained his point. On rising from my knees I was unable to stand, for the time; a kind of *fallen* and *crushed* feeling seemed to paralyze me, both physically and mentally. He smillingly attributed it to the length of time I had been kneeling, and commenced talking on the most indifferent subjects, with as great freedom and coolness as though I had no cause for one unpleasant thought; and talked on thus for an hour. At the end of that time a lady of my acquaintance called upon him, and after another half-hour thus consumed, we left together. She was the mother of a family, and a devoted Catholic, as pure I believed in heart as life; and as I walked home by her side, I looked at her in wonder. I could not smother the questions which *would* arise within me, as to the purity of the duty I had just been performing. What would I have given to have thrown myself on her maternal bosom, and have asked, *Do you, can you* know of these things? and if so, will you bring your children up exposed to such horrors? What would I have given for even *one* friend to whom I could fully have opened my mind, capable of understanding and advising me. But the fetters were on me, and I soon awoke as from a sinful dream, to torment myself with the enquiry, whether *such reflections* were not *wrong?* while conscience, or the friend—whispered they ought to be *confessed.* From this dilemma indeed, I only at length escaped by the conviction that they were involuntary, and absolutely unavoidable. I merely name this to shew the galling nature of my chains, and my case is not solitary. By scruples and doubts of a ridiculous, and even a more puerile character, I have seen one or two most sincere Catholics driven to the very verge of distraction: I have known them go to confessor after confessor, and wander hither and thither, at great loss of time and money, to get relief to their minds, without being a whit nearer the goal they aimed at. Every *thought* on which rests a *doubt,* should be confessed, they are told, and the scrupulous *see* this doubt in the thoughts of each day and hour. Hence there is no end to their misery if they once become severely exact. God's love and the Saviour's mercy, are all here made subverient to the dictum of a priest, if not entirely lost sight of, by the poor dupes of their fanaticism. What a terrible idea, that instead of the simple faith which justifies, such a figment as the merit of his own performances, should be held out as the only means of man's salvation, still farther to distress the mind of the already distressed sinner. How entirely justification is made to *depend* on *this merit,* and also how completely the really sincere are priest-led, I would just give this exemplification. One of the ladies slightly involved in the affair with the bad priest already alluded to, on becoming aware how widely the scandal had extended, went to the *religieux* to whom I have adverted, who had received several confessions on the subject, in order to add her testimony to the general mass of evidence. She was an innocent-minded, and I believe most guileless girl, and sincerely anxious to save her soul, which she believed was to be accomplished by obedience to the commands of her church. Not more than four months before, or five at farthest, she had, after a great deal of anxiety on the subject, made a general confession of the sins of her whole life. It was only the last of several; but as she had been most painfully particular, and had sought out a confessor famed for his guidance of souls, she hoped it was for the best, indeed the final one; for I have myself heard her say, that if she knew she was going to die, she should not wish to make another after this. The knowledge she had possessed of the irregularities of this immoral priest, however, from a charitable wish to screen him, and also because she really doubted whether she ought to speak ill of him, she had not alluded to in this confession, and for this reason—founded in charity as well as respect for his office — the arbitrary *religieux* told her, that her long and difficult confession was invalid, and good for nothing; and commanded her to repeat it to him. Deep as was her reverence for the ministers of the church, she would not for a time believe him, and refused to comply with his demand. He remonstrated, persuaded, and resorted to all the authority of which he was master,—still in vain. She lowered her position so far as to admit, however, that what he said might be true; but if so, she would not make her general confession to him. He then spoke of her self-will, and endeavoured to make her sense of pious submission to the church, the means to extort compliance. Ashamed at this, she pleaded her state of health—which was then so precarious, that he himself had predicted in six months she would be in her grave—and the mental anxiety it would occasion; also how likely this would be to retard her recovery, and asked at least for a little respite, until she could gather more strength, when she promised to make it without loss of time. But all was fruitless. Her very argument became his stronghold. What if she should become worse instead of better, and so, more unfit for such a task, and then die without absolution? In short, he shook the rod of spiritual terrors so effectually over the debilitated, and really sincere-minded victim, that she had no alternative, and was compelled to obey him; which she actually did, without any other reason than his despotic and sovereign *will*. But did her perplexity end here? Oh! no! believe it not. She was subsequently reduced to the verge of the grave, from the same complaint under which she was at that time suffering, and lay for many weeks as on the borders of eternity. In that state I saw her repeatedly, and was witness to her agitation and distress of mind. Constrained against her conscientious sense of right, to perform a duty hastily, which her scrupulosity required a long time and much thought to perform at all, she was filled with doubts and fears of the most harassing character; and instead of being supported by the Christian's certain hope in a season of such extremity, upon her sick bed she was wasting the little strength she could summon, in writing painful letters to this harsh arbiter of her spiritual fate, (she was then at a great distance from him,) to express her difficulties, confess her supposed direlictions, and obtain her passport to heaven. Of the *comfort* he afforded her, I *could* speak, but it is useless. Suffice it to say, her weary soul was *not* pointed to the pitiful Saviour, for free and unmerited forgiveness and peace, but after keen and protracted anxiety, and much mental conflict, she was at length permitted to calm herself as well as she could, by the assurance, that now she had at length done her best, she might at least hope for heaven. Thus were the means taken to prevent the commission of priestly crime, converted into a source of pain and annoyance on every hand; which was well nigh enough to make one question, whether the remedy was not almost as bad as the disease. In its effects upon many minds, I believe it may have proved so. I speak advisedly. The one was infamy, whose very bold blushing face appalled, and placed you somewhat on your guard; the other was an insidious shape of abomination, screened by a holy name. It was, forsooth, the *sacrament* of penance. But here I may be reminded by the advocates of the dogma, that whatever had to be endured, arose out of the *nature* of the confession to be made. Willingly I grant the plea. I do not unqualifiedly blame the confessor. But the *fact* is worth ten thousand arguments upon the subject, and speaks more than all the homilies ever written, for the direful character of the institution. For if such sufferings and annoyance had to be borne at the hand of one who professed to regard his fellow-minister's crime with abborrence, in the very *confession* of that crime; if such consequences resulted only in the *legitimate* use of a sacred thing, what must be its awful effects where the priest himself is faulty? and what must be the fearful amount of contamination, when it is converted into an instrument of abuse? Oh the frightful influence of guilt in an individual placed in a position of such tremendous trust and responsibility. No more dangerous or subtle snare, for those beneath his control, could be devised by the combined malice of the powers of darkness. The most virtuous may not say that they are proof against it. The sternest in their strength of purpose, cannot assure themselves ' so far will he go but no farther.' Those who have hitherto fled each thought of impurity as defilement, here *know not its guise*. The very principles seem in danger of becoming perverted, one's ideas of right and wrong confounded; the judgment to be hood-winked, and utterly bewildered; while evil wears a mask so treacherous, that the victim to its influence is led on blind-fold. The very confession of guilt to an individual, who seems bound by his character and office to detest and reprehend it, instinctively precludes the idea of the possibility of it, in connection with *himself*. The very humiliation of supplicating for pardon at his hands, seems to place him so far above the petitioner, that the *thought* of suspecting *him* becomes a crime; while the familiarity with such subjects between him and his penitent thus induced, intuitively lessens by degrees the horrors on both sides. Thus the mind may be debased to an extent fearful to contemplate, before the sufferer is aware of the danger surrounding her. *Then* if temptation comes—to God's preventing grace alone is it to be attributed, if she is proof against it. I have known an individual, who, in the confessional, has been severely rebuked for the bare *permission* of a fault in connection with *another*, the very next week exposed to a worse, from the confessor himself; and on some kind of remonstrance being attempted, she has been told that to *him* it was no sin, because *he meant* none. And even worse instances than this have come under my observation. Here, however, justice compels me to say, that I have met with noble exceptions, instances of pure and exalted virtue, where such abomination would be abhorred, and the slightest approach to it shunned as pestilence. But of the too common effect of the confessional, after extended experience, I can have *no doubt ;* and my impression may be stated in few words. That while to pure and heaven-guarded souls it *may* be pure, to those of an opposite character it is a source of terrible temptation, the baneful results of which eternity perhaps only will reveal. Oh that this, my bitter experience, may warn some, and fain would I pray, appeal to some Catholics also; but I fear *this* is a hopeless wish. Excepting those who have similarly suffered, none would believe me; and even they, who in their *hearts know* that I am speaking truth, are so deeply infatuated, that they regard such instances of turpitude as that I have narrated but as abuses ; never for an instant looking *from them* to the *originating cause.* In proof of this, when I was really burdened in mind almost beyond endurance from the painful knowledge I possessed, I sought, after much reflection, the counsel of a really pious and sincere young Catholic Lady, laying before her, even with tears, a small part of what so distressed me. What was her conduct? She doubted my statements, and though I gave her proof *unequivocal,* to a mind not in the most degree prejudiced, she disbelieved me; even carrying the fact of her having listened to me, to confession, as a sin on her own part against charity and the reverence due to the character of her spiritual guides. Nay, I had some reason afterwards to believe, from indirect information I received, that she had taken it to the very Priest himself whom I had implicated."

CHAPTER XIX.

More visits to the imprisoned Nuns—Their fears—Others temporarily put into the Cells—Relics—The Agnus Dei—The Priest's private Hospital, or Holy Retreat—Secret Rooms in the Eastern Wing—Reports of Murders in the Convent—The Superior's private Records—Number of Nuns in the Convent—Desire of Escape—Urgent reasons for it—Plan—Deliberation—Attempt—Success.

I often seized an opportunity, when I safely could, to speak a cheering or friendly word to one of the poor prisoners, in passing their cells, on my errands in the cellars. For a time I supposed them to be sisters; but I afterwards discovered that this was not the case. I found that they were always under the fear of suffering some punishment, in case they should be found talking with a person not commissioned to attend them. They would often ask, " Is there not somebody coming?"

I could easily believe what I heard affirmed by others, that fear was the severest of their sufferings. Confined in the dark, in so gloomy a place, with the long and spacious arched cellar stretching off this way and that, visited only now and then by a solitary nun, with whom they were afraid to speak their feelings, and with only the miserable society of each other; how gloomy thus to spend day after day, months and even years, without any prospect of liberation, and liable every moment to another fate, to which the Bishop or Superior might condemn them! But these poor creatures must have known something of the horrors perpetrated in other parts of the building, and could not have been ignorant of the hole in the cellar, which was not far from their cells, and the use to which it was devoted. One of them told me in confidence, she wished they could get out. They must also have been often disturbed in their sleep, if they ever did sleep, by the numerous priests who passed through the trap-door at no great distance. To be subject to such trials for a single day would be dreadful; but these nuns had them to endure for years.

I often felt much compassion for them, and wished to see them released; but, at other times, yielding to the doctrine perpetually taught us in the Convent, that our future happiness would be proportioned to the sufferings we had to undergo in this world, I would rest satisfied that their imprisonment was a real blessing to them.

Others, I presume, participated with me in such feelings. One Sunday afternoon, after we had performed all our ceremonies, and were engaged as usual, at that time, with backgammon and other amusements, one of the nuns exclaimed, " Oh, how headstrong are those wretches in the cells—they are as bad as the day they were first put in!"

This exclamation was made, as I supposed, in consequence of some recent conversation with them, as I knew her to be particularly acquainted with the older ones.

Some of the vacant cells were occasionally used for temporary imprisonment. Three nuns were confined in them, to my knowledge, for disobedience to the Superior, as she called it. They did not join the rest in singing in the evening, being exhausted in the various exertions of the day. The Superior ordered them to sing; and, as they did not comply, after her command had been twice repeated, she ordered them away to the cells.

They were immediately taken down into the cellar, placed in separate dungeons, and the doors shut and barred upon them. There they remained through that night, the following day, and second night, but were released in time to attend mass on the second morning.

The Superior used occasionally to shew something in a glass box, which we were required to regard with the highest degree of reverence. It was made of wax, and called an Agnus Dei. She used to exhibit it to us when we were in a state of grace: that is, after confession and before sacrament. She said it had been blessed in the very dish in which our Saviour had eaten. It was brought from Rome. Every time we kissed it, or even looked at it, we were told that it gave a hundred days' release from purgatory to ourselves, or if we did not need it, to our next of kin in purgatory, if not a Protestant. If we had no such kinsman, the benefit was to go to the souls in purgatory not prayed for.

Jane Ray would sometimes say to me "Let's kiss it; some of our friends will thank us for it."

I have been repeatedly employed in carrying dainties of different kinds to the little private room I have mentioned, next beyond the Superior's sitting-room, in the second story, which the priests made their " HOLY RETREAT." That room I never was allowed to enter. I could only go to the door with a waiter of refreshments, set it down upon a little stand near it, give three raps on the door, and then retire to a distance to await orders. When any thing was to be taken away, it was placed on the stand by the Superior, who then gave three raps for me, and closed the door.

The bishop I saw at least once, when he appeared worse for wine, or something of the kind. After partaking of refreshments in the Convent, he sent for all the nuns, and on our appearance, gave us his blessing, and put a piece of pound-cake on the shoulder of each of us, in a manner which appeared singular and foolish.

There are three rooms in the Black Nunnery which I never entered. I had enjoyed much liberty, and had seen, as I supposed all parts of the building, when one day I observed an old nun go to a corner of an apartment near the northern end of the western wing, push the end of her scissors into a crack in the panelled wall, and pull out a door. I was much surprised, because I never had conjectured that any door was there; and it appeared, when I afterwards examined the place, that no indication of it could be discovered on the closest scrutiny. I stepped forward to see what was within, and saw three rooms opening into each other; but the nun refused to admit me within the door, which she said led to rooms kept as depositories.

She herself entered and closed the door, so that I could not satisfy my curiosity; and no occasion presented itself. I always had a strong desire to know the use of these apartments: for I am sure they must have been designed for some purpose of which I was intentionally kept ignorant, otherwise they would never have remained unknown to me so long. Besides the old nun evidently had some strong reasons for denying me admission, though she endeavoured to quiet my curiosity.

The Superior, after my admission into the Convent, had told me I had access to every room in the building: and I had seen places which bore witness to the cruelties and the crimes committed under her commands or sanction; but here was a succession of rooms which had been concealed from me, and so constructed as if designed to be unknown to all but a few. I am sure that any person who might be able to examine the wall in that place, would pronounce that secret door a surprising piece of work. I never saw anything of the kind which appeared to me so ingeniously and skilfully made. I told Jane what I had seen, and she said at once, "We will get in and see what is there." But I suppose she never found an opportunity.

I naturally felt a good deal of curiosity to learn whether such scenes as I had witnessed in the death of St. Frances were common or rare, and took an opportunity to enquire of Jane Ray. Her reply was, "Oh yes; and there were many murdered while you were a novice, whom you heard nothing about."

This was all I ever learned on the subject; but although I was told nothing of the manner in which they were killed, I supposed it to be the same which I had seen practised, viz. by smothering.

I went into the Superior's parlour one day for something, and found Jane Ray there alone, looking into a book with an appearance of interest. I asked her what it was, but she made some trifling answer, and laid it by, as if unwilling to let me take it. There are two book-cases in the room: one on the right as you enter the door, and the other opposite, near the window and the sofa. The former contains the lecture-books, and other printed volumes. The latter seemed to be filled with note and account books. I have often seen the keys in the book-cases while I have been dusting the furniture, and sometimes observed letters stuck up in the room; although I never looked into one, or thought of doing so; we were under strict orders not to touch any of them, and the idea of sins and penances was always present with me.

Some time after the occasion mentioned I was sent into the Superior's room with Jane to arrange it; and as the same book was lying out of the case, she said, "Come, let us look into it." I immediately consented, and we opened it, and turned over several leaves. It was about a foot and a half long, as nearly as I can remember, a foot wide, and about two inches thick, though I cannot speak with particular precision, as Jane frightened me almost as soon as I touched it, by exclaiming, "There you have looked into it, and if you tell of me, I will of you."

The thought of being subjected to a severe penance, which I had reason to apprehend, fluttered me very much; and although I tried to overcome my fears, I did not succeed very well. I reflected, however, that the sin was already committed, and that it would not be increased if I examined the book.

I therefore looked a little at several pages, though I still felt a good deal of agitation. I saw at once that the volume was a record of the entrance of nuns and novices into the Convent, and of the births that had taken place in the Convent. Entries of the last description were made in a brief manner, on the following plan : I do not give the names or dates as real, but only to shew the form of entering them.

   Saint Mary delivered of a son, March 16, 1834.
   Saint Clarice ,, daughter, April 2.
   Saint Matilda ,, daughter, April 30, &c.

No mention was made in the book of the death of the children, though I well knew not one of them could be living at that time.

Now I presume that the period the book embraced was about two years, as several names near the beginning I knew ; but I can form only a rough conjecture of the number of infants born, and murdered, of course, records of which it contained. I suppose the book contained at least one hundred pages, that one-fourth were written upon, and that each page contained fifteen distinct records. Several pages were devoted to the list of births. On this supposition there must have been a large number which I can easily believe to have been born there in the course of two years.

What were the contents of the other books belonging to the same case with that in which I looked into, I have no idea, having never dared to touch one of them ; I believe, however, that Jane Ray was well acquainted with them, knowing, as I do, her intelligence and prying disposition. If she could be brought to give her testimony, she would, doubtless, unfold many curious particulars now unknown.

I am able, in consequence of a circumstance which appeared accidental, to state with confidence the exact number of persons in the Convent one day of the week in which I left. This may be a point of some interest, as several secret deaths had occurred since my taking the veil, and many burials had been openly made in the chapel.

I was appointed, at the time mentioned, to lay out the covers for all the inmates of the Convent, including the nuns in the cells. These covers, as I have said before, were linen bands to be bound around the knives, forks, spoons, and napkins, for eating. These were for all the nuns and novices, and amounted to two hundred and ten. As the number of novices was then about thirty, I know that there must have been at that time about one hundred and eighty veiled nuns.

I was occasionally troubled with a desire of escaping from the nunnery, and was much distressed whenever I felt so evil an imagination rise in my mind. I believed that it was a sin, a great sin, and did not fail to confess, at every opportunity, that I felt discontent. My confessors informed me that I was beset by an evil spirit, and urged me to pray against it. Still, however, every now and then I would think, " Oh, if I could get out !"

At length one of the priests, to whom I had confessed this sin nformed me, for my comfort, that he had begun to pray to St. iAnthony, and hoped his intercession would, bye and bye, drive away the evil spirit. My desire of escape was partly excited by the fear of bringing an infant to the murderous hands of my companions, or of taking a potion whose violent effects I too well knew.

One evening, however, I found myself more filled with the desire of escape than ever; and what exertions I made to dismiss the thought proved entirely unavailing. During evening prayers I became quite occupied with it; and when the time for meditation arrived, instead of falling into a dose, as I often did, although I was a good deal fatigued, I found no difficulty in keeping awake. When this exercise was over, and the other nuns were about to retire to the sleeping room, my station being in the private sick room for the night, I withdrew to my post, which was in the little sitting room adjoining it.

Here, then, I threw myself upon the sofa, and being alone, reflected a few moments on the manner of escape which had occurred to me. The physician had arrived a little before, at half-past eight; and I had now to accompany him, as usual, from bed to bed, with pen, ink, and paper, to write down his prescriptions for the direction of the old nun, who was to see them administered.

What I wrote that evening I cannot now recollect, as my mind was uncommonly agitated; but my customary way was to note down briefly his orders in this manner—

1 d. salts, St. Matilde.

1 blister, St. Genevieve, &c., &c.

I remember that I wrote three orders that evening, and then, having finished the rounds, I returned for a few minutes to the sitting-room.

There were two ways of access to the street from those rooms; first, the more direct, from the passage adjoining the sick room down stairs, through a door, into the nunnery-yard, and through a wicket gate; that is the way by which the physician usually enters at night, and he is provided with a key for that purpose.

It would have been unsafe, however, for me to pass out that way, because a man is kept continually in the yard, near the gate, who sleeps at night in a small hut near the door, to escape whose observations would be impossible. My only hope, therefore, was that I might gain my passage through the other way, to which I must pass through the sick-room, then through a passage, or small room, usually occupied by an old nun: another passage and staircase leading down to the yard, and a large gate openin into the cross street. I had no liberty ever to go beyond the sick-room, and knew that several of the doors might be fastened! still I determined to try; although I have often since been astonished at my boldness in undertaking what would expose me to so many hazards of failure, and to severe punishment if found out.

It seemed as if I acted under some extraordinary impulse, which encouraged me to do what I should hardly at any other moment have thought of undertaking. I had sat but a short time upon the sofa, however, before I rose with a desperate determination to make the experiment. I therefore walked hastily across the sick room, passed into the nun's room, walked by her in a great hurry; and almost without giving her time to speak or think, said—" A message!" and in an instant was through the door, and in the next passage. I think there was another nun with her at the moment; and it is probable that my hurried manner, and prompt intimation that I was sent on a pressing mission to the Superior, prevented them from entertaining any suspicion of my intention. Besides, I had the written orders of the physician in my hand, which may have tended to mislead them; and it was well known to some of the nuns that I had twice left the Convent and returned from choice; so that I was probably more likely to be trusted to remain than many of the others.

The passage which I had now reached had several doors, with all which I was acquainted; that on the opposite side opened into a community-room, where I should probably have found some of the old nuns at that hour, and they would certainly have stopped me. On the left, however, was a large door, both locked and barred; but I gave the door a sudden swing, that it might creak as little as possible, being of iron. Down the stairs I hurried, and making my way through the door into the yard, stepped across it, unbarred the great gate, and was at liberty.

NOTES, FACTS, CONFIRMATIONS, &c.

AFFIDAVITS IN PROOF OF MISS MONK'S STATEMENTS.—On page 135 we promised to give the affidavit of Mr. Hilliker, and statement of the Rev. Mr. Tappin. We subjoin the same :—" The affecting circumstance in which Mr. Hilliker and his associates first discovered Miss Monk, after her arrival in New York, are briefly stated in the following affidavit. It is to this kind and humane gentleman that the world is indebted, under a benign Providence, for the preservation of Miss Monk's testimony, by rescuing her from a premature grave, into which she was then rapidly sinking, after having spent several days in the forlorn situation in which she was thus discovered. I envy not the sensibilities of that man who can read it unmoved. 'John Hilliker, being duly sworn, doth depose and say— that one day early in the month of May, 1835, while shooting near the Third

Avenue, opposite the three mile stone, in company with three friends, I saw a woman sitting in a field at a short distance, who attracted our attention. On reaching her we found her sitting with her head down, and could not make her return any answer to our questions. On raising her hat we saw that she was weeping. She was dressed in an old calico frock, (I think of a greenish colour,) with a checked apron, and an old black bonnet. After much delay and weeping, she began to answer my questions, but not until I had got my companions to leave us, and assured her that I was a married man, and disposed to befriend her. She then told me that her name was Maria, that she had been a nun in a nunnery at Montreal, from which she had made her escape on account of the treatment she had received from priests in that institution, whose licentious conduct she strongly intimated to me. She mentioned some particulars concerning the convent and her escape. She spoke particularly of a small room where she used to attend, until the physician entered to see the sick, when she accompanied him to write down his prescriptions; and said that she escaped through a door which he sometimes entered. She added that she exchanged her dress after leaving the nunnery, and that she came to New York in company with a man, who left her as the steamboat arrived. She further stated that she expected soon to give birth to a child, having become pregnant in the convent; that she had no friend, and knew not where to find one; that she thought of destroying her life; and wished me to leave her—saying, that if I should hear of a woman being found drowned in the East River, she earnestly desired me never to speak of her. I asked her if she had had any food that day, to which she answered, no; and I gave her money to get some at the grocery of Mr. Cox, in the neighbourhood. She left me, but I afterwards saw her in the fields, going towards the river; and after much urgency prevailed upon her to go to a house where I thought she might be accommodated, offering to pay her expenses. Failing in this attempt, I persuaded her, with difficulty, to go to the Almshouse; and there we got her received, after I had promised to call and see her, as she said she had something of great consequence which she wished to communicate to me, and wished me to write a letter to Montreal. She had every appearance of telling the truth; so much so, that I have never for a moment doubted the truth of her story, but told it to many persons of my acquaintance, with entire confidence in its truth. She seemed overwhelmed with grief, and in a very desperate state of mind. I saw her weep for two hours or more without ceasing; and appeared very feeble when attempting to walk, so that two of us supported her by the arms. We observed, also, that she always folded her hands under her apron when she walked, as she has described the nuns as doing in her 'Awful Disclosures.' I called at the Almshouse gate several times and inquired for her; but having forgotten half of her name, I could not make it understood whom I wished to see, and did not see her until the last week. When I saw some of the first extracts from her book in a newspaper, I was confident that they were parts of her story, and when I read the conclusion of the work I had not a doubt of it. Indeed, many things in the course of the book I was prepared for from what she had told me. When I found her I recognised her immediately, although she did not know me at first, being in a very different dress. As soon as she was informed where she had seen me, she recognised me. I have not found in the book anything inconsistent with what she had stated to me when I first saw her. When I first saw her in May, 1835, she had evidently sought concealment. She had a letter in her hand, which she refused to let me see; and when she found I was determined to remove her she tore it in small pieces, and threw them down. Several days after I visited the spot again and picked them up, to learn something of the contents, but could find nothing intelligible, except the first part of the signature, 'Maria.' Of the truth of her story I have not the slightest doubt, and I think I never can until the nunnery is opened and examined. JOHN HILLIKER.

"Sworn before me, this 14th of March, 1836.
"PETER JENKINS, *Commissioner of Deeds.*"

"The following statement respecting the origin of Maria Monk's Disclosures and her first acquaintance with Mr. Hoyt, has the sanction of the Rev. Mr. Tappin, Chaplain, for several years past, of the Humane and Criminal Institutions of the city of New York—a gentleman of unblemished character.—In the summer of 1835, Maria Monk, authoress of the 'Awful Disclosures,' was seriously ill, and, as she supposed, on the borders of the grave. In this situation, she sent for me, and with all the solemnity of a dying hour, she communicated to me the principal statements respecting the Hotel Dieu Nunnery of Montreal, which she had since published to the world, in her disclosures. She did this by way of penitential confession. Her object appeared to be, not to criminate others, but to confess her own guilt, and thus relieve her troubled conscience; for she felt that she had, in some sense, been a participator in the horrid crimes which she divulged. At the time, it was evident to my mind, that she had no idea that her disclosures to me, would ever be made known to the public. The impression, which I then received of her honest sincerity, remains to this day uneffaced. This was some time before her acquaintance with Mr. Hoyt; who, having recently arrived in New York from Canada, and having heard of her case, called on me to make inquiries respecting it, and was, by me, introduced to her acquaintance.'

CONCLUSION.

The following circumstances comprise all that is deemed necessary now to subjoin to the preceding narrative:—

After my arrival in New York, I was introduced to the almshouse, where I was attended with kindness and care; and, as I hoped, was entirely unknown. But when I had been some time in that institution, I found that it was reported that I was a fugitive nun; and not long after an Irish woman, belonging to the house, brought me a secret message, which caused me some agitation.

I was sitting in the room of Mrs. Johnson, the matron, engaged in sewing, when that Irish woman, employed in the institution, came in and told me that Mr. Conroy was below, and had sent to see me. I was informed that he was a Roman priest, who often visited the house, and had a particular wish to see me at that time; having come, as I believe, expressly for that purpose. I showed unwillingness to comply with such an invitation, and did not go. The woman told me further, that he sent me word that I need not think to avoid him, for it would be impossible for me to do so. I might conceal myself as well as I could, but I should be found and taken. No matter where I went, or what hiding-place I might choose, I should be known; and I had better come at once. He knew who I was; and he was authorized to take me to the Sisters of Charity, if I should prefer to join them. He would promise that I might stay with them if I chose, and be permitted to remain in New York. He sent me word further, that he had received full power and authority over me from the Superior of the Hotel Dieu Nunnery at Montreal, and was able to do all she could do: as her right to dispose of me at her will had been imparted to him by a regular writing received from Canada. This was alarming information for me, in the weakness in which I was at that time. The woman added that the same authority had been given to all the priests; so that go where I might I should meet men informed about me and my escape, and fully empowered to seize me wherever they could, and convey me back to the Convent from which I had escaped.

Under these circumstances, it seemed to me that the offer to place me among the Sisters of Charity, with permission to remain in New York, was mild and favourable. However, I had resolution enough to refuse to see the priest Conroy.

Not long afterward I was informed, by the same messenger, that the priest was again in the building, and repeated his request. I desired one of the gentlemen connected with the institution, that a stop might be put to such messages, as I wished to receive no more of them. A short time after, however, the woman told me that Mr. Conroy wished to inquire of me, whether my name was not St. Eustace while a nun, and if I had not confessed to Priest Kelly in Montreal. I answered, that it was all true; for I had confessed to him a short time while in the Nunnery. I was then told again that the priest wanted to see me, and I sent back word that I would see him in the presence of Mr. T———, or Mr. S———; which, however, was not agreed to: and I was afterwards informed that Mr Conroy, the Roman priest, spent an hour in a room and a passage where I had frequently been; but, through the mercy of God, I was employed in another place at that time, and had no occasion to go where I should have met him. I afterward repeatedly heard, that Mr. Conroy continued to visit the house, and to ask for me; but I never saw him. I once had determined to leave the institution, which gave me time for further reflection; and I *was saved from the destruction to which I should have been exposed.*

As the period of my accouchement approached, I sometimes thought that I should not survive it; and then the recollection of the dreadful crimes I had witnessed in the nunnery would come upon me very forcibly, and I would think it a solemn duty to disclose them before I died. To have a knowledge of those things, and leave the world without making them known, appeared to me like a great sin, whenever I could divest myself of the impression made upon me by the declarations and arguments of the Superior, nuns, and priests, of the duty of submitting to every thing, and the necessary holiness of whatever the latter did or required.

The evening but one before the period which I anticipated with so much anxiety, I was sitting alone, and began to indulge in reflections of this kind. It seemed to me that I must be near the close of life, and I determined to make a disclosure at once I spoke to Mrs. Ford, a woman whose character I respected, a nurse in the hospital in number twenty-three. I informed her that I had no expectation of living long, and had some things on my mind which I wished to communicate before it should be too late. I added that I should prefer to tell them to Mr. T——, the chaplain; of which she approved, as she considered it a duty to do so under those circumstances. I had no opportunity, however, to converse with Mr. T. at that time, and, probably, my purpose of disclosing the facts already given in this book, would never have been executed, but for what subsequently took place.

It was alarm which led me to form such a determination; and when the period of trial had been safely passed, and I had a prospect of recovery, any thing appeared to me more unlikely than that I should make this exposure.

I was then a Roman Catholic, at least, a great part of my time; and my conduct, in a great measure, was according to the faith of a Roman Catholic. Notwithstanding what I knew of the conduct of so many of the priests and nuns, I thought that it had no effect on the sanctity of the Church, or the authority or effects of the acts performed by the former at mass, confession, &c. I had such regard for my vows as a nun, that I considered my hand as well as my heart irrevocably given to Jesus Christ, and could never have allowed any person to take it. Indeed, to this day, I feel an instinctive aversion to offering my hand, or taking the hand of another person, even as an expression of friendship. I also thought that I might soon return to the Roman Catholics, although fear and disgust held me back. I had now that infant to think for, whose life I had happily saved by my timely escape from the nunnery; and what its fate might be, in case it should ever fall into the power of the priests I could not tell.

I had, however, reason for alarm. Would a child, destined to destruction, like the infants I had seen baptised and smothered, be allowed to go through the world unmolested, a living memorial of the truth of crimes long practised in security, because never exposed? What pledges could I get to satisfy me, that I, on whom her dependence must be, would be spared by those who I had reason to think were wishing then to sacrifice me? How could I trust the helpless infant in hands which had hastened the baptism of many such, in order to hurry them to the secret pit in the cellar? Could I suppose that *Father Phelan, Priest of the Parish Church of Montreal,* would see *his own child* growing up in the world, and feel willing to run the risk of having the truth exposed? What could I expect, especially from him, but the utmost rancour, and the most determined enmity against the innocent child, and its abused and defenceless mother.

Yet my mind would sometimes still incline in the opposite direction, and indulge the thought, that perhaps the only way to secure heaven to us both was to throw ourselves back into the hands of the Church, to be treated as she pleased. When, therefore, the fear of immediate death was removed, I renounced all thoughts of communicating the substance of the facts in this volume. It happened, however, that my danger was not passed. I was soon seized with very alarming symptoms; then my desire to disclose my story revived.

I had before an opportunity to speak in private with the chaplain; but as it was at a time when I supposed myself out of danger, I had deferred for three days my proposed communication, thinking that I might yet avoid it altogether. When my symptoms, however, became more alarming, I was anxious for Saturday to arrive, the day which I had appointed; and when I had not the opportunity on that day which I desired, I thought it might be too late. I did not see him till Monday, when my prospects of surviving were very gloomy; and I then informed him that I wished to communicate to him a few secrets, which were likely otherwise to die with me. I then told him that while a nun in the Convent of Montreal I had witnessed the murder of a nun called St. Frances, and of at least one of the infants which I have spoken of in this book. I added some few circumstances, and, I believe, disclosed, in general terms, some of the crimes I knew of in that Nunnery.

My anticipations of death proved to be unfounded; for my health afterwards improved, and had I not made the confessions on that occasion, it is very possible I never might have made them. I, however, afterwards felt more willing to listen to instruction, and experienced friendly attentions from some of the benevolent persons around me, who, taking an interest in me on account of my darkened understanding, furnished me with the Bible, and were ever ready to counsel me when I desired it.

I soon began to believe that God might have intended that his creatures should learn his will by reading his word, and taking upon them the free exercise of their reason, and acting under responsibility to him.

It is difficult for one who has never given way to such arguments and influences, as those to which I had been exposed, to realise how hard it is to think aright after thinking wrong. The Scriptures always affect me powerfully when I read them; but I feel that I have but just begun to learn the great truths in which I ought to have been early and thoroughly instructed. I realize, in some degree, how it is that the Scriptures render the people of the United States so strongly opposed to such doctrines as are taught in the Black and Congregational Nunneries in Montreal. The priests and nuns used often to declare that of all heretics the children from the United States were the most difficult to be converted; and it was thought a great triumph when one of them was brought over to "The true faith." The first passage of Scripture that made any serious impression upon my mind was the text on which the chaplain preached on the Sabbath after my introduction to the house—" Search the Scriptures."

APPENDIX.

From Preface of last American Edition.

I would now appeal to the world, and ask whether I have not done all that could have been expected of me, and all that lay in my power, to bring to an investigation the charges I have brought against the priests and nuns of Canada. Although it was necessary to the cause of truth that I should, in some degree, implicate myself, I have not hesitated to appear as a voluntary self-accuser before the world. While there was a hope that the authorities in Canada might be prevailed upon to bring the subject to a legal investigation, I travelled to Montreal, in a feeble state of health, and with an infant in my arms only three weeks old. When all prospect of success in this undertaking had disappeared, and not till then, I determined to make my accusations through the press; and although misrepresentations and scandals, flattery and fear, have been resorted to, to nullify or to suppress my testimony, I have persevered, although, as many of my friends have thought, at the risk of abduction or death.

I have, I think, afforded every opportunity that could be reasonably expected, to judge of my credibility. I have appealed to the existence of things in the Hotel Dieu Nunnery as the great criterion of the truth of my story. I have described the apartments, and now, in this volume, have added many further particulars, with such a draft of them as my memory has enabled me to make. I have offered in case I should be proved an impostor, to submit to any punishment which may be proposed, even to a re-delivery into the hands of my bitterest enemies, to suffer what they may please to inflict.

Now in these circumstances, I would ask the people of the United States whether my duty has not been discharged? Have I not done what I ought to inform and to alarm them? I would also solemnly appeal to the government of Great Britain, under whose guardianship is the province, oppressed by the gloomy institution from which I have escaped, and ask whether such atrocities ought to be tolerated, and even protected, by an enlightened and christian power? I trust the hour is near when the dens of the Hotel Dieu will be laid open, when the tyrants who have polluted it will be brought out, with the wretched victims of their oppression and crime.

Extracts from the Long Island Star of Feb. 29th.

"Since the publication of our last paper, we have received a communication from Messrs. Howe and Bates, of New York, the publishers of Miss Monk's 'Awful Disclosures.' It appears that some influences have been at work in that city, adverse to the free examination of the case between her and the priests of Canada; for thus far the newspapers have been most entirely closed against every thing in her defence, while most of them have published false charges against the book, some of a preposterous nature, the contradiction of which is plain and palpable. * * *

"Returning to New York, she then first resolved to publish her story, which she has recently done, after several intelligent disinterested persons had satisfied themselves by much examination that it is true.

"When it became known in Canada that this was her intention, six affidavits were published in some of the newspapers, intended to destroy confidence in her character; but these were found very contradictory in several important points, and in others to afford undesigned confirmation of statements before made by her.

"On the publication of her book, the New York Catholic Diary, the Truth Teller, the Green Banner, and other papers, made virulent attacks upon it, and one of them proposed that the publishers should be 'lynched.' An anonymous handbill was also circulated in New York, declaring the work a malignant libel, got up by Protestant clergymen, and promising an ample refutation of it in a few days. This was re-published in the Catholic Diary, &c., with the old Montreal affidavits, which latter were also distributed through New York and Brooklyn; and on the authority of these, several Protestant newspapers denounced the work as false and malicious.

"Another charge, quite inconsistent with the rest, was also made, not only by the leading Roman Catholic papers, but by several others at second hand—viz. that it was a mere copy of an old European work. This has been promptly denied by the publishers, with the offer of 100 dollars reward for any book at all resembling it.

"Yet, such is the resolution of some, and the unbelief of others, that it is impossible for the publishers to obtain insertion for the replies in the New York papers generally, and they have been unsuccessful in an attempt in Philadelphia.

"This is the ground on which the following article has been offered to us, for publication in the Star. It was offered to Mr. Schneller, a Roman Priest, and Editor of the Catholic Diary, for insertion in his paper of Saturday before last, but refused, although written expressly as an answer to the affidavits and charges his previous number had contained. This article has also been refused insertion in a Philadelphia daily paper, after it had been satisfactorily ascertained that there was no hope of gaining admission for it into any of the New York papers.

"It should be stated, in addition, that the authoress of the book, Maria Monk, is in New York, and stands ready to answer any questions, and submit to any inquiries, put in a proper manner, and desires nothing so strongly as an opportunity to prove before a court the truth of her story. She has already found several persons of respectability who have confirmed some of the facts, important and likely to be attested by concurrent evidence; and much further testimony in her favour may be soon expected by the public.

"With these facts before them, intelligent readers will judge for themselves. She asks for investigation, while her opponents deny her every opportunity to meet the charges made against her. Mr. Schneller, after expressing a wish to see her, to the publishers, refused to meet her anywhere, unless in his own house; while Mr. Quarter, another Roman Catholic priest, called to see her, at ten o'clock, one night, accompanied by another man, without giving their names, and under the false pretence of being bearers of a letter from her brother in Montreal."

Reply to the Montreal Affidavits, refused publication by the Catholic Diary, &c.

(To the Editor of the Catholic Diary.)

"Sir,—In your paper of last Saturday, you published six affidavits from Montreal, which are calculated, so far as they are believed, to discredit the truth of the 'Awful Disclosures' of Maria Monk, a book of which we are the publishers. We address the following remarks to you, with a request that you will publish them in the 'Catholic Diary,' that your readers may have the means of judging for themselves. If the case be so plain a one as you seem to suppose, they will doubtless perceive more plainly the bearing and force of the evidence you present, when they see it brought into collision with that which it is designed to overthrow.

"First. We have to remark, that the affidavits which you publish might have been furnished you in this city, without the trouble or delay of sending to Montreal. They have been here two or three months, and were carefully examined about that period by persons who were acquainted with Maria Monk's story, and were desirous of ascertaining the truth. After obtaining further evidence from Canada, these affidavits were decided to contain strong confirmation of various points in her story, then already written down, only part of which has yet been published.

"Second. It is remarkable that of these six affidavits, the first is that of Dr. Robertson, and all the rest are signed by him as Justice of the Peace; and a Justice, too, who had previously refused to take the affidavit of Maria Monk. Yet, unknown to himself, this same Dr. R., by incidents of his own stating, corroborates some very important parts of Miss Monk's statements. He says, indeed, that he has ascertained where she was a part of the time when she professes to have been in the Nunnery. But his evidence on this point is merely hearsay, and he does not even favour us with that.

"Third. One of the affidavits is that of Miss Monk's mother, who claims to be a Protestant, and yet declares, that she proposed to send her infant grandchild to a Nunnery! She says her daughter has long been subject to fits of insanity, (of which, however, we can say, no traces are discoverable in New York;) and has never been in a Nunnery since she was at school in one, while quite a child. She, however, does not mention where her daughter has spent any part of the most important years of her life. A large part of her affidavit, as well as several others, is taken up with matter relating to one of the persons who accompanied Miss M. to Montreal last summer, and has no claim to be regarded as direct evidence for or against the authenticity of her book.

"Fourth. The affidavit of Nancy M'Gan is signed with a cross, as by one ignorant of writing; and she states that she visited a house of ill fame, (to all appearance alone,) although, as she asserts, to bring away Miss M. Her testimony, therefore, does not present the strongest claims to our confidence. Besides, it is known that she has shewn great hostility to Miss Monk, in the streets of Montreal; and she would not, it is believed, have had much influence on an intelligent court or jury, against Miss M., in that city, if the latter had been fortunate enough to obtain the legal investigation into her charges, which, as Dr. R. mentions, she has declared to be the express object of her visit to that city, in the last summer, and in which she failed, after a month's exertion.

"Fifth. The affidavit of Mr. Goodenough is contradicted in one point by the letter of Mr. Richey, a Wesleyan minister, which you insert, and contains little else of any importance to this or any other case. * * *

"Sixth. You copied in a conspicuous manner, from a Catholic paper in Boston, a charge against the book, the groundlessness of which has been exposed in some of the New York papers, viz. that large parts of it were 'Word for word, and letter for letter,' (names only altered) copied from a book published some years ago in Europe, under the title of 'The Gates of Hell opened.' We have not seen in your paper any correction of this aspersion, although the assertion of it has placed you in a dilemma; for, if such were the fact, as you asserted, the Montreal affidavits would have little application to the case. Besides, that book having proceeded from Catholics, and relating, as was intimated, to scenes in European Convents, divulged by witnesses not chargeable with prejudices against them, is to be taken for true with other names; and therefore the charge of extravagance or improbability, which is so much urged against our book, is entirely nullified, without appealing to other sources of information, which cannot be objected to.

"But before closing, allow us to remark that you, who claim so strongly the confidence of your readers in the testimony of witnesses in Montreal, who speak only of things collateral to the main subject in question, must be prepared to lay extraordinary weight on evidence of a higher nature, and must realise something of the anxiety with which we, and the American public generally, we believe, stand ready to receive the evidence to be displayed to the eye and to the touch, either for or against the solemn declaration of Miss Monk, whenever the great test shall be applied to which she appeals, viz. the opening of the Hotel Dieu Nunnery at Montreal. Then, sir, and not till then, will the great question be settled—is our book true or false? Affidavits may possibly be multiplied, although you say, 'Here, then, is the whole!' Dr. Robertson may be again called to testify, or receive testimony, as Justice of the peace,—but the question is not, what do people believe or think outside of the Convent? but 'What has been done in it?'

"By the issue of this investigation Miss Monk declares she is ready to stand or fall.

"You speak, sir, of the 'backwardness' of persons to appear in defence of Miss Monk's book. We promise to appear as often on the subject as you are willing to publish our communications. In one of the paragraphs you publish, our book is spoken of as one of the evils arising from a 'free press.' We think, sir, that 'a free press' is exposed to less condemnation through the

'Awful Disclosures,' than the 'close Nunneries' which it is designed to expose.

"Respectfully, &c.

"New York, Feb. 22, 1836."

The above was afterward copied in other papers. The following certificate appeared in the Protestant Vindicator and other papers, in March, 1836, introducing the two first witnesses.

The truth of Maria Monk's 'Awful Disclosures' amply certified.

"We, the Subscribers, having an acquaintance with Miss Maria Monk, and having considered the evidence of different kinds which has been collected in relation to her case, have no hesitation in declaring our belief in the truth of the statements she makes in her book recently published in New York, entitled 'Awful Disclosures,' &c.

"We at the same time declare that the assertion, originally made in the Roman Catholic newspapers of Boston, that the book was copied from a work entitled 'The Gates of Hell Opened,' is wholly destitute of foundation; it being entirely new, and not copied from any thing whatsoever.

"And we further declare, that no evidence has yet been produced which discredits the statements of Miss Monk: while, on the contrary, her story has received, and continues to receive, confirmation from various sources.

"During the last week, two important witnesses spontaneously appeared, and offered to give public testimony in her favour. From them the following delineations have been received. The first is an affidavit given by Mr. William Miller,* now a resident of this city. The second is a statement received from a young married woman, who, with her husband, also resides here. In the clear and repeated statements made by these two witnesses, we place entire reliance; who are ready to furnish satisfaction to any persons making reasonable enquiries on the subject.

"W. C. BROWNLEE,   "AMOS BELDEN,
"JOHN J. SLOCUM,   "DAVID WESSON,
"ANDREW BRUCE,   "THOMAS HOGAN."
"D. FANSHAW,

The following challenge was published in the New York

---

* The affidavits of Mr. Miller and others here alluded to, have been given in previous pages of this work.

Protestant Vindicator for six or seven weeks, in March and April, without a reply.

"CHALLENGE.—The Roman Prelate and Priests of Montreal—Messrs. Conroy, Quarter, and Schneller, of New York—Messrs. Fenwick and Byrne, of Boston—Mr. Hughes, of Philadelphia—the Arch-Prelate of Baltimore, and his subordinate Priests—and Cardinal England, of Charleston, with all other Roman Priests, and every Nun, from Baffin's Bay to the Gulf of Mexico, are hereby challenged to meet an investigation of the truth of Maria Monk's 'Awful Disclosures,' before an impartial assembly, over which shall preside *seven* gentlemen; three to be selected by the Roman Priests, three by the Executive Committee of the New York Protestant Association, and the seventh, as chairman, to be chosen by the six.

"An eligible place in New York shall be appointed, and the regulations for the decorum and order of the meetings, with all the other arrangements, shall be made by the above gentlemen."

From the New York Protestant Vindicator, April 6, 1836.

"THE CHALLENGE.—We have been waiting with no small degree of impatience to hear from some of the Roman priests. But neither they, nor their sisters, the nuns, nor one of their nephews or *neices*, have yet ventured to come out. Our longings meet only with dissapointment. Did ever any person hear of similar conduct on the part of men accused of the highest crimes, in their deepest dye? Here is a number of Roman priests, as actors, or accessories, openly denounced before the world as guilty of the most outrageous sins against the sixth and seventh commandments. They are charged before the world with adultery, fornication, and murder! The allegations are distinctly made, the place is mentioned, the parties are named, and the time is designated; for it is lasting as the annual revolution of the seasons. And what is most extraordinary,—*the highest official authorities in Canada know that all those statements are true, and they sanction and connive at the iniquity!*—The priests and nuns have been offered, for several months past, the most easy and certain mode to disprove the felonies imputed to them, and they are still as the dungeons of the Inquisition, silent as the death-like quietude of the convent cell; and as retired as if they were in the subterraneous passages between the nunnery and Lartique's habitation. Now, we contend, that scarcely a similar instance of disregard for the opinions of mankind, can be found since the Reformation, at least, in a Protestant country. Whatever disregard for the judgment of others, the Romish priests may have felt, where the

Bring me before a Court
Maria Monk

Inquisition was at their command, and the civil power was their Jackal and their Hyæna, they have been obliged to pay some little regard to the opinion of Protestants, and to the dread of exposure. We therefore repeat the solemn indubitable truth—that the facts which are stated by Maria Monk, respecting the Hotel Dieu Nunnery, at Montreal, are true as the existence of the priests and nuns—that the character, principles, and practices of the Jesuits and nuns in Canada, are most accurately delineated—that popish priests, and sisters of charity in the United States, are their faithful and exact counterparts—that many female schools kept by the papist teachers, are nothing more than places of decoy through which young women, at the most delicate age, are ensnared into the power of the Roman priests—and that the toleration of the monastic system in the United States and Britain, the only two countries in the world, in which that unnatural abomination is now extending its withering influence, is high treason against God and mankind. If American citizens and British Christians, after the appalling developments which have been made, permit the continuance of that prodigious wickedness which is inseparable from nunneries and the celibacy of popish priests, they will ere long experience that divine castigation which is justly due to transgressors who wilfully trample upon all the appointments of God, and who subvert the foundation of national concord, and extinguish the comforts of domestic society. Listen to the challenge again! *All the papers with which the Protestant Vindicator exchanges, are requested to give the challenge one or two insertions.*" (Here it was repeated.)

FURTHER CONFIRMATIONS AND GENERAL REMARKS.

We have promised our readers to give them extracts from a volume entitled —" Confirmations of Maria Monk's Disclosures;" and shall now do so, giving all that is interesting and to the point; and shall here close our labours, without swelling out the book to an unreasonable extent with extraneous matter.

In the notes attached to this work already given, we think there is sufficient to satisfy the mind of any impartial reader of the truth of the assertions made by Miss Monk; but as we wish not to leave a doubt on the minds of any; we give further confirmations. The volume from which the greater part of these extracts are taken, was edited and partly written by the Rev. J. J. Slocum, an esteemed minister of the gospel, at New York.

"The following is taken from an able article in the New York observer.—

"'Popery forbids its priests and ecclesiastics to marry, and encourages the devotion of each sex to a single life. Hence convents are provided both for monks and nuns, to which they may respectively retire from the world, and lead a life of holy seclusion, as it is termed, from the temptations of the flesh. Nature cries out against this unnatural and forced separation of the sexes. Reason condemns it as monstrous and absurd, and religion pronounces upon the unnatural and absurd prohibition its severest denunciations, '*forbidding to marry*,' being expressly classed with the '*doctrine of devils.*" We cannot escape from the conclusion that a course which nature, reason, and religion unite to condemn, must be productive of evils of a kind and extent commensurate with the folly, absurdity, and impiety of the parent evil. We here see one of the strongest passions of human nature, a passion implanted in man for the wisest purposes by the God of nature, unnaturally restrained by pains and penalties. What power has unhallowed vows to bind where God has not required the sacrifice—where he has, in fact, prohibited it? Need I pursue the details of the degenerating process to show the easy steps by which passion thus restrained descends to crime? How the nun, at the confessional, must pour into the ear of a man the secret conflicts of her own breast with regard to this very passion; how the priest questions; and how he may advise his fair penitent in secret? Need I depict the voluntarily incurred temptations to which both are exposed by this most unnatural intercourse? It can scarcely be otherwise than that crime should be the result. Both priests and nuns are kept from its commission by no *human* restraint, and certainly by no promise of *divine* assistance, but they are left weak and unaided to contend with, and to be vanquished by, this strongest of human passions. Love thus perverted is lust, and every one knows that the secret servant of lust is murder. In reason's name I would ask, what is the object of female cloistered convents? Why congregate an assembly of youthful females, and then bind them, not only with bolts and bars, but with the most solemn and superstitious vows and oaths, never more to have any communication with the world? Why deprive such of that liberty which the God of nature has given to all mankind? To imprison an individual for life, and thus deprive him of his liberty, is considered to be next to the highest punishment that can be inflicted for crime. But of what crime have the helpless victims of female convents been guilty prior to their becoming nuns? Can it be said that the religion of the Son of God demands such imprisonment? If so, where is the chapter and verse? I have never been able to find it. But I do find that Christ was "*To proclaim liberty to the captives, and the opening of the prison to them that are bound.*" The voice of Christianity therefore, is that the doors of these female prison houses be opened, and that the captives be set at liberty. Christianity is from heaven. It came into the world, not to derange and break up the institutions of man's social nature, but to hallow and purify them. Did the God of nature make woman for society, or to shut her up in a nunnery? Let the advocates of nunneries read the second chapter of the first book of their Bibles, if they have any; and they will learn that woman was made for man, not to be shut up in a prison. Revelation, therefore, is against nunneries. Reason still presses the inquiry, why should inoffensive and unsuspecting young ladies be decoyed from the path of life which Christianity prescribes, and be entombed for life within the walls of a convent? *Young ladies*, I say, for the priests will have no others, unless it should be some who were very rich, and received for the sake of their wealth. This fact proves to a demonstration that the object cannot be of a religious character, for if it were, then the aged and the infirm, who are now excluded, would of all others, be received. I am aware of the fact that a religious profession is the bait by which young females are enticed by the priests and their panderers into nunneries. They are made to believe that the moment they enter a convent they are thenceforth removed from all worldly temptation, and are, during the remainder of their lives, to be devoted exclusively to the holy duties of religion. But that this is untrue is evident, not only from the testimony of eloped nuns and others, but from the above-named fact, viz. that the aged and infirm, to whom such retirement and religious employment might possibly be desirable, are the very persons who are excluded. Nor can the object be for purposes of charity, such as educating poor children, and nursing the sick. I am aware that the latter is connected with the Hotel Dieu—that there is a fine hospital there, and that many of the sick have reaped essential benefit from it. But, I ask, what necessary connexion there is between this charity, and the imprisonment for life of scores of young and tender females? Cannot the sick be taken care of without doing such violence to the laws both of God and nature? The sick are nursed, and the poor are educated, to say the least, among Protestants, who have no occasion for nunneries, as well as they are among Catholics. The truth is, this charity business is a mere outward garb—fair to appearance, like a 'whited sepulchre,' designed, in connexion with a 'Religious profession,' to conceal from the public eye the real object which the priests have in view in sustaining cloistered convents. Roman priests are required by their religion habitually to violate a primary law of the human constitution, in being required to live a life of celibacy. But nature protests against the requisition, and determines on seeking relief from some other source. But concealment is requisite in order to give external consistency to their professions of chastity. How then can gratification and concealment be secured? A cloistered nunnery, under the colours of peculiar sanctity and charity, presents itself as affording both the requisites. Concealment, however, requires something more than the most arrant deceit and hypocrisy. Children and refractory nuns must be disposed of; and to secure this, habitual murder is necessary, as well as a system of the most severe and tyrannical discipline. Sin, in its progress, being downward, where will it stop? What bounds can you set to it, when unbridled, as in a convent, concealed from the public eye? The Hotel Dieu is of long standing, and has grown ripe in iniquity. Hence but a small portion of its diabolical abominations can be disclosed by Maria Monk in the world. There are others which ought not to be 'Once named, as becometh saints.' It seems, then, that the real object of cloistered nunneries is, so far as they respect the priests, their own licentious gratification. Now I do not say that this was their original intention. I think it was not. But they soon degenerated into it. Hence the ultimate design of the scores of incipient nunneries in these United States. Oh, that they were rightly understood by mothers and by daughters! Then we should hear of no more taking the veil. The conclusion therefore, of the whole matter under this head is this—That the Disclosures of Maria Monk are just what might rationally be expected from the nature of the case; from priestly celibacy in connexion with cloistered females. How futile, then, is the following question of the priests— 'Now we ask the ten thousand readers of the book (Awful Disclosures) if the deeds therein alleged are not incompatible with human nature,—if anything that is known of man's capacity for crime can render them credible?' What is the history of Popery but, to a great extent, a history of just such incompatibilities?"

Some of our readers may not, perhaps, be aware that the priests of Montreal published a book, entitled, "Awful Exposure of an atrocious Plot, formed by certain individuals against the clergy and nuns of Lower Canada, through the intervention of Maria Monk;" in which book they vainly attempted by sophistry, deceit and glaring falsehood, to disprove Maria Monk's statements. But from good authority, we learn that nearly the whole number of copies printed of this book, were sold at waste paper price. The style and writing of the said book is characterized as vulgar and wretched in the extreme. They deny that ever Maria Monk inhabited the convent; but that she did reside in the Hotel Dieu Nunnery we have already given our readers abundant proof.

Another point upon which an attempt is made to overthrow the Disclosures, is—the subterranean passage. The priests deny that any such passage exists, or ever existed; but that it did and does exist, we have abundant testimony; *although they threw the Nunnery doors open for the public to examine the building;* and it could not be seen; for we are very credibly informed, by a gentlemen who recently visited Montreal, that while the road was being opened to lay down either water or gas pipes, *the subterranean passage was discovered.* We take this to be a very important feature in the evidence in favour of Miss Monk; inasmuch as the priests pretend that the non-existence of the passage is good proof of the imposition. The following extract proves that Maria Monk was a resident of the Nunnery, and also, that the passage does exist.

"The subjoined testimony of Mr. Miller and Mrs. Hahn has been some time before the public. That of Mrs. Hahn is the more important. It is that of an old companion, and of course there can be no mistake as to her acquaintance with Miss Monk. Mrs. Hahn described the person of Miss Monk, and stated the substance of her testimony before she saw her; and before Miss Monk knew any thing of Mrs. Hahn's residing in New York. Collusion, therefore, between the parties, is out of the question. Mr. Jones, while in New York, inquired of me what I should say respecting Mrs. Hahn's testimony, if she herself were to acknowledge that it was false. I replied that it would not in the least shake my confidence in its substantial truth, for such were the circumstances connected with the giving of it, that my reliance was chiefly upon them. Mrs. Hahn, however, remains unchanged as to the truth of her statements. Mr. William Miller, a resident of New York for several years past, and formerly an old schoolmate of Maria's in Montreal, testifies that, on a visit to the latter city, in 1833, he called on Mrs. Monk, the mother of Maria, and inquired for Maria; and was informed by her that her daughter Maria was *then in the nunnery.* See his affidavit, Awful Disclosures, page 73.—The priests, in their work, dispose of this affidavit by exhorting Mr. Miller to *repent!* Mrs. Hahn, now a resident of New York, and formerly a schoolmate of Miss Monk, testifies that she was with Maria in the school of the Congregational nunnery for about two years: that she was present at the time that Maria was received as a novice in the Hotel Dieu; and that she saw her some time after this, while she was yet a novice: and that she saw her a veiled nun, towards the close of the winter of 1833-4, in the hospital of the Hotel Dieu, which she at that time frequently visited, in order to see a sick friend: and that 'a short time afterwards,' she saw her again in the same place among the veiled nuns. The gentleman who penned her works, is a gentleman of high standing in the community, for literature, integrity, and piety. No man could have felt a deeper solicitude on the subject, than he has felt. He has felt, that not only his own reputation was at stake, but that truth —to him priceless—was to achieve new victories, or receive detriment, according as Miss Monk's testimony should prove true or false. Hence he has spared no pains to get at the simple truth of the case, whatever that might be. I trust that the reader will not consider it out of place, for the writer of these pages to add his own opinion to the above. It is now some eight or nine months, since Miss Monk came to reside among the people of my pastoral charge. During this time I have seen her in a variety of circumstances; have heard her converse with friends and enemies, Protestants and Catholics, and men of all professions; have improved every opportunity, which God in his providence has given me, to ferret out the truth in relation to her claims—and as the result of the whole, I deliberately say, that I have never seen any thing which led me, for any length of time, to doubt the general truth of her story; but on the contrary, the evidence of its truth has been constantly augmenting, so that I could almost as easily believe any supposable impossibility, as to believe that she has been acting the part of an impostor, in what she has done. It is known to many, that there is a subterranean passage, leading from the priest's Seminary to the Hotel Dieu. In addition to what is said on former pages of the Awful Disclosures, respecting this passage, the following, taken from St. Alban's Franklin Journal, is subjoined. Even Mr. Jones, the publisher of the "Awful Exposure," admitted, to several gentlemen in New York, that there was such a passage; but that it was not more than thirty feet long! The existence of this passage is known to many in Montreal. What is the object of such a passage? Can any thing virtuous require that a house of priests should be thus united, by a concealed, under-ground passage, to an establishment of secluded women? And I would further ask, how a man, who believes in the existence of such a secret communication, can disbelieve the 'Awful Disclosures' of Maria Monk? If the priests are such licentious hypocrites, as to need a dark, under-ground passage to the women of the Hotel Dieu, from the commission of what crime would they abstain, which they considered necessary to conceal their infamy from the public eye? Would they refrain from the murder of infants and nuns? That man has but a slight acquaintance with human depravity, that can believe they would. The following is the communication alluded to.—'As there is some excitement in the community upon the subject of Popish licentiousness and vice, from the Disclosures of Maria Monk, and as some affect to disbelieve and ridicule her work, as totally false, being in possession of some strong evidence that will confirm her statements, I give the public these facts. In conversation with a gentleman, who was some months since a Roman Catholic in Montreal, but has renounced their blasphemous dogmas, and is now a professed Christian, he told me, that he had been employed to labour in the cellars of the Priest's Seminary at Montreal, and while there engaged, he discovered a door in the wall of the cellar, which on opening, he found it connected with a passage under ground. He entered the passage and passed through it until he came to some stairs, at the head of which was a trap-door. From the direction and distance of the passage, he was perfectly certain that it must be a subterraneous communication between the Seminary and the Convent. He further informed me, that from the testimony of many females, his relatives not excepted, that the priests were in the habit of asking the most licentious and revolting questions that could be propounded, not only to married ladies, but also to girls of thirteen years. Likewise from the habiliments of the nuns, and their appearance at times, he was wholly confirmed in the belief that that their course in the nunnery was any thing but virtuous. At the time of his making these disclosures, I think Maria had not written her book. I think testimony of this kind is powerfully corroborative, and that these things exist, I fully believe. It is truly painful to come before the public with so offensive a subject, but believing the contagion of death to be spreading through the community by Catholicism, leaving putrescence and woe behind, I feel constrained thus to appear. 'E. SPRAGUE.

'*St. Albans, July,* 1836.'"

"The ensuing statement is from a gentleman who was for many years a resident in Montreal For reasons satisfactory to himself, his name is withheld. His testimony is undoubtedly true. 'I often heard of a subterranean passage, from the Seminary to the Hotel Dieu nunnery, years ago; and while the cathedral was building, I often saw that part of it which was opened in digging for the foundation. It was near the foundation. It was near the east corner of the cathedral, where the waterworks were laid along St. Joseph's Street. Several years before, I saw the same passage opened in another place by the workmen, who had removed several stones and exposed it to view. I have often heard it spoken of, as a thing very generally known; and never heard any doubt of its existence, until the appearance of Mr. Jones' book, and Mr. Stone's pamphlet.'

"The following documents on the subject of the subterranean passage, are extracted from the American Protestant Vindicator, of November 2, 1836. They have appeared since the above was written :—The first witness is the Rev. *Oliver Wetmore*, of Utica. In a late conversation with that beloved minister of the gospel, he thus remarked—Mr. Stone says: 'No subterranean passage between the Seminary and the Hotel Dieu nunnery, at Montreal, was ever seen or heard of!' *That is not true!* When I travelled as a missionary in the northern parts of the State of New York, *thirty-three years ago*, I was frequently at the house of Judge Moer, who resided about a mile from the Canada line. That gentleman repeatedly talked with me respecting the Roman priests and Popery, in Montreal, which he had often visited. He spoke of the *subterranean passage between the Seminary and the Nunneries*, as a matter of most public notoriety; and detailed the dissolute habits of the priests, their habitual gambling, intemperance, and profligacy, as well as the licentiousness of the female convents of Montreal; which Judge Moers said, were as open matters of talk at that period, in that city, just as much as the common affairs of life. Judge Moers also represented to me the priests and nuns of Montreal, from his own personal acquaintance with them, in exactly the same light and character, *thirty-three years ago*, as they have lately been exhibited before the American public. Mr. Stone, therefore, to my own certain knowledge, has published that which is not true!'"

"It appears, from this statement, that the existence of an underground passage, between the priests' Seminary and the nunnery, has been a matter of conversation for many years. The next statement is from the Rev. George Bourne, of New York:—

"'I most solemnly affirm, that the late Rev. Mr. Christmas, conducted me in the year 1825, I believe, for I have but one criterion by which I can determine the first time that I saw it, to visit the subterranean passage, between the Seminary and the Hotel Dieu convent; and that we frequently afterwards stood over that passage together. At other times, in company with different Christian brethren, I have also examined that underground avenue from the Seminary to the Nunnery: at least, that part of it which was open for common inspection for a considerable period, during the completion of the cathedral in that city.

"'GEORGE BOURNE.'"

"The following is the affidavit of Mr. Hogan, now a respectable member of the Methodist church, of New York, but formerly a Roman Catholic student of the Seminary of Montreal:—

"'*New York*, October 26, 1836.

"'Thomas Hogan, of the city of New York, being duly affirmed, doth say: That in the year 1824, he was a resident of the city in Montreal, Lower Canada—that at that period, the existence of a subterranean passage between the Seminary in Notre-Dame Street, and the Hotel Dieu convent, was a matter of the most public notoriety; and that he himself has been in that passage, having entered it from the door in the Seminary—and the said Hogan doth further depose, that to his own personal knowledge, the Roman priests were constantly in the practice of visiting the nuns, for the purpose of licentious intercourse, by that secret passage.

"'THOMAS HOGAN.'

"'Affirmed this 26th day of October, 1836.
"'Before me, William H. Bogardus, Commissioner of Deeds.'"

"Who, after this, can doubt the existence of such a communication between the two establishments? And the question may be reiterated, what is the object of such a passage? Can it be any thing lawful? If so, what is it? The world would be glad to know what it may be. It is hardly necessary to remind the reader of the fact, that the above testimony furnishes a high degree of evidence in confirmation of the general truth of the 'Awful Disclosures.'"

The conduct of Miss Monk's opponents, furnishes another argument in her support. The position, which they have taken, that she is an impostor, and never has been a nun, if true could have been proved beyond all doubt with one thousandth part of the labour, which they have fruitlessness bestowed in their several attempts to prove it. They admit, that till within a short time of the publication of their book, she lived in about Montreal. Could they not then, with very little trouble, have shewn where, and with whom she lived, during the time she professes to have been a nun in the Hotel Dieu Nunnery? The Rev. J. J. Slocum continues:—

"But let us look at their conduct a little in the detail. When Miss Monk visited Montreal in the month of August, 1835, and there presented her criminal charges against the priests and nuns, it was denied that she had ever been a nun in the Hotel Dieu nunnery. In proof that she had been an inmate of that convent, Miss Monk offered to furnish a description of its interior—its apartments, its persons, and their occupations, &c.—and urged the examination of the nunnery, with a view to the application of the proposed test. Certainly this was fair on her part. Why, then, did not the priests comply with the proposal? If she had been an impostor, what easier and more ready mode of proving it, to the satisfaction of all concerned, could they have required? The reply often made, that she and her friends were unworthy of their notice, and that the convent was a sacred place, not to be inspected by men from the world, is not less insulting than it is untrue; for they did notice her, by collecting and publishing things against her; and men from the world, such as they have been pleased to select, have been admitted into the nunnery to inspect it. Does not their conduct in this particular betray guilt?

"A short time after Miss Monk returned to New York from Montreal, her opponents made an attempt to prove an alibi—to show that she was elsewhere than in the convent, during the time in which she declares herself to have been in that establishment. They collected and published six or eight affidavits. Five of them refer exclusively to matters subsequent to her arrival in Montreal. The other two are those of Dr. Robertson and her mother, Mrs. Monk. Dr. Robertson states, that on inquiry, he had ascertained that she was at service in Sorel and St. Denis, a portion of the time which she professed to have been in the nunnery; and Mrs. Monk says, that she once told certain persons, that her daughter had not been in the nunnery. This is the amount of their testimony; and, if Maria Monk had been an impostor, can any man believe that the priests and their advocates, would have rested their cause on a foundation so substantial as this? Does not the weakness of their defence, show the unsoundness of their cause?

"The next step worthy of notice in the conduct of the priests, is the visit of Father Phelan of Montreal to New York, in order to decoy Miss Monk away from her friends in that city. This was in the winter of 1835-6. As this priest came to New York in disguise, leaving an impression in Montreal that he had gone to spend a few weeks on Nun's Island, it is presumed, that his visit to this city will be denied. It can, however, be proved that he was in New York at the time specified, and that the impression was made in Montreal that he had gone to the Island. It has been published again and again, without being as yet contradicted, from any responsible source. Why then should that priest visit New York under such circumstances, unless it were in some way to destroy Miss Monk's testimony? He knew her feelings towards himself as the father of her child; and he knew that a special intimacy had been formed and cherished between himself and her, during her residence in the nunnery; in a word, he knew that if any man could draw her away from her friends in New York, or induce her to withhold her testimony, he was the man. Out of regard to him, Miss Monk was perfectly silent respecting his visit to New York, until after the abduction plot, during the following summer, had been developed. It was, however, noticed by her friends, that her feelings towards him, during this lapse of time, were different from what they were, prior to this visit. Now if Miss Monk were an impostor, is it supposeable that this priest would have thus visited her? And does not this visit stamp with the seal of truth her claims as an ex-nun? What stronger evidence can be demanded?

"The design of the plot was to induce Miss Monk voluntarily to leave New York. The plot was well formed, and well conducted; and would have succeeded, had it not been thwarted by the untiring vigilance of Miss Monk's friends. Miss Monk was completely deceived by her uncle until the time specified by her in her narrative of the affair, when a gentleman called on her, and made known to her the true nature and design of the plot. I was present at the time when the gentleman called, and I regret that it is not permitted me to mention, at present, particulars as to the betrayal of one of the enemy, by which the ultimate object of the scheme was communicated to her. Now they knew whether or not Miss Monk was an impostor: on this point they could not possibly be mistaken. Would they, then, be at so much trouble and expense to decoy away a known impostor? The supposition is preposterous in the extreme. It is therefore evident that she is not an impostor.

"The next attempt on the part of the priests to vindicate themselves, worthy of special consideration, is to be found in their book entitled, 'Awful Exposure.' The contents of this book have been examined, and it is believed that the candid reader is prepared to unite in pronouncing the attempt to be an entire failure."

There are two things in the disclosures of Maria Monk which render them comparatively incredible to the public. First, the enormity of the crimes which she declares to have been perpetrated in the Hotel Dieu Nunnery of Montreal; and secondly, the coldhearted manner in which they are said to be habitually practised in that establishment. But we shall now furnish our readers with a few extracts from a standard Catholic author, for the purpose of illustrating the character of convents, and of shewing that the statements made by Miss Monk are in perfect keeping with the past history of those infamous dens. The priests, who published and edited, the "Awful Exposure," (the reply to Maria Monk's Disclosures,) again and again refer to the life and writings of Scippio de Ricci, a Roman Catholic Bishop, whom they represent as a model writer on convents. We, therefore, take the following extracts from his writings. And it should be borne in mind, that these disclosures of Scippio de Ricci, were made, *not in the dark ages*, but *only* some fifty or sixty years since. Further, it should be borne in mind that Scippio de Ricci, was not a Protestant, or an enemy to Convents, but a friend and a staunch Catholic. And it should be remembered also, that this prelate, not having been connected with convents, knew nothing of them but what he learned by report, and in his attempts to reform them. But the case with Maria Monk was different. She was an inmate of the convent for years, where she had every opportunity of witnessing its abominations. Reader! ponder well the subjoined extracts; and say whether you do not see therein abundant historic confirmation of Maria Monk's Disclosures.

"The Dominican Monks, who were members of one of the most numerous ecclesiastical orders, had been the scandal of all Italy, during one-hundred-and-fifty years, for their total corruption: and their direction of the female convents had degenerated into a scene of the basest profligacy. Long habit had so accustomed them to the greatest licentiousness, that scarcely any respect for public decency remained.'"—"Memoirs of Scipio de Ricci, pages 96, 97, vol. i."

"The nuns of Pistoia testified that the monks taught them 'every kind of vice,' and that they should look upon it as a great happiness, 'that they were able to *satisfy their libidinous desires, without the inconvenience of children.*'"

"It was necessary to raze from the foundations a monastery and a female convent of Carmelites, which were in fact joined by means of subterranean passages."—Vol. i. pages 98, 121.

"A Hindoo brahmin, having become a Catholic priest, says: 'The Roman priests in India, are like the bonzes of Japan. The nuns are the disciples of Diana, and their nunneries are seraglios for the monks. They were more often pregnant than married women in general. The Jesuits had become brahmins, in order to enjoy the privileges of that caste; among which were exemption from death for crime; and the right of enjoying the favours of every woman that pleased them, it being generally received, that a brahmin priest sanctifies the woman whom he honours with his attentions.'"—Vol. ii. pages 216. 217.

"'The monks, confessors of the convents, openly taught the Tuscany nuns atheism; encouraged the most disgraceful libertinism; and filled them with impurity, sacrilege, and debauchery of the foulest kinds. Immorality was thus added to profanation; and corruption brought forth impiety. By tolerating these crimes, the pope plainly announced his indulgence of them; and by encouraging the commission of those iniquities, he became an accomplice.'"—Vol. ii. pages 263, 264.

"'The false or forged virtues of the monks and nuns, are but a tissue of hypocrisy, and a stimulant to the most odious vices. The institutions called *Virginales*, were schools of corruption and licentiousness: and the *soi-distant* tribunal of *penitence* is the constant source of infamous wickedness, by those infamous jugglers, whose authority depends on the blindness of man. The monks, the nuns, their superiors, and even the pope himself, not only tolerated these disorders, but took no measures to arrest the infidelity and impiety of those who were daily adding new victims to their atheism and inordinate voluptuousness.'"—Vol. ii. pages 276, 277.

"But enough of such filth; for it is filth of the darkest dye; and as such ought not to be named, did not the cause of humanity, virtue, and religion, demand it, for the same reason that the Son of God divested the ancient scribes and Pharisees, the embryo prototypes of Romish priests, of their hypocritical robes, and thus enabled the people to see that they were 'FULL OF DEAD MEN'S BONES, AND OF ALL UNCLEANNESS.' Matt. xxiii. 27. The Saviour knew that there was no other way to destroy the superstitious veneration with which the Jews regarded their priests, just as the Catholics, only in a much higher degree, regard theirs. The naming of such vices, should be regarded as an evil, the object of which is the removal of a much greater one; just in the sense in which many a medical prescription is an evil, absolutely necessary, however, to be administered, in order to remove disease, and secure health. The unqualified condemnation, therefore, of this moral medicine, on the ground that some writers deal in it too freely, is as absurd as it would be to condemn the 'healing art,' because unskilful men abuse it.

"Before leaving this subject, I wish to add a single remark further. And that is this: That all the vices spoken of by Maria Monk, as practised in the Hotel Dieu, (yea, and more too,) are abundantly inculcated by the standard writers, on morals of the order of Jesuits. If any man wishes proof of this assertion, I would refer him, among others, to Paschal's Provincial letters, a work of undying celebrity. Paschal was himself a Roman Catholic, but opposed to the Jesuits.

"According to these moralists, a priest may commit lewdness on the ground of self-gratification; and then on the ground of self-defence or defending his reputation, he may lawfully murder, deceive, lie, and swear falsely, or employ others to do the same for him. I know that these principles are horrid beyond conception. But they are true; and I hold myself pledged to prove them, giving chapter and verse, if the priests, in any responsible manner, have the audacity to deny them.

"Who, then, after reading the preceding part of this chapter, can seriously question the general truth of Maria Monk's statements respecting the character of the Canadian priests and nuns? Especially when it is recollected, that a large portion of these priests are foreign Jesuits, expelled from foreign countries, as an order of men too infamous to be tolerated by civil governments. They have been expelled, as an order of men, from almost every country in Europe, by Catholic as well as Protestant governments. Hence they come in swarms to the North American continent, bringing along with them their ill-gotten gain, by which they build colleges, churches, nunneries, &c. The 'Disclosures' of Miss Monk, therefore, are unquestionably true, and they would be substantially true, even if it should be proved that she had never been a nun in the Hotel Dieu. This is the opinion of the mass of the Protestant people in Canada. It is to be hoped, therefore, that the testimony of Maria Monk will no more be disbelieved on the ground that she discloses practices so abominable, as to cause virtue to hide its blushing face at the very mention of them.

"In conclusion, I will mention two facts, which ought not to be forgotten. 1st. A large number of the Canadian priests are Jesuits, from France: and 2nd. The fact that when Bonaparte broke up the convents in France, bones of murdered infants were found in great abundance. Can it then be supposed, that the French Jesuits are any better in Canada, than they were in France?"

Although Miss Monk repeatedly challenged an impartial investigation of the matter no notice was ever taken of it; in consequence of which, a party of gentlemen, in America, formed themselves into a committee; and at one of their meetings, formed the following resolutions; of which, let the reader remember, the priests have never to this day, attempted to take any notice.

"At a meeting convened in the American Tract Society's Rooms, at the call of several gentlemen, for the purpose of considering the controversy existing between Maria Monk and the Romish Priests of the Montreal Diocese, Francis D. Allen, Esq. was called to the chair, and the Rev. Octavius Winslow appointed as Secretary. The following Preamble and Resolutions were unanimously adopted:—

"Whereas, Maria Monk has hitherto appealed in vain to the Canadian Authorities, both civil and ecclesiastical, to bring her charges against the Romish priests of the Montreal Diocese to some equitable tribunal for investigation; and whereas she now appeals to the people of the United States, invoking them to interpose in her behalf, and demand that justice be rendered to her, a lonely girl, in her peculiarly trying and unequal controversy with the priests of the Romish church; and, whereas the people of the United States—besides being always disposed to listen to the voice of the friendless and the persecuted—have a deep and solemn interest in the matter in dispute, in consequence of the rapid increase of Popery, and of Popish institutions in their country; and also in consequence of the contiguity of the Canadian nunneries, and their intimate connexion with, and influence upon, the rising institutions of America:—Therefore,

"Resolved, 1st. That it is the sense of this meeting that the appeal of Maria Monk to the American people ought to be promptly and efficently responded to, so far as the nature of the case will admit of.

"Resolved, 2nd, That the conduct of the Romish Montreal priests and their advocates—(1) in attempting, by every means, to asperse and vilify the character of Maria Monk; and (2) in attempting, through the most artful deceptions, to decoy her into their hands; and (3) in refusing, for the space of one full year, to allow the matter of controversy to be brought to a fair trial; bespeaks anything rather than manly honesty and virtuous innocence.

"Resolved 3rd, That the recent examination, said to have been made, of the Hotel Dieu Nunnery of Montreal is altogether unsatisfactory; because (1) the gentlemen engaged in it have been, from the beginning, *strongly and actively prejudiced* against Maria Monk. Mr. Jones, editor of a Romish paper, under the auspices of the priests, and principal mover in getting up the book against Maria Monk, which is about to appear, containing, among other things, the results of this party examination, was their leader. And because (2) *material alterations are said to have been made in and around the convent during the past year*—alterations such as doubtless would easily deceive *such* a committee of examiners. For these reasons any report unfavourable to Maria Monk, made by these disqualified examiners, ought to have no influence in deciding the controversy.

"Resolved, 4th, That the recent effort of the priests and their defenders to make it appear that Maria Monk, instead of describing the Hotel Dieu Nunnery and its inmates, has described a place which they call a 'Magdalen Asylum;' and also, their attempts to prove, by the affidavits of some unprincipled profligates and infidels, calling themselves protestants, and of ignorant papists, that she never was a nun, but that she has been of a bad character, living in brothels, &c., is highly characteristic of Jesuitism; adapted to blind and bewilder the public mind, and turn it away from the single point to which it ought to be directed, viz., *an impartial examination of the convent.*

"Resolved, 5th, That the demand made and reiterated by Maria Monk during the space of a full year, viz. that herself in person, accompanied by her friends, as well as enemies, should be permitted to explore the Nunnery, is perfectly reasonable and right; and that a further refusal in the present state of the case, forthwith to comply with it on the part of the Hotel Dieu Ecclesiastics, *ought to be considered as equivalent to an acknowledgment of the crimes alleged against them by Maria Monk.*

"Resolved, 6th, That a committee of four gentlemen be now appointed, with power to fill vacancies and increase their number, either in the United States or in Canada, to accompany Maria Monk to Montreal, as soon as the authorities of Canada shall afford suitable protection to such a committee, and shall grant them the necessary permission and facilities for thoroughly exploring the Hotel Dieu Nunnery, and such other establishments as are said to be connected with it, viz. the Priest's Seminary, and the Congregational Nunnery, connected by subterranean passages; and also the Black Nuns' Island, which seems to be a component part of the Hotel Dieu Nunnery of Montreal; and that the following gentlemen be appointed on that committee—George Hall, Esq., late Mayor of Brooklyn, Professor S. F. B. Morse, David Wessen, Esq; and Rev. J. J. Slocum.

"FRANCIS D. ALLEN, *Chairman.*

"OCTAVIUS WINSLOW, *Secretary.*
"New York, August 8, 1836."

ATTEMPTS TO ABDUCT MARIA MONK.

SEVERAL attempts were made at various times to entrap Miss Monk, after the publication of the present volume. They would fain have rid themselves of such an enemy, by again immuring her in their infernal dens; and, perhaps, ere long she would have shared the same fate as St. Frances, and several others. We give the account in her own words:—

"I have had various trials to undergo since my escape from the Nunnery, many of which I have particularly stated. Other trials, however, have been my portion, some of which may have arisen in part from my want of acquaintance with the world, and others from the peculiar station in which I was placed, among persons as ignorant of me, as I was of them. I have met with none, or at most but very few indeed, who were at first prepared to believe my story; and some have long remained incredulous, at least in part. * * * * I received a letter which excited my curiosity in an uncommon degree. I had directed the penny-post to bring to my lodgings any letters addressed to me, because several intended for my hands, had been lying a long time in the Post-office. He left one for me one day, dated in New York, written in Canadian style, half French and half English, and signed F. P., which I, of course, understood for the initials of Father Phelan, the father of my child. I presumed, at first sight, that the letter must be a forged one, for I could not persuade myself that Father Phelan would visit New York, at so inclement a season, or that he would invite me to hold an interview with him. Yet, on the other hand, the style and language of the letter, as well as the signature, reminded me strongly of him; and my curiosity was excited, to discover who it could be, that had made so good an imitation. The letter invited me to go, between the hours of two and three, to the corner of Franklin Square, and Ferry Street, as the writer had something important to say to me.

"I thought there could be no danger in going there, to see who the impostor might be; and the distance being short from my lodgings, although the weather was bad, I went. Near the corner I saw a man, whom I immediately recognized. It was father Phelan; and he accosted me with mildness, told me he had something of importance to say to me, but wished to avoid observation, and proposed that I should go somewhere to a more retired spot.

"We proceeded to a very considerable distance from the place of meeting, he asking questions, and making remarks about my Disclosures, &c.; and at length he pointed at a house, which he proposed to enter, that we might converse at leisure. I, however, pointed at another, which had a shop, and looked something like an inn, and told him I would not object to entering there. He consented; and we seated ourselves in a room which was shewn us, I telling him, that I would not trust myself in his power, as I had reason to fear the consequences, but that in that place I was not afraid of him. He spoke as if to quiet my apprehensions; and then entered into a long conversation, in which he showed that he was well acquainted with the contents of the affidavit I made in Montreal, in August, 1835, and which was left in the hands of Mr. Ogden, the King's Attorney.

"He made different inquiries about my plans and intentions, and spoke of my intended publication with much solicitude. He remarked that the priests in Canada did not blame me for what I had done, being disposed to throw it all on my advisers. He said he was glad I had not mentioned his name in speaking of the death of St. Frances.

"He inquired whether I had any difficulty in getting the work published. I told him that in the present state of things, money was wanted to carry it on, which I had not at my command. The stereotype plates had not been paid for. He immediately said, that he would supply me with money, to a large amount if I wished, if I would let him have the plates. It was evident that the prospect of getting possession of the plates, raised great hopes in his mind; and he showed much earnestness in pressing his request.

"Although Father Phelan had invited me to an interview, on the pretence that he had something of much importance to me to communicate, our conversation took such a turn, during most of the time I was in his company, that the promised information was left out of view. He several times adverted to things in Canada, but told me nothing of much importance of any thing there. Once or twice also, he spoke of our child: but in such terms as to displease me very much, making some such expression as this, that he would rather it should have its brains knocked out, than be brought forward as a witness against him.

"After a long interview, we parted; with an agreement to meet on a future time at a particular place where I was to acquaint him with my determination concerning the sale of the stereotype plates. On the same day, I intimated to one of my acquaintances, that I knew how to obtain money, if it was thought best, in exchange for the plates; but this caused an alarm among those who felt interested for me, and measures were soon taken which rendered the assistance of Father Phelan unnecessary.

"Accordingly, at the second interview, he learned from me, that the work was beyond his reach, which appeared to produce a momentary regret; but he soon remarked that that was a matter of no very great importance, for there was to be a publication in opposition to the work, as soon as it should appear, which would prevent the people of the United States from believing it; and besides, if I would leave New York, return to Canada, and reside there, as he wished me to do, I could come out with a public denial of it, and that would have all the effect he could desire.

"Soon after this time I changed my residence, and stayed a while at Wehawken, in New Jersey, opposite New York. As I occasionally visited the city, he found opportunities to meet me several times, in different places. He sometimes requested me to see him again, always professing to have something more to say to me. It might, perhaps, be thought, that it would have been more safe, proper, or judicious, in me, if I had refused all interviews with him from the first: but I began with a belief that some one had attempted to impose upon me; and after I had found it to be Father Phelan himself, who had come on from Canada, and was urgent to converse with me, I found no particular objection to make against another and another interview; and feeling more and more confident that he dared not make any attempt to do me injury, or to get me into his power, while I conducted with caution, I saw him time after time; and if any one is to suffer from this publication of it, it seems to be himself rather than I.

"When Father Phelan proposed a place for meeting me, it was commonly a different place from that where we had met last, and I uniformly refused to meet at the place proposed, and chose another. He informed me one day, that there was a priest with whom he had been conversing, who wished to see me, and asked my consent to an interview. I refused, and so resolutely, that although he appeared to wish it, he soon ceased to urge that request, but proposed to let him stand at a distance, so that he might see me, while we were conversing together.

"Father Phelan wrote me a letter, while I was at Wehawken, enclosed in one superscribed to the person at whose house I stayed, requesting me to meet him on one of the occasions above referred to. It was not signed; but I knew the author from the hand, and other internal evidences. After my return to the city, and while in a retired situation in the upper part of it, near the Dry Dock, he sent me another letter, by two boys, in which he desired that I would meet him at a particular corner near the Park, at nine o'clock; and although I was not on the spot till about eleven, he came up and accosted me, and prevailed on me to take a turn down Spruce-street, and one or two others, while he communicated some requests with much cogency. There was, he said, a woman in another part of the city, somewhere above Broadway and Canal street, who was much disposed to befriend me, and in whom I might place entire confidence. He recommended to me to go and see her, and take up my abode with her, as I should be sure of good treatment. He added that the lady was much more a friend to me than to him; which led me to suppose that she did not wholly confide in the character of priests, and was suspicious of his intentions towards me. What he said was calculated to make me think she might be one of those Roman Catholic women, who know something of what I know, and at the same time that she possessed humanity enough to afford me aid and protection, while she credited my story. I refused to visit the house he indicated to me; but the character of the lady, I did not forget. This was the last time I saw Father Phelan."

Shortly afterwards Miss Monk continues :—

"A woman in a plain black dress, and accompanied by a boy, obtained an introduction to me one day, by making fair representations to some of my friends, on pretence of having been converted from the Roman faith, after receiving an education in a Convent in France. She said she had always entertained a high idea of the sanctity of nuns, and could not be persuaded to doubt it, by any of her friends, until she had read my book, which she was now unable to disbelieve on account of the internal evidence of truth which it presented. She wished to converse with me, and put a few questions, that her mind might be a little further enlightened. She was therefore introduced, after giving her name and address, which was that of a teacher of a private school in the lower part of the city.

"This lady, having expressed a wish to see me in private, we withdrew for some time, during which she said some things which led me to suspect her being a Roman Catholic in disguise. She put several questions to me, which I think must have been put into her mouth by some priest. From other expressions I became convinced that she knew much of nunneries. She then turned to ask some questions about my infant, and remarked that she could not bear to see the child of a priest—she thought it a pity it should live—it would be a kindness if somebody would take it out of the way—she could hardly keep her hands off from it—she wished its neck was wrung. I began to be somewhat agitated, and was glad to get back into the other room among the family. But there, strange as it was, she repeated one or two of these expressions about my child; yet left a piece of money in its hand on going away. The impression this interview left with me was painful, although so unintelligible was the stranger's conduct.

"She afterwards made me two or three calls, when she seemed still more wild and crazy than before; for she once brought a young man with her, whom I never saw before nor since, but whom she told me she had induced to consent to marry me, urging me to take him without delay for a husband. I answered the woman very shortly, but it did not discourage her. One of my friends soon afterwards called at her school, and informed her that she could not be again admitted to see me; when her appearance and manners were so equivocal as to excite some suspicion that she had some project in view, but nothing further has ever come to our knowledge in relation to her."

After these occurrences, Miss Monk received more letters from her seducer, Father Phelan reiterating his former propositions. She also received letters from her uncle at New York; and held interviews with several Canadians—all of whom it would seem, were employed to decoy her once more to the convent.

In connexion with Maria Monk's statements, of the attempts made to abduct her; she gives us some very important

FURTHER DISCLOSURES,

explanatory of those given in this volume. We shall just give a few extracts from this, which we think will suffice for the present.

"While I was a novice, there was a young lady of our number from the Tannery, (a village a few miles from Montreal,) named Angelique Duranceau, with whom I was somewhat acquainted, and of whom I had a favourable opinion. She was about eighteen, and at the time of her entrance had every appearance of good health. After she had been there a considerable time, it might be about seven months, (as I know she was not near the period when she could make her general confession, that is, at the end of the first year,) I saw her under circumstances which made a strong impression on my mind.

"I had received a summons from the Superior to attend in the Novices' sick room, with several other novices. When I entered, I found Fathers Savage and Bonin reading a paper, and Miss Duranceau on a bed, with a look so peculiar as quite to shock me. Her complexion was dark, and of an unnatural colour, her look strange, and she occasionally started and conducted very singularly indeed, though she never spoke. Her whole appearance was such as to make me think she had lost her reason, and almost terrified me. The Superior informed us that she wanted us as witnesses; and the priests then coming forward, presented the paper to Miss Duranceau, and asked her if she was willing to give all her property to the church. She replied with a feeble motion of the head and body, and then, having a pen put into her hands, wrote her name to it without reading it, and relapsed into apparent unconsciousness. We were then requested to add our signatures, which being done, we withdrew, as we entered, I believe without the sick novice having had any knowledge of our presence, or of her own actions.

"A few hours afterwards I was called to assist in laying out her corpse, which was the first intimation I had of her being dead. The Superior, myself, and one or two other novices, had the whole of this melancholy task to perform, being the only persons admitted into the apartment where the body lay. It was swelled very much. We placed it in a coffin, and screwed on the cover alone. On account of the rapid change taking place in the corpse, it was buried about twenty four hours after death.

"Not long after the burial, two brothers of Miss Duranceau came to the Convent, and were greatly distressed when told that she was dead. They complained of not being informed of her sickness: but the Superior assured them that it was at the urgent request of their sister, who was possessed of so much humility, that she thought herself unworthy of attracting the regard of any one, and not fit to be lamented even by her nearest friends. 'What was she,' she had said, according to the declarations made by the Superior, ' what was she that she should cause pain to her family?' "

Of the deceptions practiced in the Hotel Dieu Nunnery, Maria Monk further says—

"There was a young girl, named Ann, who was very stout and rather homely, but not of pleasing manners, though of a good disposition, seventeen or eighteen years of age, to whom I took a liking. She was a novice with me, and the time of which I am to speak, was not long after I returned from St. Denis. The Superior also displayed a partiality for her, and I found she was much in favour of having her received as a nun, if it could be accomplished. She was very handy at different kinds of work; and, what I believe chiefly induced me to regard her with kindness, she was a fatherless and motherless child. She had a beau in town, who one day called to see her at the nunnery, when she was going to confession.

"I was with the Superior at the time, who, on being informed that the young man was there, and of his errand, requested me to go into the parlor with her, to meet him. He put into the Superior's hands a parcel and three letters, requesting her to give them to Ann. She took them, with an expression of assent, and he withdrew. Just as he had gone, Ann came hurrying into the parlor, saying that some one had told her that the Superior had sent for her. The Superior rebuked her sharply, and sent her back, without shewing her what she had promised to give her. Ann said, that she understood a young man (mentioning her visitor) had called to see her. This the Superior denied, telling her never to come till she was wanted.

"When Ann had gone, the Superior told me to go with her to her room, which I did. She there first made me promise never to tell of what she was going to do, and then produced the letters and package, and began to open them. One of the letters, I remember, was folded in a singular manner, and fastened with three seals. In the parcel was found a miniature of the young man, a pair of ear rings, a breast pin, and something else, what, I have now forgotten. The letters were addressed to her by her lover, who advised her by all means to leave the Convent. He informed her that a cousin of hers, a tailor, had arrived from Scotland, who was in want of a housekeeper; and urged her to live with him, and never renounce the Protestant religion in which she had been brought up.

"It is not uncommon for priests to recount anecdotes of what they have seen and done; several stories which I have heard from some of them I will briefly repeat.

"A country priest said one day that he knew a priest in a parish better off than those of the Seminary, for he had seven nuns all to himself.

"A priest said to me one day that he had three daughters in Montreal, grown up. Their mother was a married woman. One of the daughters, he added, now occasionally confessed to him, ignorant, however, of any relationship.

"Another said he was once applied to by a man for advice, in consequence of suspicions he had of his wife, and quieted his suspicions by telling him a falsehood, when he knew the husband was not jealous without cause, he himself having been her seducer.

"It may, it must, offend the ear of the modest to hear such exposures as these, even if made in the most brief and guarded language that can be used. But I am compelled to declare that this is not all. I shall stop here, but lest my readers should infer that it is because there is nothing more that could be said, I must first make the solemn declaration, that *there are crimes committed in the Hotel Dieu Nunnery too abominable to mention.*

"One of their favourite topics is Confession. One of them shewed a watch one day, which he said was worth a hundred dollars. He had received it at confession from a fellow who had stolen it, telling him that he must see it safely restored to the owner, while his intention was to get it into his possession to keep, which he did, and boasted of what he had done.

"I have known priests to sit and talk about what they had done in the Confessional for three or four hours at a time; and I have heard one give another instructions how he might proceed, and what he might do. One priest, I know, paid another fifty dollars to tell him what was confessed to him by a young woman for whom he had a partiality, or what he called love. Sometimes one will request another to send him a particular lady to confess to him, either on account of her beauty or her property: for considerable sums are in such cases obtained from the rich.

"In the country the common practice is, so far as I know, to fix the price of Confession for the year at some particular rate: as two bushels of wheat out of twelve; or if the person is not a farmer, a sum of money.

"A priest one day said to another in my hearing, you confess such a young lady, mentioning her name. She does not like you, I understand, because you kiss her. She is rich, and you have more rich persons to confess than I think is your share.

"I knew a country priest, on a wager, drink a shoe-full of wine. I was once near the priest's parlour (as I have called it) when I heard two of them in an altercation about the speed of two insects; which led to a wager, on the question whether that insect would move quicker over a hot brick or a cold one. They told me to put a brick in the cold, while they heated one on the stove; and when both were prepared they actually tried the experiment. This scene caused great excitement, and loud talking. I have mentioned it to give an idea of the manner in which much time passes in the nunnery."

Of the means resorted to for the purpose of frightening nuns into obedience, Miss Monk relates the following.

"One night, when I was going up to bed, the Superior called me into her room, and told me she wanted me to frighten another nun for her. St. Charles, she said, had been concealing something from her confessor for two or three weeks; and the way to make her bring it out, was to terrify her.

"I had some acquaintance with the nun of whom she spoke. She was a young woman who had been occasionally in the apothecary's room, and I had conceived a considerable regard for her. I did not like the thought of doing any thing unfriendly to her; but the Superior's will was not to be opposed, and I was not accustomed or prepared to show any backwardness in complying. She told me that I was to disguise myself as the Devil, and, in his character, urge St. Charles to persist in withholding her confession.

"She then went to a cupboard, and brought out a sheet, which she put round me, and a singular thing, which, on being unfolded, proved to be a cap, with lappets to hang down the back and over the face. The former was black and the other white; it had two cows's horns sticking out at the sides.—This she placed upon my head; and after some instructions sent me to the apartment in the common sleeping room occupied by the young nun. I proceeded cautiously along, according to the Superior's direction, stepped in, as I believe, unnoticed, and took my stand beside the bed of St. Charles. The light was feeble, and she could have had only an indistinct view of her unexpected visitor. I instantly perceived that she was extremely terrified. She had only the power to cross herself and say, 'Sainte Marie, Joseph, &c., have pity on me.' I however staid near her, told her that I was pleased that she had resisted the persuasions of her confessor, and hoped she would continue to disobey him. She repeatedly crossed herself, and murmured over and over her prayers to the saints for mercy; and at length, presuming I had done enough, I withdrew, returned to the Superior's room, was relieved of my disguise, and permitted to go to bed."

We close the volume with the following remarks by the Rev. J. J. Slocum, in his concluding observations to the confirmations.

"What then is the result of the whole matter? We have, in the first place, examined the 'Awful Exposure,' published in defence of the Canadian priests and nuns; and have found it to be an entire failure; nay, we have found it to furnish strong evidence, in confirmation of Miss Monk's claims to public confidence. Thus also in reference to every attempt made by them for the same object. We have, in the second place, briefly noticed the principal arguments in support of Miss Monk's claims to our confidence, as an ex-nun, derived from a consideration of her incapacity to have acted the part of an impostor—of her minute and extensive nunnery knowledge—of her comparative ignorance of other matters — of the marks on her person, produced by the infliction of penance and nunnery violence—of the forlorn condition in which she was first discovered in New York—of her supposed dying penitential confession to the Rev. Mr. Tappin—of her consistent conduct with the demands of her supposed truth—of the internal evidence of her book—of the moral impress, stamped on her mind—of the testimony of others, direct and indirect—of the failure of her opponents in their varied attempts of self-defence—of revelation, reason, and nature—of the past history of the Roman priesthood and convents. And now, I reiterate the question, what is the conclusion? Is there a particle of ground for suspense? If so, what is it? Is there a single position, taken by her opponents unswept away? If so, let it be named.

"But, perhaps, some will say, after all, there is a possibility of her being false, of her being an impostor, and of course, of the priests and nuns being innocent of the crimes charged upon them. Yes; there is a possibility in the case; and so there is a *possibilty* of her being changed into a '*pillar of salt.*' But is there any *probability* of it? The ground of rational conclusions, is *not possibilities*, but *probabilities.* When gentlemen, in their reasonings, substitute the former in the place of the latter, they place themselves beyond the limits of reason.

"With reasonable men the case is different. It is believed that the foregoing arguments are sufficient to establish them in the belief, that Maria Monk is not an impostor, but is truly what she professes to be, and that she has told substantially the truth, respecting the nunnery. Such will readily perceive the importance of the 'Awful Disclosures,' as a means for opposing the conventual system, as also the spread of popery.

"Let Protestants, then, act reasonably in appropriately using them for these objects, Let them remember the deplorable state of more than one half of Christendom, in consequence of popery. Let them look at wretched starving Ireland. Let them behold bleeding and distracted Spain, as well as South America. Let them consider the ignorance, poverty, and oppression of papal countries in general. Let them call to mind the condition of Canada; a vast majority of whose inhabitants are so ignorant, as to be incapable of reading or writing their names. They are sunk not only in ignorance, but in vice. Intemperance abounds to a fearful extent, the priests, their spiritual guides, setting them the example. Let the American people especially, open their eyes upon their own beloved country, and see with what rapid strides, popery has been spreading itself, for a few years past, over the length and breadth of the land. Let them count the number of its churches, mass-houses, convents, colleges, academies, and newspapers, all devoted to the dissemination of a religion which is fundamentally hostile to every thing that is truly American. Let them count the number of its devotees, all of them marshalled and kept in the most abject subjection to these foreign Jesuits: ready to go anywhere, or to do any thing which their unprincipled leaders may direct. And then, let them remember, that the God of their fathers has put into their hands, this powerful instrumentality, with which they may oppose and break the unholy power of the Roman priests in their country."

FINIS.

THE PUBLIC
Proclamation
OF THE
PONTIFICAL GOVERNMENT
TO
DESTROY THE BIBLE,
AS DECLARED IN THE
SPEECH
OF THE
REV. DR. ACHILLI,
AT ST. ALBAN'S.

WITH

AN URGENT APPEAL TO PROTESTANTS
FOUNDED THEREON.

FIFTH THOUSAND.

LONDON:
HOULSTON & STONEMAN, 65, PATERNOSTER ROW:
MANCHESTER: W. BREMNER, PICCADILLY;
South London Religious Tract Depository, 14, Bermondsey New Road: and ot all Booksellers.

PRICE ONE-PENNY.

NEW WORKS;

Just Published, by HOULSTON and STONEMAN, Paternoster Row.

To be had of Mr. BREMNER, Piccadilly, Manchester; at the TRACT DEPOSITORY, 14, Bermondsey New-road; and of all Booksellers.

THE TRUE OBJECT AND NATURE OF PRAYER: the Morning Sermon at the re-opening of the Surrey Tabernacle, by Mr. JAMES WELLS, on Lord's-day, October 20th, 1850.—Price Three Half-pence.

No spiritual lover of truth can read this discourse without profit. It is an able, experimental, and really useful sermon. When we read it, and thought of the commodious place that has now been provided for Mr. WELLS's ministry; and the immense crowds that flock to hear him, we said to ourselves, no other minister of truth in the neighbourhood of the Borough will now be required: about half-a-dozen of us may go into the country, where the loss of a living ministry is sadly deplored. But, the direction of our steps, as well as the extent of each man's usefulness, is so entirely with the Lord, that with Him the whole matter must be left. We have, in this sermon, first, a striking contrast between that *adversity* which is the result of the fall; and that *prosperity* which arises from vital union to Christ. We have, secondly, a discriminating exposition of "*Prayer as an essential part of the Gospel order of things.*" We expect this opening discourse will be perused by many thousands of Christians, not only in this our native land, but by many in the Colonies, who have gone forth to seek in those far-off lands the bread that perisheth.

WESTMINSTER: being Explanations, &c. of some things connected with the Ministry of G. J. Atkins.—Price Twopence.

A New Work for Faithful Ministers, and the Churches of Christ generally.

MEMOIR OF THE LATE MR. WILLIAM EACOTT. We have this month just published, a very precious little work, written by MR. JOSEPH RUDMAN, entitled "The Warfare Ended; the Course Finished; and the Crown put on; or, It is Well: a MEMOIR of MR. WILLIAM EACOTT, late Pastor of the Baptist Church at Southwick, near Trowbridge, Wiltshire. To which is added his Funeral Sermon, a Short Sketch of his Character, Extracts from his Writings, &c., &c." Mr. Rudman has certainly rendered the churches of Christ very essential service in furnishing them with so interesting and striking a Narrative as this little work contains. It is entirely *free* from anything that could offend, or be a stumbling-block to any of the Lord's family; while it is *full* of facts illustrative of the power of God in arresting a poor, ignorant, wicked soldier; and of the richness and fruitfulness of saving grace in calling such an one, and for many years, keeping him, in solid usefulness, as a faithful servant of Christ. We sincerely hope the work will be extensively useful to saints and sinners; and when we further add, that William Eacott was mainly instrumental, not only in bringing MR. JOHN WARBURTON into Trowbridge, but also in first opening a place for the pure gospel of Christ to be preached in that town; the full account of which, together with a most remarkable record of the origin of, and persecutions endured by, one of the oldest baptist churches in Wiltshire, under the pastorate of the venerable and noble-minded Andrew Gifford, is given in this work, we think there are but few lovers of gospel truth but will read it with unusual pleasure. The work is very neatly printed, and is bound in a stiff neat wrapper, price FOURPENCE. It is published by Houlston and Stoneman, Paternoster Row; and can be had of any agent for the *Earthen Vessel*, or from any bookseller in the Kingdom.

Third Edition, Price Six-pence.

THE MOST POWERFUL BLOW that has ever been struck at the Spirit of POPERY in these days, is the publication of that astounding Narrative, entitled—ELIZA BARRY, The CHILD of a CLOISTER. Dedicated to "His Holiness," Pope Pius the Ninth; but more especially to all British Roman Catholics, by their best friend, the Rev. JOHN TEODOR, D.D. This narrative is a fact of the present day: it will do more to discover the hideous nature of Popery than ten thousand arguments. The Pope himself, and many Priests, are hot in rage against it: but its circulation cannot be impeded. Every thinking person will read and wonder.

Also, just published, price Two-pence,

GORHAM *Versus* BISHOP OF EXETER: or, what do you think of Baptismal Regeneration now? By "UNCLE JOSEPH." The rapid sale of the First Edition well bespeaks the utility and value of this striking book. Its Author is an Independent Pastor, whose desire is to awaken the attention of his fellow men to the vital principle of Regeneration. It is a most pleasing dialogue. Every Christian Minister and Religious Society should aid in extending its circulation.

In Handsome Embossed Cloth, Price One Shilling,

A CLOSET COMPANION FOR THE DAUGHTERS OF ZION: being ORIGINAL POEMS, on the Person, Work, Sufferings, and Triumphs of our Lord and Saviour, Jesus Christ: and some on the Longings and Labours of Living Souls. By HELEN MARIA ALLINGHAM.

"This Work, as regards its Binding and Printing, is one of the handsomest we have seen for some time. Some of the pieces are exceedingly rich; especially 'A Dialogue between a Father in Israel and a Babe in Grace:' this is calculated to be useful to seeking souls. Another entitled, 'Fellowship with Christ from Gethsemane to Glory,' is a most soul-transporting poem. In short, we may say this is altogether a valuable little Companion for the Christian, either when travelling, or in his retired moments."

Price Two-pence.

THE "OLD INFIDEL'S PROGRESS TO CHRISTIANITY: or the Grace of God Exemplified in the Conversion of WILLIAM HOLMES.

"The Old Infidel's Progress to Christianity: or the Conversion of W. Holmes" is a plain, positive, and undeniable testimony in favour of saving and sovereign grace.—*Earthen Vessel*.

Just Published, Price 2d. (at the particular request of many Christian friends, and intended principally for the use of Sunday Schools, and for Village distribution,)

A remarkable, deeply interesting, and faithful narrative of the Conversion—Vital Experience—and glorious Death of MATTHEW HEPBURN. This narrative was published in the EARTHEN VESSEL, for July 1850; and excited such feelings of gratitude and wonder at the amazing grace of God, as displayed in the child, that many friends have offered various sums of money to have it re-published in a cheap separate form for universal distribution. It is a question whether the whole range of Literature, (ancient or modern) can furnish a more genuine and beautiful illustration of that portion of Scripture (Isaiah lxv. 20.) "A child shall die an hundred years old," than this striking and faithful narrative does. It is published in London by Houlston and Stoneman, Paternoster Row; may be had of all booksellers in the kingdom. Where large quantities are taken very considerable allowance will be made; and every information given by addressing a line to the Secretary of the South London Religious Tract Depository, No. ,14 Pagoda Terrace, Bermondsey New Road, London.

BRITISH PROTESTANTS

READ THIS FACT,

AND therein learn, that in connection with what is termed the Papal Aggression, there is a deep-laid scheme to overturn the Protestant faith; to set up the Romish whore, and to abolish those privileges which we, as British Christians, have been permitted, so long to enjoy.

A most important and heart-thrilling speech was delivered by Dr. Achilli, on Friday evening, November 8th, at St. Alban's; where a public meeting was held in connexion with the Evangelical Alliance.

This speech ought to be circulated and to be read, by the many millions of our fellow-men; and solemnly indeed doth it behove them to consider deeply the character, the conduct, and the consequences of the foe who would take from us heaven's richest earthly boon—the Book of books.

Without further introductory comment, we here give the Dr.'s Speech entire.

After several other gentlemen had addressed the meeting, the Rev. Dr. Achilli rose, amidst loud cheers, and spoke as follows:

It gives me great joy to find myself in a religious meeting free from sectarian divisions; where no disputes can arise about unimportant doctrines and useless forms; but where we meet to speak of catholicity (in the true sense of that ancient word) of Christian union, and of Evangelical alliance. No conflicting opinions, no theological theories, which may whet the intellect without touching the heart, have any place here. May the spirit of faith, in the purity of the Word, reign amongst us for our mutual edification. May God prosper this alliance, and call from every side spiritual men to unite themselves together in harmony of essential faith and community of hope; and may brethren here below, who call themselves, indeed, by different names, ever remember that they are members of one family, have the same Father, and the same glorious inheritance. Such an Evangelical alliance is that to which it is my boast to belong. In this union of all Christian denominations I find my Church. And I assure you, brethren, that this is the feeling of all those newly converted, as I am. It would be useless to attempt to draw us exclusively to any party. We will not belong to any party; we will be brethren with all who love the Lord. In such a spirit is progressing the new Reformation in Italy, of which, with your permission, I will give you some tidings. I am, indeed, expressly charged so to do. Early in the present week a dear brother arrived in London, who is the bearer of most consoling news from Rome itself. He has been driven out of Rome because, himself a follower of the Word of God, he did not believe the lies of the priests, nor bow down to the idol of the Vatican; and another powerful reason for his banishment is, that he is bound to me in close bonds of faith and of kindred. Before his departure, that Government chose to take possession of some of his private property, and amongst other things, of a pocket Bible, which our dear brother was in the habit of carrying about with him. He cautioned the agent of the police saying to him, "Observe, this little Bible is in English, and I am an Englishman." "The Pontifical Government," replied the agent of police, "The Pontifical Government has resolved upon destroying the Bible, *wherever* and *however* they find it." These are the precise words used, and I repeat them to you, in order that you may repeat them far and wide. Whenever you have occasion to speak of the Church, of the priests, and the Government of the Pope, repeat these words—words which we followers of that blessed Book of God must hold in horror—"*The Pontifical Government has resolved to destroy the Bible* WHEREVER *and* HOWEVER *they find it!*" These words were addressed officially, by the Inspector of Police Signor Volponi, in the name of his Government, in the presence of two Caribineers to Henry Hely, on the 21st day of September last. Weigh these words well, in order that you may see something of the real character of the Government of the Pontiff, and of the Church of the priests—persecutors of the Bible wherever and however they find it. Can you have fellowship with such men? Since they proclaim themselves haters of the Bible, I will have nothing in common with them; and were it not that I am full of confidence that that evil government must soon cease to rule in that unhappy land, I should be ready to renounce every claim to it as my country—every title, and every right. It is in Rome itself that this persecution is principally carried on. The material Book is burned; the doctrines of the Book are hated, and the followers of that Book are accused and condemned by the Inquisition. It is not very long since I escaped miraculously from those prisons, where twice I have been confined for the same cause. Some are imprisoned there now, while others are deprived of employment, and reduced to misery, or else are sent into exile with heavy personal loss. All are more or less slandered in a thousand ways. You are probably aware what things they have dared to say of me, and you know who is the slanderer. All whom Rome has hated for their love to the Bible she has accused of countless enormities. It would make you shudder to hear the things they have said against such holy men as John Huss, Jerome of Prague, Martin Luther, and the whole band of Reformers. There is no iniquity, no crime, which has not been imputed to them. I am not ashamed of the same lot. I, poor and miserable as I am, least amongst all the servants of God and of the Lord Jesus Christ, have this to boast of, as much as the highest of them. And it is written, "Blessed are ye when men shall revile you, and persecute you, and shall say all manner of evil against you, lying, for my sake. Rejoice, and be exceeding glad, for great is your reward in heaven." My brethren, as long as they persecute me, I have learned in the school of the Gospel to bear with them, and when they desist, to forgive them. But shall I bear with the persecutors of the Bible? the persecutors of the true Church? the company of believers? Shall I forgive those who persecute and calumniate the brethren, and bring ruin and desolation everywhere? I, thank God, have nothing to fear for my own person; your laws, your very friendship protect me, and assure me; let them cry out against me as loudly as they please; I hold it as the braying of the ass, or the barking of the dog. But I will not stand still and quietly bear what they are doing to others. I will not forgive the ills they daily are doing to the spouse of Christ. It is well that I have escaped from thence, according to the precept, "Come out of her, my people; that ye be not partakers of her sins, and that ye receive not of her plagues." I was able to do this by fleeing at the risk of my life. But I have many brethren in Italy—in Rome—who would come out but cannot—who are resolved to flee, but have no way to escape. These enemies have shut the gates and blocked up the roads—they have fortified themselves in their own city, and actually presume to invade other nations, and attack other cities. For a long time they have been sending to these islands, those good soldiers of Popery—the Jesuits. England, and Scotland, and Ireland is full of them. These soldiers have not only planted their tents among you, but they have built for themselves barracks. They have erected churches, founded monasteries, schools, and convents. You permitted them—you gave them liberty to fortify themselves in your very midst. "Oh!" said they, "it is only that we may go through our exercise." False. It was that they might make war upon you. Some people told you of this, and cautioned you, but you would not believe them. You have the fullest proof of it now. The army of fighting men is here, and now they send the generals—twelve in number, (one of them bearing the title of this very town, St. Albans), and at their head they place a general-in-chief. What are the instructions? What commands have they received? I will tell you. Neither more nor less than to prosecute heresy—that is, the Bible; and to make war with heretics—that is, Protestants—to exterminate them from the face of the earth. Do you not believe it? They have already taken the oath. One of your own newspapers has given you the formula of the oath which all Roman Catholic bishops take on the day of their consecration. My friends, whoever has told you hitherto that such men are not to be feared, has deceived you. They are enemies of your faith, persecutors of your Bible, and betrayers of your liberty. They want to bring your nation under the Pope's dominion, as it was up to the time of Henry VIII. They would make you a present of their doctrines of dependence and servitude, they would gladly establish (and at a very cheap rate too,) a good traffic in indulgences and holy relics, and they would gladly make you worshippers of images and of the wafer god. I stop here. I know that you are already aroused enough, and moved with indignation against this new invasion of Rome. But it is my duty to say—and protest before you—that it is not the Roman people who do this—on the contrary, they detest this audacious act, more, even than you do. It is priests who have done it. Men who have no country—no homes—wanderers on the earth, like the gipsies; some who have been born by chance in Rome, think themselves at the same time Englishmen—Frenchmen—Germans—lords and masters of the wide world. I here protest, in the name of my fellow-citizens and fellow countrymen, that we respect the rights of others, and believe that the Church of England has every right to be governed by her own pastors, whether called bishops, or by any other name. Let those who follow the Church of Rome, remain within the limits of Rome's jurisdiction Here she has no jurisdiction. And therefore, whoever comes here with such a title, is not the shepherd of the sheep who comes in by the door, but, according to Christ's Gospel, a thief who climbs in by the window. And we few Italians—and especially Romans—tossed about by priestly persecution, political and religious—we, members of an Italian Church, declare that the Bishop of Rome—called Pope—is an ursurper of rights that belong not *to* him, and deserves to be punished for his daring. Do what duty prompts for the preservation of the most sacred of your possessions—the first of all your rights—faith, and liberty of conscience, and God will be with you. He who has said of that whore, whom we will no longer call the Church of Rome, for such is no longer the Church of the Roman people, but the Church of the priests. "For her sins have reached unto heaven, and God hath remembered her iniquities. Reward her even as she rewarded you, and double unto her double according to her works: in the cup which she hath filled, fill to her double. Even so, in God's name. Amen."

At the close of the Dr.'s Speech, the Rev. W. Arthur, spoke and made some remarks which are worth their weight in gold. It is time indeed, it is time, most seriously to THINK—most fervently to PRAY—and most UNITEDLY TO ACT. We are concerned to furnish the material for thought—God alone can give you hearts to pray; but, verily, we do believe that if the hands of our praying Israel now hang down, a day of darkness and distress for the Church of God is not far off.

The Rev. W. Arthur, in urging the point that " The Persecutions and the Efforts of the Church of Rome, are aloud calling for the union of Evangelical Protestants," said—

Rome makes use of her boasted unity in propagating her soul-destroying errors. Everything that will weaken *us* ought to be discarded, and everything that will strengthen our common foe ought to be done away. Papists pointed to our disagreements, and made a great deal more of them than we were aware of, and more than we did ourselves. We cannot display our differences without lessening our power. If we take occasion to decry Episcopacy, Presbyterianism, Independancy, or Methodism, we must do honour to that which is above all, and better than all—vital godliness. The Papists direct their attacks against our *Bible* and not against our *denominations*. If Paul and Peter had been consulted upon Church government at the same time in two different streets of Jerusalem, it is highly probable that they would not both have recommended the *same* form. Little confidence should be put in education or in the spirit of the times. If the Papacy is met in an effectual manner, it must be met by the life of the Lord Jesus Christ in the soul; for the power of the Gospel is a purely spiritual power. Union will never be found in strength.

Having thus stated THE FACT—we close with an Appeal to all British Protestants. We wish not to alarm them. No. The old Pope has only been feeling England's pulse; and finding her so docile, so calm, so universally charitable, so unconcerned, and so undecided for the glorious Gospel of Christ: finding that nearly all sects and parties in England are dwindling down to a mere form of godliness, having a name to live, while, it is to be feared, in the great masses, she is spiritually dead—finding this to be her position, he thought he might venture to take some advantage of her generosity, and palm upon her his beautiful CARDINAL WISEMAN.

But, vainly, we hope, he will find he has made a mistake. In order, however, to convince him of this, it will be needful for us to awake out of our sleeep, and give him full proof that we are on the Lord's side.

In the language of Richard Swaine, we ask—

Can English Protestants forget for a moment, or be indifferent to Papal Rome's sworn motto, made known to us by Wiseman's predecessor in dignity,

Cardinal Bellarmini, "With heretics keep no faith; it is even lawful to slay them." Be assured this is a motto their "sacramental oath" calls on them to realize whenever their interests urge, or opportunities present, to have it so, or whenever Satan's reign predominates.

Up then, Protestants of England! Defend firmly but peaceably your high and privileged position as inheritors of the blessed and glorious Reformation, as worshippers of one only true God and a Redeemer, as believers in his most holy word, and in it alone, as Defenders of the faith once handed down to the saints; but as contemners and despisers of that Romish Mythology about to be extended more widely and metriciously amongst you—that "slough of a slavish superstition" that calls on its unfortunate votaries to worship many gods instead of one God—to receive the traditions of men, instead of those of the "Holy Ghost"—to look for salvation in the merits of their martyrs, their indulgences, their purgatories, more than in faith on the Lord Jesus Christ and his all sufficient atonement.

Call meetings in every parish—let every bishop address pastorals to his clergy, and let every rector call a meeting of his parishoners—let petitions pour in from all quarters to her Majesty, praying her power and authority to crush in time the arrogant assumption of Rome's potentate; else ere long her Holy Bible, her religion, her supremacy, her crown will be swamped in Popery. This of a verity, I predict without any pretensions to prophecy. My past experience as a Popish priest, of Romanism, and my sight and hearing of Popish boasting by British apostate priests, that ere long England will see her sons, Spencers, Wards, and Newmans, force on the prediction. Did not the idolatry and superstition of ancient Pagan Rome conquer and overrun the few nations who knew and believed in the one only true God, Jehovah.

Protestants of England! this is the advice of one who knows Popery well, and her insatiable thirst after temporal and spiritual power. Receive it, and you may again rejoice—or reject it, and you may mourn its loss.

THE BIBLE PREACHER.

SPIRITUAL CONQUEST AND ITS PRIVILEGES:

A SERMON BY MR. JAMES WELLS,

Preached at Jewin Crescent Chapel, April 5th, 1850.

"To him that overcometh will I give to eat of the hidden manna; and I will give him a white stone, and in the stone a new name written, which no man knoweth, saving he that receiveth it." Rev. ii. 17.

These words were addressed to the church at Pergamos. This place still exists under the name of *Bergamo*, with a population of about fourteen thousand; made up of Greeks, Armenians, and Turks; but in a state of great degradation, ignorance, and superstition. One of the chief temples of Æsculapius, the god of medicine, was at Pergamos, and the worship carried on by acts the most vile and revolting; and yet so perverted were the votaries, and so darkened their understanding, that they thought they were doing that which was right.

This temple of serpent worship is, in this address to the church at Pergamos, called satan's seat,—"I know thy works, and where thou dwellest, even where *satan's seat* is." And there were professors who brought into the Christian Church the doctrines of the grossest idolatry, as well as some who brought in the doctrines of the Nicolaitanes; doctrines, as report goes, that denied the divinity of Christ, abolished matrimony, and everything hallowed and orderly. We here see how very early men began to corrupt the Word of God, and what abominable idolatry, what dark superstition is there; what vile and murderous practice has ever been followed by the Pagan world, which has not been mixed up with the pure truths and holy institutions of the gospel?

We do not suppose they were all real Christians at Pergamos: this address is to them as a body of *professed* believers in Jesus Christ, and those who were joining the worship of satan with the worship of God were, on the ground of their professed discipleship, exhorted to repent; (see verse 16); and if they did not, by a renunciation of their error, prove the *reality* of their profession, they were to be dealt with by the sword of the Spirit; that is, they were (for so I understand it) to be cut off, and cast out, and banished from the presence of the Lord and from the glory of his power. But notwithstanding these gross faults, the church of Pergamos was not without its excellencies, nor without true disciples, who were earnestly contending for the faith once delivered unto the saints, and that unto death I know thy works; thou holdest fast my name, and hast not denied my faith even in those days wherein Antipas was my faithful martyr, who was slain among you, where Satan dwelleth.

The first clause in our text is a test to distinguish the real possessor from the mere professor;—"*To him that overcometh.*"

Rightly then to understand this address to the church at Pergamos, we may observe a certain caste of character among them giving way to the spirit and religion of the times, just as professors in the present day shape their course according to the spirit and religion of this world. But as now, so then, there was a remnant who knew, loved, walked out, and effectually contended for the blest realities of eternal life. Both the reproofs and gratulations in this address are capable of a great variety of application as necessity may require, or as the Lord may be pleased to apply them.

Pergamos, we have said, still exists; but where is its Christian church? Its ministers are no more: instead of holy men of God, there are the poor benighted vassals of despicable ceremonies. There flows the water, not of life, but of death; there moves, not the holy inspiration of the spirit of God, but the poison winds of error pestilential. There rises not the Sun of Righteousness with healing in his wings, but the smoke of the bottomless pit, with vapours fatal to the souls of men; there appears not the bright, the morning star, but the star called wormwood, (Rev. viii. 11,) leaving nothing for dying man but the bitterness of death; no "golden vials full of odours sweet," but humanly devised prayers and praises, and which are an abomination in heaven's most holy eyes. In a word, Pergamos is now spiritually without form and void, and the heavens give no light; there is no man to plant another church; all the birds of paradise that there warbled out the notes of redeeming love, are fled to their "eternal home;" but the Lord liveth, and the word of his grace still lives, and his people live, and Jesus hath said, "Because I live, ye shall live also, and to all these is given victory through the blood of the Lamb; and now may that holy Word which he hath preserved unto us be above all things profitable unto us! We notice—

I. *The distinction*—"To him that overcometh."

II. *The privilege*—"Shall eat of the hidden manna."

III. *The bestowment*—"I will give him a white stone, and in the stone a new name written, which no man knoweth saving he that receiveth it."

I. *The distinction*—"To him that overcometh." There are two evils under the dominion of which are all men by nature. If these two evils can be overcome, or where they are overcome, all other good consequences follow; and there is a divine discipline essential to victory over these two evils, and which discipline none but living, spiritually living people can submit to; and these two evils are *ignorance* and *enmity*. Happy then is the man whom God correcteth; therefore, —"despise not thou the chastening of the Almighty, for he maketh sore and bindeth up; he woundeth, and his hands make whole." Job v. 17, 18. And when and where this is felt, how empty are the things of time and sense known to be; its highest advantages mere husks and vanity of vanities! The word of holiness becomes sealed home upon the conscience; the ear is opened to discipline; righteousness, temperance, and judgment to come are matters that enter like iron into the soul, and as death into the bones; a dreadful sound is in the ears,—"Prepare to meet thy God;"—"Be ye also ready; for ye know not the day nor the hour when the Son of Man cometh;"—"Every idle word that men shall speak, they shall give account thereof in the day of judgment." Thus arises in the soul dread of eternity, enough to make the stoutest heart tremble, and be miserable, gloomy, fearful, discontented, restless, suspicious that all is not right before God, that the heart is not right, the life not quite right; and where these convictions are, there will be separation from a vain, a pleasure-taking, and ungodly world. "Arise and depart," saith a voice more than human; "arise and depart, this is not your rest, it shall destroy you even with a sore destruction." And thus is the spirit led to make diligent search, and reflect thus:—"If the *wrath of God* abide on me, what would be the whole world to me, if I shall at last lose my own soul? If my soul be lost, all is lost; and if this life, with all my attachment to it, shall so weary me that it can bring me not to inherit a throne of glory, but, instead of this, shall bring me to the dust of death, for dust I am, and unto the dust must I return, then what good shall such a vain life do me? Hitherto the question of vital godliness has not troubled me; but now I see, and wish I could still more deeply feel that it is everything. I can no longer trifle with such questions as these, 'How wilt thou do in the swelling of Jordan? and how wilt thou contend with horses? who shall help me out of all my sin and woe?' 'Vain is the help of man, and as for me, I am altogether as an unclean thing;' 'my righteousnesses are as filthy rags;' 'I fade as a leaf, and my iniquities, like the wind, have taken me away;' 'I am a worm, and no man;' 'surely, I am more brutish than any man, and have not the understanding of a man; I neither learned wisdom, nor have the knowledge of the holy; so ignorant am I, I am as a beast before thee.' And do I labour to be holy and righteous? Alas, I find, that out of the heart proceed evil thoughts; that in me is all manner of concupiscence; that I am carnal, sold under sin — God is holy, and looks on the heart. How, then, can a holy God do otherwise than reject me and cast me away for ever; for, 'by the works of the law shall no flesh living be justified.'"

Now, let a man be thus taken captive by the Word and power of God; let the terrors of the Almighty be thus set in array against him; this will make him willing to be saved by grace; willing to be nothing that God and Christ may be all in all. Now that he has seen an end of all creature perfection, and the commandment made to appear exceeding broad. Now, I say, he will be glad to hear that "Jesus Christ came into the world to save sinners," and that "Christ is the end of the law for righteousness, to every one that believeth."

When the weight and solemnity of eternal things are thus felt, there is a willingness to undergo anything rather than give up seeking the Lord. The stony ground, thorny ground, and wayside hearers never had such convictions, such heart searchings, such hungerings and thirstings for God and godliness; or they would not have been so easily offended, the word would not have been so easily choked, nor could the enemy have taken the word out of their hearts; no, there would have been an honesty of purpose and a willingness to endure any, and every thing, so that they may come to a saving knowledge of the truth; for they well know that all things are as nothing to the excellency of the knowledge of Christ. These may be, and are tempted to give up, are ready to halt, and seem to seek the Lord in vain; but still the question and acknowledgment come with force, "Lord, to *whom* shall we go? *Thou hast the words of eternal life;*" these are they that accept not false deliverances. Opportunity to return they may have, but they desire a better country, and God never will be ashamed to be called their God, and he hath prepared for them a city, and to this city of the living God they shall surely come.

Here then, *ignorance* and *enmity* against God are overcome; but still here is yet something more to be achieved; here is yet to be realised the mercy, and love, and peace of God; and if not realised to full assurance, must be so known as *supremely to endear the Saviour*. There is something lacking in your faith if Christ be not precious unto you; therefore, saith the apostle, "to them which believe he is precious." And in this manifestation with power of the salvation of God, when he is pleased to say, ".I am thy salvation," there is freedom of heart and soul from the guilt of sin, from the dread of eternity, and from the powers of darkness. The order of God's covenant is seen; the immutability of his counsel is opened up; the pure gospel of all-sufficient grace is understood; error is victoriously rejected; and the liberty of the gospel is held fast; the heavens are opened to be closed no more, (except in appearance); the gates of righteousness are open day and night, "They shall speak with the enemy in the gate." Here judgment is given in favour of him that believeth. The Saviour's blood cleansing from all sin, and his righteousness imputed justifying from all things, give them the victory, so that their enemies shall be found liars unto them. Here then, by life, and light, and faith, and hope, and love *in* the soul, and the mediation of Christ, God's love and counsel, and the Holy Spirit's mighty power, *for* such they have the dominion. God *giveth* them the victory; and an unspeakable gift it is; it is a gift that brings into oneness eternal with Christ Jesus; and in this oneness they endure to the end; they shall be ignorant of Christ no more; they shall be at enmity against him no more; they shall not hurt or destroy in all God's holy mountain, for their souls shall be filled with the knowledge and love of God as the waters cover the sea."

They are, by faith and love, one with Christ; being moved with fear, from being warned of God of things not seen as yet. They hold fast the revelation made to them; thereby working out their own salvation; nor cease to labour spiritually, as Noah did literally until "the Lord shut him in."

They journey, like Abraham, until they find the promised land; and wrestle with God, like Jacob, until they prevail. They suffer on, like Joseph, until the visions of God to them become established. And they wait in solitude, like Moses, until the God of victory appears to them, puts down all their suspicions and fears, and arms them with all that wisdom and power which shall enable them to meet and overcome the mightiest foe, to subdue kingdoms, and tread upon principalities and powers, and foresee sure possession of the promised land; and like the woman in the gospel, they press through the crowd to touch the hem of the garment of Jesus of Nazareth; and like the blind men by the way side, the more they were rebuked, the more they cried, "Thou Son of David, have mercy upon us."

These are the saints of the Most High; compassed, it is true, they are with infirmity; beset with temptations; hated by the world, especially by the mere professing world; yet, the Lord careth for them, and through him they shall do valiantly, for he it is that treadeth down their enemies.

Now these things must be known and felt. "To him that overcometh," is the promise; and if only such are to eat of the hidden manna, then it follows that all others must perish. If *only* him that overcometh is to have the white stone, with the new name; then it follows that all others fall under condemnation, and are lost in the desolations of the Adam fall transgression.

Under ignorance and enmity it is men crucify Jesus, despise his truth, hate his people, and thus sin against God and their own life. "Be not deceived, God is not mocked; for what a man soweth that shall he also reap; he that soweth to the flesh shall reap corruption; he that soweth to the Spirit shall reap life everlasting:" To him that overcometh belongeth—

II.—*The Privilege.* "I will give to eat of the hidden manna." This supposes, First, *Participation.* Many who partook of the typical manna were destroyed; for they went back in their hearts into Egypt. They apostatized and despised the manna, calling it light bread; and the people spake against God and against Moses, "Wherefore have ye brought us up out of the land of Egypt to die in the wilderness, for there is no bread, neither any water, and *our* soul *loathed this light bread*?" (Num. xxi. 5.) But not so with the antitypical bread. It is true, there are apostates under the New as well as under the Old Testament dispensation; but shall their unbelief make void the faith of God's elect?

The Word of God is the food of the soul, and Christ is the life and substance of the Word; so that by the Word we are fed with knowledge and understanding.

Now, look for a moment at the manna, and let us see *how* it accords with the promise to feed us with knowledge and understanding. 1st. Did it not give them, at least the right-minded among them, to *know* that the Lord could provide for them in the *direst necessity?* Here they were in a desert land and *nothing* to eat. The wrong-minded among them (and the name of this company was Legion, for they were many) were for going back to Egypt again; but the right-minded knew that they need not depart, for God was able to give unto them. "Is anything too hard for the Lord?" The promise of life in Christ Jesus, thus becomes a matter of life and death; that is to say, without Christ Jesus, without this word of life by him, by the power of his Spirit, we must perish. Now the Lord will hear the prayer of the destitute; and when, instead of sinking into black despair, we do by the Word of Life rise into heavenly hope and love, and thus know that our necessities do not and cannot go beyond what the Lord has done and will do; and when we are favoured to enjoy holy things; when the word is made unto us spirit and life, and comfort and peace. What is this but eating of that bread which strengthens man's heart? And this gives us such knowledge of Christ as enables us to believe that the Lord can and *will* provide; and that while unworthy of the least of his mercies, he bestows upon us the greatest, and thus are all our springs in him.

2. We are by this led also to know that he provides *suitably* for us, feeding us with food *convenient* for us. How suited was the manna to the necessity, to the *health*, the *strength*, the *cleanliness*, and *social comfort* of the Israelites. So the word of God in Christ Jesus: how suited to our necessity, assuring us of a God of love, who will neither leave nor forsake us; and how strengthening to our hearts, and what health is his wholesome word unto us; and how purifying: for who can doubt but the manna was of a purifying quality, healing many diseases, but inflicting none. "Thy word," saith one, "is very pure, therefore thy servant loveth it." He sends his holy word with all that power that heals all our diseases. Whether the leprosy, lunacy, withered hand, a bowed down back, or a burdened heart, he healeth us. And what is this but partaking of holy things? What is this but eating of the hidden manna?

And what *social comfort* is there also in this heavenly bread; by it we have fellowship with God, for it is the bread of God; by it we have fellowship one with another: this is and will be an heavenly feast, at which the poor and needy, the hungry and thirsty, the weary and heavy laden shall meet, lose all their troubles, and part no more.

3. How *ample* also is this manna: there is no lack, it is abundant: its sources are those which a God unbounded

in love and power has at immediate command: it is free, without money and without price; and there shall no fatal or final want be to them that fear him.

4. This manna is also *constant:* it will not forsake us all our journey through: yea, it endureth unto everlasting life: he that partaketh of this bread shall never die. We need not depart from our God, though we may be as in a desert place, yet he will go before us, and make his goodness pass before us in the way.

But this manna is said to be *hidden* manna. Does not this imply, first, that it is hidden from the people of God (as from all others) while in a state of nature, and also while they are in legal bondage? While in this state, they know not how good the Lord has been in providing for them, mercies and blessings unnumbered, of which they are ignorant: they know not, while shut up in legal darkness, the things which are freely given to them of God; but when the enlightening, enlivening words of truth come with power, saying, "Hear, and your soul shall live; and I will make an everlasting covenant with you, even the *sure mercies* of David," then the abundant provisions begin to be revealed, and then it begins to appear that "the Lord is rich unto all that call upon him, that call upon him in truth." Now is revealed the truth, that in our Father's house is bread enough and to spare for all that come to God by HIM.

But still it is hidden manna, "it is meat which the world knows not of:" they may hear thereof, that God sendeth bread from heaven; but they have no faith to receive it, no understanding to enter into it, no experience to enable them to appreciate it, and no abiding anxiety to be partakers thereof: they prefer ashes to living bread; yea, "they labour for that which is not bread, and spend their strength for naught." "If, then, our gospel be hid, it is hid to them that *are lost*, in whom the god of this world hath blinded the minds of them that believe not, lest the light of the glorious gospel of Christ, who is the image of God, should shine in unto them."

But may it not also be called hidden manna in the *comparative* sense, as being as yet but partially revealed and but partially known. How little as yet is known of the blessedness of the gospel. "We know only in part, but when that which is perfect is come, then that which is in part shall be done away." We have as yet but a few clusters of fruit from the promised land compared with the abundance in store.

But may not *hidden* manna mean also *reservation?* The golden pot of manna was reserved for a memorial; but there is a better and more enduring substance laid up in the better Ark—of a better testament, established upon better promises, of which Jesus, the better Mediator, being made, as the Son of God, so much better than men or angels, have for us an inheritance which fadeth not away, *reserved* for us in heaven.

The manna, before it descended, was not within the reach of either friend or foe; and therefore, could not, by the bad management of the one, nor the enmity of the other, be destroyed or injured; it was *ever fresh.* So however we be robbed and plundered of what we have in *hand*, that cannot be lost which we have in *hope* so that we are saved by *hope*, and kept by the power of God, through faith, unto salvation. Well may the apostle say, "Love not the world, neither the things that are in the world; for the world passeth away, and the love (or as our version has it, the *lust*) thereof; but he that doeth the will of God, abideth for ever." Happy those who hear, and are drawn by wisdom's voice speaking to them, and saying, "Whoso is simple let him turn in hither; as for him that *wanteth* understanding (and who that knows his own ignorance, does not want understanding?) she saith to him, Come away from all your wrong and vain pursuits, and false and fleshly hopes, come eat of *my* bread and drink of the wine that I have mingled; forsake the foolish and live; and go in the way of understanding."

III.—*The bestowment.* "I will give him a white stone, and in the stone a new name written, which no man knoweth, saving he that receiveth it."

This white stone alludes, as is well known, to an ancient custom of voting for or against a person by black and white stones, and whichever exceeded in number, such was the decision of the court for or against a person, whether the votes referred to official or to criminal matters. Now this being the allusion, the promise when applied spiritually, has a great fulness of meaning. As the black stones were the symbols of disfavour, or of condemnation, so the white stone becomes the symbol of everything favourable and pleasant; the import of the new name is not at all difficult to understand: this symbol, then, of good things will mean:

First, *Acquittal*—Now, the Lord *delighteth* in mercy; and as a father pitieth his children, so the Lord pitieth them that fear him; and as far as the east from the west, so far hath he removed our transgressions from us. The first great characteristic of the gospel, is of the *remedial* kind; raising the dead, opening the eyes of the blind, taking and commiserating the poor man that is fallen among thieves, pouring in oil and wine, finding means to carry him when he is not able to walk; staying with him through the darkness of the night, furnishing the host wherewith to keep him, and becomes responsible for whatever may be needed. Every fault, every sin freely forgiven, and for ever blotted out; the blood of Jesus taking away all sin; not one enemy shall be left; not one voice spared to be raised against a sinner; pardoned by the blood of the Lamb, pardoned by the love and authority of God; pardoned by the sealing power of the blessed Spirit of grace; pardoned by the testimony of truth; his sins as entirely silenced as were Pharaoh and his host in the Red sea. He has cast their sins into the depths of the sea; there shall not be an adversary or evil occurrent. "The sins of Israel and Judah shall be sought for, but they shall not be found; for I will, saith the Lord, pardon those whom *I* reserve." Wherefore then look ye so sadly to-day, his mercy will not depart from you, nor doth his promise fail, nor hath he forgotten to be gracious; *he changeth not.*

Our sins are nothing new to him. He *knew* that our brow would be as brass, and our neck as an iron sinew; he knew what folly we should sink into, and what worthless mortals we should become, and yet "loved us notwithstanding all;" yea more, our sins were taken away at an infinite cost. If he did these things for us when we were enemies, much less will he forsake us now, after having reconciled us to himself, and hath united our hearts to his holy name and heavenly truth. No; his blessed word still saith, "I, even I am he that blotteth out thy transgressions, and will not remember thy sins."

2. *Freedom* is also implied in this white stone. This follows upon the acquittal; justification being in the Gospel inseparably connected with forgiveness of sin, so that here is freedom of the city of God; "no more strangers and foreigners, but fellow citizens with the saints and of the household of God." It is a liberty that gives access to the tree of life, to the water of life, to the bread of life, to the crown of life, to the promise of life, to the God of life, and ultimately to all the joyfulness of eternal life.

3. *Acceptance.* The white stone will imply acceptance, so as not to be banished from the kingdom; and it is in the kingdom of God only that lines can fall to any one in truly pleasant places; no where else can any one have a truly goodly heritage. So then, God will not cast away his people which he foreknew; he does not cast them away, but accepts them to all the honours and advantages of oneness with his dear Son.

4. *Defence.* The person to whom this symbol of *favour* is given would come under the defence of public law. So he who has a sincere love to the Saviour is defended by all the laws of Zion. "Their place of defence is the munitions of rocks." Bread *shall* be given—mark, their *bread shall be given them.*

"The black horse of error, and the devil on his back," (Rev. vi. 5) may go forth with a pair of balances in his hand, to dole out to his followers their creed and prayer books, and forms and ceremonies; and at the same time labour to hinder the gospel of Christ, trying with all his satanic might, by all the agents he can command, to hinder and keep back from dying man the bread of life; but he shall not so prevail as to render null and void, in whole or in part, God's truth. Bread shall be given, water shall be sure: the bread comes down from heaven, and therefore is sure; the waters spring from the mighty deeps of everlasting love; these are waters that fail not.

A black horse, and he that sat on him had a pair of balances in his hand. Some of our best biblical scholars say the word balances would have been more correctly rendered, not balances, but *yoke;* and then this black horse would mean a religion, not of light and purity, as represented by the *white* horse, but of *darkness* and *death.* It is the black horse, directly opposite to that of the white horse; this black horse, and he that is said to sit on him, are a power hostile to the gospel.

He that sits on him is certainly either the devil, or one of his representatives. It strikes me it is the Pope; and whatever the Pope may be as a *man*, he is in his *official* capacity, as good a representative of the king of the bottomless pit, as any mortal on earth can be. Nor let any one think that the Pope has been thrown from his horse lately; for though he was obliged to run away from Rome, still this black horse went with him; he is Pope still, and the Catholic world wondered after the beast and made large contributions for his support. Now the black horse of error, and his rider, would deprive, if they could, the saints of the Most High, both of the kingdom and of the bread of God; but a *voice* from the *midst* of the four *living creatures*, the tabernacle in the wilderness, was placed in the *midst* of the host of Israel. This voice, then, from the midst of these living creatures, was a voice from the *mercy seat*, commanding daily bread for the saints of the Most High; a measure of wheat for a penny, and three measures of barley for a penny. A penny was, as we may see from the labourers in the vineyard, (Matt. xx.) the pay for a day's labour; so that a measure of wheat for a penny, and three measures of barley for a penny, will mean that living, working believers shall have their daily bread; sometimes barley, and sometimes wheat, that is, shall sometimes fare a little harder, and sometimes a little easier, as the matter may require; when in captivity, he shall be fed, as it were, with barley bread; that is, he shall, as it were, just live, and that is all. Yet a good free-grace barley-cake has made an army tremble, and strengthened a Gideon's heart and hands, and those that were with him; but when we gain victory, and have peace, we are fed with the finest of the wheat: these are feast days.

But, if we take the barley and the wheat to mean also providence and grace, the command still stands good, that the Lord will prepare a table in the presence of, or in spite of all our foes. He will give us our daily bread; and not only so, but there are stores of good things to come. Hence the command, "See thou hurt not the oil and the wine." The oil and the wine are a figure of good things to come: the one referring to the blessed anointing of the Holy Spirit; the other, to the blood of the everlasting covenant. Give us these two, the anointing of the Holy Spirit, and the blood of the everlasting covenant, and we then have all things; and these the enemy cannot fatally hurt.

Purity and perfection are among the favours meant by this *white* stone. A purity and perfection in the provisions of the covenant, in the mediation of the Saviour, and in the power and faithfulness of God, which leads to holiness here, and to a perfect possession of perfect peace when this dying life shall be no more.

Well, therefore, may the Psalmist say, "Let all those that put their trust in thee rejoice: let them ever shout for joy, *because thou defendest them.*"

But in this white stone is a *new name*. This new name arises from a *new* birth, a new state, and new relationship and new possessions. This name would be a name of *essential* use and of *great honour*, and therefore of great value in the eyes of him that hath it. And who will undertake to describe the *depth* of the necessity there is for the NAME of Immanuel? Who will attempt to set forth its full value, or to open up in order the honour that all the saints have by him?

Our Adam name is associated with evil, and only evil. Now to keep this old name would, in a sense, be to perpetuate the evil: it would, as it were, be a continual reproach unto us; but we are to *forget* the shame of our youth, and not to remember the reproach of our widowhood any more. To term the church forsaken, would be, as it were, to reproach her, to call her desolate,—would be a very discourteous way of speaking of her whose great and new name is *Jehovah our righteousness*. This is the name of her husband, and by whose name should she be called, if not by that of her husband; but though she be thus named after her husband, yet she shall have also a name of her own, but it shall be a new name, which the mouth of the Lord shall name; and so it is written, "Thou shalt no more be called Forsaken; neither shall thy land any more be termed Desolate: but thou shalt be called Hephzibah, and thy land Beulah: for the Lord (if no one else does) delighteth in thee, and thy land shall be married." (Isa. lxii. 4.)

So completely is our old Adam name to be at an end, that it is to be remembered no more. Hence it is we have to die to all the old Adam associations and interests, in order to be completely alive to all the associations and interests we have in Christ; but while we have to die unto old things, and those old things are not worth living for, yet we die *wonderfully hard;* it takes, dying mortals as we are, a very great deal to kill us to the old Adam, and to make us alive to God. With men this is impossible, but with God these things are possible.

What an expression is this *new name* of the love of God in thus abolishing all that can be against us, so that every name connected with evil is taken away; and this old name is taken away *honourably*. A new birth, and that of God, certainly entitles to a new and godly name.

Here then is *Saul* the sinner, and *Paul* the saint. We may suppose for a moment, that sin, and death, and Satan, yea, and the law, as the avenger of blood, are all in hot pursuit for *Saul*. Sin says, "Saul is mine." Death says, "Saul is mine." Satan says, "Saul is mine." The Avenger of Blood says, "Woe be unto Saul." Presently *Paul* appears. Sin says, "This is not the man; its Saul (not Paul) that I want." Death looks and says, "No, this is not the man. This is not Saul, my friend. This Paul is an enemy to me. This is not the man." Satan looks at him and says, "Oh, no; this is not the man. This is not Saul, my servant. This is *that Paul* that does me so much mischief." The Avenger of Blood steps in, looks, and says, "This is not the man; this is not Saul. Saul was a murderer; but this is Paul. This Paul is a man against whom I have no law. No, I must not touch this Paul, for he is complete in Christ, and is a friend of God, and of the household of faith."

What then is become of Saul? Why he is *dead*. Sin, and Death, and Satan retire in despair, knowing that Saul is dead, and the Avenger of Blood seeks no more after him. And thus was Saul, by his new birth, new state, and new *name* so *altered*, that he was not known by his old companions, so that they can bring nothing against *Paul*, and *Saul* is *dead*,—old things are passed away, all things are become new. Time forbids me reading out the various import of this new name any farther than just to observe, that it means all that we have in oneness with the dear Saviour; and means freedom from all condemnation, and after, and by this new name, the Lord will judge his people. "Even according to that worthy name by the which they are called." (James ii. 7.)

But it is a name which no man *knoweth* saving *he that receiveth it*. We may, from the last verse of the 13th chapter of Revelation, see that it was customary of old to give names in *mystic* characters, or in *numerical* letters. Now, to this person to whom this white stone was given there would be given also an *explanation* of the letters or characters making up the name; so that, of course, a *stranger* would be altogether at a loss to divine the meaning.

Now the Lord makes his new covenant name known to his people, but it is by such experiences, and exercises, and trials, and manifestations of himself to them, that none can know saving he that receiveth it. "To you," said the Saviour to his disciples, "to you it is given to know the mysteries of the kingdom of heaven." But to others it is not given. "The natural man receiveth not the things of the Spirit of God." But God revealeth them to his people: he makes them know the meaning of those Scriptures which are expressive of soul trouble, and of those which are expressive of deliverance, and of those Scriptures expressive of the certainty of his everlasting covenant. He teaches his disciples privately, as well as publicly, so that they shall "know in whom they have believed;" and the Holy Ghost will root in them a persuasion that "he is able to keep that which they have committed unto him against that day." Let us then hear the conclusion of the whole matter, and it is this, "That we may know him, and the power of his resurrection, and the fellowship of his sufferings, being made conformable unto his death."

The Bible Preacher

Is intended (D.V) to be published occasionally. No. II. contains:

A SERMON BY Mr. J. MOODY,
Of Walworth.

London: J. Paul, 1, Chapter House Court, Paternoster Row; and sold at the Religious Tract Depository, 14, Bermondsey New Road.

THE THREE GREAT ESSENTIALS

IN OUR GOSPEL ZION:

PRAYER TO GOD:
PREACHING THE PURE WORD:

AND

THE PREVAILING POWER OF THE PRINCE OF PEACE.

BEING,

THREE SERMONS

PREACHED AT THE OPENING OF ZION CHAPEL, GOLDINGTON TERRACE, OLD ST. PANCRAS ROAD, LONDON.

ON MONDAY, SEPTEMBER 16, 1850.

FORMING

No. 10, 11, and 12 of the "Bible Preacher."

LONDON:

HOULSTON & STONEMAN, 65, PATERNOSTER ROW;
JAMES PAUL, 1, CHAPTER-HOUSE COURT, ST. PAUL'S.

To be had also, at Zion Chapel, Goldington Terrace, Old St. Pancras Road, on Wednesday evenings; of Mr. MARKS, 78, Brewer Street, Somerstown; of Mr. TOPLEY, Trafalgar Road, Greenwich; of Mr. PACKER, 21, Free-school Street, Horsely-down; of Misses HIGHAMS, Chiswell Street; of Mr. KISSICK, Bookseller, Tottenham Court Road; of Mr. BREMNER, Publisher, 15, Piccadilly, Manchester; of Mr. WILKINSON, Bookseller, Poultry, Nottingham; and of all the Booksellers in Europe.

Price Three-pence.

NEW WORKS

PUBLISHED BY HOULSTON AND STONEMAN,
65, PATERNOSTER ROW; AND BY
JAMES PAUL, 1, CHAPTER HOUSE COURT.

A STONE OF EBENEZER RAISED IN THE VALLEY OF FALLEN MISERY, on which is inscribed the Love, Mercy, Wisdom, Power, and Forbearance, of Jehovah, in Calling by his Grace, Preparing for his Work, Supporting in the Valley of Death, and Calling to his Eternal Kingdom. Likewise, the Founding of the First Gospel Church, the First Addition thereunto, their Strict Obedience to the Command of their Sovereign Lord, and the Gross Inconsistency of Mixed Communion. By JAMES NUNN, Minister of the Gospel, Beulah Chapel, Somers'-town. Price Six-Pence.

In Handsome Embossed Cloth, Price 2s. 6d,

JEHOVAH-JIREH: or, the Provisions of a Faithful God: as Manifested in his Wonderful Dealings with the late Mrs. Eliz. LACHLAN, formerly of No. 6, Upper Portland Place, London. Written by Herself; and now Collected, Edited, and Revised, by a PHYSICIAN, who was brought out of Nature's Darkness into Christ's Marvellous Light, and turned from the Power of Satan to the Kingdom of God's dear Son, through the instrumentality of this devoted Sister in the Lord, now fifteen years since.

Also, in one Handsome Volume, Price Five Shillings,

MAGDALENA'S VOYAGES AND TRAVELS

Through the Kingdom of this World into the Kingdom of Grace. By the late Mrs. ELIZABETH LACHLAN, formerly of 6, Upper Portland Place, London. Edited by A PHYSICIAN. Embellished with Three beautifully engraved and colored Maps. ☞ A suitable Present to a Friend.

In Handsome Embossed Cloth, Price One Shilling,

A CLOSET COMPANION FOR THE DAUGHTERS OF ZION: being ORIGINAL POEMS, on the Person, Work, Sufferings, and Triumphs of our Lord and Saviour, Jesus Christ: and some on the Longings and Labours of Living Souls. By HELEN MARIA ALLINGHAM.

"This Work, as regards its Binding and Printing, is one of the handsomest we have seen for some time. Some of the pieces are exceedingly rich; especially 'A Dialogue between a Father in Israel and a Babe in Grace:' this is calculated to be useful to seeking souls. Another entitled, 'Fellowship with Christ from Gethsemane to Glory,' is a most soul-transporting poem. In short, we may say this is altogether a valuable little Companion for the Christian, either when travelling, or in his retired moments."

JAMES PAUL, Chapter House Court, Paternoster Row, has just published, Price One Penny, A Funeral Sermon, Occasioned by the **Death of the late James Osbourn**, who Died in North Carolina, August 24th, 1850. Also, a Beautiful Edition of "A Remarkable, Deeply Interesting, and FAITHFUL NARRATIVE of MATTHEW HEBPURN, who was Born at Hampton, in Middlesex, and Died on April 30, 1846, when only Ten Years of Age."—Price 2d. Also, Price 2d., "'THE OLD INFIDEL'S' PROGRESS TO CHRISTIANITY: or, the Grace of God Exemplified in the Conversion of WILLIAM HOLMES." Also, "The Controversy between Mr. G. ABRAHAMS and Mr. GODSMARK on 'The Resurrection Body' Examined, and the Doctrine of the Resurrection Expounded;" being Nos. 7 and 8 of the BIBLE PREACHER.—Price 2d. Also, Price 2d., A SUPPLEMENT to the EARTHEN VESSEL, for September, 1850; containing, Baptism Controversy Concluded; C. W. Banks Reproved; "Gorham v. Bishop of Exeter" Reviewed; Mr. Joseph Irons Paraphrased; An Address to Mr. Finney, the American Revivalist, on his Effort to Convert London; containing an Awful Account of some Popular Ministers in Great Cities. May be had of all Booksellers and Agents for the "Vessel."

JEHOVAH THE SPRING AND MAINTAINER OF ALL OUR BLESSINGS.
A SERMON BY MR. JAMES NUNN.
Preached at the Opening of Zion Chapel, Goldington Terrace, Somers' Town,
on Monday, September 16th, 1850.

"Save now, I beseech thee, O Lord; O Lord, I beseech thee, send now prosperity." Psalm cxviii. 25.

One might imagine that being brought through a variety of difficulties, and having obtained a position so long desired, a part of this language might be dispensed with, and that is the former part—" Save me," or, "Save now, I beseech thee, O Lord;" but when the Holy Ghost, who indited this language, in the heart of him who was brought forward as the instrument to open it, and to put it in this form, that individual by the same almighty power was brought to know that what he here penned was necessary in every word and in every letter. Why so? Because we, as creatures, are so soon excited and carried away, or else we are crushed, and, as it were, sink into despair, unless there is an omnipotent and unseen hand to lay hold of our hearts, our affections, and our feelings to put them right. The very deliverances of the world; the very position in which Jehovah has more particularly manifested himself, that is in raising us out of our distress, secures, according to human reason, the most righteous feeling in our hearts; and yet, my friends, they are the very circumstances which, without the immediate sanctifying power of the Holy Ghost. if left to them, only we should be carried away with, instead of having our hearts lifted up with grateful feelings to him who gave us what we do possess.

We find, therefore, that the Psalmist must have been taught by One who knew the human heart, who knew the necessity of all that was connected with it in its workings, and the power that was necessary to guide it in its proceedings. We are like a ship; we may be very quick; we may have everything favourable in the tackle, in the compass, and in the helm, but if left to ourselves we should find that without a pilot we should soon be wrecked, and soon come to nothing. We may have sentiments as clear as a bell; we may have privileges innumerable; we may have every-thing that the heart can wish; but if we have not God Almighty to take possession of the helm, to guide us in all that is before us, we shall soon find that we shall make sorry work. The prayer then, my friends is a very important one.

We had only yesterday before us two very important portions of Scripture: "I will go into thy house;" looking at it as God's house; not your house, nor my house—God's house—where God dwells —where God displays his glory. " I will go into thy house with sacrifice." What for? "To pay my vows that I made when my soul was in trouble." We find, then, that when the soul is in trouble the vow is sure to be connected. How? "Bring my soul out of trouble." Does it end here? No. "That it may praise thee." That is the end of the vow; that is the inseparable feeling of the heart when it is taught rightly by the Holy Ghost. " Let my soul live," says another. What for? "That it may praise thee." Here is the vow, he says, " I will enter into thy house, or go to thy house with sacrifice of fatlings, I will not take the leanest of the flock." I will not take that which I can comfortably spare, but I will take the best from the flock; I will take as it were the first thing connected with my movements; and my going forth to the house of the Lord shall be as it were devoted unto him, The next portion was, " If thy presence go not with us, let us not go hence." What would it all be without the presence of God? And what is our prayer this morning? " Save now." We have been anticipating; we have arrived at the hill; we have taken possession of the house; and now we want the God of the house, and the almighty power of that God put forth in perpetual operation to keep us in a right position, that we may enter in with the Psalmist, " Save now, we beseech thee, O Lord." O Lord I beseech thee, send now prosperity.

A multiplicity of mingled feelings arise in my poor heart; and I dare hardly attempt to speak, lest I should be overcome by those feelings. But let it all be wrapped up in this as it may be, I am brought through the tender mercy of God to view myself merely an instrument in his hands. I bless him for his grace, that, notwithstanding all the calumny, and all the opposition which has surrounded me, God Almighty has, in spite of mine enemies, opened his hand, spread my table, and prospered me. I feel greatly my debt to him; and I am humbled whilst I rejoice in viewing the friends and friendship that I could not have calculated upon, who have ministered in every way that my heart could wish: but, I say while I rejoice in all these things in the goodness of God in connection with it, I feel a trembling. And why trembling? At God's word? At what it contains? There the Lord gives us advice that is very necessary—that we should not "Lean to our own understanding;" that there are lustings of the flesh and the lustings of the spirit, and the lustings of the one perpetually war with the other; and it is only as God in a special and perpetual manner puts forth the same power that created this world in which we live, that power which created the sun and moon, and governs all the planets in their course, who moulds a tear, and bids it trickle from its source; that is the power we want to work upon our heart and put it right, and when it is right to keep it so.

There are three things, my friends, that I must come to more particularly, that appears evident from the language before us.

I. The persons exhibited.—I and thee.

II. The period that is mentioned—"Now."

III. The prayer presented—"I beseech thee send *now* prosperity."

First, then, the persons. There is a suppliant, and there are persons to whom the supplication is presented. These are necessary for our examination and consideration. God can only be worshipped as he is "Worshipped in spirit and in truth;" and if this house were full of living beings, without the living principle of vital godliness in the heart, God would neither bow the listening ear to hear, nor would he manifest himself. Why? Because the "Sacrifices of the wicked are an abomination." Not the prayer, but the sacrifice of the wicked, that is, by the sacrifice I understand the form of worship. The wicked may bring, as the Jews brought, bullocks and lambs; but God Almighty said, "Who hath demanded this at thy hand?" "He that killeth an ox is as if he slew a man." Isa. lxvi. 7. So that it is not the mere position of the body, but it is the heart that God looks at. I conclude, therefore, that the individual was no hypocrite who penned the language before us. I conclude that it was not a mere nominal matter; that he was not a mere poet, and therefore exercised his poetical skill only, but that he was one whose heart God had laid hold of, and that from his heart he gave expression to the feelings of his soul.

There are three things very necessary to be understood here. First, we must be brought to this consideration—that the person or persons supplicating possess a knowledge, and this to be a right knowledge must be a divine knowledge, because we are told that "The wicked know neither Christ nor his Father." John viii. 19. If it be a divine knowledge, then there is none but the Divine Being could give it; and this must be a knowledge that far surpasses every other knowledge presented to our view upon the platform of time. We may gather in all sciences; we may view every stage of the most gigantic strides of the human mind in all its intellectual force, gathering things that make us stare with amazement; and yet this knowledge gained from the bowels of the earth and the heavens above, all that is connected with the ingenuity of man sinks into comparative insignificance when compared to a knowledge of God in Christ, as Jesus the Saviour of mankind. It surpasses it all. The poor soul crippled by sin, panting after God, blessed with a knowledge of God in Christ as a just God, claiming everything that his righteousness can claim, and yet a Saviour; blessed with a knowledge of the complete work of Christ; such an individual is blest beyond all philosophers, astronomers, or any other science that you can name among men, because he is blessed with a knowledge of him who can do all that he can possibly require of him.

In connexion with this knowledge, my dear friends, it is a moral impossibility that it can be in exercise without our being brought to know our necessities, and our entire imbecility. To know our necessities; to talk about individuals knowing Christ; that is, having an experimental knowledge of him, and not knowing that they are sinners, and need all that he has provided is, my friends, a complete paradox to me. I must be be brought into a position spiritually, as I must be naturally. If I were to learn one science, and entering into that science, found that in its connective links it opened up a variety of other subjects, I must be brought to see my deficiency before I should feel a desire to pursue the inquiry further. When I am brought individually, or you are brought individually to a true knowledge of God as a just God and a Saviour, we must be brought to know that he would be just in sending us to hell, but that he is merciful in the person of Christ, and just in demanding all from the substitute; and that having received all that his righteous nature could demand, he breaks forth in mercy's streams to meet our varied necessities.

What do we need, friends, when we come to the house of God? Is the company of friends sufficient? Are the smiles of our acquaintance sufficient to feed our souls, comfort our hearts, strengthen and nerve our minds? No! What else do we want? The presence of him who causes angels to strike their lyres, and sing their Maker's praise. We want all that; and you will want it perpetually. Not only so, but there is another branch of knowledge; and that is, (if we are taught by the Holy Spirit) we are brought to know the source of all our supplies,—to know the Lord,—to know that in him dwelleth all fulness, that he is life's fountain; and that every thing emanates from him. And this made the Psalmist say:—"All my springs are in him." My faith springs from him; my love springs from him; my hope springs from him; joy and every grace spring from him. It is all from God; bless his adorable name that it is so! If your hope was in yourselves, it would soon be extinguished; if your faith were merely centred in, and derived from yourselves, it would soon be obliterated. But it's all in God—all there!

There is another idea—that wherever this knowledge is, there is life divine. That is a blessing! to know we are born of God. Knowledge, literally, my friends, cannot be where there is no life; we do not expect dead men, or dead women to know anything. But we do expect that where knowledge is mentioned, there is life; and, as this is divine knowledge, there is the life of God in the soul. And these are the living tokens of that life—the eye that sees, the ear that hears, the heart that moves, the mouth that gives expression to what the heart feels; that heart and soul longs for salvation; and as the living in Jerusalem, they pray from life, and the man who has that life can never die, because it is eternal; it is the springing up of that life which is hid with Christ in God, produced by the power of the Holy Ghost carrying the heart up to God from whom the holy stream of life emanates.

The next idea—the person or persons addressed. How necessary in natural things are all these connections. We know not how to frame our petition if we are ignorant of the person we are going to. But if we are acquainted with him, and know that the person is not only liberal, but that he stands in such a connection, in such relationship, and in such a position as to command influence, especially when we have got his promise, and have got, as it were, the very parchment on which we can write our desire. We have got the very seal with which we can stamp it, and that is recognized as his own engagement; and the suppliant is emboldened to go to him. In looking at this, we must do so very briefly. We find here the language—Lord, Jehovah; and from that language I understand Jehovah, Father, Son, and Holy Ghost. And "prosperity" in the soul will never be realized and enjoyed, unless we are brought by the spirit of the Lord to view it rightly. Therefore, when we look at the Father, we are brought to look at his all-wise plan; when we look at the Son, we are brought to look at his ever completed work; and when brought to look at the Holy Spirit, we are brought to look at him as now officiating, as the promised Comforter; it is he who in the day in which we live is rejected and insulted, for where this knowledge is not possessed, men go on in their own strength; and they tell us in every quarter that all that is wrapped up in religion now is mental persuasion, without divine operation. It is a lie! forged, my friends, by the enemy of souls to deceive you. The divine operation in every thing is necessary, and no heart presses to God; no heart is quickened unto life, but by the spirit of God, who transformed us out of nature's darkness into marvellous light. Looking at it in this light we are brought at once into another position; that is, that the appeal is made to him who knows all; the appeal is made to him who sees all; the appeal is made to him who sustains all; the appeal is made to him who rules all and manages all. Can we go to a better? Is not the very thought delightful—that we go to God himself? that when we bow the knee, or when we think of him as we enter into Zion, we are entering the presence of him who knoweth all things? When a man's soul is shut up, and he cannot give utterance to what he feels within, by the mysterious dispensation of God, if he hath this knowledge; a spring of delight riseth up in the mind, as he remembers—my God knows all my necessities; my God knows all my desires; my God knows all my afflictions; my God knows all my feelings; my God knows all my enemies; all my difficulties, and all that is connected with my deceitful heart. He knows every evil propensity, every temptation, the power of the enemy, the darkness with which the soul may be assailed; and this knowledge is brought by the power of the Holy Ghost into the heart and mind—that that God before whom he is going, and is becoming dumb, knows the utterances that are wrapped up in a tear, wrapped up in a sigh, wrapped up in a groan; and that he not only knows all, but sees all. He sees the cottager as well as the king; he sees the prisoner with all his fetters, binding him in the dungeon, as well as he sees those who are walking at liberty; he sees the very motive and the very intention, as well as the action: and this brought the Psalmist to say—"Lord thou knowest me altogether, there is not a word in my tongue even before it is uttered, but thou art thoroughly acquainted with it." This is what I want to see generally acknowledged; and by the blessing of God, though I may never live to see it flourish in all its fruitfulness, I have seen it planted; I believe it will be watered by God, because it arises from God. I want to see in all your proceedings in the house of God the persuasion that God sees your every act, your every motive, and your every desire. I trust that you will not want the praise of men; that you will not want the encomiums of your fellow creatures; but that you will do what God gives you the ability to do; and that you will do that as in the sight of God; and that, as the apostle says—"Whether we eat, or drink, or whatsoever we do, we may do it to the glory of God." I cannot expect, I do not expect, to see it branch out in all its various forms; but my soul does exult in the thought that the Lord should think me worthy of being raised as an instrument to present what I believe in my soul is strictly according to his Sacred Volume. What a consolation it is to know this—that whatever poor fellow creatures may think, if you give but a halfpenny in the house of God, if you give it according to your ability and your conscience, you have done well; for the Lord does not require where he has not strewed. The heart leaps with gladness in the very idea. The Lord knows what I have done; and he knows that what I have done, I have done according to my ability. There will never be any warfare in the conscience when this is the case, my friends.

He not only sees all, but he sustains all, my friends. Ah! that is one part of the subject quite necessary for us to remember. Have we got the lively feeling now? Have we got the living principle in exercise now? Do we not feel that the Lord God has sustained us and brought us thus far? Do you not feel, to-day, that if God were to withdraw his power, we should be paralyzed in a moment? If you are permitted, to-day, to enter into the Zion that he has provided, be assured he must sustain it that gave ti. Do you not see, then, the beauty of the prayer, "Save Lord, from a return unto Babylon! Save, we beseech thee, O Lord, by thy sustaining power! If the Lord has been pleased, in mercy, blessedly to develop and exhibit himself, let me not forget him; let me keep him in remembrance! Save, thou blessed Jesus! and thus maintain and sustain the living picture in all its lively forms, that my soul may be spared! Save, O blessed Spirit! Put forth thy power, and keep up the living feeling." Do you think it will go out? What do people tell us—that so long as we stand on our watch-tower, as long as we attend to our duty, that God is so good that he will never forsake us, but sustain us! That is all right; but it is not beginning at the right end. The fact is, I may have natural bodily health to-day; I may use the means necessary to sustain my natural life, and my natural vigour; I may take food, and it may be food wisely taken; but that God who put my machinery into action, must cause that food, which I take, to act properly; or otherwise, the food which I had taken consistently and wisely, would produce disease and inflammation, or a variety of other things might arise to produce death. We are not the mighty giants we imagine; we are not so independent, as natural creatures, of that God who made us, as we are sometimes told. We are every moment dependent. Why does one man drop down suddenly after eating a meal? Why does another when about to proceed upon a journey fall into the arms of death? Because God withdraws his breath, and man ceases to live. How is it that we sleep in the night; and that whilst others are seized with disease, and agonised with pain, we find comfort and repose, and get up refreshed? Because God takes charge of us; because that God, who holds our life in his hands, sustains us in the arms of slumber and repose; for he keeps all. We do not think much of it; we have comparatively, but a small share of the knowledge of the goodness of God; and of the necessity of a God to sustain us in everything spiritual, as well as in everything natural. The appeal, then, is made to the right quarter; the right object is selected, because he is the source and the spring of all grace.

Not only so; but he who is applied to, rules all. He may allow the carpenter, to encourage the smith; he may allow another to make an instrument for destruction; and we may be anxious, and wonder what the Lord is doing, and tremblingly cry, "Wilt thou pursue a worm to death?" But he who allows it all, puts a stop to it all. He is like a man who knows every part of the machinery; the moment it is said, "Stop her!" the hand is on the point, and the thing is executed. He says, "He creates the destroyer to destroy." I have often thought of that passage, where he says, he has "broken the jaw-bone of the enemy." There is no animal that can swallow us when the jaw-bone is broken; it may injure, but it cannot devour us; the Lord has broken the jaw-bone of the enemy; he may attack and bite us, make us feel, and cry out, but he can never swallow us. This is the Lord's mercy; there is such a blessedness here, that I hardly know how to leave this point. I am not speaking theoretically, but experimentally; and I want, instrumentally, to convey this blessing to your souls. You may have many dark nights; you may have many rough paths; you may have many crookways; but God Almighty, if he is your Friend, can make the darkness light, and crooked places straight, and enable you to say,—I have got such a Friend— I have got such a Shield—that the assassin may be in the dark shades of night, with his dirk ready to take my life—but God stands between me and the assassin, and, unknown to me, breaks his arm, or paralyzes it, and I am saved! I am saved! I may be in the midst of fire; but he can protect. This is what the church felt; the persuasion that the God to whom it appealed, overruled, or ruled all, they said, "God is our refuge and our strength, a very present help in time of trouble." Therefore, we will not fear, though the earth be removed. "What nonsense!" some may say, "earth removed, and you a creature! What will you stand on then?" That God in whom we trust, even when the pillars of nature shake, and are broken—when all nations are, as it were, in confusion and dismay —when he pours out the vials of his wrath on the city—he will keep that man and woman in perfect peace whose trust is in him! When faith is brought into blessed exercise, upon the true sentiment that God has revealed, it can smile at death and poverty, and everything that may appear in battle array. Here is where I wish to live, my dear friends; here is where I wish the Lord may bring us all to live—to live on the naked arm of his faithfulness — to feel as Abraham felt, that when God goes directly opposite to our desires, we may bow softly with submission, in the firm persuasion, as he did, "Shall not the Judge of all the earth do right?" If he strikes at our natural comforts; if he breaks down that on which we are building or leaning; in the midst of it, may he maintain the holy frame of mind in us as of one of old, when he said, "It is the Lord, let him do what seemeth him good." Nothing happens by chance; chance is the mere phantom of a perverted mind; it is not the creation of God. Everything that he does is directed with a precision worthy of his high character.

My dear friends, when we are brought to this, that we have to do with God, we begin to talk with God, to lay our case before God, in proportion as the mind is impressed, and the soul engaged, so, in proportion, is the mind impressed that the Lord's hand is in it.

Secondly, the period. It is a period of deep interest and desire, a period of hope, that has been prayed for—that we should have a house for God—that there should be nothing to prevent it in its erection and completion—that we might live to see the day when we should enter into our earthly Zion. This is the period; and now let us offer up the prayer, "Save now, we beseech thee, O Lord; O Lord, we beseech thee, send now prosperity." We cannot do anything without God, though we have got the house. We cannot do without the God of the house, though he has thus graciously condescended to answer our prayers; though he has brought us into a position so desirable and so pleasing. It is a period very pleasing to my mind, and sometimes it is too much for me, when I think how God, in his mercy, has inclined the hearts of my friends, not only to stand by me, but liberally to contribute to my necessities, and joyfully to come forward to enable me to go beyond my own personal necessities,—to enable me to carry out my heart's desire in the Sick Visiting Society, to give them some assistance in the hour of affliction, when they had nothing, perhaps to support them, when nature required the most. They have come forward, I say, liberally, in every way—too numerous for me to mention; but I thank God for all. Though, even now, having obtained all this, we are poor creatures! I have had so much in God's mysterious way, to pass through, that I cannot lay hold of one friend, without I lay hold of that friend in God; because the heart of man is so deceitful. The Lord hath said, "He that trusteth in his own heart is a fool;" and I have found it so many times; and I have been taught, alas! by painful lessons, that he who trusteth another man's heart, must be a *double fool!* If we cannot trust our own heart because it is so deceitful, we know nothing about another person's heart; we only judge from words and actions. But then, you and I are so bad, perhaps we may injure the best of friends, in our foolish moments of peevishness and irritability; perhaps we may overturn, by our own folly, the very platter from which we receive our meal. We dare not trust ourselves; we must, therefore, come to God to "save us." Having obtained help, we continue to the present moment. But there is a future journey: and *now*—this very period—may be a time of great necessities: for, I believe that every fresh door opened in providence, is a fresh opportunity for the devil to get behind that door, secretly, to prepare his stratagem to mar our comfort—secretly to come forth with fresh temptations. He has been endeavouring to mar all—he has been endeavouring to frustrate all: but look on the beautiful house that God has given you. Though you must not think that because you have arrived at such and such a position, you have nothing else to think about. You will want now, my dear friends, as much of the goodness of God, and the power of God to keep you persevering, as you did, to bring to your present state. What will be the house—the Zion—without him? What will be the place without the God of the place? Nothing!

There is another thing, my friends, that I wish to bring to your notice, to shew you that this prayer is right. We will look at it briefly—and yet it must be very briefly. Suppose you plant a tree: the tree may be very healthy when you plant it; but, my friends, if you want it to prosper, what must it have? Water from heaven. If it were ever so healthy when planted, and it could get no water, it would decline and die. I want you to look at it as represented by the Lord taking a vine out of Egypt, (Psa. lxxx. 8.) It has been planted and hedged round. What is necessary now? Have we nothing to fear? Yes, we have. We have "the wild boar of the woods;" he may "break down the hedge and devour the vine." We want the same protecting power, and the same gracious and Almighty operations—we want the help of the Holy Spirit to keep alive the flame in our souls, to produce right feelings in our hearts, right motives in our actions, and right intentions in our pursuits. The language, then, applies beautifully, "Save *now*, we beseech thee, O Lord!"

This is a time of necessity. We are

something like a garden which has been planted; there is a variety of flowers and shrubs. We must remember. May God make us remember it—that we have different constitutions; and having different constitutions, we are just as different in our feelings and passions; like plants we want the skill and care of him who knows how to treat us; then they are all in beautiful form and order; but we cannot take care of them. No, we must not try to do the work of God; we must do our work. What is our work? To cry unto the Lord. This reminds me of the poor black man of whom I heard once: he was working among a number of profane men, who were constantly cursing and swearing; and when he spoke to them about it, they laughed at him, jeered him and cursed him. At last, his soul was overwhelmed, he ran up in a loft, prostrated himself on the floor, and said—"Lord, speak to the devil; he is too much for me." That is just what you and I shall want to do. With all our crooked tempers, with all our perverse feelings, we shall want to do it for ourselves and one another; we must say, "Speak, Lord, unto them." If that feeling reign in our hearts, we shall baulk the devil as sure as he is a fallen angel. We want God's help for this. We are like a house, a married couple having got the house; is that all they want? No, what else is required? Furniture, my friends. We have got the house; but what will the house be to us if it is not filled with the furniture of the Lord. What is it that we want? the sacrifice ever kept alive before our minds; we want the High Priest with his breastplate—sprinkled with his blood going into the holy of holies; we want the mercy seat, where Jehovah has said, "There will I commune with thee!" We want the covenant ark, for in the ark are the tables of the law given in their unbroken state; we want Aaron's rod budding with all the yea and amen promises; and we want much incense to arise to heaven on our behalf. We want the furniture of the house; this is the Lord's house; and we want the Lord God to preserve it. We want God, you see. We have God's house; but I would sooner die this very moment than press forward, without God in the house. Here is the period then.

There is something yet. What is that? Thirdly, the prayer. Here we are, I hope a goodly number of us if not all of us, blessed with a knowledge of ourselves and our God—a knowledge of our necessities, and a knowledge of him as the source and the only source of our supplies, a knowledge of the position in which we are through mercy interested, a knowledge of our weakness and inability to stand, or to maintain anything, unless God stand by us. And now what is the eager pursuit? what is the souls longing desire? what is the aspiration of the mind now we have got the house and presented our prayer? What is it that we want?—"O Lord, we beseech thee, send now prosperity," this is a supplication; not a dictation. This is that which shows the soul is brought low and the man is in his right mind—clothe me with humility—"O Lord, I beseech thee!" not standing forth to argue arrogantly; and say, "Lord, you promised so and so, now do it; it is thy promise; thou canst not fail." I do not like such dictation. I tell you candidly, that when my soul is rightly affected, I find myself then in the very character of a child before my Father. I cannot demand. Would an earthly parent like the child to come with argument, or, as it were with dictation, and say, you promised so and so, therefore I demand it, the parent would not like this. The parent would like to be reminded perhaps of his promise; and the child would say,—"Father, you were kind enough to say you would present me with so and so; I am now in much need of it; there are such and such circumstances in which I am placed, and I need that which you have promised; will you be so kind as to fulfil that promise?" the parent's heart would seem drawn out with affection to see a child thus brought low and clothed in his right mind. And so it will be with us, my friends, when God brings us rightly to feel. This is a petition, as I have said, for something—"O Lord, I beseech thee, send now prosperity." What is prosperity? an advance, an enlarging, an increase. When a man is looking for prosperity, if he begin with a sovereign, and maintain only that position, does he call that prosperity? certainly not. But when he adds one to another, he feels that there is an increase, he is aspiring; he imagines that by and by, he shall grow a great man, and to a great estate, he becomes enriched. Again, a man plants a tree; he sows the acorn. Do you expect that the acorn will remain an acorn if it be healthy and prosperous? No! it will strike up into a stem; it will spread its branches; it will appear the gigantic oak, arising from the small acorn. Now, we have got the acorn of hope, the acorn of desire, the acorn of longing after God, and we say, "O Lord, we beseech thee, send now prosperity." Make it shoot up; make its branches spread out and bear much fruit to the glory of thy name! Blessed be his name, it will be fruitful if he has planted the acorn in our souls. He has suffered us to come up to Zion; and this is our earnest as I understand it of an increase. An increase of what? An increase of that alone which can make us happy. You must know that we are upon spiritual subjects and spiritual promises; and therefore we mean that we want spiritual enlargement, spiritual increase in spiritual things. What are they? The feeling heart does not want an unfeeling religion. I want the power of God to go with the Word. It matters not how fluently it may be preached; it matters not how truly scriptural I may speak; or however frequently I may utter the most consistent word of truth; if the power of Almighty God does not go with it from my mouth to your hearts, it will produce no fruit. "Send, Lord, prosperity!"

Friends, I am not standing here, merely to fill up an hour preaching; nor am I coming here, from time to time, to please your fancy? God Almighty forbid! I want to speak to your souls. Here I want to be instrumental in bringing you to the well of Jerusalem. "Send now prosperity, O Lord!" An enlargement—an increase—not only of feeling, but of fervour. We want fervour as well as feeling here, in Zion. We do not merely want words and acts, but fervour of soul, that we may draw nigh unto God with sincerity; living power, with warm and affectionate feeling. I have felt (through mercy) myself a poor, ruined, and worthless sinner; and many times I have gone and told God about it. Truly the words uttered, have appeared like icicles—so cold—no heart's warmth —obliged to put my hand to my mouth, and my mouth in the dust. I could only groan. We want fervour, my friends; that is, we want a live coal from the altar, that it may warm our hearts, and gather in the things of Christ's to the glory of the Lord. "Send, Lord, prosperity!"

We want faith, my friends. "What nonsense!" say some: "the Christian ought to have faith." Indeed! assertions are easily made—but they are not so easily proved. Now if you know anything of your own heart, I need not detain you long upon this point; but I will bring you at once to the question. Are you ever dark, uncomfortable, shut up, miserable? Oh, yes! Then you are a fool to be in the dark for a moment—to be shut up for a single second. I would always be at liberty, always be light, always be lively. I would live above the world; live and triumph in my God perpetually. But, if you cannot do it, where are your nonsensical ideas about "the Christian ought to have faith." Tell me to stop the earth in its course—tell me to command all nature to yield its supplies!—the one is as easy as the other. This brings you and me, and every poor helpless soul, in our right place before God. It empties us of self; it shews us that God daily supplies us with faith, and "grace upon grace;" and thus he keeps us alive, and our graces, every moment, all our journey through time. "Send, Lord, prosperity!" In what? In much fellowship with thee. What! is the Christian brought to this? Oh, yes! the real Christian, is brought to this feeling of soul. What! is it not enough that God has entered into covenant? Is it not enough that you are elected? Is it not enough that heaven will be your portion? No; it is not. Is it not? No! What else is wanting? We want to enjoy it whilst we are travelling here below. What else do we want? We want to be sanctified to God's glory. It is not even the persuasion that hell is for ever barred; it is not the persuasion that God has laid himself under a solemn obligation, that he will carry me on to the end, and raise me up to eternal glory, that will do. What more do I want? The Holy Spirit's sanctifying power, to put my mind right, my affections right, and to guide and keep me right! What a conflict there is! Some individuals go on smoothly, where they are not brought to this; but here there is a striving: there is a law of the members and a law of the mind. The law of the members says, "I would not be so particular about religion; I think you might relax here, and give up there." But when the soul is brought to a right position, it says, "Oh, hold me up, Lord! Open thou mine eyes, that my soul may see wondrous things! Here is my heart—Lord take it; I will give up all to thee—take and seal it; seal it from thy courts above!"

Thirdly, "Send prosperity." In what way? In spirituality of mind. It is life and peace. Oh! how carnal we are at times. Are we not? What are we doing when we are carnal? Trying to "make our nest." What are we doing when we are carnally minded? Trying to save up all we can to make provision for the flesh; to shuffle as we can, so that we may escape the cross. When carnality of mind is in exercise the individual is working without his God, and the individual is working away from God; but when spiritual-mindedness is brought, it carries the soul upwards; the thoughts are employed about eternal things; and the mind and thoughts are engaged in the blessed realities of heaven; it is life and it is peace. You are never at peace when you are carnally minded; you have never got enough; if you get £50 you want £100; if you get one house you want ten; if you get one field you want five; and when you get ten you want a hundred, or a thousand, and if you get a thousand you want a million. But when the mind is directed and influenced by the Spirit, there is a stream that flows that supplies the Israel of God through the wilderness. Faith brought into exercise sees God, trusts God, and rises above carnal things. I do not mean that individuals should be improvident. I do not harbour the idea that individuals should not act as consistent creatures; I am only arguing in this form that you may act consistently by not giving more than you can afford; give just what, as in the sight of the Lord, you know you can afford.

To be spiritually-minded, then, my friends, is to be kept looking at spiritual things—the covenant of God—the complete work of Christ—the perpetual operations of the Holy Ghost—and the full and final glory that is inseparably connected with them. I cannot go into them, time will not allow. You will want all this when you come to die; I often tell you so, because I feel it to be so: then what is the good of putting off what we must have to make us truly happy? Supposing we get thousands upon thousands laid up? Suppose we get, by conniving the smiles of all the world, and supposing we have every thing that the heart can wish, when we come to die what good will that be to us? If they were all to bless us who stood around us, and were all to smile upon us, they could not ease one pang of the heart, nor remove one stain of guilt from the conscience. What is it we want then? To be spiritually-minded, is to have the mind "swallowed up" with spiritual things. It is the fulness of God in Christ, the complete work of Jesus atoning for our sins, going to the end of the law for righteousness, which must bring us to that blessed position described by Toplady:—

"Jesus, thy blood and righteousness
My beauty are, my glorious dress:
'Midst flaming worlds in these array'd,
With joy shall I lift up my head."

Where spiritual prosperity is, there is enlargement of heart; the soul's power is employed in the the things of God, the will of God, and the ways of God. The gathering in of sinners to Jesus, the prosperity and peace of Zion, the comfort, happiness, and prospery of the people of God is then earnestly longed for; it is then the soul longs to be made useful to sinners, useful to saints, and useful to the cause of God; it is then faith, fervour and fellowship are united in soul prosperity. I beseech thee, O Lord, send prosperity.

Perhaps it is necessary (though I must attend to it very briefly) to state some little in reference to the principles upon which we have proceeded. As I have already said, I view myself only as the instrument of God. I had no thoughts of taking the position not a month before I did. I had for years been uncomfortable in my mind respecting church government, from the existence of various circumstances that I have passed through, and seen others pass through. I felt a longing disposition to see a change, yet I felt a difficulty and diffidence in bringing forward myself that which would break up long-standing customs which had long been a standard with the people of God. There I should have remained till this time—till I had died, had not God allowed things to break out. Still I wanted to go, as it were, inch by inch; afraid, fool like, to launch out; but God drove me out by allowing one attack upon another, so that I was driven into a corner, where I must have submitted to degrade every principle I professed, or else stand forward shield and sword in hand, and say, "Here I am; follow me who will, and if you follow me not, then I will live by myself. God has mercifully brought me out; twelve months have rolled round, and he, as I have stated, has supplied all my wants; there has been no necessity for begging, for entreating, for using carnal arguments to induce. I have thought for years that there cannot be a greater insult offered to christians than the idea that they have not got principle enough to induce them to give, unless they are well worked upon by carnal arguments. I don't believe it, and therefore I would not insult christians in the profession of their righteous principle—spirituality of mind. I would not so insult them as to say I cannot trust them to give what they think is right. What is it but to say that they have not got principle enough, that they have not got light of conscience enough to do that which conscience says they ought as in the sight of God. I say I will not so insult them. Therefore we make no charge for seats, nor receive any money for seats. It may be said, how do you do then? We have persons standing at the door after each service for any one, and every one to deposit there as the Lord gives him or her the heart. I love the principle. The more I look at it, the more I long to see it carried out, and the more I rejoice in it. Why? Because it branches out in a variety of ways. A parent can train up a child in principles, and here is a point and principle by which the child may be taught practically to do that which is right in reference to the supporting that place where they profess to worship. Thus it teaches children, as they grow up, that the house of God should be supported. Not only so, friends, but I have seen some of God's people weep and weep with joy because of the principle. Why? Because when the quarter came round, under the old system, it was announced perhaps rather unexpectedly: probably they had two or three sittings to pay for, and this amounted to six, seven, or nine shillings. This had been an unpleasant quarter—(affliction, perhaps)—and they had not got the six, seven, or nine shillings to pay: thus they were obliged to drive it off; hoping the next would be better. But in the next quarter there was sickness, perhaps, or something else, that they could not pay; and then they thought the pew-openers were always looking at them as defaulters, as they felt they were; by which they were made uncomfortable in the house of God. Now they have nothing of the kind. If the Lord prospers them—if they have a good week, and their hearts are right—they can put a sixpence, or a shilling, into the box: the next week may not be so well with them, and then they can put a halfpenny, or a penny, as circumstances will allow.

I have now to announce that we have provided a dinner; and that at the dinner we are carrying out the same principle. Some one said to me, "I don't know— it seems so singular; I shall not know what to give." Why, I am not speaking to persons who have got no judgment. If they go and see a table spread with certain things, their judgment may lead them to think, " Well, this may have cost the proprietors a shilling; if I give eighteen-pence, that will be a shilling for the dinner, and sixpence for the building."

May the Lord bless you all—may he come down with his presence to your hearts—may he keep us—and be with our brethren, who will assist us in the afternoon and evening of the day! Amen.

GOOD SEED AND GOOD SUCCESS:

Being, the Afternoon Sermon at the Opening of Zion Chapel, Goldington Terrace, Somers' Town:

BY CHARLES WATERS BANKS.

"For the seed shall be prosperous; the vine shall give her fruit, and the ground shall give her increase, and the heavens shall give their dew; and I will cause the remnant of this people to possess all these things. And it shall come to pass, that as ye were a curse among the heathen, O house of Judah, and house of Israel; so will I save you, and ye shall be a blessing; fear not, but let your hands be strong." Zech. viii. 12, 13.

Now, I will tell you my mind, at once, friends—that I think the ministry is good for nothing unless it comes from God; and unless the same power that gave it, applies it to the hearts of men. It is no use a man talking about the things of God, nor the word of God, nor the will of God, if God has not written these in his heart; and if he has not made them life and power in his soul; if God has not given him an experimental knowledge of them, it is all empty talk, and amounts to nothing. But if God writes the truth in a man's heart and makes it life and power in a man's soul, and then gives him authority to declare it, and clothes that declaration with power, the glory of God shall be seen; his presence shall be enjoyed; the blessing of God shall rest on the people; the text will be fulfilled.

After my day's work yesterday, I sat down in my bed-room: I asked the Lord to give me a word from himself; I felt I could not lie down to rest until something I had obtained. I sat there thinking and praying a little—not much—and presently I turned to an old volume of Erskine's sermons; I opened right on a dirty bit of paper, and on that paper was written, "December 10, 1846.—Going to Richmond—got nothing to say; but turn to Zech. viii. 12, 13." Well, I dropped Erskine's sermons, I dropped the bit of paper, and took up the Bible; and turning to Zech. viii. 12, 13, the first part was sealed upon my heart—"The seed shall be prosperous." Two or three times in the night I awoke—"The seed shall be prosperous." When I got up this morning—"The seed shall be prosperous." All the way coming here—"The seed shall be prosperous." And I thought when your minister was praying this morning for prosperity, I must have burst out and said, Prosperity shall come, for the Lord has sealed this upon my heart—"The seed shall be prosperous." And, therefore, as he came this morning in a praying spirit, pleading, supplicating, and beseeching, I hope I may say that I am come this afternoon in a good spirit when I tell you that the Lord will accomplish his own word, when he says—"The seed shall be prosperous; the vine shall give her fruit, and the ground shall give her increase, and the heavens shall give their dew; and I will cause the remnant of this people to possess all these things. And it shall come to pass, that as ye were a curse among the heathen, O house of Judah, and house of Israel; so will I save you, and ye shall be a blessing: fear not, but let your hands be strong."

You notice four things in this chapter. The Lord speaks, in the first place, of a certain result—They shall inherit his Jerusalem. He says, "I was jealous for Zion with great jealousy, and I was jealous for her with great fury." That is very remarkable indeed; you know this; you will not be offended if it stands in accordance with the word of God and your experience. God has been jealous for Zion with great jealousy and great fury. He is speaking here after the manner of men. And, perhaps, you may know that in days when you were seeking after a spouse, there might have been some disagreement between you, there might have been some falling out between you; and you parted for a time. But there was a feeling of jealousy in the breast, because there was real love in the heart; and where there is real, pure, and powerful love in the heart, though an offence should cause a separation for a time; though division may come, yet love allures, jealousy burns, desire works; and presently the separated hearts come together, as the Lord and his people will. Does the Lord express this feeling for Jerusalem? He says, "I was jealous for Zion with great jealousy, and I was jealous for her with great fury. Thus saith the Lord; I am returned."

The Lord goes on to speak of certain

effects of his return, of the benefits resulting therefrom. He speaks in cheering terms. He says, "Let your hands be strong, ye that hear in these days these words by the mouth of the prophets." He then describes a state of captivity; and then he says, "But now I will not be unto the residue of this people as in the former days, saith the Lord of hosts. For the seed shall be prosperous." There are three things. First of all, a cluster of promises; secondly, a beautiful transition shall come to pass—"That as ye were a curse among the heathen, O house of Judah, and house of Israel; so I will save you, and ye shall be a blessing;" and then there is a double admonition— "Fear not, but let your hands be strong."

In the first place, there is a fourfold promise here, that the Lord in his mercy joins together in his word, and joins together in the experience of his people. And I am sure it has been my private prayer, and it is my publicly expressed desire, that every part of this divine promise may come down in rich, and in large abundance upon you as a Christian people: what the Lord has said, can never fail.

Here is a figure employed. The word of God is compared to seed. The seed is the pure word of truth—the word of God. And this appears to be adapted to meet the threefold discouragement that our Lord gave in the days of his flesh, when he said, speaking of the gospel, it is like a sower who went out to sow; and he sowed the seed—but what became of it? Some fell by the way-side, some fell upon stony ground, and some fell among thorns. There are three classes of hearers who will hear the word. Some will support the ministers of the word, and will help to build up houses for the word of God to be preached in, but who do not receive the word into the heart, and consequently are not truly saved. This, therefore, appears to me a threefold discouragement that the minister may expect to meet with. We shall have people sometimes receiving the word gladly, whilst their hearts are in the world; their minds are choked with the cares of the world. Carnality and fleshly things so occupy their minds, that the word has no true entrance; it has no abidance; it is not prosperous, and brings not forth fruit. This promise then, I say, meets a threefold discouragement, when the Lord says—"The seed shall be prosperous."

The figure employed here is not without meaning. The seed itself is contemptible—small in its appearance; and so is the word of God in the eyes of the world. But what a beautiful Bible you have got here!—a very handsome Bible indeed! the handsomest book that ever I saw in a pulpit in my life. What is it that makes it valuable? The contents— the word brought by the power of God to act on a sinner's heart. Man, in his natural state, cares nothing for the word of God; it is contemptible to him; it is not valuable in his estimation; but when God carries home the word to his immortal soul—his living heart, then it is precious; more precious than gold.

My friends, look at the figure for one moment to see it in its smallness and contemptibility. Some of you may be staggered; but you cannot dispute what I say. There are some who profess the gospel, who despise the fundamental principles of it, as an Independent minister told me. He said, (speaking of the grand truths), "They are written in the word; but I think it not safe to preach them." That is despising them; that is treating them with contempt. If the fundamental principles of the word, the great bulwarks of Zion, the basis of our salvation are left behind, and kept out of the sight of the people, that is treating the word with contempt. If God does not bring thousands of such men to a solemn book, I am sadly mistaken. God will let them know whether the doctrine of divine election is to be laid aside; whether divine sovereignty is to be hidden, or finished redemption kept back. These are the very things that the children of God feed upon. Everything that helps the poor sinner; everything that helps the broken-hearted and contrite soul; everything that brings heavenly blessings down to the poor sinner, must be fully and faithfully declared.

There are some on the other hand, who preach doctrines high enough, but despise the experience of God's people. I do not know how it is with my brethren; but I am sometimes obliged to read the 88th Psalm; I am sometimes obliged to read the 51st Psalm; I am sometimes obliged to read the 7th chap. of Paul's Epistle to the Romans; and I sometimes feel these things as well as read them. I know that "in me, that is, in my flesh dwelleth no good thing." And, depend upon it, my friends, that the man who despises the deep experience and experimental knowledge of the things of God, and keeps these back from the church of God, rejects one part of God's word, and treats one part of God's word with contempt. How many ministers and servants of God (as they pretend to be) do despise the travail, the conflict, the poverty, the brokenness of heart, and deep distress, that many of God's people are subject to. They say "that is corruption preaching—we want Jesus Christ." You want Jesus Christ preached out of the sinner's heart. You must have Jesus Christ preached as he is revealed in the sinner's heart—you must have Jesus Christ preached as he is made manifest in the sinner's heart; and if Jesus Christ be not preached in this experimental way and manner, it is not food, it is not bread and meat for the church of God.

There is another part of the word of God that is despised, and that is, the preceptive part—that part which tells the Christian what he ought to be, and tells the Christian what he ought to do. You may say,—We cannot bear with your "oughts" to day. I cannot help it, my friend. It was said once of an old man—an old minister—that he went to the 1st chap. of Paul's Epistle to the Ephesians, and there stopped; but the servants of God must read Paul's Epistles through, and they must preach them through; and must know the doctrines of them, the experience of them, and the practice of them. I beg to say that the precepts in the word are as important as the promises; and the promises as important as the doctrines: and he despiseth the precept despiseth God's word.

Now, then, the word of God is compared to seed. It is not said the doctrine shall be prosperous; the experimental preacher shall be prosperous; the practical man shall be prosperous; but "the seed shall be prosperous." If the word of God be preached in its length, its breadth, its fulness; if the word of God be preached in its points and principles—if the man of God go from doctrine to experience, and from experience to practice; if he stand honestly and humbly in the fear of God, that word shall prosper; nay, it shall bring glory to God, and life to redeemed souls.

"The seed shall be prosperous." In what way shall it be prosperous? I may say in a sevenfold point of view, the seed, the word of God, shall be prosperous. What is good seed without good land? If you have a thousand bushels of good seed and that is not put into good land, it produces nothing. What is the good of good land without good seed? If there be a thousand acres of good land and no good seed be put into the land, it produces nothing but weeds and briers. No, my friends, there must be a conjunction—a coming together of good. The land must be ploughed and prepared, the seed cast into it; and then with the rain of heaven a blessing shall come.

Now, then, "The seed shall be prosperous," in that it shall drop deeply into hearts prepared. How sweet is the work of God the Holy Ghost! He prepares sinners' hearts for the word. Do you not remember (if ever you received any good thing from God,) there was a favourable providence that first brought you to hear the word. You had lived, it may be, for years careless about the word, heedless about the word, but at length a singular circumstance took place, a providence occurred; you were led towards the house of God, and you came without prayer, without concern, without desire, without devotion, without any specific object to the house of God; there was an arrow shot into the heart, fear and trembling rushed into the soul. A man writing to me, said, "Don't you know what I went to chapel for, sir? It was from no good motive. But, when the man read the text it rolled into my soul; it took possession of my heart; it broke me down in melting tears and sighs; and I shall never forget that time—I never shall." No, my friends, the blessed word of God is only fit for prepared hearts; and when the Spirit applies the word to the sinner's heart, it sinks down deep, and then the Spirit will make the word life and power in your never-dying souls: then "the seed shall be prosperous." This is the church's foundation for prosperity. When the word of God is carried with power into a sinner's heart; then the sermon is not tedious, the service is not tiresome; there is no weariness, nor dryness, nor deadness about the word then; when the Lord opens a man's heart, and opens a man's mind, and opens a man's spirit, he takes in the word; it drops into the heart where it lays, never to be taken away. You will never get to heaven without this, friends. I believe that God's great instrument in preparing his people for heaven, is by his precious word; and I believe it is by the application of it, by the deep dropping in of it, by the powerful operations of it in the soul, that sinners are brought near to him and prepared for glory. You that have a Zion here, the Lord grant that you may sometimes be blessed to pray that God would bring in sinners whose hearts are a little touched, whose souls are a little softened, and in whose minds there has been some revelation of the glory, the greatness, and the majesty of God; that they may hear, and feel, and fear, and repent, and sigh, and pray; and may the word of God be prosperous in them! "The seed shall be prosperous."

Secondly. "The seed shall be prosperous," when it works deep conviction of sin; when it gives the sinner an experimental knowledge of the nature and consequences of sin.

The gospel is of no value; Jesus Christ appears of no value; the atoning blood of Calvary appears of no importance; the ministers and servants of God are not esteemed; the house of God is not prized; the ordinances of Christ are not valued, unless the sinner feels his sin. But when God has smitten him, when the Holy Ghost has convinced him, and when the bitterness and blackness of sin is felt in and by him, he smites on his breast; he feels his guilt, the burden and weight of the curse in his heart; and he begins to cry out, as they did of old, "Men and brethren, what *must* I do to be saved?" One parson down our way (Mr. C——) went, I understand, round among all his inhabitants; he said, he found many professing Christians, but a broken-hearted sinner he could not find. I thought that a most solemn testimony for a clergyman to give. You may depend upon it there are plenty of strong Calvinists, and plenty of bold Calvinists, staunch doctrine men; but of broken-hearted sinners there are but few to be found; they are "few and far between;" there is but here and there one whom God has thus brought; but he has said, "The seed shall be prosperous."

Is there one in this house to-day with a real broken heart before God? Or, did you come up and say—"Well, I think I will go and hear this afternoon." Sometimes people have said, I thought I would come and hear you, because I have understood you have been a great sinner, and in a great deal of trouble; and I thought you would understand my case. You may depend upon it, friends, that if poor sinners get trouble in their hearts about sin; if they get a sense of sin in their consciences; if they get condemnation in their souls; if they get the fear of death and hell in their spirits, they begin then to look out, to seek out, and try to find out the servants of God who can speak to their case. If there be here, this afternoon, one poor broken-hearted, contrite sinner, who is bleeding in his soul, sinking in his heart, and quaking—waiting, as it were, to be condemned, I say, read this text: "The Lord is nigh to them that are of a broken heart, and saveth such as are of a contrite spirit." That text has been my staff to lean upon; that text has been my bread and meat; that text has been my consolation and comfort for many years. The Lord will never forsake him who hath a broken heart and a contrite spirit; he will not turn his back upon them; they shall be saved with an everlasting salvation. Oh! the deep convictions of sin! Is that the way in which the Holy Ghost makes a Christian? I would not give you a fig for a chapel full of professors, if they have not had broken hearts for sin. It will not be worth a fig; for, as a dying saint said last week—"For the want of a knowledge of the law in the soul, in convincing the soul, thousands will sink to hell that make a good profession." Oh! my friends, depend upon it, it is so. The word of God is sent for sinners; the dear Redeemer's blood was shed for sinners; the Holy Ghost comes with saving grace to broken-hearted sinners. "The seed shall be prosperous," then, when deep conviction is worked in a sinner's heart. This is the way in which God lays the foundation for Zion's prosperity. He prepares the sinner for a mighty conflict. You and I little thought, when he first came to us what we should have to suffer and endure, the conflict we should have to pass through, and what trials we should have to bear. Oh! some say, if I had known it, I should have never had gone through it; but you may depend upon it, the Lord will bring his people through all; he will bring them out of all; bring them over all—all that distresses and opposes them in their way to glory. A minister said to me last week—"These are they which came out of much tribulation." My friends, my christian brethren, the path to heaven lies through a deep, a thorny maize; but the Lord has gone before and goes with his people, therefore we shall overcome. "The seed shall be prosperous."

Thirdly. "The seed shall be prosperous," in the hands of the Holy Ghost, to produce heartfelt and fervent prayer to God. I wish to speak openly for the good of souls, for I have thought—here are a quantity of souls who will be presently in eternity. You and I must presently stand before God; and I do not want to day "a flash in the pan"—something just alive for a moment, and then gone out. I pray that Almighty God will seal the word on your hearts, so that there may be prosperity—that there may be success—that there may be a divine blessing resting on the word this day. The seed is prosperous then, when it produces fervent prayer to God. "Behold, he prayeth," says God. He took notice of that. Saul of Tarsus had never prayed before; that self-righteous man had never been in prayer before; he had never bowed his knees, or his heart to God before. No! my friends, it was not till now that Saul, this Saul of Tarsus, began to flee to God. What his prayer was made up of I cannot tell, but I will be bound to say, it was in accordance with the poor publican's—"God be merciful to me, a sinner." Oh! how many a Christian has experienced this! They have been brought to go into the fields, or into a garret, or to get into some retired place to pour out their hearts before God. Prayer to God is a solemn test of interest in Jesus Christ. I believe there never will be a soul get to heaven but is brought to a throne of grace, is brought to the mercy-seat, is brought to seek God in prayer.

This is one thing that the prosperity of the word stands in, when it is laid in a sinner's heart, it produces seeking after God; it produces fervent prayer to God: prayer that shall be answered. It is a holy position too, when a minister has a praying people. There is a good deal of talk about prayer-meetings and monthly missionary meetings; but when God gathers sinners together for heartfelt prayer, and when there are united cries to God in prayer; when many wrestling Jacobs come together for prayer, you may depend upon it the Lord will bless that people, that place, and that minister. Let your minister have your fervent prayers to God, and you may come and expect a blessing. I tell you what I thought of this morning, and this encouraged me to come—that from the earliest dawn of the awakening of my soul, I can speak and testify in great affection, I know that God is he who hears and answers prayer. Temporal provision and spiritual provision come in answer to prayer. The application of the word of God to the sinner's heart brings him to the throne of grace.

The seed is prosperous, my friends, when it produces (by the Spirit's power) a revelation of the person of Jesus Christ in the sinner's heart. There is a time appointed by God; there is a time fixed by the Spirit of God, when the sinner shall not only pray for pardon, but when he shall see Christ's work; when he shall have a clear view of the sacrifice that has been made; when he shall have a clear view of the dear Redeemer; when he shall see in the person and work of Christ, all that his never-dying soul requires. What a solemn time is that! What a sacred season is that to the life-seeking sinner when the dear Redeemer is revealed in his heart; when He is held up to the view of his mind; and when by precious faith he sees the great sacrifice for sin, and by divine faith lays hold on that fountain of pardon and peace which shall never be forgotten in time or eternity either! And where Christ has been once seen; where he has been once embraced, there is eternal life in that soul. You ask the people that make a profession of the gospel—(although I do know that I ought to say this, because I am not on my own ground)—but, if so be that you are desirous of having prosperity and peace, ask the people who come to join you in church fellowship, when it was, and how it was, that they got rid of their burden, and a sense of their sin; and how it was they got peace in their spirits; and if they have really, by precious faith and by the Spirit's power, seen the Son of God, been brought to know him, and have found pardon and peace in him, they can and will testify the same: and will tell the saints of God what the Lord has done for them. I do not think it will do to preach much about this if you have a very large company. I think if you stand for vital things; if you stand for deep, solemn, and experimental things, it may be that but very few can really and cordially receive them into the heart. But "the seed shall be prosperous" when Jesus Christ is revealed in the sinner's heart. As the gospel is the great instrument, it follows that the preaching of Jesus Christ is of vast importance.

The Bible is a large book, and there are many types and many figures of Christ's person and work. John Owen makes one remark that strikes my mind. He says, there is a vast amount of glory—there is that tremendous weight of glory in the person of Jesus Christ, that if it had all been concentrated in one word, and if the whole glory of Christ's person had been revealed in one word, it would be more than mortal man could bear. He says, there is a little of Christ here, and a little of Christ there, all through the precious word of God; there is a little opening of the mystery of Christ here; a little type and representation of Christ there; and these help the minister to explain him and proclaim him to the people; and I must say I dearly love to get picking out types, and figures, and prophecies, and declarations about the Lord Jesus Christ. That appears to me the health of the gospel; that appears to me the life of the gospel; that appears to me the glory of the gospel—"the Lord Jesus Christ, the same yesterday, to-day and for ever," the sinners' friend, the Saviour of our souls. I pray, I do pray that our brethren, the Lord's servants, may be brought, more than ever, to know that God the Holy Ghost will honour, and does honour, and greatly honour the exaltations of the dear Redeemer. Let him be preached out of a clean heart, with clean hands, by a clean man—a man washed in blood—and the Holy Ghost says sinners shall be converted, and saints shall be comforted; the church shall prosper; the blessing of heaven shall rest on the place: but anything short of this is death, darkness, bondage, and good for nothing. "The seed shall be prosperous" in revealing Christ in a sinner's heart. What a diversity there is in the work of the ministry! Sometimes, on a Sunday morning —I cannot tell how it is—but I find such distressings, such despondings, such sharp temptations!—I cannot see Christ; I cannot enjoy Christ; I cannot talk about Christ!

But I find that after I have been preaching out this sorrow—this darkness and distress, it was just to be dropped into some poor sinner's heart; it was some poor sinner's case; to meet this is to let the Lord's servants know that they will have peculiar trials, temptations, conflicts, and darknesses; and that these, instead of casting them down, in the estimation of the children, will raise them up.

At other times, the Lord Jesus Christ warms our spirits and draws out our souls; so that we preach with great warmth and fervour; and then, indeed, the gospel is peace to our souls. "The seed shall be prosperous" in bringing the family of God into the whole truth. The Word of God is designed, in the hands of God the Holy Ghost, to lead his people experimentally, extensively, and permanently, into the whole truth. They shall not only just come into the outer court—but they shall be like Ezekiel of old, get up the stairs into the chambers, and into the different galleries, round about the temple; sometimes to one part of divine truth, and sometimes to another; the Scriptures shall be opened to them; and the gospel becomes interesting, edifying, and establishing, as new glories and new scenes are opened up to their minds; and thus the mind is fed, the heart established, the soul comforted; and thus it is that "the seed shall be prosperous," when the glory of God is revealed, in and by the Word. The minister of Jesus Christ is not to be like a brewer's horse, just running round one track; beginning, as some do, with conviction, and ending with some faint hope of deliverance: and, whether it is winter or summer, whether it is seed time or harvest time, it is just in one line of things. As they told me down in the country, "Our minister is a good man; he is a man of God; but we always know his prayer and sermon before we hear them." It is bad when this is the case; and you may depend upon it, that when the Holy Ghost applies the gospel, there is a newness and a freshness, a variety and a beauty in the glorious gospel; and that when he preaches it, "the seed shall be prosperous.

With this house—this beautiful house—if there be not a variety in the ministry, if there be not a beauty in the ministry, if there be not a freshness in the ministry —in the unfolding of the gospel, the people will leave the place, and the parson will have it to himself.

You may depend upon it, my friends, there must be a coming out, and a coming in of the power of God's Word; it must be broken up and unfolded; and then the people will be kept alive.

"The seed shall be prosperous" again, I say, in giving the saints of God union to one another. The true Word of God cements us together: Christ's gospel joins us, heart and hand. Yes! and it often does that. Do you remember going to chapel, and there was a friend there, between whom and you there had been some little bad feeling previously? There had been some difference of feeling between you, and you had been shy, and distant, and cold; aye, and you would not speak; but the word of God dropped into your heart; the word of God melted down your soul; and you said, "I do love my brother now; I will go and speak to him for I feel this morning that the word of God has done me good." Do you remember this? Yes, the Word of God brings saints together, joins them together, unites them together. The Word is prosperous then, when the saints of God are taught to walk in union, love, and power.

If I do not finish this sermon, I will leave it for my brother Gwinnell, I will say as much as I can, and leave the rest for him.

In the next place, "The vine shall give her fruit. By the vine, I understand the church of God, in union with Christ. In the Word of God, sometimes Christ is called the Vine; and at other times, the church, or churches, are called vines. I believe it is the Christ of God, in union with Christ! "The vine shall give her fruit."

Now there is no tree weaker and more dependant for support than the vine. It will drop on the earth, lay on the earth, run along upon the earth, if it is not held up and supported; so the churches of Jesus Christ are in themselves weak; they fall and lay down unless they are supported. There is no tree more fruitful than the vine. I have not borrowed this, brethren, but I believe it to be quite true that the vine is in itself the weakest tree, and in its nature the most fruitful. Such is the church of God: she, in herself, is the weakest, and cannot stand without support; she cannot stand without defence; she cannot stand without protection. What poor, weak, and worthless members are we! What daily need we have of strength, of support, and of a refuge to flee to!

I say, the church of God is not only in itself weak, but she is by grace divine, made fruitful, yea, most fruitful. There are no people on the face of the earth so fruitful as the saints of God: and what fruit is that which the vine shall give? She shall give a divine experience. She shall tell out faithfully, savingly, and experimentally what the Lord has done for her; her ministers shall declare in the heights of Zion the works of the Lord their God. If the Lord has broken the heart, and healed; if the Lord has transformed the spirit and sanctified it; if the Lord has wounded the conscience, and afterwards cleanses it; if the Lord has made it feel the guilt of sin and has afterwards taken that guilt away; if you have groaned under your burden and are now brought to rejoice, you will have something to tell the saints about, and you will say, "Come, and hear what the Lord has done for my soul." "The vine shall give her fruit." The dear saints of God tell one another what the Lord has done for them; how the Lord delivered them: how the Lord helped them, and how the Lord blessed them; and as they tell out what the Lord has done for their souls, the church is comforted, saints are drawn together, the word prospers, the minister's hands are held up, and ten-thousand blessings come down.

There is nothing more profitable and comforting to the church of God than experience—the experience of really converted sinners. I think I may say, and say it not in an isolated way or manner, that the very best meeting I was ever at, has been when the church has been brought together, when converted sinners, when delivered souls, when saints have come together, and poured out the dealings of the Lord with them. Oh! what solemn feasting we have had! how we have been comforted in truth! how the minister's heart has rejoiced! how the church has blessed the Lord for his faithfulness! and how with one heart and voice they have praised the Lord! and thus the Lord means to say that where "The seed is prosperous" there shall be a manifestation of it.

"The ground shall give her increase." By the "ground," I understand the elect of God as they lay in the fall. "The ground shall give her increase," that is, by the power of God the Holy Ghost, his dear elect vessels of mercy which lay hidden in the fall, in the ruins of the fall, in the world, in the earth, shall come up out of sin; out of satan's haunts; out of satan's power, out of satan's darkness; the earth—the ground shall give her increase, and they shall come into Zion, into the church of God, and they shall say, "We will go with you, for we perceive that God is with you."

There is one thing that seems to make me at times uncomfortable. I do not know how it is with other ministers, but this one thing appears sometimes to damp my spirits—there appears to be in these days but very little of the converting power of God manifest. We have believers, we have professors; we have friends to Zion. There are some growing up who seem to bid fair, and some look well; but we have very little of powerful demonstration; very little mighty manifestation of the power of God in plucking sinners "as brands from the burning" is to be seen! This is not what I say, it is what the ministers of Christ say all round this professing England—that the convincing and converting power of God appears, as it were, lost in our day. The Lord grant that the Spirit may come and convince rebellious sinners *in* their hearts!

"But the ground shall give her increase." The Lord's elect shall be gathered; He will bring them from the North, from the South, from the East, and from the West, and they shall come to Zion. As our brother said this morning, every door opened in providence is a fresh opportunity for satan to stand behind it. I thought he was going to say every house that is opened, every minister raised up, is a manifestation of God's intention to bring sinners to himself. Although there may appear to be a lack of the convincing and converting power of God the Spirit in plucking sinners as brands from the burning, yet this house is not erected for nothing: God has a hand in this; God's power shall be manifest in this. "The ground shall give her increase;" sinners shall come with broken hearts, and contrite spirits shall find salvation at the cross of Christ; "The ground shall give her increase, and the remnant of his people shall possess all these things." What else? Why, "The heavens shall give their dew." The dew falls in the night; the drops fall gently; it is still and soft.

We are told in Scripture language that the Lord was not manifested in the earthquake, the Lord was not manifested in the fire, but "In the still small voice;" and I am satisfied that when the Lord gives the word, when the Lord applies the word, there shall be the soft distilling power of the Holy Ghost. The word shall be preached savingly; the word shall be preached with anointing power; the word shall get root in the feelings and in the consciences of sinners; the word shall be with salvation to their souls; and God the Father, God the Son, and God the Holy Ghost will give their divine blessing; and there shall come down from heaven that invincible grace which shall make the word almighty, so that it shall change the sinner's heart, and bring glory to his name. "The heavens shall give their dew." I am hastening on to the close of my subject, lest I weary you, knowing what an afternoon's service is.

I will just go on to speak of the transition—"And it shall come to pass, that as ye were a curse among the heathen, O house of Judah and house of Israel; so will I save you, and ye shall be a blessing." Blessed be God, we are living witnesses of this! What were we in our natural state but a curse? A man living in his sin, a woman living in her sin, is a curse to the neighbourhood, a curse to the place in which he or she live. But when the Lord has changed the heart, turned the affections, and brought the soul to Christ; when the man becomes a preacher of Jesus, having faith in Jesus, he becomes a friend to the people. "You shall be a blessing." My friends, every servant of God is a blessing in his day: every true believer in Christ is a blessing in his day: they that wear Christ, walk Christ, and are practical preachers of Christ, are blessings in their day. Do you not think that every true believer is a preacher of the gospel? Preaching the gospel is not confined to sermonizing; it is not confined to preaching in the pulpit. Every christian man who wears, walks, and practices Christ, is a practical messenger of the gospel: yea, I think, my friends, that as much is done by the silent practice of devout christians, as is done by all the sermons that were ever preached in the world. Let a man walk Christ; let a man manifest Christ; let a man live Christ; let a man bear the image of Christ; so that sinners may see him; and God sometimes convinces them that they are a blessing to the people: "And ye shall be a blessing."

Therefore, the Lord says, "Fear not, but let your hands be strong." This double admonition, I come to, hastily, because of the time. "Fear not, but let your hands be strong." This exhortation is necessary, as well as beautiful. The Lord seems to say, Fear not that these promises shall have effect: fear not that this promise shall come to nothing: fear not that sin, satan, and the world, shall be too much for you. "Lo, I have spoken," says the Lord, "and my word shall stand; my promise shall come to pass. Give not way to fear; believe my promises; do not doubt them. Believe what I have said; I have said it; I have spoken it," said the Lord. "The seed shall be prosperous, and the heavens shall give their dew." Fear not! Whatever clouds of darkness, distress, and temptation may come, when the Lord speaks he speaks with Almighty power, and that promise shall be fulfilled. There is a vast deal of comfort and encouragement contained in this exhortation, as spoken to the hearts of God's people: I do not know whether you know what I mean: but there are times and seasons when the Lord delivers his family clean out of fear. They do not fear temporal things; they do not fear eternal things; the Lord stands with them, stands by them, stands for them, and goes before them; the Lord delivers their souls; they trust in his righteous name. Then the Lord speaks here and says, Fear not; whatever dark dispensations await thee; whatever heavy trials come upon you; whatever dark valley you have to pass through, believe what I have said—"I will never leave thee, nor forsake thee, world without end." Therefore, "let your hands be strong." For a man's hands to be strong, there must be cleanliness, and unity. If a man stands in the ministry, and his hands be not clean, God will not bless him; the Lord will not honor him; the Spirit will not help him. But, if they are—if his conscience is clean; if his motive is pure, then the Lord will stand by him, and bring men to stand by him too. Clean hands gather many friends, and overcome many foes; and if a minister stands with clean hands, he stands blessed in the sight of God. "Let your hands be strong." This says to me, if not to you—be careful how you walk, and what you do; see that you ponder well the path of your feet.

"Let your hands be strong." For your hands to be strong, they must take hold of eternal life: the man that holds fast by Christ; the man who, by faith, has embraced Christ, is a strong man that nothing shall overcome or cast down, though he may sink for a time—fear not; he has got hold of the Son of God, and the strength of God, and by the strength of God, he shall stand.

I will not keep you looking for my leaving off, my friends, but I pray that God may bless, prosper, preserve and keep your hearts in the truth! May his precious promise be for many years verified and substantiated in your experience. May the word of God expand; may the word of God be prosperous; may the heavens send down their dew; may his people stand together, with clean hands and united hearts; rejoicing as a people fearing God, and walking in his truth.

I feel a humble persuasion that this is a solemn beginning of greater things for our esteemed friend. May the Lord send his blessing for Christ's sake!

You know what our brother said this morning—that there are no rents here for pews; no anniversaries here; but this is just a free and open place of worship, upon voluntary principles. I am, in my spirit, quite in accordance with the spirit of our brother: I think it is not a voluntary principle unless the people take their places where they like, and pay what they can. Let them do as they do in Scotland: a friend of mine said to me, "Sir, in Scotland we hold the plates at the door every time the people go into the house of God. When they enter the house of God we stand there, and hold the plates; and they give what they please, as an offering to God." Well, it matters not whether it is before or after; because upon this principle it is a voluntary gift, according to conscience. May you be helped and enabled to give.

May God's blessing rest upon you. Amen.

THE POWER OF CHRIST'S WORD:
BY MR. J. GWINNELL.

BEING THE EVENING SERMON AT THE OPENING OF ZION CHAPEL, GOLDINGTON TERRACE, SOMERS' TOWN.

I DO not know whether you have been thinking of nothing but opening a chapel all day; but my thoughts have been led to dwell upon a topic that is more exciting and comforting to the souls of God's people, than merely the opening of a chapel. I hope and trust that the desire of our heart is, that this day may be a memorable one in the history of some poor sinner, who may have attended this house of God. And if the Divine Being condescend to make his word power and life to some immortal soul to day, surely this day will never be forgotten. If ever I felt all the responsibility and solemnity of the work, I really feel it to night; and that not merely because so many people are here, although that is a source of encouragement to the minister of Jesus Christ. But, my dear hearers, upon looking round, and seeing so many who are more aged in the ministry, and better qualified for public occasions than myself, as a young minister, I feel these things. However, if the divine Spirit be here to help the preacher, and help the hearers, the design will be prosperous, our souls will be blessed, and we shall be enabled to glorify God.

This morning, you had a very suitable subject for the occasion. What could be more suitable than that portion of Scripture which was so blessedly dwelt upon, with reference to the Lord's sending prosperity to this place.

This afternoon, some of you heard what was meant by the seed—the word of the Lord; and that it shall prosper. I understand that was very delightfully dwelt upon, as many of you must have felt, and some of you must have been comforted.

The portion of Scripture which seems most powerful upon my mind, is rather a singular one. It is recorded in the 8th chapter of the Book of Ecclesiastes, and part of the 4th verse:

"*Where the word of a king is, there is power.*"

Various are the opinions of men as to who was the writer of this book. You, who read the works of Divines; you who peruse them, in order to have their help in the ministry, know that some have thought it was one man, and some have thought it was another. Various are the opinions of men, as to whether it was Solomon, or whether it was not; and if any come to the conclusion that it was Solomon, then they vary in their opinions, as to when he wrote it. Some think he wrote it before he fell into the sin of adultery, and into the wanderings of his heart from God. Others think that he wrote it after his restoration; and so I think; for you will find that the book of Proverbs, while it is a chain of links of no small value, he says but very little in reference to the vanity of things here below; but in this book you will find that he comes to this conclusion—after having well weighed every matter, and tried every thing, in order to gain pleasure and satisfaction, in speaking of the things of time, he says, "Vanity of vanities; all is vanity." You will find him, my dear hearers, speaking also upon the solemn realities of eternity—the necessity of a preparation for that awful period, when the tabernacles of clay will be dissolved; and when the spirit must return to God who gave it. It occurs to me here, that Solomon is speaking in this chapter in reference to those who are wise; and the effects produced by wisdom. My dear hearers, although the language seems to have reference to those who have literally rule over us, it seems to me that it refers to the eternal world—"Where the word of a king is, there is power."

You know some of you, and if not, you can go home and look at it, what the seventy writers say upon this point. You will find that they come to the conclusion that the king in our text, is the Lord Jesus Christ; and that the word alluded to, is no other than the word of that king.

Now what power is there connected with the word of a natural king in comparison with the word of the King, Jesus Christ?

Now, in a very simple manner to night, perhaps it may not be very pleasing to some of you, but that I must leave—in a very simple manner to night, let us notice—

First—The King. And,

Secondly—Try to make some remarks

upon the power of the King and his word. Oh! that the divine Spirit whose office it is, whose prerogative it is to bless, may accompany his own truth with his own power; so that we may be enabled to go home and say, Surely, "where the word of a king is, there is power."

Now, I think of taking this up in the following form: first, let us endeavour to find out in what way Jesus Christ may be called a King. First, kings are generally the descendants of a noble family; a family that is termed of *high blood*. This is the law of the land: that the kingdom falls under the government of one who is heir to it—one who is born of kings. Now, if we look at the dignity which rests upon human families; if we look at the heir to the throne, the descendant of a noble family, what comparison is there with the King, Jesus Christ? Whom did he descend from? Why, my dear hearers, he descended from God himself: he was the only begotten Son of God, "full of grace and truth." I shall never forget Mr. Jay, of Bath; I believe he stood up, and took for his text, "The word was made flesh, and dwelt among us, (and we beheld his glory, the glory as of the only begotten of the Father,) full of grace and truth." And, my dear hearers, when he dwelt on the fulness of his grace, it vibrated through the whole place. Jesus Christ is the only Son, if I may so express myself, of the Eternal Father; the *only* Son! Yes, say you, angels are termed in some parts of Scripture, the sons of God; sinners converted by sovereign grace are termed the sons of God. But this King is *the only begotten Son of God;* the only heir to the kingdom; and, descending from so high a parentage, he has a right to govern the universe.

2ndly, Kings have, or ought to have, exceeding great and proper qualifications. They ought to be acquainted with the laws; and they ought to be acquainted with the station and circumstances in which their subjects are placed. But where can we find a king so qualified as the Lord Jesus Christ? If you read the 7th chapter of the book of Proverbs, he makes the statement, "That he was brought up as one by him; that when he made the mountains, he was there." Yes, he had all the qualifications that were essentially necessary to enable him to govern. If there was but that one expression in the New Testament, which I am about to repeat—that one declaration, it would satisfy my mind that he had every qualification necessary in order that he should be a King. What was that? "Jesus said unto him—Simon, son of Jonas, lovest thou me more than these?" "*Lord, thou knowest all things.*" Did you ever see the beauty of that expression? Oh! here is a qualification!—a knowledge, a perfect knowledge, not only of all that is transacting, but of all that has been transacted, and that ever will be transacted. And it is a blessing to know, that whatever trials we are to bear; however deep our tribulation; however heavy our doubts and our fears, this King has a perfect knowledge of our state of mind, Oh, what a comfort to our souls that is! We have a sovereign of this realm, but thousands of her subjects are distressed, and she knows nothing about it; not so with the Lord Jesus Christ.

I was spoken to in a friendly manner, although there was hardly much need of it, not to be long this evening, because the place is so full. I shall be just as long as the Lord gives me strength.

Now, in the next place, we notice, and will just pass on it quickly; that sometimes kings are chosen. Now, in the Old Testament dispensation, we have instances of their being chosen. The shepherd boy was chosen of God to be a king over Israel. And Jesus Christ was chosen by God the Father, to be a King in Zion—a King over his people.

Once more, under the Old Testament dispensation, we read of kings being anointed as well as chosen. It was a customary thing in Samuel's day; and when Saul was chosen, you will remember that Samuel anointed him. Now, the King spoken of in my text, has been anointed; the apostle Paul tells us in the first chapter of his Epistle to the Corinthians, that "he was anointed with the oil of gladness above his fellows." One day I was reading (it is a solemn fact) that this king was passing through a certain place, and he went into one of the Synagogues, and took up the Scriptures—the Old Testament—and opened it at a portion where it is said, "The Spirit of God is upon me: and hath anointed me." What to do? "To preach glad tidings to the poor; to heal the broken hearted; to bind up their wounds, and to give them the oil of joy for gladness, and the garment of praise for a spirit of heaviness." You see Christ is not only a descendent from a royal parentage in heaven; he is not only possessed of great qualifications; he is not only chosen; but he has been anointed for the sacred office.

Once more: kings when they enter upon their reign, as a general plan, are proclaimed; there is a proclamation. Yes, some of us remember when her present Majesty was proclaimed heir to the throne; when she was put in possession of the sceptre, and when she was seated upon her dignified throne. And Jesus Christ was proclaimed. How? First he was proclaimed by Angels. Now, you will observe, my dear hearer, that when "the fulness of time was come," when this king was to be made heir to the earth, and to take upon him the form of humanity, angels proclaimed him to the world. Where? We might have said—though that would have been going from our subject; that angels proclaimed him before he made his appearance. But let us keep to our text. It is said that when the shepherds had seen the stranger— "Presently, there was with the angel a multitude of the heavenly host." My poor soul has been made glad many times when I have thought upon this subject. It appeared to me that there was not a happy spirit in yonder world, but felt so interested in the proclamation of the king, that all were at the portals of the sky. And what was their song? "Glory to God in the highest; peace on earth, and good-will towards men." But the angel proclaimed him to the shepherds. A light shone round about the poor shepherds, and the proclamation that the angel made was—"Fear not; for unto you is born this day a Saviour; which is Christ the Lord, and this shall be a sign unto you." All the scientific performance of music; all the echos of a huzza; all the loud cheers of the human family when a natural sovereign is elevated to the throne is but "as dust and ashes;" nay, it is not worth comparing with the proclamation from heaven of the event of this King. Yes, Christ was proclaimed first by an inhabitant of yonder world, who came forth to proclaim his dignity.

He was proclaimed, in the second place by a star. A star! Yes, a star proclaimed him. I have had some sweet thoughts upon this part of the subject, my friends. I have indeed. And when the inquirers came towards the spot where this king lay, they said—"Where is he that is born King of the Jews; for we have seen his star in the east, and are come to worship him. I will tell you what my thoughts have been—but perhaps you will say it is all nonsense and try to make it so if you can—I have thought that that star was both made and created for the very purpose of the proclamation of the advent of our God. "*His* star!" why was it "*his* star?" Oh! it was *his*, because *he* made it. My dear hearers, although no voice proceeded from the star itself, there was a power which convinced the shepherds, and directed them on their way to this precious King—to where he was born, in all the acclamations that they could bring to this heavenly messenger.

Once more, he was proclaimed by the shepherds. Dear me! see what a union there is subsisting between God and his people! What Jesus Christ is interested in, poor converted shepherds had something to do with! What that star which shone in the east denoted, they felt interested in. Yes, what the wise men were in search of, this star directed them to. Think of the condescension of God, who brought poor shepherds from the field to give them the honourable privilege of proclaiming the Saviour of mankind!

Also, lastly, he was proclaimed by children. You remember when this King was riding upon the foal of an ass,—

"The children all stood singing,
Hozannahs to his name.
Nor did their zeal offend him,
But as he rode along
He left them, still attending,
And smiled to hear their song."

What was their song? "Behold the King cometh in the name of the Lord. Hosannah to the King! I do not believe there are any children in hell. I don't like the high sentiment men, who preach children in hell. I don't know what would become of my feelings, if I thought that children who died without coming to a knowledge of the truth, were lost. Do you think that this King would allowed these infant children to sing hosannas to his name for an instant, if they were ever lost? I am not one of those straight-laced men, who talk so much about God's elect; you know me too well for that; to say that they are grown up people, and that children have nothing to do with it. Children in hell! No such thing! I believe, my friends, that the greater part of the inhabitants of yonder world of joy is composed of infants! I do indeed! The children proclaimed this King.

Once more, kings have their attendants; and, my friends, their attendants are not always visible in every part of the court at one time. Jesus Christ is King; and who are his attendants? Angels. Indeed, after his birth, they were with him. In the wilderness, after his sorrowful trial of temptation, they came and ministered unto him when he needed it. In the Garden of Gethsemane, the attendants were there. Yes, my hearers, and when he burst the barriers of the tomb, divine justice gave order to some of the intelligent beings to go and let the Saviour free! to shew that justice was satisfied, and hell overcome! And hence we read, that angels came and rolled back the stone from the door of the sepulchre, and sat upon it. Matthew Henry says, that the angels sat upon the stone, defying the power of hell to roll it back again! And, secondly, it was to comfort the poor distressed women who were coming to seek their Lord. They attended; and, mark! they attend him now. They are ministering spirits; they attend him wherever he goes; they are sent forth with the "word" of the King; and they attend all his subjects.

A man said to me, in reference to this subject, that kings have their prime ministers—and that Christ's prime minister was the Holy Ghost. Oh, I said, that will not do for me to advance in the pulpit; because the prime minister is below the king; and that would be taking the Godhead from the Holy Ghost. I don't believe that. There is a coequality between Father, Son, and Holy Ghost; and if you take away the Godhead from the Holy Spirit, we are lost. I was telling my people of this, last night, I am a curious man. Before I go up into the pulpit, I am almost distracted. Last night, before I went into the pulpit, I picked up a little pamphlet; the Lord placed that little book in my hands. A Church minister was visiting a poor sick man; and he asked the man who was praying—"Where did you get that book from?" "Book, massa! Me no books, massa!" "How could you pray like this without a book?" "The light of the Holy Ghost, massa!" "Why you good for nothing fellow; there has been no Holy Ghost since the apostles' days." No Holy Ghost since the apostles' days! What are the people talking about? May we feel his power, to-night, accompanying these remarks to the comfort and strength of our souls!

Once more, and then we will try and get away from this part of the subject; that is, that where kings are sitting upon their thrones, they have the prerogative of receiving appeals, and of communicating pardon to criminals. Now here we see the beauty of our King; here we see him exalted "to be a Prince and a Saviour, to give repentance and remission of sins unto Israel." What an infinite mercy is it that he should always be waiting, always be ready, always willing to receive the broken accents of poor condemned criminals, who can say no more than this, "God be merciful to me a sinner!" He will never send any one away; he is just as ready to communicate pardon to the petitioner, as he is to hear the petition. Now, all petitions sent to Her present Majesty, must go through a long preamble—they must go through the minister's hands, and the valet's hands —and there are hundreds of petitions she never sees at all! But, however simply the brief may be drawn up; however broken the language of the poor cottager may be; whatever may be the form of the petition; if it comes from the heart, Jesus Christ will hear it. There are some in this chapel, to-night, who have said, "Lord have mercy upon me, a poor wretch; I deserve nothing but thy hottest displeasure!" But Christ has said unto them, "Thy sins, which are many, are all forgiven." Thus much for the King. He is a very blessed King; yes, he is a very loving King; and he is such a King as you and I want: and if we have not this King to rule over us; if we are not his loyal subjects, we shall never sit upon his throne, and never wear his crown.

Now then, as to his word, "Where the word of a king is, there is power." Now having brought this subject to bear on Jesus Christ, let us view him now in the exercise of his power in the creation of the universe. Now the word "Create" implies the making out of nothing. Does it, or does it not? Now we are lost. The word "Regenerate" implies the making anew out of something; but the word "Create" embodies such a mystery that the mind of man can never fully enter into it. I think Charnock somewhere says; and some of you have got Charnock, perhaps, and you will say a parson will steal from every one that he can, in order to feed the people; I think he somewhere says, speaking of the work of God in the creation, that the musician may bring forth sweet tones from the music; he may perform so as to bring pleasure and delight; he may cause the sound to vibrate so as to charm our ear; but he must have something to play with and play from. The chemist may operate upon different herbs and drugs, and bring the result to answer his purpose, but he must have something to work with. The painter may draw a likeness, but he must have the likeness either in his own mind or before his view before he can do it. Man's thoughts may range into the celestial hemisphere in contemplation, but man's thoughts must have something to work upon. Now in the work of creation this was not so. When I come to contemplate that God, before whom we must all appear, and hear him say "Let there be light, and there was light," is not there a power with his word? He has but to say let the world be brought into existence, and there it appears. Sinner! thoughtless, unconcerned sinner! this is the God that thou wilt stand before; the God who can make millions of worlds from nothing, and bring them into existence from nought. Oh! is there not a power with his word?

Let us pass on to see this King in the wonderful acts and miracles which he performs. One day, in the days of his flesh, he was passing along the street, and there was moving along in solemn procession the funeral train of the only son of a poor widow, for aught I know, her only support. He is being carried to the grave as this King comes along, and he says, "Stop! you that are carrying the corpse." In those days, if I mistake not, they had no coffins; the corpse was bound up in a linen cloth, and carried on a board to the tomb. Such was the case here perhaps. He stops the bier, and the next thing he says is—"Young man, I say unto thee, arise!" Every eye is upon the speaker; every one is in amazement; the young man at once sits up, and he is delivered to his disconsolate mother. Have you ever thought upon these things? "Where the word of a king is, there is power." Again, Lazarus had been dead four days, and of course there was no hope of his coming to life again; Jesus is brought to the sepulchre; he stands there like a sovereign who has the power of raising the dead to life, and he says—"Lazarus, come forth." The next thing that we read is that "He came forth bound hand and foot in his grave-clothes;" and instantly this King saith, "Loose him, and let him go." Again, see his miracles wrought on the diseased. See the leperous man saying, "If thou wilt, thou canst make me clean." Jesus says, "I will, be thou clean." Oh infidel! perhaps thou dost not believe these things. "And immediately the fever left him;" immediately the leper departed; and he became sound and whole as another man. Again, see him walking upon the water: see his disciples at sea, tossed here and there, and overwhelmed with sorrow and despair; but this King comes along, he speaks to the waves of the sea, and immediately there is a calm. Aye, my friends, the mariners said to themselves, and I do not wonder at it, "What manner of man is this that even the winds and the sea obey him!" Ordered by the chief magistrates of the land, gone with the multitude to bring him up for open persecution and death. "We will bring him back safe enough, (say they,) we will put this troubler out of existence." They return. "Well, have you not brought him," says the magistrate. Brought him indeed! "Never man spake like this man." So that you see if you look at the word of this King in the miracles which he wrought in removing diseases, in bringing the dead to life, and in overcoming the hearts of his enemies, I think you will say to-night, "Well, 'Where the word of a king is, there is power.'"

Let us come to a more precious subject, and one that I hope and trust you are interested in; "Where the word of a king is, there is power," in reference to the work of conversion. However men may be led systematically to preach from the word of God, and sail round it in the boat of deepest study for ideas, if you leave out the work of conversion, what is preaching? "Where the word of a king is, there is power." There sit two men in one seat in the Chapel; they come in thoughtless and prayerless; they are there because others are there, little thinking of what might take place; and behold! there is a trembling and a fearing with one; and if you could just bow down your ear to the throbbings of the breast, you would hear this language, "What must I do to be saved?" What a change has taken place! What has been the cause of it? Christ has spoken through the means of his word to the poor sinner's heart, and he instantly feels that there is something the matter; he is instantly levelled to the earth: he is like poor Saul of Tarsus; he is brought down to the ground; and when a man feels that he is an enemy to God he instantly cries out, "Lord, what wilt thou have me to do?" I can tell you this much that I would not give the snap of my finger for all the preaching in the universe without the power of God. That is what you, my brethren in the ministry, have been kept by; and I have had enough to pay me to-day, I have indeed. Passing through the vestry to-day, a dear friend seized me by both hands, and asked me how I did; and she said, "This is one of your children, one that the Lord gave you in Beulah Chapel when you preached for our pastor there. Thank God! I can only hope that he will give me another one to-night.

I should like to have a little more time to dwell on this part; but let us observe once more that "Where the word of a king is, there is power" in the application of his promise. Some say when you are in darkness you should read the promises, you should apply the promises. I thought our brother Nunn came out rather abruptly this morning for a clever talking man. I really looked at Mr. So-and-so, and Mr. So-and-so, whom I knew were here. I said that is enough. He actually said you were fools because you did not exercise faith. Don't you remember it? So say all arminians. "Faith!" Oh yes, I have heard them say so nicely—come to Jesus, just now, come and roll your cares upon him, just now, you poor soul, who are cast down, come and apply his promises. The promises are locked up; the Bible is locked, and where is the key? Ah! my dear hearers, I know whether these things are true or not. There have been instances in my experience when I would have given ten-thousand worlds to experience those promises; but when Jesus came along and spoke, what power there was.

Eighteen hundred years ago, when the disciples were on the way, and that their Lord was dead, when they were mourning, perhaps, poor fellows! one with the other, and saying, "Our Jesus is gone! We have lost him; this is the third day, and there are no signs of him." When this was taking place, the King comes along, and he was disguised so that they should not know him. As soon as he comes to them, he asks—"Why are ye so sad?" He knew all this before. "What communications are these that ye have?" "Oh, art thou a stranger in Jerusalem, and hast not heard tell of these things that have taken place?" What things? And then, when they talked together, and he began to expound the Scriptures, to them, beginning with Moses and the prophets, and telling of things concerning himself, what power there was in his word! Their hearts were warmed. It was a short visit; and he was off again. That is just like him sometimes. The disciples said—"Did not our hearts burn within us?" Oh, my brethren and sisters, you who know anything of the spirit of grace in your experience, you know that when Jesus has whispered one word, there has been a burning within. Poor Mary, when she saw Jesus, though she thought it was the gardener, said, "They have taken away my Lord, and I know not where they have lain him. If thou hast borne him hence, tell me, that I may go and see him." And Jesus said, "Mary!" in all the accents of comfort and consolation; and there was such a power with his word, my dear hearers, that she instantly knew his voice.—"Where the word of a king is, there is power."

Finally—the Christian has to die. Sinners have to die: the solemn event will take place with every child of God. Death is a solemn thing! Ah, you may tell me, some of you bold champions, that you have no fear of death, and I do hear some professors talk about having no fear of death. Joseph Clift, of Bradley, in Wiltshire. Some of you know Bradley—he was a poor home spun weaver like myself, a preacher of the Gospel. He preached encouraging tidings of Jesus. When he had one foot in the river, his son went to him; and he said, "Father, how is it now?—All dark, boy. I fear that after having preached so often, I may be cast away." Poor Benjamin was so distressed that he went a second time—"How is it now?—All dark." He went the third day—"My dear father, how is it now?—All right. Jesus has spoken to my heart; and all fears are gone."

"Where the word of this king is, there is power; and at the Judgment Seat of Jesus, when he shall say,—"Come ye blessed of my Father, inherit the kingdom prepared for you from the foundation of the world," will there not be a power?

I cannot quit the subject without observing, that "where the word of a king is there is power," in reference to the destruction of his enemies. How often have we seen the wicked cut down in their rebellion, and hurled from the land of existence into the world of spirits! My dear hearers, this Jesus is "the same yesterday, to-day and for ever" in the word of his power; and he is the same yesterday, to-day and for ever, in the administration of his justice upon the ungodly. And, my dear hearers, you who know nothing of his power and his grace to change your hearts, will know something of his power to destroy. God grant it may be otherwise!

We might make some remarks upon the fact that "where the word of this king is, there is power in commanding the building of places for his worship. My dear friends, have patience for a minute or two. I congratulate you upon this occasion. I confess I have been alarmed at your proceedings. The first movement of this principle shook me to the centre. Aye! it did indeed. I have been watching and inquiring how you were getting on with this voluntary principle. I have said—" How does it work? Very well." I have expected every time it would be not quite so well. But so late as yesterday, the last day in the old place, I believe the collection amounted to as much as, or more than it ever had since you had been there. One of the deacons told me not to say a word about money to-night; you have given a good deal to-day I know. I know it is a voluntary principle; but you want a little stimulous sometimes, do'nt you? Now I tell you what my firm persuasion is—that before this day seven years I may be dead and gone—the transactions of this chapel will be brought under the notice of the House of Commons, and there discussed. It has got already into the hearts of some, and you may depend upon it that there is many a minister in London who would like to be in Nunn's place. They are afraid; their deacons have not got courage. If it were a general thing, there would not be so much groaning about the quarter's sitting money coming due as you heard this morning. I watched the people one night at Gower Street; and if there was any one in the way of the box, they pushed them out of it. May it be thus here, and may many a sinner be brought to God in this place.

I suppose you will look rather cross at me when I come down from the pulpit. But I shall not like it at all if the evening's voluntary principle does not come on quite as well as in the former part of the day. You may say, you are not a voluntary man. I am to the back-bone; and if the Lord give me strength, as soon as I can put my finger on the principle I will. I have not got it yet; but Nunn has, and I hope by the blessing of God he will bring it to bear. "Oh" said a parson to-day, "we tried it at our place; but it did not act well." I thought, though I did not say, perhaps there was not very good preaching there, that will not be the case here. You have a man of talent and wisdom. It is aggravating to some; they are jealous about it.

May the Lord be with you in this place! May he bless you with the tokens of his presence! May you be ready to enter that rest that remaineth for the people of God, where you shall sing for ever and ever—"Where the word of a king is there is power!"

www.ingramcontent.com/pod-product-compliance
Lightning Source LLC
Chambersburg PA
CBHW080244170426
43192CB00014BA/2554